THE

GREAT HARMONIA.

VOL. II.

THE TEACHER.

THE

GREAT HARMONIA;

BEING

A PHILOSOPHICAL REVELATION

OF THE

NATURAL, SPIRITUAL, AND CELESTIAL UNIVERSE.

BY

ANDREW JACKSON DAVIS,

AUTHOR OF "THE PRINCIPLES OF NATURE, HER DIVINE REVELATIONS, AND A VOICE TO MANKIND."

Spontaneous and profound Questions are living representatives of internal Desires; but to obtain and enjoy those pure and beautiful responses, which are intrinsically elevating and eternal, the Inquirer should consult not superficial and popular Authorities, but the everlasting and unchangeable teachings of Nature, Reason, and Intuition

VOL. II.

BOSTON:
BENJAMIN B. MUSSEY & CO.
29 CORNHILL.

1854.

STEREOTYPED BY
RICHARD H. HOBBS,
HARTFORD, CONN.

AUTHOR'S PREFACE.

In accordance with an announcement in his first volume, the author here presents to the world the second volume of the Great Harmonia. And again he is moved to repeat, that he will not consent to be considered as an Infallible "teacher" of science and philosophy; but addresses his revealments to the Intuition and Reason of the human soul. He feels it to be his duty to devote his life and interior powers to the promotion of human progression, happiness, and spiritual illumination—to individual and social harmonization. And to obtain means and principles adequate to the accomplishment of these sacred ends, he is impressed to seek, (as far as his abilities will permit,) the Natural, Spiritual, and Celestial departments of God's Universal Temple; and to write, and suggest the proper application, of such general truths as man's physical and spiritual organization evidently requires.

It will be perceived, by examining the contents of the chapters which follow, that the author has incorporated in this, as he did in the preceding, volume, several articles which have before appeared. The present volume is entitled the "Teacher," on the ground that most of its contents refer especially to the common themes and interests of every-day life. According to the amount of manuscript in the author's possession, and that which he is yet to write upon the subject, it is supposed that the chapter concerning the Deity, will extend to the center of the third volume. And the reason, which he is impressed to assign, why the present work is not wholly devoted to the discussion of this sublime and holy theme, is this—the nature and expansiveness of the subject, especially in its concluding divisions, render it too laborious for the general reader, and too lengthy for that variety which is deemed essential to the welfare of any publication.

In the first chapter will be found, preceding an account of the author's early experience, several testimonies concerning his powers and achievements while in the capacity of a seer, or subject of interior illumination. And those who would seek more information on this head, may consult the account which is given in the author's first work, "Nature's Divine Revelations." With regard to the writings of the author there is a great variety of opinion. George H. Lee, M. D., a very candid and honest writer, thus remarks respecting them :—

"Many critics have expended their powers in analyzing the sentiments of the book known as 'Nature's Divine Revelations.' It may be that their conclusions on the merits of this book are correct in some respects and erroneous in others; but all should understand that Mr. Davis does not recognize infallibility either in himself or any other human being. He says: 'Let what I am impressed to state, then, be received as true, or rejected as false, according to its appeals to your judgment;' and again he says, 'I know I shall, like all others, progress eternally; therefore I do not promise to believe to-morrow exactly what I believe to-day, for I may know more.' It is true that the writings of Mr. Davis may partake somewhat of the individuality of his own mind, like the productions of all other authors. The written ideas of every person are in a measure the expression of his own individuality, or a symbol of the inspiration peculiar to himself. The several books of the Bible bear an obvious impression of the individual minds of the persons by whom they were written. Hence arise the different styles and modes of expression which are here apparent. Moses, David, Isaiah, and St. Paul, all had their peculiar styles of writing, according to the measure or degree of inspiration. It is so, also, with modern writers, both poets and theologians.

Some persons question the propriety or consistency of entitling the book referred to, 'Nature's Divine Revelations.' In reply let us ask, is not visible and invisible Nature a complete embodiment of the Divine Mind, representing both its outer and interior manifestations ?—and is not this volume a transcript of Nature in all its multiplied forms and infinite ramifications, and also of God in the unfathomable depths of his love, power, and wisdom ? If so, then does it fully possess the very character which is indicated by its title.

I would not defend the errors of Mr. Davis, if any exist. Let them be fairly and candidly pointed out. But we are compelled to regard his writings as the triumph of clairvoyance, and when we reflect that these are the work of an uneducated young man, and then consider his profound philosophy, his far-reaching powers of thought and reason, together with the surpassingly beautiful language he employs, we say that these things combined form the greatest wonder of our age. Can the history of mankind furnish another instance of a person who has thus risen, without education, and while a mere youth, to become a distinguished author on the most abstruse, metaphysical sciences—exhibiting in all these the most astonishing resources of thought and knowledge which would have cost other men, in the usual way of obtaining them, a long life-time? I say, can history clearly show a case parallel to this? And have mankind yet fully appreciated this startling development of mental power?"

With regard to the vision, contained in the chapter on the author's early experience, there are a few explanations deemed necessary. As it originally appeared, it contained several statements which did not harmonize with the author's uniform revealments respecting the entire unsupernaturalness of all human events. These statements gave rise to many criticisms and speculations, in a manner not unlike the method usually adopted by commentators to harmonize biblical averments with each other, and especially with what they conceive such averments should be made to signify. The objectionable points alluded to—those which could not be readily explained according to the author's standard, *Nature* and *Reason*—were the following:

First, The unaccountable disappearance of the author on the morning subsequent to the fastening, by himself, of all the doors and windows of the dwelling; which the young man, who slept in an adjoining room, asserted, notwithstanding the author's disappearance, he found in precisely the same condition on his descension from his bed-room to the lower story of the house.

Second,—The extraordinary journey which the author supposed he accomplished in the brief period of sixteen hours—making the speed, according to human experience, utterly supernatural.

Third,—The mysterious and apparently unaccountable manner in which he crossed the Hudson river, in order to seek the Catskill Mountains.

Fourth,—The walking past all wagons, and other vehicles on his route to Poughkeepsie; and the author seeing the persons in them, but they not perceiving him—thus implying his invisibility at the time.

When the vision, alluded to, was first published, the author candidly announced his inability, at the time, to furnish the public with the proper solution of these seemingly supernatural and contradictory statements,—alleging it as his reason, that he had truthfully related all he remembered, while in his interior state, of the incidents of the vision; and the circumstances with regard to the doors, windows, &c., he related according to the allegations of the young man who was the first to observe the condition of the fastenings on the morning of the initiatory vision, related in the first chapter.

About eight months ago, however, the author obtained, by an interior retrospection of the whole experience, a clear insight into the minutiæ of the above occurrences; and, in consequence of the entire simplicity and almost inutility of the explanations of the mysterious incidents of his vision, he has adopted this manner of presenting them to the public, rather than incorporating them in the main body of his volume.—Though, it must be confessed, that a very instructive lesson, to biblical commentators and to speculators upon supernatural occurrences, might be obtained from the author's explanations Showing, as they evidently do, that all " mysteries," when properly understood may be traced to one of three causes, namely:—to Nature's immutable principles; to the misapprehension of individuals; to the misrepresentations of enthu siastic zealots.

The author discovers, on his interior and retrogressional examination of the statements referred to, that his friends were confounded with wonder at the mysterious nature of his egress from the house, on the supposition that the doors and windows were all tightly secured in the morning, as the young man stated --all, because this young man, desiring to aggravate the curiosity of the already excited citizens, and to enjoy the speeches occasioned thereby, did not tell the exact truth. For the author ascertained that he arose soon after retiring, while in the somnambulic state, prepared himself and noiselessly passed down stairs and out of the back door of the dwelling, through an adjoining yard, into the street. This is all the mystery there is in this circumstance, which has given rise to several elaborate speculations.

The explanation of the extraordinary journey is found in the fact, which the author has ascertained, that he was absent from Poughkeepsie nearly five hours longer than he was first led to suppose. This renders the traveling not more extraordinary than has been accomplished by several celebrated pedestrians; though it is evident that the author's natural speed of walking was much increased by the high excitement and strength which magnetism had imparted to his entire system.

Perhaps no portion of this vision has excited more curiosity and speculation, than the author's mysterious passage over the Hudson river. But on examination, he discovers that he walked across the river on the ice, which had not then disappeared. This is very reasonable, when it is remembered that his vision was obtained on the seventh of March, at which time the Hudson river, in the region of Catskill, is mainly covered with ice.

The next mysterious portion, referring to the author's implied invisibility to persons on his walk from the grave-yard to Poughkeepsie, is all explainable, he discovers, on the ground that he confounded the flight of his spirit in that direction, in advance of his body, with the act of traveling in his ordinary state. He was then so young in spiritual exercises and experience, it was difficult at times for him to accurately discriminate between the passage of his mind, during its partial disengagement from the physical body, and the ordinary manner of walking. This explains why he perceived the persons in the vehicles on the road to Poughkeepsie, and yet was himself invisible to them. He discovers that his spiritual perceptions passed over the road to the village; then returned to the grave-yard where his body was left in a death-like state, but which his spirit afterward completely re-entered; and then he naturally walked home; but did not remember the latter circumstance in his first relation of the vision, in consequence of the intense excitement which the more essential portions of that interesting experience produced upon his mind.

The author has announced his intention of devoting the ensuing year to public lectures and the teaching of the principles of the Harmonial Philosophy; and his readers will, therefore, not expect from him, at the end of this year, the third volume of the series.

Mr. R. P. Ambler, editor of the Spirit Messenger, institutes the following interesting comparison between Nature and Theology:—"The term *Nature* is properly used to express all the innumerable forms, both visible and invisible, existing in the whole universe, which are an effect and manifestation of the Creator's power. It comprehends not only those things which may be seen with the outward eye, but also those subtle and refined elements which, from their exalted position in the progressive scale of existence, are beyond the reach of the human vision. Nature, therefore, embraces both the *physical* and the *spiritual*, for one is as properly a work of God, and as necessarily subject to established laws, as the other. In short every thing in the whole universe may be comprehended in two great departments—God, the Cause—Nature, the Effect. The supposition, then, that there is, or ever has been any thing, less than the Divine Mind itself, which is supernatural or above nature, involves an impossibility and absurdity.

I am aware that the plan of the old Theology is based, to a great extent, on the occurrence of events which are regarded as supernatural. The basis, how ever, which is here recognized, is as frail and untenable as the system itself is corrupt and false. The events supposed to be supernatural have been so regarded, merely because the laws by which they were produced have not been understood.

Standing as it were in the vestibule of creation, we are able to penetrate but a small part of its sublime mysteries, and hence, not comprehending all the essential principles operating in Nature, we have been inclined to limit them to the boundary of our own vision, and imagine that those occurrences which can not be readily explained, must be *above* or *beyond* nature, resulting from some special exercise of divine power. When, however, we take a more extended survey of the Creator's works; when we consider that every thing below God which exists as an effect of His power is a part of nature, and that those creations which are spiritual and invisible to the outward sense, are governed by laws as fixed and immutable as those with which we are acquainted in this material sphere, we shall realize that there is and can be nothing supernatural, but that all events, however mysterious and wonderful in their character, are the result of established principles, which, though not at present comprehended, shall be known as we advance in knowledge, and the light of a superior wisdom breaks upon the soul." In the midst of much that darkens man's future pathway, there stands a bright and pure theology which leads the honest searcher of Truth to the contemplation of Deity in all the ways and methods of his being. And those who would partake of such sweet enjoyment as naturally flows from a philosophical consideration of this high and lofty theme, will find the beginning principles of that enjoyment in this volume.

A. J. D.

HARTFORD, *May* 21, 1851.

CONTENTS OF VOLUME II.

THE

GREAT HARMONIA.

MY EARLY EXPERIENCE.

READER, by the senses, your spirit perceives the characters hereon impressed, and thereby forms an acquaintance with mine: for by these characters my spirit expresses its *inner* thoughts, which thus come in contact with your spiritual perception; and thereby reflection is excited, and questions arise demanding answers. Personal experience teaches me to anticipate some questions which the following vision may suggest; and to these I feel prompted to reply as follows:

From childhood, I have evinced a constant tendency to meditation, solitary rambles, and somnambulism, which have periodically come on me, and sometimes continued for a protracted period. My parents have known me frequently to leave my bed in the night time, construct machines, draw landscapes, and paint various objects. Once, in the village of Hyde Park, I arose eight nights in succession, and painted, upon a little canvass three feet square, a beautiful landscape, which, when completed, was found to represent the *Garden of Eden*, as I imagined it from historical account.

The testimony of others, however, concerning this power of independent vision, will be more convincing to the skeptical reader.

"In subjoining a few remarks," says Rev. Gibson Smith, "I respond to an urgent call, which is almost universally made, for some account of the *Clairvoyant*, and a brief statement of the circumstances under which, from time to time, his disclosures and experiments have been made. In this, however, I shall give only a very few statements, as a specimen of the many which I could present.*

Mr. Davis is well known here—he has resided, for the first twelve years of his life, at Hyde Park and its vicinity, a place five miles distant from this. Since that period, a term of about six years, he has resided in this place. He has neither been favored with privileges by which to obtain an education, nor has his mind at all been turned to the investigation of scientific matters. These statements are capable of the most satisfactory confirmation. I have said that Mr. D. is not an educated man, nor has he now, in his wakeful state, the least idea of those sublime and lucid representations which he gives in the clairvoyant state, only as some one who hears his revelations may describe them unto him.

I have been located in this place seven months. Previous to my settlement here, I have for many years been a believer in Mesmerism, but a very decided unbeliever in Clairvoyance. But the frequent attestations which I have witnessed as given by my neighbor, Mr. D., have convinced me of the truth of this new and wonderful development of mind,—its powers in Clairvoyance. Experiments have been so varied and multiplied, that I can no longer remain an unbeliever. The truth is irresistible, and I am compelled to believe it.

At the first of my observations, Mr. D. examined my own sys-

* This account was written nearly six years ago. It refers to the author's early experience.

tem, telling me very accurately where a disease with which I had long been afflicted was located—its cause—describing also the pain which I suffered from it, and the weakness occasioned by it, most perfectly. Further: he prescribed medicine for me which cured my disease, and from which I am now perfectly free. He also gave me a phrenological examination, speaking of a peculiarity in the arrangement of the organs, which others had named, and which, with the general representation, he explained most satisfactorily.

I next witnessed his examination of a young lady. He described her condition perfectly, as was acknowledged at the time—pointing out the seat of her disease and pain, designating the different organs by their technical or scientific names, and locating every part of the system which he had occasion to name, with the most astonishing readiness and propriety.

Since the examinations named above, I have witnessed his examination of some seventy or eighty persons, the seat of whose diseases and pains, together with their causes, symptoms, &c., he has described with equal readiness and truth—many of which persons were brought in before him after he was put to sleep, and of whom he had no previous knowledge. Indeed, there can be no reasonable doubt that the human system is transparent before him when he is in the clairvoyant state.

At the time of my examination, as above alluded to, I requested Mr. Davis to go to the house of Mr. A. P. ——, in New Portland, Me.—a distance of some five hundred miles at least, to examine his house, describe his family, &c. He gave an accurate description of the house from cellar to garret, speaking in the outset of the unusually tall chimney, and then proceeding to a very definite representation of the rooms, and a most accurate and minute description of the various articles of furniture within them—pointing out even the number of pictures in a certain room. He described also Mr.

—— and wife, and a child of adoption with them—stating their height, size, complexion, &c.; and most correctly did he describe the disease with which Mr. —— had for some years been troubled, stating that it was occasioned by injuring the spinal cord when lifting a heavy burden, some three years previous to the time of this examination. He described also other houses in the place, recognizing and pointing out my portraiture in a certain room, and making many other most truthful representations altogether too numerous and minute to mention in this account.

Among the many other instances of his power in describing distant objects and events which I witnessed, I would speak of his visit to England. Mr. Wm. Brown, of this place, feeling anxious about his wife and child, who were on a visit to their friends in England, requested Mr. D., the Clairvoyant, to go and inquire after their health and welfare. He went and returned, and informed Mr. B. that his wife and child had been very sick—described their complaints, and said they were then recovering. He also gave a representation of the house in which they resided—of many other things in its vicinity—speaking particularly of an antiquated meeting-house which stood near. He stated that there were four persons in the house at which Mrs. B. was visiting, and that one of them appeared, from the soot upon his clothes, and from his complexion, as a coal-man. For his own satisfaction, Mr. B. immediately wrote to England, making inquiry with reference to all these items, and received an answer confirming the entire account as given by Mr. D. A man of the household was engaged in the coal business; the account of the antiquated building was also true; and the wife and child had been sick as represented above, and were convalescent at the time of Mr. D.'s examination.

As another instance which I will name, as a specimen of the powers of the Clairvoyant, I would relate the fact that Mr. D——, a young man of this place, had long been absent at sea, and his friends becoming very anxious about him, requested that Mr. Davis, the Clairvoyant, be requested to go in search of him. He accordingly went, and found him at a distance of eight thousand miles. He told his precise condition: that by a fall he had broken his leg; and that at this moment he was in a long building, confined to his bed—that he was then talking with a tall man dressed in white pants, with a green jacket, and that he, Mr. D——, was weeping, being in conversation relative to his mother, whom he then expected never again to see. Mr. Davis, the Clairvoyant, however, said that the young man would return home again to his friends. The young man has since returned according to the testimony of the Clairvoyant, and he has also confirmed the entire statement of the Clairvoyant. He had received the fall,—his leg was broken; the long building was a hospital, to which he was taken after receiving his calamity—he had conversation with a tall man, as named above, in reference to his mother, whom then he did not expect again to see; and he wept on the occasion, as testified by the Clairvoyant;—all of which account can be confirmed to the abundant satisfaction of any inquirer. When the young man arrived, his friends told him they knew the accident that had befallen him; at what distance it occurred; the conversation which he held with the tall man, &c.; all of which was readily acknowledged and confirmed by the returning son.

I will in this place present a letter which I have received from a gentleman whose character for discernment, candor and integrity, is not to be questioned.

ORONO, May 9th, 1845.

Friend Smith,—Agreeably to your request, I send you the following statements, in reference to the mesmeric experiments which I witnessed in Poughkeepsie, some few weeks since, as given by Mr. Davis, the Clairvoyant, of that place. And I would first speak of his examination of my own person. By what power he made his discoveries, or formed his decisions, I know not; but certain I am they were correct. He very accurately pointed out certain difficulties of the stomach with which I had long before been afflicted, but which the energies of my system had resisted and thrown off, and from which I was then free. He also pointed out certain other difficulties, which, from much exposure, I had experienced, with such exact precision, that I could not doubt that my system was transparent in his view. I made some inquiries, upon which he replied that I was not diseased—that my lungs and chest were sound, save a slight irritation upon the bronchial tubes, occasioned by much exposure, and a bad cold with which I was then most manifestly afflicted.

I would further state, that I requested the Clairvoyant to go to Orono, Me., and examine a man of my acquaintance. He went and found him, (the name having been given,) and described him, his height, size, &c., and spoke also of a large scrofulous tumor on the side of his neck. He described the size, shape and appearance of the tumor very accurately and minutely,—much more so than I could have done, although I had frequently seen the man thus afflicted. The Clairvoyant also spoke of the method and gave the directions by which the tumor could be removed.

Among other examinations and prescriptions which I witnessed, was the case of a child in Poughkeepsie, afflicted with the croup. The father of the child came into the room in much apparent excitement and anxiety, and requested that Mr. D., who was then in the clairvoyant state, be requested to prescribe medicine for his child. The Clairvoyant paused for a moment, as he usually does before an effort of the kind, and then proceeded to prescribe. The Clairvoyant was then requested to go and look at the child, and see how he might be at that moment. He went, and having evidently beheld him, said, yes—he is very sick; he lies in the woman's lap now; he chokes very much; he is very black; and, speaking to the father, said, you had better go quick, the medicine I have named will be good for him. The remedy, as prescribed, was immediately applied; and in a short time the child was relieved, and recovered. These facts can be confirmed, to the satisfaction of any one, by the most indubitable testimony.

And now, dear sir, having carefully and very truthfully penned the above, I remain, with much respect, yours, &c.

L. P. RAND.

I would remark in this place, that I could give very many testimonies like those presented above, but I deem what I have already presented, authentic as they are, sufficient to show that Mr. Davis, when in the clairvoyant state, has powers most wonderful and sublime; and that his knowledge entirely surpasses the ordinary conceptions of man. In fact, it would seem that when in this state the powers of his mind expand indefinitely, extending to every department of science and knowledge, grasping not only the minutest intricacies in the vegetable and animal kingdoms, but also the vast mechanism and laws of the planetary worlds. He seems equally familiar and at home, whether speaking of the earth's atmosphere, its extent, its gases, its mists and clouds, or of the heart and its appendages, with the life-current that flows through it to the ten thousand avenues of the human form—the same, whether giving a botanical description of the herb of the field, explaining the formation of a dew-drop, or expounding the principles by which the fierce comet is controlled in its fiery path! Now, he talks of the brain, its structure, its formations; of the formation of mind, as acting in connection with the physical organization; and now he speaks familiarly of the unspeakable gifts and capacities of superior beings in the angelic state. The sick man is brought in before him, or he is requested to visit him, hundreds of miles distant, and his system being transparent in his view, he examines, detects the cause, describes the disease, and prescribes a remedy. When he has thus pointed out the disease, he pauses for a moment, as if to look through the whole arcana of nature, then analyzes, compounds and prescribes with the most perfect readiness and propriety. Nor is it less astonishing, that having given long and minute prescriptions, embracing a great variety of ingredients—prescriptions given with wonderful rapidity—he should accurately remember the whole, even the quality and quantity of the smallest article, to any number of weeks and months afterward, when in the transic state. His diction is generally free from errors or blunders; he speaks rapidly and correctly, using words suited to his subject,—giving the scientific name to the medicine he recommends; and converses freely and accurately in any language he has occasion to use. I confess that these statements would seem to be almost too much to publish to the world, but they are nevertheless true."*

Such facts are external evidences that the spirit can command the body to do its will, though outer light, or other ordinary aids, be not employed,—which fact to me is manifest in a more perfect degree, while in an interior mood.

Concurrently with the foregoing testimony, calculated to establish the reality and reliability of spiritual perception, are many of the interior experiences of Emanuel Swedenborg. As he is the individual who came to me in the vision, soon to be related, I will furnish the reader with *three* instances of undoubted spiritual perception, from his own experience, as a seer. They illustrate the manifestations consequent upon mental illumination.

First Instance.—"Swedenborg," says Wilkinson, in his biography of that Swedish philosopher, "was probably in London during the latter part of 1758. * * * We find him returning to Gottenburg from England on the 19th of July, 1759, and here he

* The powers here described were mainly developed subsequently to the *vision* about to be related.

gave a *public proof* that he had a more spacious eyesight than was usual in his day. Immanuel Kant, the transcendental philosopher, shall be our historian of the occurrence that took place.

'On Saturday, at four o'clock, P. M.,' says Kant, 'when Swedenborg arrived at Gottenburg from England, Mr. William Castel invited him to his house, together with a party of fifteen persons. About six o'clock, Swedenborg went out, and after a short interval returned to the company, quite pale and alarmed. He said that a dan gerous fire had just broken out in Stockholm, at the Sudermalm (Gottenburg is three hundred miles from Stockholm,) and that it was spreading very fast. He was restless, and went out often. He said that the house of one of his friends, whom he named, was already in ashes, and that his own was in danger. At eight o'clock, after he had been out again, he joyfully exclaimed, 'Thank God! the fire is extinguished, the third door from my house.' This news occasioned great commotion through the whole city, and particularly among the company in which he was. It was announced to the governor the same evening. On the Sunday morning, Swedenborg was sent for by the governor, who questioned him concerning the disaster. Swedenborg described the fire precisely, how it had begun, in what manner it had ceased, and how long it had continued. On the same day the news was spread through the city, and, as the governor had thought it worthy of attention, the consternation was considerably increased; because many were in trouble on account of their friends and property, which might have been involved in the disaster. On the Monday evening, a messenger arrived at Gottenburg, who was despatched during the time of the fire. *In the letters brought by him, the fire was described precisely in the manner stated by Swedenborg.* On the Tuesday morning the royal courier arrived at the governor's with the melancholy intelligence of the fire, of the loss it had occasioned, and of the houses it had damaged and ruined, not in the least differing from that which

Swedenborg had given immediately it had ceased; for the fire was extinguished at eight o'clock.

What can be brought forward against the authenticity of this occurrence? My friend who wrote this to me, has not only examined the circumstances of this extraordinary case at Stockholm, but also, about two months ago, at Gottenburg, where he is acquainted with the most respectable houses, and where he could obtain the most authentic and complete information; as the greatest part of the inhabitants, who are still alive, were witnesses to the memorable occurrence.'

Kant had sifted this matter, to the utmost, by a circle of inquiries, epistolary as well as personal. * * * His account comes, therefore, as a suitable testimony. But what proof is so good as the re-appearance of the facts? Powers and events of the kind are now common enough not to excite surprise from their rarity. Mesmerism produces a per centage of seers equal occasionally to such achievements. Nay, but the faculty of transcending the horizon of space and the instance of time, is as old as history: there have always been individuals who in vision of a higher altitude, saw the refractions of the distant and the future painted upon the curtains of the present. At any rate, Swedenborg was aware of the faculty long before he became a seer. Thus in his *Animal Kingdom*, Part VII., p. 237, when speaking of the soul's state after death, he has the following, illustrative of its powers: 'I need not mention,' says he, 'the manifest sympathies acknowledged to exist in this lower world, and which are too many to be recounted: so great being the sympathy and magnetism of man, that communication often takes place between those who are miles apart. Such statements are regarded by many as absurdities, yet experience proves their truth. Nor will I mention that the ghosts of some have been presented visibly after death and burial,' &c., &c. To account for events like Swedenborg's vision of the fire of Stockholm, (which also

Robsahm says that he foretold,) we need not pierce the vault of nature; this world has perfections, mental, imponderable, and even physical, equivalent to supply the sense. The universe is telegraphically present to itself in every tittle, or it would be no universe. There are also slides of eyes in mankind as an Individual, adequate to converting into sensation all the quick correspondence that exists between things by magnetism and other kindred message bearers."

Second Instance.—"Supernaturalism," continues the same candid historian, "has charms for every society, whether atheistic or Christian, savage or civilized, scientific or poetic. May we not say, that it is the undercharm of all other interests, and that from childhood upward the main expectation of every journey, the hope of every uncovering, the joy of every new man and bright word, is, that we may come at length somewhere upon that mortal gap which opens to the second life. Supernaturalism in all ages has had also a commercial side, and has been cultivated as a means to regain *missing property*, or to discover hidden treasures. The good people of Stockholm were perhaps spiritual chiefly in this latter direction. It was in 1761 that Swedenborg was consulted on an affair of the kind by a neighbor of his, the widow of Louis Von Marteville, who had been ambassador from Holland to Sweden. Curiosity too was a prompting motive in her visit; and she went to the seer with several ladies of her acquaintance, all eager to have 'a near view of so strange a person.' Her husband had paid away twenty-five thousand Dutch guilders, and the widow being again applied to for the money, could not produce the receipt. She asked Swedenborg whether he had known her husband, to which he answered in the negative, but he promised her, on her entreaty, that if he met him in the other world, he would inquire about the receipt. Eight days afterward Von Marteville in a dream told her where to find the receipt, as well as a hair-pin set with brilliants, which had been given up as lost. This was at two o'clock in the morning, and the widow, alarmed yet pleased, rose at once, and found the articles, as the dream described. She slept late in the morning. At eleven o'clock, A. M., Swedenborg was announced. His first remark, before the lady could open her lips, was, that 'during the preceding night he had seen Von Marteville, and had wished to converse with him, but the latter excused himself, on the ground that he must o to discover to his wife something of importance.' Swedenborg dded that 'he then departed out of the society in which he had been for a year, and would ascend to one far happier'; owing, we presume, to his being lightened of a worldly care. This account, attested as it is by the lady herself, through the Danish General, Von E——, her second husband, was noised through all Stockholm. It ought to be added, that *Madame* offered to make Swedenborg a handsome present for his services, but this he declined."

Third Instance.—"It was in the same year, (1761,) that Louisa Ulrica, a sister of Frederick the Great of Prussia, and married to Adolphus Frederick, King of Sweden, received a letter from the Duchess of Brunswick, in which she mentioned that she had read in the Gottingen Gazette, an account of a man at Stockholm, who pretended to speak with the dead, and she wondered that the Queen, in her correspondence, had not alluded to the subject. The Queen had no doubt heard of the Marteville affair, and this, coupled with her sister's desires, made her wish to satisfy herself by an interview with Swedenborg. Captain de Stahlhammer, out of many authorities, is the one whose narrative we select of what passed at that interview.

'A short time,' says Stahlhammer, 'after the death of the Prince of Prussia, Swedenborg came to court, (being summoned thither by the senator, Count Scheffer.) As soon as he was perceived by the Queen, she said to him, "Well, Mr. Assessor, have you seen my brother?" Swedenborg answered, "No;" whereupon she replied,

"If you should see him, remember me to him." In saying this, she did but jest, and had no thought of asking him any information about her brother. Eight days afterward, and not four and twenty hours, nor yet at a particular audience, Swedenborg came again to court, but so early that the Queen had not left her apartment called the white room, where she was conversing with her maids of honor and other ladies of the court. Swedenborg did not wait for the Queen's coming out, but entered directly into her apartment, and whispered in her ear. The Queen, struck with astonishment, was taken ill, and did not recover herself for some time. After she was come to herself, she said to those about her, "*There is only God and my brother who can know what he has just told me.*" She owned that he had spoken of her last correspondence with the prince, the subject of which was known to themselves alone.'"

So far as this evidence goes, so far are we persuaded of the spirit's independent entity; not that the spirit is independent of the body, but that it is, or at least should be, the *master;* the body being subordinate. At death, when present partnership between body and spirit is dissolved, the spirit inhabits another sphere; the *body* is discarded as being no longer a fit habitation for the elevated soul, whose promised residence is in "a mansion not made with hands, eternal in the heavens." All this may be, and yet an invisible relation may exist between the *lower* and *higher*, or *earth* and *heaven;* for we do constantly acknowledge that there is a world within and a world without. And so I *reason* with myself in this manner: "If I should lose my form this moment, then I should only be dead by *outer* sense, to outer things; but there is a world within yet unexplored, and so I shall be alive, by inner sense, to inner things; and this is far superior and more glorious."

The question of mere *locality* is of but little importance; for new sensations are not so much created by coming in contact with new objects, as by one's own *development*, which elevates the spirit to a proportionate degree of enjoyment, consisting of higher and wiser modes of action. Wherefore, if I *never* change *locality—never* leave this individual globe—I shall be immortal in the world within—growing in *wisdom* and *happiness*, which constitute *heaven*, whether obtained in this room, in society, or in spheres beyond the power of fancy to conceive. Now, reader, from principles unfolded in personal experience, I am convinced that the mind is capable of endless expansion, of unutterable enjoyment, and of an unbounded growth in wisdom; but there was a time when I did not think so, because my thoughts were directed by popular religious teachers.

At first I attended the Presbyterian church, studied its catechism, and believed in a God clothed in Calvinistic attributes; also in His eternal decrees of election and reprobation, and also in many other points of faith ascribing unamiable qualities to the Deity scarcely discoverable in any of his creatures. An old gentleman, who was my Sunday School teacher, would occasionally expound Scripture to the class, and frequently to me, as I was ever inclined to listen. One day, after reflecting upon the subject of "election," I called upon the old man, and said:

"Uncle Isaac, you told me that *God is love?*"

"Yes, my child."

"And that he *is wise*, too?"

"Certainly, my little son."

"Well, you say I must be good, and love my parents, or else God will send me to hell forever?"

"Yes."

"Now, uncle Isaac, "if *God is wise*, he *knew*, before he made me, whether I would go to hell or to heaven; and if *he is love*, I think he would have been too good to create me."

"Oh! my child, you must n't talk so; the ways of God are past finding out; our hearts are depraved; our *reason carnal;* the *devil tempts you* to have such thoughts of God."

I went no more to Sunday School; but my mind was painfully agitated. New circumstances soon placed me in the way of Methodism. I attended their meetings, and prayed that the spirit "all sinful and hateful before God," might lead me to the altar. But it was no use; the more I desired, the further I receded; for it seemed foolish and absurd. After being in this state of suspense for a long time, the residing and much esteemed Pastor came one day where I was engaged at my work, and inquired:

"Well, brother Davis, how do you feel?"

"Very well, Sir," said I.

"No, no, I have reference to your *spiritual* welfare—have you made peace with your God?"

It seemed impossible to answer. I never have had any disturbance with him in all my life, thought I. But in my embarrassment I stammered out, "No, sir."

"Well," continued he, "don't you *fear* your God?"

"No, Sir," said I, "I am not afraid of God."

"O, unconverted youth!" said the Pastor, "I fear the day of grace *is past.* I fear you will be damned forever!"

On thus saying, he turned and left me. O, reader, can you imagine my thoughts, as he closed this sentence? The love of my nature was chilled into the coldest hate. For a moment I feared no one; nor did I love life, myself, man, earth, heaven, or God! A long life, thought I, is before me—why not turn *robber* or *pirate* at once? If I live a pure and blameless life, damnation will be my destiny; and if I should be desperately wicked, it could make no difference in my final estate; for if the day of grace *is* past, I am eternally lost—lost in hell! I hesitated a moment, and *a though* told me, "be calm—the Pastor is wrong." O, how I did rejoice

By another year I was inclined to Universalism. Its teachings were more congenial with my better nature. I rejoiced that some persons entertained a more exalted conception of the Father. But

I could not believe the system of theology as a whole; it was too complicated; it involved too many contradictions, and required too many verbal criticisms—admitting the *Bible* to be as true a *revelation* of God as is Nature, which we *know* can not be made by man. And so I was in this state of anxious apprehension until occurred the vision to be related on subsequent pages; and *this* will *explain* the horrid fears I experienced on *first* passing into the Magnetic condition.

And now, reader, if you have any similar experiences, *do* not consider your "heart depraved," your "reason carnal," "the ways of God past finding out"; but investigate them, as I did, as all should do; and you will not only discard all *isms*, and their absurdities, but will prove yourself a lover of Nature and her laws, which are "God's ways," and be a pure and happy spirit, and a wise child of the all-wise Eternal Father!

The Magnetic State.

Situated in close relation to the one who intends to produce the physical sleep, I am compelled, in order that it may be properly effected, to sit in an easy position, entirely quiet, with mind free from external intrusions and internal desires. The mind and thoughts should be concentrated to accelerate the accomplishment of the end. I become wholly passive, while the operator is active; and due care is taken to exclude all unfavorable circumstances, which might, in any particular, render the operation unsuccessful. Thus conditioned, for the first time, I remained perfectly tranquil, desiring to know the result flowing from a reciprocal exchange of sympathy and sensation. The following account embodies the result of the first, which also in its main features represents subsequent processes:—

I felt the chilly hand pass and repass my brow and chamber of thought. The living blood, which had flowed undisturbed through my youthful form during its brief existence, seemed well-nigh arrested. Its ten thousand avenues were immediately illuminated with the livid flames of electric fire; and anon it was intensely dark within. Dreadful and strange feelings passed over my body and through my brain, in rapid succession. My emotions were painful. I had heard of the horrid sensations of dying! Oh! could this be the period of my physical dissolution—of the spirit's transformation to a higher sphere! Yes! the heart discontinued to perform its office so powerfully as before—its beatings were less frequent! I felt the different senses which connect the mind with the outer-world, gradually close—alas! were they closing forever?

All my senses yielded imperceptibly to the subduing power. I could no longer hear the busy and active world without, nor feel the touch of any object, living or dead. No longer, thought I, can I behold the system of nature, whose light, life and beauty have prompted me to the deepest admiration. The sweet and fragrant forests and fields are gone, and are never more to be the scenes of happy contemplation!

Thoughts like these flashed rapidly through my awe-struck mind. But what was I to do? To resist the sensations would have prevented the effect hoped for and anticipated. But to remain in this condition much longer, thought I, will result in closing forever, from my spirit, the beauties of the material universe.

But the query now occurred, whether all this was any more than the illusion of the imagination? "Certainly I *think*. I feel strange; but do I actually *know* that my sensations are real?" Thus questioned I myself, without making the least exertion to satisfy my judgment as to the truth or reality of what I experienced. I sat almost breathless, a few seconds longer, encouraging a hope that the experiment might not succeed, meanwhile involuntarily assisting to produce it. "I am alive yet," thought I, "for I hear the operator inquire the hour—I hear him respond seemingly to something said by another—but I do not hear any other person speak! Is not this exceedingly strange?" Another silence occurred, during which I endeavored to analyze my feelings, which had penetrated the innumerable recesses of my whole structure. But again I heard a low, distant, strange, unpleasant sound proceeding from the operator, as if from the human world, calling me back to earth, which I was seemingly leaving far behind. Then my sense of hearing—those chambers along whose delicate halls has reverberated the pleasurable music accompanying the sacred voice of pure affection and friendship, are closed!—and closed to seal the reality of an eternal silence? Can this indeed be so? thought I, while the most dreadful darkness encompassed me. "The moment has arrived—I will submit no longer to this dangerous and dreadful experiment; and never shall my marvel-seeking mind again lead me into such fearful perils. I will speak and protest against a further continuance of this operation." But oh! how frightful!—my tongue, seeming instantly to be enlarged, clung violently to the roof of my mouth. My cheeks seemed extremely swollen, and my lips were joined as if by death, and apparently to move no more. Another thought passed through my brain, and I instantly obeyed its suggestion. I made a desperate effort to change my position, particularly to disengage my hands; but, horrible beyond description, my feet, hands and body were entirely beyond the control of my will! I could no longer claim the proprietorship over my own person. All was lost—it seemed—irretrievably lost. Yes! I felt convinced that external life and being were for me no more. What was I to do? I could exercise my mental faculties to the highest degree—could reason with perfect clearness; but I could not hear, see, feel, speak, or move! I had no means of ascertaining my true physical or spiritual situation. Thus I mused and queried within myself: "I have a body, a tangible body—I reside in the *form;* but is it my natural or spiritual body—one adapted to the outer-world, or to the sphere of the inner-life? Where am I? Oh! I am lonely! alas, if *this* is the "Spirit-Home!" A natural consciousness, however, pervaded my mind—preconceived ideas were evolved from my inmost memory; and what surprised me more than any thing else, was the gushing forth of novel and brilliant thoughts, apparently extending over the vast landscape of the "Spirit-Home," and comprehending more than it is possible for me to relate. These conceptions were, I am persuaded, an influx of interior and immortal truth.

This moment demanded an absolute decision. Death of the outer, and life of the inner being, seemed an inevitable consequence of my situation. Every moment I approached nearer and nearer the dark valley, which lay before me. I felt a perverseness, but this only impelled me onward. Again and again I retreated in mind, but every wave of thought wafted me nearer and nearer the fearful vale of inconceivable darkness. Now is the time for a powerful exertion; resistance is necessary, or else I shall be lost in yon impenetrable gloom forever. But, alas! I advanced nearer and nearer. In thought, I leaped back suddenly, and lo! I stood on an awful margin, that seemed lashed by waves of mad despair, that rolled up from the ocean of an eternal night! The warmth of my whole person was exchanged for death-like coldness. Horrid thoughts of disorganization continued to distress me. Naught but an eternal midnight clothed my tender spirit, and I was filled with terror. The darkness became more dark and appalling. And now I was seized with an unearthly shudder, and—terrible to relate—I found myself revolving in that blackened gloom with an inconceivable velocity! I seemed to be revolving in a spiral path, with an orbit, wide at first, and every revolution on my descending flight contracted my movement. Down, down I sank, till immersed in that mighty ocean, where conflicting elements were swallowed by a mountain wave of darkness, which grasped me within its mighty folds, and I sank to the lowest depths of forgetfulness !*

How uniform and immutable are those powers which are constantly manifesting themselves throughout every department of Nature ! I am deeply assured by a knowledge of their unfailing righteousness, that nothing can possibly occur opposed to the highest well-being of the innumerable Worlds, forms, and compositions which are developed by them, and intrusted to their exclusive and eternal control. So I am compelled to believe ; and that, too, by the force of those explicit evidences constantly presented to my mind. However, all minds are not susceptible to, or capable of, receiving similar impressions. Nevertheless, the reality of the evidences on which they rest, can not be doubted by those inclined to natural observation. And that my inward conviction upon this point rests upon a substantial basis, the reader will be prepared to admit when I relate the account of the mysterious restoration of my lifeless body and distracted mind to the enjoyment of external Nature, and the kind smiles of beloved friends.

I awoke into consciousness while revolving in a circuitous form, in that hideous darkness. I rejoice with exceeding great joy. This darkness continued, with the movement, to increase and expand, till I arose to the margin, which bounded the ocean of oblivion, whose restless waves conveyed me to the high, happy land of thought and wakefulness !

* The horrid sensations which the writer experienced on first entering the magnetic state, were in a great measure attributable to the gloomy views of death, and of possible subsequent conditions, instilled into his mind through early theological teachings. These sensations were not experienced on subsequently entering the state.

My senses, the windows of the soul, were opened; light broke in upon my dimmed vision; sound vibrated through the labyrinths of my ear; sensation flashed over my whole frame—and I moved, spake, and opened my eyes. But how surprised! I was living in the body, on earth, and in precisely the same position as when I first seated myself for the experiment. Many were sitting near and around me, with countenances indicating awe, pleasure, and astonishment. For a moment I felt dissatisfied. I could not realize that I had returned from the "dark valley of the shadow of death." But another penetrating glance about the room, and upon the familiar faces of those around, convinced me; and I arose as if from the chamber of death, with strength renewed, and greeted the amazed and delighted witnesses.

Methought, how strange that so much time should have elapsed, of which memory had preserved no record!—and that unremembered period, too, yielding more interior and immortal truth than any other period in my life! How strange a phenomenon witnessed by inhabitants of this and the spirit-world, and meanwhile unknown to the subject's memory! I could not suppress these thoughts, for the operator informed me that I had been *in that condition over four hours*, during which time I had manifested some of the most solemn and surprising demonstrations of spiritual sight. I had developed some of those many powers which we *now* know only rest in the soul's deep bosom; whose interior recesses are unfolding heat, light and knowledge, which are faith, love, and wisdom.

I had described the internal condition of many persons, and als had described their residences,—had visited various portions of th town and country—with which, in my nominal state, I was totally unacquainted. All this I did, spiritually, to the perfect satisfaction of those who requested the descriptions. "Can this," thought I, "be prophetic or apostolic power, mental hallucination, spiritual or imaginative ecstasy, a fantastic display of satanic influence,—or is it a beautiful truth, developed by a kind of natural incantation ?" Many similar queries entered my mind, in rapid succession, and passed it unanswered; for they were all *caused* by the mental impressions—arising from the gloomy religious ideas of my youth, which were absurd, though popular and generally believed.

For several weeks, experiments of the kind which I have decribed, were successfully continued. Each day new truths and interesting wonders made their appearance and spread their influence over the community. But the heart of that monster, Ignorance, was touched, and prejudice began to be aroused. The various denominations arose in rebellion against the developments, and especially against their careful investigation. In proportion to the surprise and persecution of the inhabitants of the village, did my anxiety increase; and I earnestly prayed to be informed, from some reliable source, whence came this power, and what constituted its true nature and purpose.

Know, then, gentle reader, that these things which I have related, comprehend all the actual recollection and knowledge in my possession* concerning the interior reality of this marvelous faculty of Spiritual Sight.

Thus remained all external affairs, until occurred the following revelation:—made manifest to me personally, under some of the most remarkable circumstances ever truthfully related.

On a chilly, disagreeable evening, in the year 1843—March 6th, —we (operator and myself) proceeded to the residence of some friends at No. 24 Garden Street, to comply with a solicitation by them made, to have me inspect their diseased constitutions. On our arrival, few words were exchanged previous to being placed in that strange condition before described. I experienced nearly the

* That is, when the author experienced the above phenomena.

same mental transformation, except that intense excitement and sense of novelty, which characterized my first attempt.

The engagement being fulfilled, at the expiration of the ordinary period, which is two hours, the operator endeavored to relieve me of that mysterious influence which I term Spiritual Sympathy; but it seemed impossible. Again and again he made the attempt, and as often it proved unsuccessful. Not long, however, and I felt returning life streaming through my form, and became, as I supposed, free from the subtle influence, to which I had been subjected.

After conversing a few moments, with those present, I felt an aversion to their several spheres, which impelled me instantly to leave the house. By the stair-way I descended to the street, at which time I imagined that my system retained a minute portion of the imparted influence. This was confirmed by a sudden illumination of the brain in the region of the intellectuals, which destroyed, at once, my fixedness of purpose. I stood transfixed! On leaving the room, my intention was to return home, and, not feeling quite well, to immediately retire. But thus confused, I leaned against the street gate, seemingly at the mercy and disposal of some Superhuman power. While standing thus, an intense desire sprang up within me to visit a clergyman, who resided in the same street, and for whom I had formed a strong attachment. This suggestion I speedily obeyed. I advanced to his door, rang the bell, was ushered into the sitting room; a seat was furnished, and I sat near the window. Hurriedly, I glanced over several books lying on the table. My mind was painfully distracted. The clergyman entered the room, and warmly welcomed me. I offered many apologies for my intrusion at that late hour, but each failed to satisfy his mind; for, with the cause of my visit I myself was unacquainted. Wherefore he wondered greatly as to what could be the real cause and object of my sudden appearance. He strongly desired, and frequently repeated the desire, that I should pass the night with him. This I was impressed to decline, for reasons I could not define. Without giving or receiving any satisfaction as to the cause or intention of my visit, I rather abruptly departed.

I proceeded to my home in Main Street, some time after the above unceremonious interview. With mind considerably unsettled, I entered the front door, passed through the hall, and ascended two flights of stairs to my bedchamber. With extreme agitation of body and mind, I laid me down to repose. My thoughts were few and fleeting. My physical system yielded to the sleep-inducing stillness that reigned around; and I sank into an unconscious and death-like slumber.

Behold the awful, sublime and stupendous majesty of the expanded heavens! See the ethereal curtains, whose dissolving and commingling folds conceal from the human vision the star-peopled abyss,—where ten thousand thousand orbs roll, in ineffable grace, before the *Celestial Throne* of the ever-living and omniscient King! The grandeur of the transparent sheet, around and above, is beyond the power of language to express. Divine greatness is reflected in all things! *Order* and *Form*, and *Love* and *Wisdom*, are indicated in each created object, from the lowest to the highest. From the constant re-combinations of existing materials, youthfulness is every where manifest, and Beauty grows out of, and inwreaths every spontaneous creation!

Such thoughts as these were presented to my mind, while standing at a late hour of the same night, on the side-walk at the corner of Mill and Hamilton streets, in the quiet village of Poughkeepsie. How can this be? thought I,—I distinctly remember retiring to my own chamber, and falling into a profound sleep; but what a remarkable change! The heavenly archway above is exceedingly glorious and beautiful; and the many stars stationed throughout its vast labyrinths like diamond lights, shine with an immortal effulgence to guide the traveler onward and upward to the city of eternal joy! And here I stand alone, unseen by any except the Eye of the Eternal Being, and unheard by any, except the Ear that hears the silent echoing of all human thoughts! Yes! I am clad in my usual garments, and am contemplating the most high and sublime of subjects!

Thus, I was situated and meditating—not knowing by what means I came thither, or the length of time that had elapsed since I retired; but I retained those diversified sensations of body and mind, which I experienced when I placed myself upon my bed. I felt great calmness, although I could not suppress feelings of curiosity relative to my marvelous transportation. It was spring-time. But it being a late, cold and dreary season, the sun had not yet warmed into life the beauties of Nature. The earth was clothed with a snowy garment, and the whole scene was gloomy, yet awful and sublime.

For a short time I stood meditating, supported by a wall-fence which separated the street from an adjoining field;—when all at once, a strange sound vibrated on my ear, apparently proceeding from behind me. I looked around, and lo, I beheld, with admiration, a flock of clean and beautiful sheep! Their sudden appearance somewhat excited me, but about and with them, all seemed right and good. The flock proved larger than I at first supposed it was, and their physical condition proved far inferior. Their bodies, however, were perfectly *white;* and they manifested great kindness and gentleness of disposition. I was impressed with the following interpretation, which I apprehended as evidently true, and as disclosing the *use* of the vision.

The sheep corresponded to the vast brotherhood of mankind. Their beautiful external whiteness corresponded to the innate purity and goodness of all created spirits, indicating that they are capable of material refinement, and spiritual elevation. The poverty of their bodies corresponded to the wretched physical condition of the earth's inhabitants, owing to the fact that their interests and social affections are disunited; that they are opposed to each other's highest *good* and happiness; that their spiritual sympathies are mis-directed. For mankind are connected by the senses to outer, material things; by friendship, love, and conjugal attraction, they are related socially and spiritually. They are possessed of moral powers which incline them to sentiments of veneration—to the love of good, truth, and of God. And the whole human race represents a flock of sheep, whose shepherd is the Universal Father!

These truths flowed into my unfolded and willing Spirit as freely as Wisdom flows from higher spheres to our earth. I recognized, and deeply felt their use and importance. I continued my meditation. The sheep seemed at peace, in the same position as when I first saw them. But inasmuch as I comprehended the instruction intended, they began to change their position, seemingly desiring some *Fold* wherein they might rest undisturbed. Being greatly confused, they proceeded to pass along the street in such a way as would have shown, had they been men, that their judgments were *weak* or impaired, and that they were thus incapable of choosing the proper and righteous path, which would have led them to that goal which all seemed to be seeking.

At the next moment I beheld a shepherd. His sudden appearance surprised me not, though it was strange, and I approached him. I saw that he was much perplexed, yet fully determined in purpose,—though inefficient to urge or lead the sheep hence, where peace and harmony reigned.

He had great elegance of form; and was plainly and usefully attired. He presented an air of unassuming and stately dignity, to be admired in any being. His countenance indicated purity, and his whole appearance was that of a kind and gentle being, enlowed with physical and spiritual perfectedness. On my approach he spake not, but expressed in natural language, by illuminating his countenance, the desires of his soul. I perceived that he needed sympathy and assistance. The sheep were in ignorance and confusion, which he labored to overcome; and they required gentle but regular discipline. To his request I immediately acceded. By a powerful but wise exertion, we succeeded in establishing an order among them, to which they mutually adhered;—whereupon they and their delighted shepherd proceeded down the street. Their uniform motions seemed melted into one harmonious movement, till they mingled with surrounding objects that formed the distant scene.

With impressive solemnity, the whole scene came and passed within the brief period of ten minutes. I preserved, however, general tranquillity throughout the amazing representation. The signification of its closing part was made distinctly manifest. The shepherd corresponded to a great and noble Reformer,—a good Man, *our Brother*, even Christ, whose spirit breathed "*peace on earth and good will to men;*" whose exalted wisdom comprehended the many physical and spiritual requirements of the human race; whose grand and healthy system of social and moral government infinitely transcended all others conceived by man, since life, sensation and intelligence pervaded the bosom of Nature. He investigated all natural desires, and the means for their appropriate gratification. He sympathized with the suffering, the destitute and the desponding. The suffering and needy he soothed to peace and joy; and the desponding he inspired with a "lively hope." Love to Man—of truth—of heaven—and of God, with a progressive advancement in happiness, he taught, by a righteous life and godly conversation.

The state of painful confusion into which the sheep were thrown, corresponded to the confused condition of the theological world;—to the conflicts between truth and error, reason and theology, reality and imagination, theory and practice;—and to the intense anxiety each being experiences who desires, but can not believe in, immortal life. The request which so benignly beamed forth from his countenance, corresponded to the truth that I, like others, am called to perform a duty enjoined by the Originator and Disseminator of all truth and goodness. I realized the truth thus impressed, and cheerfully bowed, in humble submission, to the sacred responsibility!

So I am compelled to speak: First, because the instruction intended by the beautiful representation, flowed into my mind irresistibly; and secondly, because my unconscious transportation to that portion of the village which I had not at that time any thought of visiting, was produced and governed by a power superior to myself, and more wise than I.

The scene now changed. I stood almost free from thought, and anon, sensation was nearly destroyed. The life-blood chilled in my exposed body; my head and chest were painfully congested; my spirit contracted violently, and seemed determined to leave my weak and prostrate form entirely! I was surrounded with a death-like darkness, and became almost insensible. I struggled and gasped for breath; but the effort failed. Life had almost fled; all was cold, dark and deathly. I made a feeble effort to escape that lonely death, and then fell unconsciously to the ground.

On the subsequent morning, an anxiety, mingled with fear and surprise, pervaded the family with whom I boarded. A young man who occupied an adjoining room, stated that he was not disturbed by a single sound during the whole night; and rising at the usual hour, and discovering my absence, he descended to the room and hall, through which I had passed on the previous evening.

* * * * * * * *

My marvelous disappearance was quickly communicated to

many of the inhabitants of the village. No one could do more than express his astonishment. Some gentlemen, among whom was the clergyman at whose house I had called on the evening previous, conceived it proper to institute a search. But no acquaintance, of whom inquiry was made, had seen me—nor could I be found at my usual places of resort. Search was at length abandoned;—and their *fear* was succeeded by a *hope*, which was modified into an assurance that *those laws* which were engaged in effecting my unaccountable disappearance, would preserve me, and that the affair would end in good. * * * *

Where, reader, do you suppose I could have been? I will relate. My natural powers were so exhausted that I was rendered unconscious of life or existence; and had not my body been re-supplied with life and energy, I could not have changed my position. But now a sweet and gentle sensation aroused me, and renewed the consciousness of life. I moved, and rejoiced. I stretched forth my hand, and felt the soft, waving and vivifying atmosphere. I could hear, and I opened my eyes! "Is it possible," thought I, "that I again behold, with natural eyes, the material creation?" In a few minutes my vision was clear, and I glanced, calmly, over the scene that lay before me. I was nearly stupefied with wonder! I was in a reclining position, elevated about seven feet from the ground. The mass on which I rested was composed of underwood and youthful trees, neatly and closely interwoven one with another, forming a well-proportioned structure, which corresponded precisely to an artificial *altar*. On each side of me was a barren, craggy and stupendous mountain; higher and mightier than any I had ever seen. I was thus situated in a deep and apparently inaccessible valley. The towering acclivities were covered with ice and frozen snow; and through this hard coating protruded large, ill-shaped rocks, between whose interstices were decayed trees. That I was lying on a line, in the direction of east and west, could be seen from the positions of surrounding objects—of this I felt fully persuaded. My head being in an eastern direction, enabled me to observe on rising, that the valley was terminated by the mountain acclivity about ten rods to the west—before me—there being an apparent opening leading to the left, around the mountain's base. On turning eastward I beheld a beautiful river, which afterward proved to be the Hudson, at the seeming distance of about four miles. On the opposite side of the river I beheld ill-fashioned and dilapidated dwellings, desolate and abrupt hills, and forests dark and gloomy.

The heavens were now shrouded as if mourning a world's death, and sorrow filled their bosom with frightful paroxysms. Dense blackness swelled into bursting convulsions, and *thunder*, like smothered groans of universal agony, rolled forth, far and wide, with terrific violence. The electric fire, like distorted smiles of hope mingled with pain, illuminated the vast concave,—succeeded by gloom which the contrast rendered blackness inconceivable! Light and darkness followed each other in instantaneous succession. Oh! it was a horrid scene. I never can forget how, as the rain descended, the heavens seemed to weep, and groan, and sigh, and laugh with angry joy; and how I, alone, did sympathize with them, and pray for power to still their troubled elements,—not having this power, I trembled and desired to escape. Terrible indeed was my exposed condition. The rain fell in torrents, and the fleeting elements, while warring among themselves, seemed to menace my destruction!

An awful and impressive solemnity pervaded the whole scene. It was a fearful *Book*, but a sublime and instructive lesson. I listened with a trembling but voluntary submission. Reposing upon an *altar*, composed of woodbine and other shrubbery, encompassed about with mountains high, frightful and forbidding—rendering escape impossible—*there* I gathered a harvest of wisdom! From the grand, but appalling representation, I learned submission ana elevation; and from the quickness of the lightning and the terrific positiveness of the thunder, I learned that "the Lord God omnipotent reigneth." I beheld my own insignificance, and meanwhile, as of all mankind, I beheld an unspeakable importance in my very existence. I learned to revere, obey, and depend alone on that Power which directs and controls the Universe!—and saw that omnipotent truth *will* consume all *error* and artificial theology, whose power is weakened, and whose corruption is revealed by the divine light of Nature's manifestations! I learned that *all evil will* be subdued and banished by the ultimate triumph of those principles that are good, *divine* and unchangeable, and that unrighteousness shall be no more;—that streams of good and healthy motives will spring up to cleanse and refresh the moral world, on whose advancing tide the race will ascend to intellectual and social harmony, and to a high state of spiritual elevation!

With composure I witnessed the disconcerted elements as they sought an equilibrium, and saw the clouds chased away, which, when apparently fatigued with their conflicting strife, changed into sparkling gems, and helped to grace the morning's drapery. Emerging from the clouds I beheld the king of heat and light, the glorious Sun, whose radiations penetrated and melted the darkest clouds into the brightest robes, which served to render more beautiful his radiance, and to increase the sublimity of his march through the heavens. Not long, and the sky was clear and serene, and the scene presented was one of grandeur and beauty wholly unsurpassed. The conviction rushed upon my mind, with great power, that every movement in universal Nature is a direct response to the mperative command of immutable Law, which is the rule of divine action eternally established by *Him*, who presides over and animates an infinite creation!

The sun seemed about two and a half hours high when the storm ceased and the sky was clear of clouds. As the representations which had suggested my reflections had passed, it appeared no longer proper to continue meditation upon them. I therefore began pondering on the unconscious and unaccountable change in the locality of my person. The last circumstance I recollected, was that of falling, in a death-like manner, at night, on the corner of the fore-mentioned streets in Poughkeepsie. How, and when I came where I then was, I could not imagine. Whether I had been there one day or one year, I could not tell; and whether I was in America, or in any foreign country, was likewise to me an unanswerable question. The place was strange; I had never seen it until then; and I felt assured, from past experience, that if I had traveled far, I should have been fatigued; but I was not. I had lain on the *mass* or *altar* of which I have spoken, during the severe storm and rain, unable to move, consequently was thoroughly wet. I was now desirous to dry my garments, and to learn if possible what portion of the earth I was in. I accordingly arose and carefully descended to the ground: and while leaning against the mass on which I had lain, I felt a dull, sleepy sensation, which was instantly followed by a reaction, and I became unusually wakeful.

The distant river rolled before me, and all things seemed remarkably romantic and beautiful. Just at this moment an indefinite sound reached my ear through the *mass*, apparently proceeding from the opposite side. I listened silently, hoping for a repetition, that I might recognize its nature and cause. Presently I heard the same several times rapidly repeated—whereupon I turned and proceeded west of the mass, and beheld one of the strangest sights imaginable! A flock of sheep in a state of indescribable confusion—painful to behold—were traversing impatiently the upper portion of the valley, running in every possible direction. Some were making exertions to ascend the *hill-side*. I saw them leap against the glazed mountain, from which they rebounded and came down, with dreadful force upon the stony basis. Others were striving to pass the position I occupied, but they were ignorant and could not stand; neither could they obtain a substantial foothold. The mountains were too high. The earth was too unpropitious, and the passage too well guarded: consequently they were compelled to submit to a wiser influence, direction and admonition! At this moment, through the opening at the base of the mountain, appeared their shepherd, who approached me with a slow but firm step.

The sheep, in their external appearance and numbers, corresponded to those I remembered seeing in the streets of Poughkeepsie, at night; and the shepherd corresponded to the one I there saw, in every particular. I advanced to meet him, and without speaking, I learned what he desired of me by observing the indications of his countenance. I cheerfully acceded to his wishes, and accordingly made a circuit around the sheep, especially those that were at a distance. At first they made a strong resistance, but on seeing the positiveness and propriety of our intentions, they yielded submissively. We gathered, and guided them into the path leading around the mountain's base, which they seemed to recognize as the correct course, and while treading therein, appeared to rejoice exceedingly! It was very remarkable, but I now discovered that they were the same that I had seen before.

A new and *unchangeable* harmony and peace characterized their physical and mental condition. The sheep and their shepherd were, for the first time, inseparably united—united forever! Eternal principles of right and good had caused and accomplished their Salvation. Even Nature had been propitious, while they were violating her Laws, and experiencing pain from their frequent transgressions. But now it was "finished," the work completed, and the people saved. The sheep departed, together with their gentle shepherd, up the valley through the opening; and I felt deeply impressed, as they retreated in the distance, with an interior conviction, that Sin had been destroyed, and transgression made an end of, and that everlasting righteousness had been brought in, for the sheep in their confused state represented the whole human world as at present; but now being united they represent the race in a state of *harmony* to which it will be brought by a similar mode of reconciliation, at no distant period hence.

Overjoyed, I returned to my resting place, and reclining upon its side, drew my garments more closely around me, and sank into deep meditation. Looking in the direction in which the sheep disappeared, I beheld a human form approaching me. He came deliberately—apparently absorbed in thought. He was a person of diminutive stature, yet had a beautiful anatomical structure. His fine symmetry, and beauty and elegance of deportment, quickly captivated my attention, which was now wholly concentrated upon him. He appeared advanced in years, and was attired accordingly, but in a style corresponding nearly to the style of dress worn by the Quakers, especially those of former times. His hair was of a living white, hanging gracefully about his neck and shoulders. His face was full and expressive, and together with the head, was unusually well proportioned. His moral and intellectual developments were prominent,—indicating an expanded mind, and an inclination to lofty Spirituality.

In his hand I perceived a clear, white *scroll.* So purely white was its external, that I felt a strong desire to take it in my hand and view it more closely. Its edges sparkled with gilding of the finest quality, and the care with which he preserved its beauty, excited in me the deepest respect. He continued to approach, and when I would have advanced to meet him, he raised his hand and gently intimated that I must remain perfectly tranquil. A most heavenly radiation played upon his countenance, as he elevated the scroll to his lips, and upon it affectionately imprinted a pure and holy kiss;

whereupon he handed it to me, to open and read. With delicacy and precision I unfolded it, and perceived *writing* in characters which I had never before seen; but I could read the writing without the least hesitation. The language was clear and comprehensive; the form of expression simple, but powerful: it contained a world of beautiful meaning, accompanied with a sweet, divine, reforming influence. It read thus:—

> "As they were, so they are;
> As they are, so they will be!"

Beneath the above was the following interrogatory: "*Now do you believe it?*" I felt its convincing power, and bowed with an internal assent:—observing which on my countenance, the messenger handed me a singular pencil, (for I had none,) with which I signified my conviction and signed my name.

This being done, he received the Scroll from my hand with a gentle bow, rolled it together, pressed it to his lips, turned and departed as he came,—slowly, firmly and deliberately,—till his form glided from my view as he passed around the base of the stupendous mountain!

"How unaccountable," thought I, "that a stranger should come, obtain my signature, and depart, without uttering one word vocally—and meanwhile so remarkably eloquent!—Can it be?" Whereupon I resolved to cease this external questioning, (for sensuous impressions do frequently contend with, and contradict the soul's purest intuitions,) and consented to obey only those instructive suggestions evolved from the interior.

Mighty and sacred truths spontaneously gushed up from the depths of my spirit, and I was impressed with the following beautiful and important correspondence:

The person who came with the scroll, represented a great Reformer,—one who had given new light upon the all interesting and sublime subjects of "life and immortality." The *scroll* represented the purity of his mission, and likewise the unblemished character of him who instructed mankind in those principles which, when duly practiced, will lead far beyond and above all physical wretchedness and moral imperfection. The contents of the scroll represented his great and good intentions, and also expressed the grand consummation which his moral teachings, when applied and devotionally practiced, will effect—viz., "Peace on earth," social and affectional reciprocation—and universal Love. The document was so concisely written, and its truth so briefly expressed, that its entire meaning may not be apprehended, if not clearly explained; wherefore *this*, it is given to know, is its signification:

"*As they were;*" As the sheep were when I first saw them,—in a state of universal confusion, wretched in the extreme, having no fixedness of purpose, no knowledge of their united interests, or of the path of progressive Wisdom that would lead them to happiness, and were therefore in a state of poverty,—"*So they are;*" So *mankind* are,—in the same disorganized condition as were the sheep. Ignorance upon natural and psychological subjects, consequently superstition, skepticism, bigotry, fanaticism, intolerance, spiritual depression and slavery, are the great evils which beset them. *These* have exerted an influence over kings and kingdoms—binding whole *empires* with the galling chains of despotism, lordly aristocracy, and social misery. They have reigned in the religious sanctuary, as in the forest homes of the untutored savage, and the undeveloped cannibal. They have elevated the potentate to a seat of uncontrollable power, and ministered to his unbounded selfish ambition,—in doing which, the weak, ignorant and submissive, have been depressed to the lowest degree of poverty and wretchedness!

"*As they are;*" As the sheep *are*,—united forever, striving for one purpose, pressing forward to one grand and glorious end, which is *happiness*; "So they," (mankind,) "*will be.*" They will be united in like manner. From all evil, they will be free! from personal misdirection and suffering; from ignorance and depravity; from pride and sectarian intolerance, free! These shall recede entirely from the earth, never to enslave and degrade humanity. This world of thought and affection, and of social relations, shall be purified, until there shall be a new heaven and a new earth wherein dwelleth righteousness. And the evils which *now* exist, shall be known only to those who will trace the history of our race; which they will do with mingling feelings of pity and regret. As the sheep were united, so all men shall be joined into one Brotherhood, and bound together by the chain of Love. Their interests shall be pure and reciprocal; their actions shall be just and harmonious, governed by a spirit of universal philanthropy; they shall be as one body, animated with an element of divine sympathy, which shall pervade and connect all its parts as one whole.

The interrogatory, "*Now do you believe it?*" was addressed to my youthful judgment,—after it had been so unrighteously impressed and directed by the traditional theology of our land,—in order that the contrast between error and truth might the more certainly effect an entire change in my convictions; and those initiatory representations were necessary in order that I might apprehend the various vicissitudes of my future life, and bear them with wisdom and patience. The question written on the scroll, appealed to my then impressed judgment, whether I would believe the instruction I had received in preference to my previous religious opinions. The truth was made manifest to my mind. I signed the scroll by internal instruction, and my thoughts became serene, elevated, and tranquil. My spirit reposed while breathing an atmosphere of *hope* and wisdom; for my convictions were immovable, and my impressions too deep to ever be changed!

My senses, and all my faculties, were restored to their ordinary state. The strange influence that had had possession of my body, predisposing me to sleep, had passed, and I stood again free from every thing but physical fatigue, and embarrassment relative to my location. I commenced descending the valley leading toward the river, for the purpose of discovering if possible my geographical situation, and to restore my exhausted form. I had not proceeded over one hundred rods before I observed a man attired in a farmer's dress, carrying a spade on his shoulder, walking leisurely in an opposite direction. I hastened to meet him, and inquired in an anxious manner,

"Sir, will you tell me the name of this place, where I can get some food, and how far it is to Poughkeepsie?"

He smiled, and gave me an inquisitive look. "This place," said he, "is Catskill, and those are the Catskill mountains; perhaps you may get something to eat at the inn. You asked me about Poughkeepsie; well, I suppose it is about forty miles from the other side of the river."

I proceeded to the river, in crossing which, feeling some fatigue, I rested in a reclining posture on the railing of the ferry-boat. How I had crossed the river before, or how I could have found that place, was a mystery. And now *sleep* came upon me imperceptibly again, as I lay reflecting on the scenes through which I had passed. I was startled when I became sensible of a return of those feelings which preceded a closing of the senses and illuminating of the internal principle. As they came on, my body yielded, as I was willing it should; external life again vanished, as if forever, and I was once more a being of the inner life.

How long I remained in that condition I know not; but, as in previous instances, I at length felt returning life streaming through my system, and was restored to a high degree of animation. I opened my eyes, and, wonderful to relate, I was seated upon a marble grave-stone about eighteen inches from the ground! The melancholy sanctuary in which I found myself, was inclosed by a huge stone wall, surmounted by top-railing, similar to farmers' ordinary fences. It was in the form of a triangle, and, I think, occupying about one acre and a half of smooth land. I could see eleven grave-stones standing, and five broken and scattered upon the ground. A dense wood obstructed the surrounding scene from my view; and I was thus sequestered in a solitary place, for a purpose of which I had not the least knowledge.

I resolved to continue in the same position as when I awoke to consciousness, and await any suggestion that might flow from within or without. At this instant I experienced a breathing sensation, unlike any other, upon the front and side of my head, in the region of the organ of ideality. Its increasing attraction caused me to turn in the direction whence it proceeded, and I beheld a *man* of ordinary stature and appearance. He approached, and, without speaking, turned to the right near me, and furnished himself with a similar seat. I observed that he was a lover of Nature and of truths,—had a constant thirst for knowledge, and strong powers of investigation. His quick perception, sustained by his highly cultivated faculties of intuition and reflection, presented a combination of intellectual powers seldom witnessed. He was a being whom I felt constrained to love—for love was prompted by his superior wisdom. And it is a truth, that I conversed with him, and he with me, for a long period, and that too, by a mutual *influx* and reflux of thought! His discourse was on this wise:

"I lived," said he, "on the earth, in the form, among the inhabitants thereof, for a length of time determined by my obedience to Natural Law. From youth, I imbibed the impressions made upon my mind by my parents, the religious world and philosophy; but artificial education served more to retard my mental progress than as an auxiliary to useful advancement. I discarded, early, these unfavorable influences, and commenced interrogating and communing with Nature and her productions, within the circumference of my vision and mental capacity—whereby I became acquainted with truths of deeper importance, and of greater magnitude. It was demonstrated to me that all the diversified external forms in this, as in other universes, are unfolded to the outer, by virtue of an element or spiritual principle, contained in each, which is their life, or Soul; and this essence, by *men*, is called God:—also, that the *external* corresponds to the inner, productive principle; that *forms* are determined, as perfect or imperfect, by the specific character of their prompting soul, which actuates them to *life* and development.

By this I learned that the gross matter, and minerals, of our earth, are formed, and governed, and sustained by a law—an inherent principle—which also operates in higher degrees and worlds of material organization. And as this principle, in various modifications, ascended in the order of Nature, higher and more perfect *forms* were unfolded, being actuated and perfected by inner life, to which the outer existence corresponded. These forms I understood constituted the *vegetable kingdom.* From this established basis, I perceived those Laws breathing forth the *animal kingdom;* and, in their next stage of ascension, developing, sustaining, and perfecting *Man!* And all this came to me, by discovering and meditating upon corresponding truths, dwelling within, about and above me.

In my analytical investigations, I discovered a threefold or triune Power in every compound,—and three essential parts to every established organization, and that such are absolutely necessary to all things in order that they may be perfectly organized.

This knowledge led me to reflect upon the many physical violations, occurring every hour, among the inhabitants of the earth,—and impressed me that these frequent transgressions of laws sustaining the human form, called for some effectual remedy to relieve the diseases caused thereby. Accordingly I founded a system upon these principles and considerations, which may be called a 'medical system of the trinity.' In this I maintained the proposition, that every particle in the human body possessed a close affinity to particular particles in the subordinate kingdoms,—and that these latter particles, if properly associated and applied, would *cure* any affected portion or organ of the human frame.

To establish this theory, I labored diligently; and *now* I have the satisfaction of knowing that my system was a *germ* enlivened by *interior truth*, whereby new and more truthful systems were developed, to bless the earth's inhabitants! Now I love truth because it begets *wisdom*; for my *love* has become *wisdom*; my *wisdom* substantial *knowledge!*" His countenance, as he closed these sayings, brightened with a delightful and beautiful smile!

Astonished at his discourse, and my mind being filled with thought concerning his revelations, I individualized one thought, which he instantly perceived and answered. I inquired, "Can I become acquainted with you, kind stranger, and your system, by appropriate means, within your power and pleasure to afford?" "Ah! 't is for *this*, that you sit in my presence," said he, inclining to the right, and raising in his hand an elegant *cane*, which I had not seen in his possession till then. "Here is a full synopsis of my System and Practice," said he, turning to me, "and I desire that *this* you should comprehend; and in understanding its fundamental principles, you will gently and justly apply its teachings to the good of your brethren, Mankind!"

Thus saying, he touched a singular spring at the top, and the *cane* mechanically parted into *three* longitudinal strips or pieces. A *rod* ran through the center, graduated in size according to the cane's shape. This rod was very beautiful, having the appearance of highly polished silver. The *parts* were neatly adjusted one to another, and when on the *rod*, formed a staff exceeding in beauty any I had ever beheld. I saw that the *pieces* remained whole when disengaged from the rod; he took these in his hand, and unfolded them piece by piece, until they completely separated. The smaller pieces now assumed the diamond form, especially when closely observed.

"Here," said he, "on these little blocks," presenting them to me, "is the name of every disease with which the human race is afflicted."

I saw and read the name of each and every disease, with many f which I was entirely unacquainted; and as I read returned them to him, one by one, in order.

Now, elevating his person, he discoursed thus: "In the *inside* of these blocks you will find a composition, which, when applied, will remove the disease named upon its *exterior*. Of this compound make you a quantity suggested at the time you see or examine the diseased individual, and sufficiently strong to be well adapted."* He restored the pieces to their respective places, and quickly joined the *cane*, so that one could not see any possible means to disunite its parts again.

"Take this," said he, handing the cane to me, "and preserve the charge devotionally; for it is a work of a lifetime, demanding equal attention, reflection and application." I received the precious gift with ineffable delight and gratification; at which he spoke:

"Moreover, that you may behold the complete correspondence between this *system* and *Nature*, I will explain the cane's signification. The pieces, when disunited in the manner observed, correspond to those principles dwelling and operating in the natural organization; and the *blocks* to the various individuals that constitute the human race. The disease specified on the *outside* of each block, corresponds to the truth that disease tends to affect *only* the *bodies* of men, and not their living, interior principle! The composition on the inside of each block corresponds to the truth that every thing's exterior is

* This system of medical treatment is fully developed in "The Great Harmonia," Vol. I.

determined precisely by the interior, creative, and moving principle;—moreover, to the truth that the spirit is the creating, developing, perfecting, expanding, beautifying, organizing, healing and eternal essence in the possession of every being.

The *rod*, which runs through the *cane*, and connects its parts together, corresponds to the principle of divine *truth* running through and sustaining this system, as well as all the vast creations both in this and higher spheres. And the rod being in the *interior*, signifies that the great law of *truth* is in the interior of all things, and especially in the *soul* of all things—dwelling there imperceptible to outer sense, yet known to be existing from the regular manifestations of a united and complicated Universe!

Inward searching after truth will lead to, and disclose, the great and important realities so delicately typified by this staff,—for it is an accumulation of interior and external evidences, assisted by the promptings of Nature, and sanctioned and consummated by the consciousness of truth indwelling in the soul."

Thus ended his eloquent interpretation. His countenance became illuminated with ecstatic delight, and his thoughts entered and were responded to by my spirit, without *even once* having the senses audibly addressed!

A sweet, gentle, but strange sensation now passed warmly over my left breast, face and head. It seemed to proceed from something immediately behind me. Impressed thus, I turned and beheld a man of an appearance very different from the one beside me. His anatomy was of wise proportions; he possessed perfect symmetry of cerebral structure, and was seemingly about six feet in stature. His head particularly attracted my attention, for I had never beheld such a harmonious combination of moral and intellectual developments. The cerebrum indicated a most vigorous and gigantic intellect,—as also an exalted power of conception, great ease of expression, and a high degree of spirituality. He drew near, and reclined against the stone the first speaker was occupying, and spake in this wise:

"By permission long granted me by the divine mercy of the Lord, to visit this and other earths, I am enabled to instruct thee, as it is becoming me to do, concerning things pertaining to thy interior life, and exterior sphere of thought and usefulness. Thy spirit is now untrammeled—has experienced a joyful resurrection from the artifices of the social world without; therefore thou hast become an appropriate vessel for the influx of truth and wisdom. Spiritually, thou hast left the world where men reside; but physically thou art there with them. Thy mission has been shown thee: and great is the Universe wherein thou shalt labor and do whatsoever thy most interior understanding shall conceive to be good, and true, and profitable.

I will be near thee in thy stewardship—pointing to the right path, and goodness of spiritual life. The things thou shalt bring forth, will surprise and confound those of the land who are considered deeply versed in science and metaphysics.

Obstructions of various kinds will affect thy external life; but they will tend more fully to expand thy interior being. Press on thy way: and love only those things tending to *truth* and *wisdom.*

By thee will a *new light* appear; it shall be *new* because it will brighten and purify that already in being, and reflect intellectually upon that heretofore conceived; and it will establish that which has been, and still is supposed to be the wildest hallucination, viz., The law and 'kingdom of heaven' on earth,—Peace on earth and good will to men.

In due time these things will be made manifest through thee, and to others, while residing in the form. By others they will be comprehended and believed, and at the end of a little season they will be generally acknowledged, their beauty and importance appreciated; and they will be loved, and proclaimed in *practice.*

At a time not far distant, I will instruct thee concerning the opening of thy interior understanding, and the laws to be observed to render thee qualified to commune with the interior realities of all subordinate and elevated things. This phenomenon when openly manifested, will testify of those divine spiritual truths, not as yet comprehended by those who admire Nature merely for the delights thereof, and by those imprisoned souls every where, who believe nothing beyond the sphere of their bodily senses. See to the promptings of thy living spirit. In a just season thy great labor will commence, which, when consummated, will elevate the human race to a high degree of harmony.

For the present I communicate no more. But now I repeat, love wisdom, which is food and light to the internal: and wisdom secureth health; and health procureth happiness. And thus strengthened, enlightened and purified, thou wilt find it congenial to seek and thirst after interior and beautiful *truths*."

Thus ended the last speaker's prophetic admonitions; and as he closed the above sentence, I saw a smile of joy and even ecstacy, pass over his countenance, which seemed sweet and heavenly—coming, as did his thoughts, with a kind of spontaneous ease.

I felt directly impelled by some influence to arise, and, with my *cane*, depart. This impulse I immediately obeyed. I went to the fence, placed my foot upon the wall-side, and raised my body to its top. On endeavoring to surmount the railing, my clothing became entangled, and I experienced a sense of irritation approximating to intense anger, because of the obstruction. This was unusual, for I had not had such feelings for many years—indeed I can scarcely remember ever being so angry. I was thus exasperated at the *rail* which, being split at the end, had caught my coat. Meanwhile those strangers were observing my feelings and movements with apparent complacency. On seeing this, I requested the one who had given me the *cane*, to hold it till I gained the opposite side of the fence.

He advanced and received the cane from my hand. Being thus free, I grasped the rail at the open portion, and tore it completely in two. I now descended to the ground and desired the *cane.* At this, the person who had last spoken came near me, and gently spake in this wise:

"Keep well the instruction given *thee:* moreover, learn to be wise and gentle; and add to gentleness, love; and to love, wisdom; and wisdom, being pure, begets illumination, and illumination, happiness. And, as it was given me to say, in a due season thou shalt return, and then this cane shall be thine; but thou must first learn not to be, under *any* circumstances, *depressed*, nor by *any* influences *elated*, as these are the extremes of an unguarded impulse, in minds not strong with pure wisdom.

From this learn meekness and humiliation, and sustain these by a proper dignity in thy natural living. Receive this thy first and sufficient lesson, and by its light lead others to seek the pathway leading to Wisdom and the Tree of Righteousness—whose fruit shall be delicious to the hungering, but untasted except they nourish the seed and cause the tree to spring up within them, when it has done which, it will reflect a refreshing shade over the spirit within, and the world without."

Thus he closed. As I stood and listened, gratitude swelled my soul into volumes of thankfulness, that the *cane* was sacrificed for such valuable instruction; while I felt assured at the same time, that the beautiful and comprehensive staff would ultimately *be mine*, and that, too, because I should be worthy of its possession.

Being on the outer side of the wall, I could now see their bodies no more, for the fence rose too high, and the ground where I stood was lower than within the yard; and whether they remained within the yard, or departed to other portions of the world, I could not discover. I remember being conscious only at intervals as I walked on the road leading to Poughkeepsie. * * *

As I approached home, my mind became exceedingly disconcerted, my mental sensations being similar to those which I experience on waking from my superior condition. I perfectly recollect meeting several acquaintances, each of which manifested great surprise on seeing me. I spake to no person. I entered the front door of my friend's residence, in Main street, and passed directly through the hall, at the termination of which, I suddenly lost my faculty of memory. But, (as I was told,) I passed through the adjoining room, up the stairs, into the dining apartments, where the family were engaged in eating.

I threw off my coat and hat, and seated myself at the table. The family were somewhat astonished at my unceremonious actions, and began questioning me in reference to my mysterious disappearance from home,—(to which, as they subsequently informed me, I made no reply.) I ate a very hearty dinner, made up of various articles of food, and when done, proceeded to wash myself at the further end of the room.

I now felt a return of normal sensibility :—as it returned, I saw a brilliant light—it flashed—and again all was darkness :—but now, another flash, and another, came, and I was completely freed from the abnormal condition.

I was absolutely frightened! The fact that I remembered entering the front door, and had lost all consciousness till that moment, and was then standing in the presence of the family, with a napkin in my hand, seemed so strange, that, for a moment, I knew not the persons in the house!

Thus ends my *fifth vision*—a vision unlike my former and more recent ones; but, to me, it is one of the greatest importance, interest and beauty, because it is so full of instructive meaning.

This vision was vividly impressed on my mind, but soon faded from my memory; and from that time until this, (September 12th,

1846,) I have been unable to convey any correct *idea* of its nature or signification.

But it revived in my mind in a brilliant manner, in the village of Danbury, (Connecticut,) on the 18th of August, 1846. I could not free my mind from the impulse to write it—prefaced with a brief history of my early religious impressions; for by the vision, all my previous religious opinions were swept completely away, and I have not been disturbed since, with such anxious apprehensions as they caused me.

I will recapitulate, in a brief form, the whole vision, together with the previous periods of external memory, and the time I was gone from home, that the reader may behold it in its marvelous connection.

On the 6th of March, 1843, I retired to my bed at half-past nine in the evening. The first that I remember after that, was standing on the corner of Mill and Hamilton streets, in Poughkeepsie; having beautiful thoughts; seeing a flock of sheep and their shepherd; assisting him in restoring order among them; and seeing hem move forward until out of sight,—and then *falling* as if dead.

Next, I remember waking while lying on a singular *pile*, in a valley with large mountains on each side; then, getting off the *pile* and suddenly seeing a flock of sheep and their shepherd, similar to those I saw in Poughkeepsie. In like manner I remember assisting the shepherd in restoring harmony in the flock,—and seeing them disappear through an opening at the upper end of the valley. I remember next seeing a small man come toward me with a scroll in his hand; taking the *scroll;* reading it; understanding its contents; taking a pencil from his hand; and, with my own hand writing my *name*, and the word "*Yes;*"—being impressed with the *meaning* of each representation, and, as I yielded assent to the instructions, losing my previous opinions.

I remember walking down the valley, meeting the farmer, inquiring the name of the place, and the distance to Poughkeepsie ;—then crossing the river, lying on the railing of the ferry-boat, and falling asleep.

Next, on waking, I remember finding myself in a grave-yard inclosed by a stone wall, and encompassed by a dense wood; then being in conversation with a small man having a cane, who it was given me to know was GALEN, an old physician; and discoursing with another, who I knew to be EMANUEL SWEDENBORG, a Swedish philosopher; I remember mounting the fence with the cane in my hand; being entangled in the rail; tearing the rail in pieces, and being briefly admonished by *Swedenborg.* I also remember leaving the cane with the impression that I should have it at some future day; then of traveling to Poughkeepsie; seeing persons I knew; entering the house in which I boarded; entering the hall; wiping my face with a napkin, and coming almost instantaneously out of *that,* into my *natural* state, and being calm and satisfied. This is all I remember.

I have *never* read a *page* either of Galen or Swedenborg, up to this moment, and at the time I had the vision I had not heard their names once mentioned. * * *

In consideration of this vision; the immense instruction it affords; the revolution it produced in my mind; and the divineness of its origin, use and purpose, I am filled with an internal sense of freedom, gratitude, and happiness.

But there are personal reflections and habits of thought, suggested by the foregoing vision, which may serve to enlighten and inform the investigator. There is an opinion rapidly prevailing at the present time, among many reformers even, that the human soul is incapable of being emancipated from error and false doctrines in a brief period; and, therefore, that such impressions are taken, after death, by the soul into the spiritual World, where they become the ruling love and distinguishing characteristics of the individual. For instance—that Luther is still believing *Lutheranism ;* that Calvin is preaching *Calvinism ;* that Methodists are advocating *Methodism ;* that infidels are still skeptics, and promulgating *infidelity.* This doctrine was taught by Swedenborg about a century since. But every day's experience disproves the statement. Behold, how men are changed or converted from cold skepticism to enthusiastic faith ; from sinners to saints ; from superciliousness to meek submission, all in a single hour ! As the inebriate, whose system is fired with the deleterious liquid and whose thoughts are leaping to and fro, like frantic steeds, is quiet and unexcited when emancipated from his intoxicating beverages ; so is the erroneously educated mind, who entertains wrong and distorted views of man, heaven, and Deity, readily changed into the perception and realization of Truth when the latter is presented to his understanding like a magnificent panorama. The human mind is the *master* of one class of influences and the *subject* of another. When the reason principle gazes upon Truth, as it is in Nature and the spiritual World, the illusions of error vanish at once. As an example of this, consider the effects which were wrought upon my mind in a few hours, by the vision. Words can not express the happy feelings and vast contemplations which were awakened in my spirit by the "new birth" thus mysteriously experienced. Without further remark, however, I refer the reader to the following chapter.

MY PREACHER AND HIS CHURCH.

The multifariousness of individuals and opinions in society, and the limited intercourse circumstances permit me to hold with them, daguerreotype upon the tablet of my ever-susceptible memory, a multitude of dissimilar impressions. And although there exists but little attraction, no department of human thought and inquiry do I enter with greater frequency, than the theological; and inasmuch as, by a concatenation of causes and events, it is my destiny and mission in this life to labor therein, I will be in the constant endeavor to fulfill it well, and thus answer to one of the many uses and ends of *my* creation.

Into the religious, the theological circle of contest and investigation, therefore, I am involuntarily drawn and deeply immersed; where every paroxysm of local thought, and convulsion of popular opinion, find their way, produce their effect, and deposit themselves within me for reflection or comment.

There are many opinions which, imbibed from birth and books, so arrest the growth of some sentiments, and impetuously accelerate the extreme development of others, that men seem armed with spear-pointed prejudices, and sword-edged ideas, ignobly used to pierce and wound the unprepared or unsuspecting; or to disappoint the hope, and obstruct the even way of more harmonious minds. A consequent and corresponding effect, on one class of individuals, is the violent denunciation of all religion, or the sometimes undeserved accusation of clerical and sectarian disingenuousness. Another effect, is the rapid generation of a cold hostility and misanthropy, which, for fear of persecution, is concealed till every sympathetic stream is chilled, every love perverted, every life-spring weakened—indeed, till the mind is seemingly barren of compassion, reason and happiness. And another effect, is resigning reason and freedom to sectarian conventional requirements; and yielding a blind consent to think, act and live in an exclusive circle, till the mind is blackened with prejudice, and each thought is fevered with anxiety and serious enthusiasm. Such are the conflicts presented; and the misdirection of religious sentiments, together with their causes and consequences, have recorded, and are recording, themselves upon the journal of my mental experience. And numerous questions are also propounded and submitted for solution. Some of them are manifestly incongruous, and even unrighteous; others impress me with their true character and importance: the former I purposely avoid; the latter I will answer, so far as I am capable.

It appears clear that, those opinions and prejudices which disturb the harmony of my mind, and injure most in community, are the partial, incorrect or angular development of pure and native sentiments residing in the soul; and that the present form of Sectarianism is not the highest expression of internal piety and worship. Hence, I conclude that something more is needed to modify and urge on the development of that central desire for every heart—the desire of unity and happiness. As an auxiliary, I feel moved to unfold and submit my interior impressions to the analysis and verdict of enlightened men. That they will respond to many cherished convictions, and tend to elucidate those momentous, and vastly interesting, questions agitating the religious world, I am confidently assured.

Prompted by the *desire* to reflect a pure light, I will be ever watchful that no thought gains an utterance through me, but what contributes to its purest gratification.

Among many other very interesting questions which have been

from time to time put to me, the following are the most frequent and conspicuous: *What church do you attend? Who do you hear preach?* These interrogatories I am now impressed to answer.

The Sanctuary, where is heard the most eloquent and profound discourses, and in which I commune with worshiping brethren, is of modest structure and wise dimensions. It was erected by a Master-builder, and stands upon a foundation which can never change. Its external form indicates but imperfectly the pleasing beauty, magnificence and Real-reality of its interior. Within, all is beautiful. The impress of Wisdom is on every thing. The adaptation—the perfect fitness—the unity of one part with another, extract the deepest admiration and gratitude. No language is adequate to breathe forth the thanks, and utter the praise, I would confer upon the Founder and Builder of the church which I am permitted to enter and call my own. Although there are millions of similar churches resting on the same foundation, constructed upon the same principles, and erected by the same hand, I am more familiar with the one I attend. And, as a knowledge of the one will lead to a general understanding of all others, I will give a description of its origin, situation and possessions.

It stands upon a spiral-like eminence, commanding an unlimited view of all surrounding scenes. In truth, it stands above, and overlooks the grand living panorama of the boundless Creation. The basis is a material combination of infinite varieties, and holds within its granite embrace the ten thousand parts which are indispensable to the formation of the three terraces, which complete and decorate the gentle eminence.

A vast collection of substances, having an original affinity for, and, consequently, resting upon the compound-base; and which are the capacious laboratory of terrestrial electricity; are so wisely arranged, that they form the first terrace, which is termed the Mineral Kingdom.

An association of superior particles, representing themselves in appropriate forms, and breathing fragrance and nourishment to all around, immediately succeeds the first, and forms the second terrace, termed the Vegetable Kingdom.

And by virtue of original design, new parts converge and congregate with philosophic precision, and ultimate themselves in the production of the third terrace, termed the Animal Kingdom.

The preparation and concentration of materials thus complete, according to the principles of holy architecture, the great Architect moved His mighty Will, and erected the living temple consecrated to my use!

With speechless veneration I tread the path of progression, leading to this mental edifice. But adoring as I advance, the Maker will be pleased, and I am rendered capable of appreciating its interior grandeur.

Over the arched entrance, in well-known characters, is engraved "PERCEPTION": and within the spacious vestibule, suspended from above, is a highly burnished mirror—the calendar of the temple, upon which is stamped "MEMORY." On this is recorded the age and character of every person (or thought) that enters from without; and, also, the image and principles of many minds, who, because of their naturalness and love of truth, are admitted, although to them unknown.

Passing memory, I contemplate the numerous living pictures which people, or ornament the vast interior. These are Archetypes, [ideas] or representatives of what is manifested but imperfectly upon, and through, the external form. Prepared and placed, also, with surpassing order, are a set of suitable windows, [Senses,] designed for the admission of light, and to inform me of outward creations, and the condition of human society. But a more mellow, resplendent, and cheering light, descends through the wreathed dome, [the faculty of Wisdom.] By the Supreme Architect's design, this dome was calculated as a medium for the influx of light [Truth] from the interior or Spirit-world, that my Sanctuary might be illuminated, and each member gladdened with joy.

Underneath the dome, and in the center, is an altar [Justice] which sparkles with divine beauty; and by that altar, in native dignity and composure, stands my Preacher, [Reason,] a Divinely-commissioned advocate of good and right! Before him, open, and resting on the altar, is a precious, sacred volume—a universal compend of Art, Science, Philosophy, Theology, and of the architectural principles upon which my church was built. It embraces the history of causes and Creation, the genealogy and experience of Nations, and contains a likeness of its Wise and Eternal Author. Its language is composed of the forms and symbols of original thoughts; its sentences admit of no transposition; and its amazing consecutiveness prohibits the possibility of human interpolation or change. To an anxious and attentive congregation composed of twelve Spirits, [Desires,] my preacher delights to expound in philosophic detail, the teachings of the "Holy Book," [Nature,] which he adores and advocates, because its Author built his church, and inspires him with a growing happiness and lovely veneration.

The central, and most prominent member, is *a desire for unity*—a great and good *layman;* as the preacher catches inspiration from the effulgent firmament of interior truth, and unfolds the sublime principles of that stupendous volume, this disciple bows in prayerful silence, and eagerly receives any suggestion or sentiment that breathes of harmony! And the statement of the principle—"Justice and Truth generate happiness, the native religion of the Soul"—my preacher considers a sufficient text, from which to preach the perpetual sermon of a righteous life, in unity with the Neighbor, the Universe, and the Father.

"*Are you ever disturbed in this Sanctuary?*"

The universal relation, and sympathetic chain bounding and

connecting all things, subjects me to the disquieting sound of religious strife without me in society. Although peace reigns triumphant, and a holy quietness pervades the spiritual atmosphere of my Sanctuary, the contention of sects, and the prejudices of men, come in and disturb me. The windows permit not only the entrance of discordant sounds; but also the conflicting scenes of theological discussion every where presented. What a contrast! In the outer world on every side I behold noble, good and learned men, but *not wise ones*, engaged in erecting and supporting churches, which, though *lifeless* representatives of the *living* church within, are pre-eminently calculated to localize each religious sentiment, and circumscribe the sphere of thought and investigation. The various sects, arrogating to themselves the possession of "true faith," presumptuously "lift a standard," according to which they exercise their judgment, and calmly pronounce a verdict of condemnation upon all dissenting minds.

From the windows of my Temple I perceive a number of highly esteemed men in the distance; though well versed in ecclesiastical history, and much nearer my church and theology than others, they are seemingly anxious to have my "religious faith" considered "unsound or deficient"; and are assiduously laboring to give the impression that "a grand demonstration" of long prepared and closely combined evils, and "pernicious delusions," are about to "break forth from the world of spirits upon the world of men." Not anticipating an invasion from without, I was for a moment surprised, and even unkindly moved; but on turning and observing my Preacher's composure, and the calm smile that played upon his countenance, I bowed and quietly listened to his brief discourse.

"*What does Reason say concerning Sectarian disturbances?*"

Reason replies that, Arrogance would as palpably show her haggard form, and the charitable injunction, "judge not," would be as unqualifiedly violated, were you to pronounce judgment upon the "moral habitudes" of any mind, because not believing as *we* believe, and not worshiping in *our* Sanctuary. And the wise admonition, "think no evil," which is the proverbial index of the "pure in heart," would be as unheeded, were you to blacken the already clouded intellects of men, by indulging in the melancholy speculation, and chimerical belief, of greater evils to befall the human race.

"There is greater cause for composure and gentle speech; for the difference between you and your church, convictions and utterances, and their church, convictions and utterances, is measured and comprehended by the fact, that they look from their position, without themselves, at you; and you look from *this* position, without yourself, at them. This causes misapprehension and censure."

Another sound proceeds from a multitude, in an oblique direction, who, for the want of liberty, capacity or inclination, doing little of their own thinking, are exceedingly clamorous in shouting, "He is the victim of delusion, or the vile instrument of imposture!" When called to the contemplation of this class of minds, in numbers by far the greatest, I am surprised that they do not see, as I see, how inconsistent and ineffectual their labors are. Though in *sound* united, I perceive that their heterogeneous and contradictory utterances, being intended to concentrate at *one point*, and perform their destructive mission, converge on their eccentric route, and equally neutralize and dissipate each other.

And I heard a voice—"*Fear not!* Error is mortal and can not live; Truth is immortal and can not die," replies my preacher, not to the vociferous multitude whose passion and high-mindedness lift them above the Voice of Reason, but to those timid intellects, who dare not think without the sphere of popular opinion.

A congregation of the weak and trembling class, far, far behind all others—and infants in theology—are represented in the act of cautiously whispering: "Beware! leave not the old paths; we know not, nor do we wish to *learn*, the way to his church ; it may lead to ruin."

" *What does your Preacher say concerning old Paths?*"

The old paths in commerce between men and cities, (replies my preacher,) were traversed by the caravan, or by hugely-built and incommodious vessels, depending for movement and success upon the capricious winds ; but *now*, the palatial steamer, the "iron steed," and "the lightning track," are paths and "mediums of communication."

And the old paths in Theology began in *Egypt*, and led, not to the "promised land" of peace and happiness, but through divided elements, over idolatrous plains, and into a wilderness of anarchy, superstition and want. But *now* they begin in the first sphere, and, illuminated by interior Wisdom and pure Philosophy, lead the intelligent traveler through a galaxy of peopled stars, to a higher sphere—into the Spiritual World.

So am I instructed, and the contentions of the outer world disturb me not. And in the purity of my Preacher, and in the holiness and wisdom of the Builder of his Sanctuary, I have a strong and undiminished confidence.

But, reader, thou hast, also, an internal preacher and a church. The latter may be closed and encompassed about by one that is external and material ; and thy preacher may be silenced, and held in subordination by an outward and superficial preacher ; but the Kingdom of Heaven, the good and the true, are *within thee!* To know this let thy Wisdom be unfolded, and from its depths will spring the holy and beautiful truths of intuition—the light of the inner world. Unmask thyself, and wear no garb but what Nature gave. Appear as thou art—the Eternal Child of an Eternal Father!

Be pure—be natural. To entomb thy living mind in the grave-like superficiality of sect or party, is not only arresting thy spiritual growth, but is doing positive violence to the sacred principles of thy being. For countless reasons, I would persuade thee to seek and know 'the truth, that thou mayest be free indeed.'

Sectarianism is not in man, except the central tendency to associate, and form groups or bodies, as the planets were made, by the spontaneous gravitation of congenial parts—the Sectarianism of the Universe! As this is the true form of association, religious and social, he should form no other.

In truth, I attend no church but my Mind; I listen to no preacher but Reason; I read no book so studiously as Nature; I love no sermon so well as a "well-ordered life"; and believe and dream of no higher, or more glorious Heaven, in this or any other sphere, than the harmonious adaptation of one Spirit to another, and *all* to the Great Spirit Father!

In order to understand each other well, I have, so far as the subject justifies it, unfolded myself to the candid consideration and just decisions of the reader, and whatever be his church opinions and creed, I can truthfully say, that the above are the purest and surest means to find, and become reasonably acquainted with, 'My Preacher and his Church.'

Reformation in any department of life or society necessarily depends upon the teaching and actions of true reformers. We have leading characters in every thing; but the lovers of universal justice and universal peace begin to call for some great governing mind—a *head* to the social and religious *body* of Humanity. And yet how different are man's conceptions of *what* or *who* a true reformer is, or should be! Different individuals are endowed with different powers and talents. Some are constitutionally qualified for Governing; some for Teaching; some for Declamation; and we have natural physicians, natural lawyers, natural theologians, and natural reformers; but it is not yet possible that any *one* individual should combine all these talents and qualifications in his own conformations of body and mind. Among nearly all reformers I perceive two rather unfortunate peculiarities of mind, which do much toward retarding their progress and impairing their usefulness to the world. I refer to two facts: first, that most reformers or teachers regard themselves as being under *the special favor of the Divine Mind*,—thus falsely elevating themselves above the natural endowments and common blessings of mankind; and second, that such minds usually consider their own peculiarities, and, perhaps, eccentricities, as *laws* calculated and destined to reform and govern the great brotherhood of Man. For example—It can not be disguised that Moses, and Joshua, and Jesus, and Mahomet, and Swedenborg, and many modern Reformers, claim to be the special Agents of the Divine Mind, under his direct guidance; and, also, that the great body of mankind, in order to be reformed, must become Moses-like, or Christ-like, or Mahomet-like, or Swedenborg-like, &c., which is simply expanding personal *idiosyncrasies* into universal principles of reformation. I am led to consider nearly all this as error. For my interior impressions upon this subject, I refer the reader to a consideration of the reply to the following question.

WHO IS A TRUE REFORMER?

This question very naturally arises at this point; and it is to elucidate this subject, in accordance with my impressions, that I submit the following reply:

The true Reformer is necessarily superior to his age. If he is not more advanced than those minds of the age from which originate all the prevailing laws and numerous customs, then he is not their superior, and can not be their Teacher. His value to his age and the world consists in his superiority to them. But in proportion as he is superior to the received and established laws and doctrines of the day, will his position be misunderstood, his motives misapprehended, his teachings misrepresented, and his intrinsic worth unknown.

The multitude, not standing where he stands, nor beholding what he beholds, may look upon him as a deceiver, a mystic, as an enthusiast, or as a philosophical madman. His position is necessarily *far* above the ordinary doctrines and theories of the day, to which the masses are constantly tending, and in which they are mostly educated. He is therefore repulsed, disliked, preached against, calumniated, and subjected to such imprisonment and torture as the liberality and civilization of his age will permit. There is necessarily a vast difference between him and the people. And it is no more unreasonable that he should *not* be understood and appreciated by the people than that he himself should not comprehend minds still superior in spheres unseen. Therefore the great, and talented, and fruitful minds, of all ages and nations, *have* suffered and *will* suffer from the combined persecutions of ignorance and prejudice which coevally prevail in the world. Therefore genius will continue to be persecuted and crucified. And, although God will *continue* to manifest himself in the souls, and thoughts, and deeds of men, blind ignorance and intolerance will concentrate their forces to deride, falsify, and destroy the medium of the revelation. The true reformer must be great and good. But unfortunately for him, his position and qualifications are powerful causes of the development of envy, jealousy, and antagonistic feelings in ambitious minds. Some deride, because they are ignorant; some deride because they are envious; and still others deride, because they have counter interests and professions. But genius is divine and eternal, and it will live and fulfill its glorious mission, though the powers of church and state join to destroy its birth-place or the medium of its sublime manifestations.

Every nation has had its reformer, and its truly original author, and its truly inspired Hero. And every age has given birth to some important truth—thus contributing something toward gratifying the insatiable thirst for Wisdom and knowledge. But every age and nation has also had its dungeons, its racks, and its stakes —*in* the mind or *out* of the mind—by which to cramp, and crush, and crucify its greatest discoverer or its most inspired prophet.

Every age and nation has also had its false reformer, its false author, and its false prophet. Some ambitious and insincere mind, perhaps, has pretended to originality in his thought, and to inspiration in his teachings. Such a mind will complain of non-appreciation, and will, perhaps, assume the appearance and position of the persecuted genius. He aspires to the martyr's crown of thorns. And he succeeds, at last, in acquiring popularity and influence among the people,—sometimes at the expense of the *true* merit, and in derogation of the inspiration of the true reformer. There is, therefore, a want of actual knowledge concerning *what constitutes a true reformer*—one, *who is* a reliable teacher. A standard must be ascertained whereby to measure and judge, with an impartial and most dispassionate judgment, who is, and who is not, the true manifestation of the divine spirit, and the true guide to the human soul. To this inquiry I now desire to direct your attention.

Far down in the depths of humanity's history, I can perceive uncultivated, simple, and enthusiastic hearts—beating for the general good of mankind. The plains of Arabia have been traversed by the savage; but some representative of refinement and civilization has led that savage onward—some cool and powerful chieftain has been his friend and father. The savage and barbarian tribes of the desert were never without God; they had some kind of a reformer in their midst—a nobleman by nature, who would unite their interests and lead them to the accomplishment of wiser ends.

Combine the indefatigable zeal and fanaticism of the savage chief, with the tender and protecting qualities of the desert patriarch, and you have an inspired patriot—a spirit replete with *power*, *philanthropy*, and Liberty. The Patriot is a man who loves his family, his nation, his country, and his God. Patriotism is emblazoned in unextinguishable characters, upon the thoughts and deeds of Abraham, Isaac, and Jacob. These patriots served their families, their country, and their God, with a zeal and devotion unequaled. They watched their sons and daughters with love in their hearts, and wisdom in their discernment. They studied their interests, and contemplated with raptures their emancipation from social bondage and affliction—such as swelled the soul of Isaiah, and attuned David's harp to heavenly praise.

But while we accord to these patriots the merit and praise du them, we must not neglect to exercise justice in reference to the Patriots of modern days. We must not forget that we enjoy privileges and liberties which no other nation enjoys, and that these privileges are secured to us by the superiority of our constitution. We *must not forget* that principles of toleration and republicanism have radiated far and wide from this center of freedom, and that they are now vitalizing, and vivifying, and energizing the soul of humanity in all parts of the world.

Combine the qualities of a Patriot with a spirit of Determination and Intrepidity, and you have a sublime Hero. And he, too, is a reformer. He rises superior to time-sanctified customs, and throws open the gates to new discoveries. His unconquerable spirit inspires timid minds with power; and his daring courage strengthens their efforts in fresh directions.

It was the *fire* and *principles* of patriotism which developed the genius and heroism of our GENERAL WASHINGTON. It was but the misdirected fire of reformation that aroused Napoleon to his desperate struggle for vast possessions. But the patriotism and energy of Washington's nature, were developed by the wants and necessities of the times; and he was a hero of many achievements on the field where struggled the *fiend* of Despotism with the *angel* of Humanity.

Washington manifested the indomitable zeal and determination for man, eminently qualified to reform the political evils of our nation. The uniform judgment which he displayed at times and under circumstances when judgment was indispensable, and the expressions of sympathy which emanated from him concerning the unfortunate sufferers of the revolutionary conflict, gave Americans reasons to hope that he would unfold the qualities of patriotism and heroism during the period of his administration.

Combine the splendid and powerful qualities of the patriot and the hero, with Thought and Deliberation, and you have a Legislator. And he, too, is a reformer. He has an indwelling love for his country and humanity; a desire to explore and acquire a knowledge of new regions of thought, and his authority is Reason. He is a man capable of developing new laws, establishing new customs, and introducing his fellow-men into new paths of progress and development. ZOROASTER was a reformer. He collected the national laws of most ancient Egypt and Persia, and from the old elaborated a new code by which to govern and reform the subjects of his empire. He was obliged to leave the old paths, and, in doing so, he impressed his spirit upon the hearts of his people and the institutions of his age. Then came the Legislator of Mount Sinai—the leader of the Israelites, and the Jewish Lawgiver. He, too, was an embodiment of the civilization and advancement of his time; and his laws were suggested by the immediate wants and requirements of his followers. Containing principles of despotism and retaliation as those laws do, they are nevertheless an improvement on the Zoroastrian code. But Moses was obliged to rise superior to the idolatrous multitudes who were his followers, friends, admirers, and enemies. His experience with his followers is not unlike that of our noble Columbus, whose crew, as the vessel was sailing to points unknown, became skeptical about the success of the adventure, and accused him of having enticed them from their homes, and even threatened his life. The laws of Moses are decisions of his own reason. The suggestions of his people, and the sanctions of his wisdom combined, formed the legislature where those principles received the Authority which they exercise over the world even at this day.

And Solon, the Athenian lawgiver, was another example of independent research, independent legislation, and independent authority. He stood far above the intellectual growth of his countrymen. He was the object of their blame and praise. He possessed great Wisdom; and was a vigorous thinker, and a sincere lover of humanity. He was an orator, a legislator, and a reformer in morals and government. But he, too, was misunderstood and dethroned. His professed friend, Pisistratus, conceived plans whereby to overthrow the Republican Liberty which Solon had established in Athens, and the people not comprehending the goodness of their lawgiver, repelled him from the seat of government and forthwith sustained Pisistratus in his sovereign and despotic rule. "Oh, my dear country," cried Solon, "I aided thee with all the assistance which my words and actions could afford! oh, my dear country! since I am the only man who declares himself the enemy of the tyrant, and since all others are disposed to receive him as their Master, I leave thee, I abandon thee forever!" Solon is not the only man who has discovered that true genius and patriotism are persecuted by the falseness of friends and the ignorance of enemies. It seems even so, that when Light shines into darkness, the darkness comprehends it not—so it is when genius reflects the light upon the world.

Solon was a reformer because his heart, his reason, his intuition, constituted his Master. He had no other authority, and he was therefore prepared to reveal truth and develop the principles of reformation. Therefore Solon stood by himself; so did Socrates; so did Plato; so did the more modern reformer, Jesus. The latter was a legislator as much in advance of Moses as were the former in advance of Zoroaster and more ancient rulers.

Jesus was a reformer because he was still more free from educational influences than were any of the previous minds. He was more simple in his mode of developing laws than they, and his laws were less numerous. Zoroaster, and Moses, and Solon, and Socrates, and Plato, unfolded laws having a progressive tendency to ultimate in a similar state of social and moral harmony; but they did not embrace, as Jesus did, in one short comprehensive sentence, the *All* of their commands. While Moses was impressed to convey his principles of social and moral government in the form of *ten commandments*, and the subsequent lawgivers their principles in more or less numerous sentences, Jesus put his down in a pure, all-embracing, Laconic style. He gave the world a new commandment—"That ye love one another." This is a concentration of the excellencies of all previous laws; and a summary statement of what Jesus was designed, or, more properly and philosophically speaking, of what he was constitutionally qualified, to reveal to Man.

But he was superior to his age, and his age comprehended him not. He was a martyr to the philanthropy of patriotism; he was a martyr to the zeal and dauntless courage of heroism; and he was a martyr to the simplest law that was ever uttered. In a word, he was above his nation and his age; he was a reformer, and his age nailed him to the cross!

But what we should bear in mind in connection with the life and teachings of this incomparable reformer is, that he acknowledged no Authority superior to his spontaneous intuitions, and the divine suggestions of his own reason. These were authoritative to him because he felt that "Our Father who art in heaven" inspired his soul with Love and his Reason with Wisdom. We should remember that Moses had no other authority; that Solon had no other; that Plato had no other; that Jesus had no other; and that therefore the true reformer can have no other; because it is *only* through the pure mediums of Intuition and Reason that truth can flow into the world unmingled with the falsities and imperfections of books and human authority.

How came Christ possessed with such infinite acquirements?

This inquiry can not be profitably and effectually answered, unless we know which view of Christ suggested it; for there are represented in the general mind two distinct Christs—one of the reason, and the other of the affections.

What is meant by the affections?

The affections are inclinations which spring spontaneously from the soul of the mind; that is, from the rudimental essence of which the mind is organized—its love. These affections are subservient to the will and government of reason, and in a well developed and directed intellect, they are thus governed; but, owing to the ignorance of men concerning themselves, reason is permitted to be trammeled and held in subordination by the affections, which receive right or wrong directions according to the favorableness or unfavorableness of influences which arise from the situations of life, from surrounding circumstances, and from education. If reason is subjected to the affections, and is not made the medium through which we receive knowledge from the outer world, then the affections will admit and ardently cherish whatever object, faith or doctrine may be presented to them clothed in captivating robes, though it may involve the most palpable errors and inconsistencies.

What is meant by the Christ of the affections?

The Christ of the *affections* is a being who is believed to be the concentrated development of special providences eternally instituted and established in the constitution of things; a being who possessed unnatural endowments and exhibited incomprehensible powers; whose whole life exhibited but a succession of supernatural phenomena; and whose death was attended with a series of corporal changes and transfigurations, altogether novel and unexampled.

The tendency and effect of this faith, is to amaze and confound the uneducated, but not to enlighten or refine them. This hereditary belief is incorporated in almost all departments of education, and is instilled into the youthful mind, accompanied with the injunction, "question not its validity." These minds develop themselves into manhood, and are talented perhaps, and commence the promulgation of this faith of the affections. And by them Christ is endowed with attributes, which are magnified beyond the simple truth, and thus he is removed from our understanding. Consequently, many minds experience a trembling delicacy whenever the name of Christ is mentioned, and never attempt to reason concerning him, or if they do, it is for the purpose of conferring more brilliant honors upon him, and rendering more highly supernatural his mission and accomplishments. Thus reality is transformed into imagination, and still seems to be absolutely true; thus the Christ of the affections is our enthroned idol, bearing but little resemblance to the Christ which reason recognizes as residing on the earth about two thousand years ago, and doing good to the children of men.

What is meant by the Christ of the reason?

The Christ of the *reason* is a good, amiable, benevolent, and unassuming man; who not only loved, but impressively taught the simple and practical truths of peace and righteousness; who relieved the diseases and sufferings of mankind, whenever and wherever he could; who was great and noble, because simple and good; and who, after living a righteous life—teaching men to know themselves and love each other as children of one Father—was crucified, according to prevailing custom, for his open and unreserved denunciation of the popular doctrines, philosophy, institutions and ceremonies which characterized the whole Jewish nation. Thus the Christ of the reason is a natural man, but the Christ of the affections is supernatural; the one is reality, the other is a creature of the imagination.

Why was Christ superior to his fellow-men?

The difference between Christ and his fellows was not conspicuous in any thing, excepting his well-constructed and comparatively perfect body, and his well-balanced and harmoniously developed mind. These are the natural and legitimate consequences of a proper conception, a proper birth, a gentle culture, and a meditative association with the objects and scenes of Nature, which tend to refine and elevate the soul. He was distinguished from other mer by two prominent characteristics: first, by a peculiarity of deportment and personal habits; secondly, by the promptness and originality of his answers to the profoundest interrogatories. The causes are plain. The one resulted from accidents of birth, and the influences of outer association; the other from the intuitions of his unsophisticated mind, because untrammeled by sect and popular superficiality. The manifestations of his simple and spiritualizing morality were ever in keeping with the circumstances of the multitudes which surrounded him, and which called them forth. The causes and their effects are visibly represented together as relating to the character of our spiritual and brotherly reformer; and all that can not be explained of him, is referable to the imperfections of ecclesiastical and biblical history, or to that which men have done for him, and not what he has done for men. Local conditions, circumstances and influences favoring a *local* development of extraordinary correctness, Christ exemplified that perfection of character and amiableness of disposition which we greatly admire. As he is represented to the *reason* as a noble child of an eternal Father, we hesitate not to consider him a model man, and as an example of what the race will be.

Was Christ an example of what the Race is destined to be?

Nature proves man to be a microcosm—a combination of all else in the material world, and the most perfect embodiment of Harmony. We believe that the race will progress and grow to the completeness and stature of a perfect man. Then will be exhibited that harmony of structure and reciprocation of justice so admirably represented in the human form. In this sense do we believe that Christ was the model man, and a living example of what the race is destined to be; and, the latter in its unity will possess and exercise his powers, which were displayed in deeds of mercy and exemplifications of native righteousness. But in order to ascertain the truth of the doctrine of this general development, we must elevate our thoughts above ourselves, and all fragmentary and individual organisms which confound the superficial observer, and calmly contemplate the substantial evidences of the great law of progress which universally present themselves in the world of matter, and the world of mind.

Jesus instituted laws and customs above the popular conceptions of his time and country. And the people crucified him for what they considered sedition and conspiracy against the Roman Government. But time and intelligence have developed the falseness of this act, and made it manifest that Jesus was misapprehended and most ignobly treated. Let us be just, and think about the reformers and developments of our country, and of our age. Are we not also fearful of sedition and conspiracy against our professions, against our government and religion? Have we not the spirit of persecution in our communities? Are we not disposed to crucify the champion of some new discovery, and cry him down as an infidel, or an impostor? I am constrained to acknowledge that we have the old spirit of bigotry, persecution, and intolerance, lurking in our midst. We crucify in our minds and speech; but, fortunately for the reformers of our day, the rack and stake have fallen into disuse—they are frightful monumental evidences of past ignorance and transgression.

Lycurgus, the Spartan lawgiver, acknowledged no Authority but reason and intuition. He was a lover of mankind; and did much toward revealing the principles and practice of Democracy. He, like the first apostles and Paul, held all things in common.

Charles Fourier, the Social legislator and reformer, lived in advance of his age. He was not appreciated nor kindly treated. He devoted his life principally to the reformation and re-organization of Society. He labored to disabuse the popular mind of those hoary-headed and time-sanctified theological errors which poison every thing they touch. He labored to exalt the passions of the Soul, and attune their acts to harmony. But let us be impressed with this fact, that Fourier lived far above the limited comprehension of the people. It was therefore *their ignorance* which let him die in poverty and obscurity; and it was their fear of sedition and conspiracy which caused them to misrepresent and defame his private character. Is it not also *our* ignorance which causes us to disrespect those who disturb our religious opinions? Do we not also defame and deride them because we fear the truths they tell us; and do we not hate them because, when we behold them, their exalted position compels us to look upward?

"*What is a Poet?*" it is asked.

I answer,—Combine the qualities of the Patriot, the Hero, and the Legislator, with a love of the Sublime and Beautiful, and you have a Poet. And he, too, is a reformer. The illumination of genius lights up the mysterious caverns of his Soul, and unfolds serene thoughts in the inmost sanctuary of his being. The sympathies of humanity expand his heart; and prophecies of future peace press his pen to utterance.

When I think of David and Isaiah, and the old prophets of the desert, I behold reformatory poets—poetically prophesying on the extirpation of social bondage and depression. They dwelt long and ardently upon subjects of solemn import, and unfolded the fullness of their internal enlightenment in language at once captivating and beautiful. The scenery and the salubrious air of the East awaken poetry in the soul, just as the landscapes and flowers of Italy exalt the nervous organization and refine the mind. Arabia is replete with native song. The simple heart but vocalizes the manifold objects of inspiration. Persia is saturated with mythology; and some of the poetical revelations which these mythological tales of the East have developed, are as yet unparalleled.

But when we step into Egypt, the grandeur and expansiveness of the prophetical poetry which break upon us are calculated to intoxicate and spiritualize the mind. Thus I consider the poetry of the Old Testament as an improvement and reformation on that of previous ages; but it was so far in advance of the age in which it was uttered that its Authors were but little understood and respected.

But Homer comes forth as a reformer and systematizer of what had gone before. He was himself an embodiment of his age more a representative of his age than its poetical reformer.

But what we must remember is, that Shakspeare, Pope, Pollok, and Milton, did not strive to represent others—that they were the direct mediums of originality and poetical inspiration. In this respect they were true reformers. Reason, feeling, and conviction were their guides to truth and utterance. Who can perfectly comprehend Shakspeare's gentle muse without being similarly organized and situated—without having the same avenues of his soul opened in the same manner, to the same sources of inspiration? Hence a full century elapsed ere Shakspeare was recognized as a most wonderful poet, and as an immortal Author. The literary excellencies or imperfections of these poets I am not now considering,—only the independent, self-representative character of their several productions. And in this respect, I say they indicate the originality and superior qualities of the true reformer.

But have we poetical reformers among us?—Very few. The cause of this is, that modern poets strive to be a Homer, a Milton, a Burns, a Shakspeare, and not themselves—not the representatives of their own intuitions. This going out of themselves for Thought and Authority, closes up the avenues of spontaneous communion with nature. It arrests the development of Genius and Wisdom in them, and renders them not true but false poets and mechanical rhymesters. In this age, poetry—*true* poetry—is more universally understood and applied to practical purposes than formerly. As the soul, and the human race, approach the era of social and spiritual harmony, which is just beginning to dawn on the world, the principle of Poetry which is music, and which is Harmony, is more easily comprehended and practiced. Thus, harmony in our souls; harmony in our families; harmony in society; and harmony among nations, is the Music of Divine order and is the Poetry of true obedience to Divine Law.

"*What is an Artist?*" inquires the reader.

Combine the qualities of the Patriot, the Hero, the Legislator, and the Poet, with a love of Refinement and Elevation, and you have a true Artist. And he, too, is a reformer. It is not difficult to decide upon the mission of the artist. He is an interpreter and a representative of nature. He is to address the feelings and attributes of the spirit through the medium of the senses—to refine and elevate them by representations of native purity and divine images. But the true artist is not understood. He has emotions and impulses which he can not communicate with his tongue or pencil to the critic. The artist lives above the multitude; and he can not receive at its most righteous tribunal, any thing like a true decision upon the merits of his work. Italy appears like a garden of Music, Poetry, and Art. The most fragrant flowers of genius bloom in that portion of the world. Every thing there seems conducive to the development of fine, emotional organizations. Italy, therefore, is highly prepared to give perennial freshness to every manifestation of Art and Song. Raphael, Titian, Angelo, and the vast constellation of contemporary and more modern artists, whose works are enshrined in the Temple of Art and in the history of Italy, were pre-eminently qualified to teach the world the beauties and mission of their profession. The Beauty, and Truth, and Love, and Education of their souls, are written in marble and on the canvas. The old Masters demonstrate that true genius lies far back of canvas, paint, and pencil. If it was not so, their works could not have lived so long. Art was patronized and encouraged, when these old Masters lived, by sovereigns, popes, priests, and princes; but yet the mysterious science was but imperfectly understood, and its advocates and devotees were not honored as the useful men of their age. And I affirm that the true mission of Art is as yet but dimly recognized by those most devoted to its defense and illustration.

Art refines and spiritualizes the feelings, and opens the interior senses to the more glorious perception and appreciation of Nature's beauties. Without this awakened perception, Nature is robbed of half its glory, and its Maker of half the homage due him. In our country, and indeed in the present age of the world, the artist has many things with which to contend, and encounters many discouraging influences. He experiences much obstruction in his progress from the injustice of critics, from the ignorance of the multitude, and from the pressure of personal and family necessities. But the most formidable obstruction to progress in his profession, is the perpetual desire on his part to study and imitate the old Masters. This devotion to Man-authority is disastrous to every attempt at progression in the science of revealing thoughts. Pictures are thoughts upon canvas—just as the objects of Nature are the thoughts of God. As nature is a mirror in which we see God, so is the Picture a mirror in which we see Nature. But Artists err when they copy from Raphael, Titian, or Rembrant, to the neglect of Nature; for the old Masters only embodied in their works their respective perceptions and interpretations of Nature, and nothing more. Our artists take the old Masters for their standard; but I wonder who the old Masters had for their standard, and as their guide to inspiration? The very fact that they were original, makes them the old Masters. They represented their own thoughts, and their own discoveries in the combination of colors. And this independence made them great and immortal! We will have New Masters when originality, and independence of popular opinion, inspires some refined and elevated spirit to express on canvas *his own* perceptions of the beauties of Nature, and *his own* intuitions of invisible things.

If it be asked—" *What is a Philosopher?*" I reply that,—

Combine the qualities of the Patriot, the Hero, the Legislator, the Poet, and the Artist, with a love of Wisdom and Knowledge, and you have the Philosopher. And he, too, is a reformer. He desires a knowledge of the causes of external things. He opens the doors and windows of his mind to the wonderful magnificence of creation; and welcomes every impulse or impression which communicates intelligence to his understanding. But he is essentially superior to the opinions and education of his age, or else he could not explore new fields of science and philosophy, without fear and trembling. The Philosophers of Greece developed a vast amount of Truth and Morality; and necessarily errors and immoralities; but independence of research and investigation rendered their revealments useful and immortal. PYTHAGORAS manifested great originality. His genius and comprehensiveness of mind were suitable qualifications for the development of the philosophy of the four Elements—Earth, Air, Fire, and Water,—of which philosophy he is the Author.

But the experience of Grecian Philosophers, and of other independent investigators previous to their day, is nothing compared with that of GALILEO. His fearless announcement of truths in Astronomy in the face and eyes of the Roman church, and all its instruments of persecution and death, by which *Christians were made* in those days, drew down upon him the bony hand of intolerance and religious ignorance.

But truth can not be crushed. It is mighty and will prevail. Therefore the Roman church, with all its popes and powers, its bulls and edicts, its racks and dungeons, could not kill nor crush the Truth, notwithstanding the threats and attempts that were made to destroy the person by whom the truth declared its power and importance. Galileo lived before his age; and his lips were sealed by the prevailing Theology, and his influence was, for a limited period, arrested by the compulsory measures instituted to enforce Theology—measures of cruelty, which are ever the handmaids of ignorance and conscious error.

It is pleasant to know that the world has been blest with fearless investigators—with some souls sufficiently strong and independent of prevailing dogmas in Science and Theology, to venture into new paths of inquiry. Thus we have the examples of Sir John Herschel, of Sir Isaac Newton, of Benjamin Franklin, and of numerous others in France, England, and Germany.

The popular church is ever ready to cry out heresy and infidelity, when a new light appears in the world of Thought and Inquiry; but the church is too full of imperfections, it seems to me, to succeed much longer in repressing the tide of intelligence. It is certain that she can not withstand its mighty current as hitherto; and I trust the time is not far off when she will be baptized in its pure Waters.

The philosophers of whom I have spoken developed many truths in their respective fields of research, which previous philosophers and the world generally, knew not of; so likewise have *we* the right to go on, encouraged by their example and strengthened by their experience, and explore the fields of immensity. As *they* unfolded truths in advance of previous minds, so may *we* unfold truths in advance of them—regardless of the perpetual opposition of the unadvanced church. The philosophers had no other authority than Reason,—so likewise should we have no other,—if we desire progression, no other should preside over our investigations.

Have we any philosophical reformers among us? We have men who talk about philosophy; but have we true, independent, unpretending philosophers? In the silence of the night, when no object intrudes upon the vision, and no prejudiced multitude disturbs one's meditation, then we are all, more or less, reformatory Patriots, Heroes, Poets, and Philosophers; but, when there is an occasion for the manifestation of this freedom of thought, do you then stand firm,—defying the popular persecutions of the day? I think we are like the artists of our age,—too devoted to the Old Masters!

When Robert Fulton first launched his steamboat upon the waters, your fathers laughed at, and at the same time deplored his mental derangement! They were skeptical as to the practicability of his midnight dream—they thought him demented. And when, more recently, the proposition was announced that steam could be employed to traverse the country on Rail Roads, it was met by the public by the same sneers and prejudices with which their fathers met the proposition of steamboat navigation.

Benjamin Franklin was a great and good man; so were his compeers in science and philosophy; but suppose Professor Morse had taken Franklin for his Old Master, would people be discoursing familiarly every day, in all parts of the country, by the Magnetic Telegraph? Suppose Mr. Porter, of New York, had taken Robert Fulton and Professor Morse as his Masters in the science of navigation and transportation, do you believe he would have dared to think about inventing an atmospherical locomotive? I think you perceive why we have but few philosophical reformers.

"*What is a Theologian?*" methinks the reader inquires.

Combine the qualities of the Patriot, the Hero, the Legislator, the Poet, the Artist, and the Philosopher, with a Love of the Unseen and Eternal, and you have a Theologian. And he, too, is a reformer. His mission is to the Soul. His duty is to cultivate its powers and elevate its impulses. He should teach the world of God. The earth, the sea, the firmament, are the Word and Work of the Ruler of the Universe; and these are the lessons which the Theologian should teach the World. But the true Theologian is superior to his age. You all remember how the intrepid Paul was persecuted—how he died that his teachings might live! The page of humanity's

History is stained with large drops of blood from the hearts of dying martyrs! How evidently is the voice of persecution the mere native language of ignorance! When you hear a man spoken against, despised, defamed, consigned to endless woe from the pulpit, he surely has some extraordinary truth and merit; and I beseech you to suspend your judgment concerning him; for he may be a Christ, a Paul, a Revelator of some important truth, and the people, Jew-like, fearing sedition and conspiracy against their old opinions, may be seeking to crucify him.

When Martin Luther first began the study of Law, he little thought of being the instrument of reforming Catholicism. But subsequent investigation convinced him that his duty was not only that of a friar, but that he should reflect new light into the darkness of prevailing Theology. Do you remember the consequences of his reformatory efforts? They were simply these,—he was calumniated, excommunicated, and denounced as infidel. He was superior, however, to the mere forms and ceremonies of the age, and consequently succeeded in impressing his doctrines upon the hearts and institutions of his countrymen. His doctrines are still incorporated in the articles of the Church of England. But he did not discover *all* the truth in religion, or else John Calvin, (the ambitious tyrant and selfish bigot, as his thoughts and deeds declare,) could not have developed a more rational and truthful system of opinions. That he did do this is generally conceded throughout Christendom. The Presbyterians, the Congregationalists, the Calvinistic Baptists, and other subdivisions of the anti-Lutheran church, are living evidences of this Theological achievement. And John Wesley also made new discoveries in the field of religious investigation; so have many minds before and after John Wesley. And have they not all suffered the penalty of their independent and straightforward course? Their history answers this question with a fearful force—a force, which strikes at the root of sectarianism and religious bigotry!

But it is now proper to ask, have we Theological reformers among us? We have men—preachers—who pretend to expound Theology; but have we any free, unprejudiced, indomitable theological reformers in our community, or even in our age? The response is that clergymen, too, are devoted to the Old Masters? They dare not leave the old paths, as if truth were not every where and in all things. They are not even so free as was good old David, who believed that if he descended into hell, God would be with him.

Luther and Calvin left the Old Masters and explored new regions of thought, and even found much truth in the old dogmas; so should we leave Luther and Calvin, and search for ourselves. They made improvements in Religion—and you all believe it,—have *we* not, then, the right, and courage, and magnanimity, to *go on with the work of reformation?* Suppose Luther had received the Pope for his Master, do you believe that Lutheranism would now be proclaimed from the pulpits of the churches of England, Scotland, and Germany; and from some of the Trinitarian, and Unitarian, and Universalist churches of our country? Certainly not. Suppose Calvin had taken Luther for his Master in matters of religious belief and duty; do you believe that Calvinism would now be preached and enforced, by the most learned and accomplished minds, from the pulpits of Presbyterian, Congregational, and Baptist churches in our community? Certainly not. Suppose the noble-hearted John Wesley had taken Calvin as his Master, do you believe that Methodism would now be preached to the world? Certainly not. Suppose, then, that WE (for *we* are disciples of one or the other of the modified forms of the prevailing sectarianism,) I say, suppose *we* consent to receive Martin Luther and John Calvin, as *our* Masters, do you believe we shall ever make any progress in religious truth and liberty?—No, never!

The time has come, then, for Reason to mount her throne, and judge the religious world universally. It is the only true Master. The experience of the past proves this, and the present enforces it. The true Theological reformer, therefore, is above the authorities of Books and Men. He can not see sects in heaven. His heaven consists in his living in harmony with the Laws of Nature; and his happiness consists in the elevation and Peace of Universal Man!

I can not leave the subject of religious progress and development without adding a few more reasons why we should advance in that department of human inquiry. They are these: we have had reformation in the science of Law—in the science of Medicine—in the science of Mechanism—reformation in Philosophy—in Temperance, and in Theology, up to this day; and now I ask if it is not reasonable that we should perpetuate the reformation in the simple science of religion! In the science of Medicine wonderful developments have been made. After *Hippocrates* and *Galen*, there came intermediate reformers, who remained very near the old school of Allopathy, until *Hahnemann* declared his important discovery, that a less quantity of medicine in a higher state of refinement and concentration, was more suitable to cure diseases in an organization where every atom is moved by the electrical principle, or by spiritual impulsions. Then came Thompson, who declared that a total devotion to physical temperature, and to the medical properties of plants as agencies in the cure of disease, with a complete abandonment of *Calomel* and *Bleeding*, is the only safe way to procure and preserve health. Then came *Priessnitz*, who declared that a total abandonment of *all* medicine, and a strict devotion to personal cleanliness by employing cold and warm water systematically, is the only true method whereby to cure all the forms and modifications of disease, and restore the body to its natural condition. Then came *Samuel Dixon*, of England, who declares, that a rejection of all learned errors in every form of medical science, and an application of the excellencies of each system in the cure of Disease—a union of all the *good* each system contains—is the only method by which to develop truth and benefit mankind. Therefore we have Allopathy, Homœopathy, Thompsonianism, Hydropathy and Chrono-Thermalism, not one of which would now exist, had not some superior mind towered above the doctrines of his profession, and declared the truths he beheld from his own position.

The science of medicine is confined to the sphere of physical suffering; and the science of religion is confined to the sphere of the mind. The former acts upon the mind through the body; the latter acts upon the body through the mind; why not, then, strive to perfect one as well as the other?—for Happiness is the object, end, and aim, in either case. Do not shrink from the attempt to reform religion! Do not believe that the world is sufficiently enlightened in that science, or that further enlightenment is impossible; for I dare affirm that your fathers laughed and sneered at things which you *now* believe to be truths. And it is not *wholly* impossible that what you now believe to be good, sound, unchangeable religion, will be rejected by your children as erroneous.

Many ceremonies of the Lutheran or of the Calvinistic church, are doubtless regarded by some of you as not essential to salvation. If those ceremonies were *ever* essential, they are *now*. The doctrine of the consignment of helpless, sinless infants to endless misery, was once esteemed as a sacred truth; but now you regard it as an error. If that doctrine was ever truth, it is true now. On the same principle of religious improvement, it may be said, that what *you now believe* to be a Divine Revelation, will be regarded by future generations—your children—as *you* now regard the Sacred Book of India, or the Koran, or as you regard the Mythology of the Arabian and Persian World.

If you would escape the sarcastic smile and the disapprobation of the intelligence of future generations, or the philanthropic compassion of advanced minds in your midst, become *yourselves* reformers. That is, keep the doors and windows of the mind open to the influx of thought. Though such thoughts may at first be *strangers*, I admonish you to entertain them; they may be truths. *Fear not to entertain Strangers, for thereby you may entertain Angels.* We now come to the main question—

Who is the true Reformer?

Combine the qualities of the Patriot, the Hero, the Legislator, the Poet, the Artist, the Philosopher, and the Theologian, with a Universal Love and a desire for Universal Harmony, and you have the True Reformer!

But before I proceed to describe the character and mission of the true Reformer, I desire to call attention to a few reflections respecting the *three* classes of reformers which the present structure of Society seems to develop—viz.: *An Oppositional class—a Theoretical class—and a Practical class.*

1st. *What is meant by the Oppositional class of reformers?*

By the oppositional class, I mean those individuals, who, becoming fatigued and disgusted with the hypocrisy, deception, and injustice of the present state of Society, strive to combat and demolish every profession and opinion with which they come in contact. Their perceptions are generally limited as to the real *causes* of hypocrisy and social antagonisms, and consequently they blame and condemn what, and where, and as, they should not. We can always know such persons by their lugubrious and misanthropic air; or by their disposition to uniformly condemn persons and things in an unkind manner. They are usually restless and discontented. I speak of this class of reformers, so called, because *undiscriminating* minds confound such individuals with those who *feel* and *act* vastly different in the field of reformation. Minds of the oppositional class are disposed to disturb public and religious meetings; and will intrude their sentiments upon individuals quite unprepared to receive them. They offend those honestly entertained opinions, which religiously educated minds have imbibed from the current expositions of the Bible and Catechism; and frequently go counter to popular customs because of their love of opposition and discussion. They talk loudly and preach strenuously *against* popular abuses, and *about* reformation; but assuredly they are not qualified to occupy the commanding position of the *true* reformer.

2d. *What is meant by the Theoretical class of reformers?*

By the theoretical class I mean those minds, who, dissatisfied with the present order of things, devote considerable thought to the searching out of new Theories for the re-construction of Society. But this class comprehends a vast variety of talents and conceptions. The most illustrious minds that ever lived were theoretical reformers. They had theories without practice. They lived centuries before their time. The philosophic Bacon lived theoretically in a new state of society of his own construction, viz., in the "New Atlantis." So did the Monk of Campanella, in his "City of the Sun." So did St. Pierre, in his "Dream of Perpetual Peace." So did St. John, in his "Millennium." So did Jesus, in his "Kingdom of Heaven on Earth." So did Fenelon, in his "Voyage to the Isle of Pleasure." So did Sir Thomas More, in his "Utopia." And so did Moses, and the children of Israel, live, theoretically, in advance of their age, in the "Promised Land." And I might quote numerous other minds, who, towering gloriously above the imperfections of present Society, have theoretically established an "Era of Peace on Earth," which they prophetically beheld from their superior position.

There is a vast difference between the oppositional class, and the theoretical class, of reformers. The difference consists in the *former* perpetually combating professions and individuals; and in the *latter* rising, Phenix-like, from out of the dust and ashes of human ignorance and misdirection, into a more glorious and harmonious future. The difference is obvious.

3d. *What is meant by the Practical class of reformers?*

By the practical class, I mean those individuals who strive to live the true life; who exercise the principles of love and reformation in their daily walk and conversation; and who are themselves the embodiments of what they profess to believe and teach the world. This class is composed of those minds which are fatigued with, and repelled by the chicanery, the frauds, and the corruptions of prevalent Society. They form themselves into communities, and strive to exemplify the beauties and joys of a new order of things. Thus we have Industrial Associations, Odd Fellow Associations, and Shaker Societies,—and, indeed, these attempts extend far down the history of Mankind. The first apostles of Christianity held all things in common; so did Lycurgus, the Spartan lawgiver; and so did Plato, in his glorious "Republic."

But more especially are the practical class of reformers those individuals whose lives and deeds are exemplifications of fraternal Love and distributive justice. Of course, the relations which the interests of such minds sustain to the conflicting interests of a community, make it extremely hard for them to live out uniformly those principles of justice which reside in the soul. But nevertheless, we have had, and have now, a few examples of practical philanthropy.

From what has been said, I think it will appear evident to every reasonable mind, that reformers of the most practical class are distinctly different, in their peculiar characteristics, from the theoretical and oppositional class; and that the practical class is the highest in the scale of natural and spiritual development, because they manifest the inherent qualities of their souls in a well-ordered life, full of temperance, patience, brotherly kindness, and glorious deeds.

"*But why is the true Reformer superior to his age?*" is here asked. I reply, that the true Reformer is superior to his Age, because he lives above it in a Temple, composed of the combined Wisdom and experience of every age, and which is built by the united assistance of every Nation. There is not a single science, a single truth, a single experience of any kind, in the vast world of Ages and Nations previous to the present century, which is not incorporated, in one form or another, in the Temple of Knowledge, in which the true reformer is at home above the earth.

The true reformer impartially judges the merits of every science, philosophy, and religion, and appropriates the good they have to the construction of his temple, which is the asylum of all nations, and the free habitation of all systems which unfold themselves in the soil of freedom and civilization. And when the world of mind beneath the reformer shall have attained his position, they can look about and truthfully exclaim—

> "'Twas but the ruin of the bad—
> The wasting of the wrong and ill;
> Whatever of good the old time had
> Was living still."

And the true Reformer is superior to his age, because,—while the world of minds are worshiping various kinds of religious or sacred books, which trammel and stupefy the spontaneous impulses of the Soul,—he has no other book than Nature. He adopts Nature as his revelation of the Divine Being. In Nature he can learn all the physical, intellectual, and moral laws of its Author; and *it is the only book* which can not be changed, misinterpreted, or manufactured by human hands; and in it no passages can be erased, or interpolated, or transposed, to suit the interest and predilections of clergymen or laymen. If any man is considered a reformer, and, at the same time, receives any other book than Nature, for his revelation and guide, then *he is not* a True Reformer.

The true Reformer is superior to his age, because,—while the world of minds about him receive men and books for their master,—he acknowledges no other master than Reason. He adopts Reason as his Master because it was given by the Creator to man; because it existed *before* men or books; and because it is the principle by which every thing we know in this or higher spheres, must be recognized, tested, and comprehended. Reason is a harmonious exercise of all the elements and attributes of the Soul; and it never controverts truth, *only* those errors which time and ignorance have caused to accumulate upon it,—just as gold is tarnished by lying in the dust of the miser's coffer.

The true Reformer is superior to his age, because,—while the world of minds about him are devoting their time and attention to the study of dead languages,—he studies the living languages of Nature. He familiarizes his mind with the flowers, the insects, the birds, the plants, the animals, the human beings, the worlds above, beneath, around; and still more the millions of worlds in Nature's more invisible developments.

His language is not so much of the tongue as of the soul,—not so much of the human, as of the Divine. Therefore, while the individual minds in his community deride and defame his character, he is far removed from their spheres, and is communing with superior worlds of thought and joy! The mineral, the vegetable, and the animal kingdoms are the words, sentences, chapters, psalms, testaments, and the thoughts, which the true reformer can read and understand, because they tell of the love, wisdom, and omnipotence of their supernal Author.

The true Reformer is superior to his age, because,—while the world of minds about him are disqualified to rule and govern themselves, and have so much duplicity as to require legislation and positive enforcement of mere human or social laws,—*he* is actuated alone by the universal and immutable Law of Love to Man. This law governs his actions in all his multifarious relations and intercourse with his fellow-creatures. It lives in his Soul, and manifests itself in his actions and life. He can acknowledge no human law superior to this, and nothing is obligatory to him which does not come within the range of the operations of this divine principle. He desires to substitute this law for the partial and unjust laws of prevalent society; but his attempts are strenuously opposed by the members of that profession, who sometimes retail justice or injustice according to the magnitude of the emolument given in exchange. The law of Love to Man rules in the Soul, and in the Universe about him; and he desires its universal adoption on earth.

The true Reformer is superior to his age, because,—while the world of minds about him are influenced by and immersed into the mythological religions of the Eastern Hemisphere, which have been systematically sublimated by highly accomplished men, and which make mankind Sectarians and bigots,—*his* Religion is *Justice.* No religion is true unless it contemplates the endless succession of creations as one just, inseparable, harmonious whole. And God, being the Great Positive Mind, must rule among the armies of heaven and the inhabitants of earth, with an unchanging and unerring government. Every thing is negative to Him. And imperfection can not from *Perfection* come! The true reformer can have no other Religion than justice to himself; justice to his neighbor; justice to the world; and justice universal! With his soul expanded and elevated above the mechanical religions of the day, it is impossible for him to assimilate with those minds who join in—

"Predestinating some without pretense
To Heaven,—the rest to Hell without offense;
Inflicting endless pains for transient crimes,
And fav'ring sects or nations, men, or times;
Or *deem it merit* to believe or teach
What Reason contradicts, or must impeach;
Or think salvation for *one class* designed,
AND HEAVEN TOO NARROW TO CONTAIN MANKIND!"

The true Reformer is superior to his age, because,—while the world of minds about him are discussing respecting what books, or creeds, or religious system, or philosophy, or about what medium contains the only true light,—*his light* is Truth. All things, whether in books or out of books, whether denounced or worshiped, contain some important truth to the true Reformer. Every thing brings life and immortality to light. The leaf that falls by autumnal winds, or the body that changes into dust, reveals to his spirit the glorious realities of another spring, or of the unspeakable beauties of another life! Truth illuminates his vaulted brow, and even while his body is racked with fatal pains, and is dissolving back into Nature, his spirit calls for—

"Light! more light still!"

Thus truth is the divine light which protects and guides the true Reformer.

The true Reformer is superior to his age, because,—while the world of minds about him are assisting to support and perpetuate the present order of things in trade, government, and religion,—*he* strives to introduce the principles of Association, and of the re-organization of capital and interests. He is pained with the injustice and dissatisfaction in society, occasioned by its false and disunited state. He would concentrate the wisdom and experience of nations, and, upon the most unequivocal basis, he would apply them to the reconstruction of individual relations and interests; and thus he would prevent three social afflictions—poverty, crime, and misery! But in this desire, the Reformer is above his country and age. If all were constituted like him, educated like him, situated like him, and harmonized internally as he is, society would at once be changed. Therefore the distance is so great between him and the world of individual conflicts, (which world the people themselves create,) that he can not associate with it, nor can it comprehend him; and so he must *expect* the scoffs, and sneers, and calumnies of the promiscuous multitude, fashionable or unfashionable, and not be disappointed.

The true Reformer is superior to his age, because,—while the world of minds desire not to leave the old paths in matters of science, politics, and religion,—*he* is inspired with the sublime idea of eternal PROGRESS! He believes in the perpetual improvement of every thing, whether that thing is natural or spiritual, scientific or religious. And therefore, in this simple but irresistible conviction, the Reformer is removed from the comprehension of popular individuals and teachers; for the latter believe and eloquently preach that mankind were better and wiser centuries ago than now, and that progress backward to Eden time is necessary to happiness. But the true Reformer strives to bring, through the law of steady

> "Progression, to the human mind,
> The light of heavenly truth and wisdom new,
> To elevate, perfect, and bless the race."

The true Reformer is superior to his age, because,—while the world of minds about him dream *not* of internal and spiritual realities being far more endurable than visible things,—*he* sees worlds in embryo—heaven—in the soul undeveloped. The law of eternal development is his guide to duty and action. When he sees a germ he knows it contains an undeveloped flower; when he sees a child he knows it contains the qualities and essences of an undeveloped Man; when he sees a man, he knows that man contains an undeveloped Angel. Therefore the Reformer would associate men, advance their interests, and develop their immortal attributes into Harmony. For harmony is the destiny of all!

The true Reformer is superior to his age, because,—while others are seeking for mere material habitations of rest,—he aspires to heaven. His heaven is not a locality—it is a state. If the elements and attributes of the soul are harmonized, the soul is in heaven. And if that soul is in America or England, or in this world or in another, the individual is in heaven. Heaven is harmony. Therefore the true Reformer knows he never can secure heaven by doing penance at the virgin's shrine; nor by praying or being prayed for; nor by building churches and hiring the gospel preached; nor by believing any system of religion, or trying to believe; but he knows that heaven is attainable only through self-development and self-harmonization. In this way he becomes acquainted with the divine within him, and the divine in others, at the expense of the oriental doctrine of human total depravity.

The true Reformer is superior to his age, because, while the world of minds about him are worshiping a God of caprice and retaliation, *he* quietly obeys the Father of All. He has educated himself in the Creator's laws, and finds it easy and natural to obey them. The Reformer can not worship a God of Abraham, Isaac, and Jacob merely, but he reveres the living Mind of Universal Nature—the Vitalizing Spirit of all existences!

The true Reformer must combine within himself the qualities of the Patriot, the Hero, the Poet, the Philosopher, and the Theologian—in a word, he must comprehend, by the exercise of his intuition and reason, the truths of science, and the nature of Man. His mission is determined by the measure of his inward capacity; and his usefulness to the world is decided by the real consistency between his preaching and practice.

In order that an Age may always know who is a true and complete Reformer, and that it may have a sure test by which to ascertain the genuineness and stability of any individual who comes forth, now or hereafter, in the character of a Reformer, I will simply add, by way of a recapitulation of what I have said on the subject, that he must be a True Man—whose Temple is the Experience and Wisdom of every age and nation; whose Book is Nature; whose Master is Reason; whose Language consists of all Forms and Kingdoms; whose Law is Love to Man; whose Religion is Justice;

whose Light is Truth; whose Structure is Association; whose Path is Progression; whose Works are Development; whose Home is Heaven; whose Heaven is Harmony; and whose God is the UNIVERSAL FATHER.

It would not be consistent with the nature of this volume to point out the various subjects which should engage the attention of the true reformer; nor am I impressed to dwell upon the methods of reformation which should be observed by all individuals who seek and labor for personal and social improvement. There will be, however, many important principles of mental or spirit culture incidentally developed in the sequel, which I confidently commend to the reader's consideration. Inasmuch as the character of this volume is that of a "TEACHER," it is not to be supposed that the subjects herein discussed will succeed each other in that progressive and consecutive manner, which usually characterizes a work devoted to the special exposition of a single thought or theory. The Harmonial Philosophy has a universal sweep, because it is a "Revelation of the Natural, Spiritual, and Celestial departments of God's Universal Temple." But as the *natural* is *first* in the order of truth, the reader may expect to find my *first* volumes on the lower or *practical* plane of inquiry. It is for this reason that I introduce subjects of more immediate interest to the welfare of society, and leave profounder themes for subsequent pages. Let us now proceed to the following chapter.

THE PHILOSOPHY OF CHARITY.

Charity is the perfection of all christian excellencies; it is the benignant angel of the human soul. Charity is the perfect image and manifestation of *Fraternal-Love:* and fraternal-love is the development, refinement, and expansion of Self-love. Fraternal or brotherly love, therefore, unfolds itself into a most beauteous form—a form embracing the elements and attributes of the self-love and conjugal-love; and this form, when manifested among men, bears the impress of an angel, and her name is Charity. The tenderness of her nature, the beautiful spontaneousness of her impulses, and the gentleness and delicate attention, which characterize her intercourse with the sick, the poor, the prodigal, the abandoned, and the disconsolate, are precious evidences of her exalted character and glorious mission.

Education and circumstances sometimes prevent the manifestation of her nature and influence in the world, and sometimes she is chained and imprisoned within the gloomy vaults and cheerless dungeons of the miser's dark and selfish heart; but when she is permitted to walk forth among men, a sweet and heavenly influence proceeds from her, like that from angels more exalted and divine, and spreads over the community in which she resides. The seal of divinity is upon her brow; and she is never more beautiful or powerful than when her works and deeds are unaccompanied with display and pretension. If charity is properly directed, and unrestrained while walking in the holy avenues of Wisdom, her deeds will unfold like heavenly violets in the garden of the Soul, and spread the fragrance of happiness wherever she treads. An individual may be distinguished for temperance, and patience, and perseverance, and for good judgment, and for sectarian sanctimoniousness, "but," says a free thinker and writer of the patriarchal age, "the greatest of these is CHARITY."

Charity teaches us to feel that one member can not suffer without all the other members sympathizing and suffering with it—that ot one individual can suffer from pain, or punishment, or exile, or destitution, or from any conceivable affliction, without positively affecting, to some extent, the quietude and happiness of every other individual. Hence she teaches that the inhabitants of this planet, and of other planets in our solar system, and the inhabitants of the planets of immensity, and all the subordinate, and superior, and celestial, and super-celestial angels, and the Father Himself—yea, that *all* would be disquieted and consequently unhappy, were one, only *one* immortal soul consigned to eternal misery!

Charity educates and expands the perceptions, and conceptions, and all other attributes of the soul. She teaches self-love to be just, and kind, and gentle, with one's self. Then she expands and teaches *self* to perfect self in another—that is, to form a *perfect union* with another and corresponding self, by conjugal relations and attractions. Then she teaches the soul to feel its individuality, to acknowledge its dependence, and cultivate the spirit of a universal relationship. Then she admonishes us to preserve and perfect our enjoyments, and attributes, and freedom, by perfecting and preserving the enjoyments, and attributes, and freedom of our neighbors. Thus our companions, and relatives, and friends, and neighbors, and all the nations of the earth, and the friends and relatives in other worlds, together with all the spiritual embodiments of goodness in higher spheres—yea, thus ALL will experience the glowing influence, will feel the genial embrace, of the angel of charity! Thus Self-Love unfolds and expands into Conjugal-Love; and Fraternal-Love elaborates the most beauteous image,—in her nature, and form, and influence, the most sweet and lovely angel; and her name is Charity.

What is Charity's field of action?

Charity's field of action is as expansive as the boundless universe. Her mission in the soul is to pervade every good act and principle with toleration; and to throw around the victim of sin and circumstances an atmosphere of lenity, forbearance, benevolence, forgiveness, and reconciliation. Her *true* labor is not so much in direct reference to the poor, as to the *causes* of poverty; not so much in reference to the sinful as to the *causes* of Sin; it is not confined to the individual, but is extended to the whole. In the steady discharge of her mission, Charity is tender, gentle, unpretending, and strong. Conscious of innate holiness and purity of motive, she never fears or feels contamination. Should she enter the most gorgeous palace, or the darkest chamber of corruption and disease—yea, should she labor in the deepest sinks of sin—she would be an angel still. The generous heart beats not merely for individual instances of suffering and depravity, but for the purification and happiness of universal Humanity. When guided exclusively by Wisdom, she confers her kindnesses, not upon the few, but upon the many,—not upon the immediate object of destitution, but upon the institutions, hospitals, and asylums, designed by her for the permanent relief of mankind, every where and in all conditions.

Whether beating in the midst of cold magnificence, or in the prison's darkest cell, the blinded, misdirected, and desponding heart should be warmed and illuminated by the sweet influence of Charity. She should mitigate the severity of every punishment, and lessen the magnitude of every transgression. Charity is not proud. She rides in the good man's bosom, but seldom in costly equipages. She sits watchfully in the inmost sanctuary of the well developed soul, but is seldom found in fashionable churches. She discourses in deeds, but seldom in words from modern pulpits. To search out the nature and extent of want; to heal the sick; to breathe benevolence and reformation into the midst of pollution and depravity; to entertain kind feelings and sentiments toward those who think and act contrary to our opinions, desires, and interests; to harmonize and adapt individual interests and possessions to the interests and possessions of the neighbor; and to concentrate labor, capital, talent, motive, impulse, and desire, to the end that selfishness, ignorance, crime, and poverty may give place for the advent of the kingdom of heaven, is Charity's constant labor, her glorious mission, and her legitimate field of action.

What are the Causes and Consequences of poverty?

Hereditary physical and spiritual deficiencies, together with a combination of vitiating, depressing, and crushing circumstances, are almost invariably the fundamental causes of individual and general poverty. But reverses in family relations, in entailed fortune, and individual occupations, among the higher and more intelligent classes, are not unfrequently the causes of great suffering and want. The delicate, cultivated, and once wealthy individual generally suffers ten times more from the deprivations consequent upon poverty, than those who are born amid its depressing scenes, and have become thoroughly habituated to its numerous consequences.

The consequences of human poverty are many and weighty Some individuals are urged into what is termed vice and wickedness, because they are poor; others are poor because they are generous. A man has a family; he must have employment by which to feed and clothe them, and pay his rent; he makes several unsuccessful applications for work; the necessities of life press in upon him; they make him desperate; he begs, *truthfully begs*, and is scarcely noticed; he steals, as the next necessary resort, and is condemned to prison. His wife and children are supported, perhaps, by the benevolent institutions of the city, or with thrice the expense and much less kindness, by its numerous strangers and resident individuals. And thus some are wicked because they are poor; and such is a legitimate consequence of poverty.

Again: A gentleman has a justly earned reputation for benevolence and philanthropy; he is in the possession of wealth; his house is beset at almost every hour of the day, from the moment he arises until he retires, by applicants for work and assistance. He gives food, money, clothing, counsel, and imparts the sweetest sympathy; he has no peace save that internal quiet which resides in the bosom of *conscious* truth and good. The world seems to him one vast sea of trouble, poverty, ignorance and corruption. He becomes desperate in his efforts to refine and elevate humanity, and breaks in upon the investment of capital, the interest being consumed to little purpose. He thus becomes embarrassed; he gives still more, and is reduced to poverty. Thus some become poor because they are generous. I know such instances are exceedingly rare, but there *are* such instances, and such are the legitimate results of local charity as exercised in the relief of poverty.

A vast amount of ignorance, vice, licentiousness, inebriety, theft, murder, and misery, can be traced to entailed poverty and circumstantial influences. But then, on the other hand, the greatest, the noblest, the most powerful and talented specimens of humanity ever known on earth, can be traced to a similar origin and class of circumstances. These antagonistic or opposite consequences depend not so much upon the immediate conditions and circumstances of birth and education, as upon the constitutional tendencies and qualifications of the individual. The *evil* consequences of poverty are illustrated in the case of the most numerous class of individuals—individuals who are constitutionally weak and inferior, and who, consequently, fall victims to surrounding circumstances; but the *good* consequences of poverty are manifest in a *few* individuals—such as are constitutionally superior to the former, and who, consequently, rise pre-eminently above the immediate circum stances, the established customs, the prevailing opinions, and the social influences of the age in which they live.

What instances does the world furnish of destitution?

New York is a miniature embodiment and true representation of the whole world. It is not necessary to visit Paris or London to become acquainted with sin and selfishness, crime and cruelty, wealth and wretchedness, pride and poverty; nor to visit the Isles of the Sea, to learn of savagism, barbaric ignorance, and enslaving superstition. The great metropolis of America embraces within itself all the forms of real and false civilization, all the conflicting elements of monarchy and aristocracy, of strife and contention, and all the attractions of refinement, opulence, and luxury.

Amid these depressing and elevating scenes, circumstances and duties have compelled me to reside. It was necessary that I should come in contact with them every day: and with my constitutional sensitiveness and disposition to sympathize with the suffering, the weak, and the oppressed, without possessing the means to render them assistance, the intercourse became exceedingly painful and uncongenial. I could not walk through a street with any degree of pleasure or satisfaction; for at almost every corner was located a representation of loneliness, distress, and destitution. Each scene was sufficient to neutralize in my mind all recollection of enjoyment and happiness, while at the same time, the counteracting effort was to remove all remembrance of personal distress, oppression, and disappointment.

Perhaps the streets were covered with snow—the wind piercing—the night dark—the weather very cold. Perhaps the scene was a child weeping, seated on a stone step or cellar door; or, perhaps, a woman with a little child, with a sick husband at home, with a month's rent unpaid,—having every appearance of hunger, and cold, and poverty; or, perhaps, an aged man—deformed, weak, trembling, and nearly divested of garments. What is a philanthropist—

whose heart is beating for human good and happiness, to do in such a case? The forlorn look, the despairing tone, the heart-rending solicitation for money and assistance, would sink with their full force into the depths of my being; and moved thus, by the spontaneous and sympathetic sensation of pity and charity, I would nervously bestow upon the child, the mother, or the old man, whatever sum I could consistently spare, and hasten on my way.

But instead of being internally approbated for, and conscious of doing a righteous act, or a permanent good to the individuals, I invariably experienced a kind of condemnation and disapproval of judgment,—a consciousness of inadequacy in the nature and tendency of the act. This consciousness of dissatisfaction invariably succeeded the act of giving, (which was generally measured by the impetuosity of the impulse,) both concerning the influence and magnitude of the bestowment, with reference to the actual condition of the solicitor. Whether I had given enough, and to the *right* one, were the perplexing questions. I desired to feel differently—to suspect the motives of the mendicants less, and to experience inward approval for the exercise of charitableness. But I found the more I listened to petitioners, and bestowed upon them, the more numerous became similar wants, objects, and opportunities. And I discovered, that instead of doing a positive good and lessening the prevailing evils of poverty and wretchedness, I was daily strengthening them, and adding more fuel to the consuming flame. I felt convinced that poverty and crime could not be thus prevented.

Having ascertained what is the origin, and nature, and mission of charity, it is necessary to institute a few practical observations concerning the various objects and scenes which address her. New York, as an example and representation of all the world, lies in the distance before me: it shall constitute the field of my present observation; and perhaps the vagrants and mendicants I now describe may have been frequently observed, and are familiarly known to many who reside in the city, and frequent its busy streets.

The *first* instance of apparent want and distress is represented in the personal appearance of a middle-aged woman and two quite young children. They are resting upon the cold stone steps of the Bank on the corner of Bowery and Grand streets. What a painful scene! The gentlemen of business, and the gentlemen of leisure, and the fashionable ladies, of the city, pass and repass the miserable objects—apparently unconscious of their existence. But the approaching philanthropist is sure to perceive them, and deeply sympathize with their situation, feeling a painful consciousness of his inability to render them assistance. The woman is evidently suffering from the effects of some disease: she seems to experience pain and aches in every nerve and muscle. Her clothing is thin, deficient, unclean and ragged. The little girl—her head resting upon the mother's bosom, with face contorted and exposed to view; her body imperfectly protected from the cold; her tiny hand extended to grasp the hand of charity—seems famishing for food.

The little boy—with body slim, shivering, half-clad—stands, with imploring look and hat presented to the passing multitude. A good Christian will sympathize with them, and think "perhaps they have no home, no place to sleep, no food to eat, no money or strength to assist themselves. The winter will soon be upon us—its deep snows—its tempestuous storms—its dark, dismal, friendless nights—its heavy and dreadful consequences, will fall upon this poor woman and her children; and our good Master teaches us to think of the poor." Charity moves within his heart; he bestows upon the poor woman some money and advice, and joyfully hastens away.

The *second* instance is an aged man. He stands on the side-walk in Broadway. His body is deformed, his senses impaired, his features shriveled; and the characters of trouble and distress are written by the hand of time and circumstance, all over his countenance. His body and mind seem the especial subjects of poverty and misfortune. The promptings of charity cause some individuals amid the busy throng, to drop now and then a piece of money in his hand.

The *third* instance is a little girl weeping,—her person and expression representing the concentration of anxiety and destitution. She follows each smiling stranger, utters no distinct words, but pantomimes the unmistakeable language of want and loneliness.

The *fourth* instance is an aged woman, sitting, with a few apples in a basket, in front of the most splendid and fashionable dry goods establishment in New York city. Her expression is sad and lonely; her external appearance indicates an experience of many weary years—years rife with distress and despair. Charity occasionally purchases an apple, pays *thrice* the sum demanded, is pained to the heart with awakened sympathy, and passes on.

The *fifth* instance is an abandoned, intoxicated, and friendless son of Erin. Apparently he is physically well, but he has many, many wants,—he wants friends, sympathy, employment, money, encouragement, and fraternal stimulation. Charity observes him, is pained deeply, but can not assist him. The watchman conducts him rudely to the watch-house; he sleeps from the combined effects of fatigue, alcohol, and disconsolation.

Numerous instances now break upon my vision. Men, and women, and children, of every nation, climate, and complexion,—having old storehouses, hulls of vessels, cold cellars, stifling rooms, and smoky attics, for their resting places and homes. Disease, and prostration, and destitution, reveal their hideous heads, and speak with melancholy tones, in almost every street and section of the city. Empower me, O kind spirit of Charity, to confine my vision to this one city; never prompt me to view, with comprehensive eye, the inhabitants of other cities, other countries, and climes; nor to *feel* for one single moment the realities of their real condition; for my heart would swell with sympathy, and be palsied with conscious inability to assist them; my joyful soul would be stilled with sadness, and my brain would almost decompose with the intensest thought concerning their relief. Yes, many, very many miserable objects inhabit the city that lies before me; I can bear the view of no more fearful and wide-spread scene than its soul-chilling instances of destitution. But it may be asked—

Are all instances of destitution real?

Inasmuch as every one experiences, more or less, the moral promptings and fraternal suggestions of Charity, it is reasonable to believe, that every one who resides in, or visits New York, must experience *some* uneasiness and depression on seeing the mendicants and horrible personifications of poverty, that walk and sit along its principal thoroughfares. Some individuals, however, become accustomed to these scenes, and pass them by unnoticed. But to abolish the seemingly benevolent custom of bestowing local charities upon these apparently wretched creatures; and to impress the *absolute* necessity of instituting more wise and effectual plans by which to remove them from the streets, and to supply their wants,—is the sole object of my present revealments.

The *first* instance—the woman and two children—was ingeniously arranged for the purposes of exciting sympathy and extracting gifts, in the following manner: The woman is not very sick, nor very well; but she would rather beg than work; and has *no* children. The little sick girl belongs to one neighbor, and the little boy to another; and they are engaged, at a trifling sum per day, to complete and act out the representation. They are not destitute,—are not deserving of the deep sympathy and money that many good citizens and strangers have bestowed upon them. I know that the statement of this discovery will seem to discourage the exercise and growth of Charity in the generous heart; that it will tend to generate conflicts of judgment and hesitation, on seeing a new, and perhaps a *real*, instance of poverty—and will tend to give birth to a cold skepticism concerning the honesty of every one who may be compelled, from the unyielding force of circumstances, to solicit alms; but if every individual possessed the power of interior perception, and had the faculty of just and quick discrimination, then a different course in reference to the relief of destitution, would be deemed expedient.

The *second* instance—which was an aged man in Broadway, and one who has caused many sympathetic pulsations and manifestations of charitableness—is in the possession of a good farm, with agricultural stock, in the state of Connecticut. When nothing particularly engages his attention at home, he visits New York on a begging expedition, and finds it uniformly more profitable than other speculations proverbially indigenous to his native land.

The *third* instance—which is a sad-looking little girl—is a *true* representation of a *true* condition, and an exact embodiment of the condition of very many others, who are less known and more retired. But she receives, in the aggregate, not more than *one third* of the assistance which is bestowed upon the above detailed instances.

The *fourth* instance—which is an old woman with apples—is more wealthy than many of the well-dressed, well-educated, and highly genteel ladies who pass by her into the fashionable store, and along the streets.

And the poor Irishman—what can be said of him? He, too, like the poor little girl, is a truthful representation of the *actual* condition of hundreds of his countrymen—both in Ireland and in the United States. And he receives not *half* the kindness and assistance which the above mentioned vagrants receive; because Charity, not being properly directed by Wisdom, expends nearly her last farthing, and sheds her last tear, whenever and wherever she is most affectingly addressed, or is spontaneously impressed to bestow them.

But let me observe further. I behold companies of beggars, dressed in their most affecting uniform, having for their leader and manager some coarse, unkind woman; and other companies, having for their head and master some coarse and cruel man. I behold an organization of German and Italian musicians, composed of men, women, and children, who play upon their harps, violins, organs, and who are scattered abroad over the city of New York, and other cities, and over the country every where; and who are employed, supplied with their various instruments, and sometimes are remunerated for their useless toil,—by a single individual proprietor. I perceive that the solicitation of alms has become a highly profitable and wide-spread business. And, thanks to the Father of Spirits, there is no want of charity in the human heart—it is a constitutional element; but there is a great, a fearful want of Wisdom in the manner of, and time for, its manifestation and exercise. Let us ask—

What is the tendency of local charities?

Having investigated the *seeming* and *actual* condition of the poor, and reflected upon the causes and consequences of poverty, it is now proper to inquire into the evil tendency of local charities. The spontaneous, local, and indiscriminate bestowment of attention and money upon apparently wretched and famishing individuals and families, is seldom attended with permanently good results. Instead of neutralizing and removing the evils of poverty and want, the practice more frequently encourages and strengthens the disposition to idleness and improvidence. Instead of lessening, it multiplies the objects and instances of seeming destitution, and transforms the natural instinct of self-preservation and responsibility into a kind of presumptuous dependence upon the more wise, and prudent, and wealthy citizens. Instead, therefore, of contracting, the practice naturally expands and perpetuates, the evil of poverty and its consequences. There are certain individuals, who are hereditarily predisposed to live by an indolent absorption of comfort and maintenance from the general fund of wealth, industry, and plenty; and these will presumptuously say: "the world owes me a living, the good people shall support me, and I will not work." And finding the generosity of the multitudes more profitable and less fatiguing than labor, such persons form themselves into begging organizations, dress themselves in begging habiliments, and go upon begging expeditions. And thus, Charity's gentle, loving, tender heart, is constantly pained, and taxed, and wearied; and at last, from the effects of over-burthen, she becomes exhausted; and is constrained to withdraw her sympathies, perhaps from the really deserving and needy, and shut them up within the seemingly selfish attribute of selfish-protection. And the individuals in whom this occurs, are pronounced uncharitable!

The practice of bestowing local charities is injurious to the progress and development of individual energies: because it creates a false reliance upon the wealth and exertions of others, and generates incautiousness and a want of true dignity and self-respect. It is injurious because it is a positive transgression of the principles of Deity as manifest in Nature. The earth is watered and rendered fertile by the united and concentrated influence of the rain and sun upon its surface; but never by *drops* of water here and there, and by spasmodic flashes of heat and light. The rain is good, the light is good, and local charities are good,—but they are permanently good only when they emanate from a central source, and in quantities appropriate and well proportioned. Charity is ever anxious to do good and conquer poverty and its evils; but the custom of directing her exertions in a disunited and abstracted manner, can not but result in lessening her power, strengthening her enemy, and impoverishing herself. Napoleon was ambitious to conquer and become Emperor of the whole world; but he, like Charity, by directing his forces in a disunited and abstracted manner, succeeded merely in lessening his power, strengthening his enemy, and accomplishing his own downfall. Charity's goodness, and Napoleon's ambition, have fought and labored for *dissimilar* ends, in a *similar* way, and have had results analogous. I know that local charity does a negative good; but, I know also, that it creates a positive evil; and hence I feel the absolute necessity of urging its immediate, but, at the same time its *conditional*, abolition. Again let us ask—

Is general charity misapplied?

The constitutional love of mankind for Humanity has expressed itself in various forms all over this country, and is beginning to speak in many portions of Europe. These imperfect expressions are our Odd Fellow Societies, Anti-Slavery Societies, Moral Reform Societies, Christian Sewing Societies, Temperance Societies, Benevolent Societies, and Prison Reform, and Anti-Capital-Punishment Societies. And fraternal love has built Alms Houses, Hospitals, and Asylums, for the sick and destitute. And Jails, and Houses of Correction, and Penitentiaries, are also, in one sense, *imperfect* and incomplete expressions of fraternal love as exercised in social protection. The latter will disappear as Wisdom is unfolded.

But I must confine my attention to New York. In New York city there are between five and six hundred thousand inhabitants. About one-fourth of the number are decidedly wealthy; and the remaining three-fourths generally occupy every conceivable plane between the sphere of the actually wealthy and the sphere of the actually poor. And I am surprised to find that in all New York city, there are not three hundred individuals—including women and little children—who are compelled to wander about homeless, in search of aid, food, and employment. But there are many, very many, who are compelled to work, day and night, for a much less sum per week, than is generally expended by a leisure gentleman at the saloon in a single refreshment upon wine, oysters, and cigars!

The sum which is annually bestowed by residents of New York, its visitors, and the public in general, upon the poor objects in its streets, in the almshouse, and upon the solicitors of alms in the city every where and in every way, is of sufficient magnitude to furnish—if systematically concentrated and wisely applied—*every poor* family in the city *with a neat house, twenty-five feet square, one story and a half high, situated upon an acre of good land!* Those persons to whom you gave money yesterday, are in the streets, and in the same condition, to-day; give them more money to-day, and to-morrow the scene will equal the scene of yesterday, if, indeed, it be not a more exciting appeal to the sympathies. The question arises—

How can local Crime and Poverty be extirpated unless Society be re-organized?

Charity never moves the heart nor hand to give without causing the individual to desire a certain assurance, an unequivocal knowledge, that the donation will be productive of beneficial results. Therefore, in order to nourish, and expand, and develop fraternal love and good will among men, and to free the streets of New York, and other cities, of mendicants and impostors, let there be immediately organized a MORAL POLICE. We have a legal or municipal police, who, as a body of men, do a *negative* good, sometimes for dollars and cents, and for the sake of office; but we want a MORAL POLICE, who, as a body of men, will do a *positive* good, for Humanity, and for the sake of PRINCIPLE. Clergymen and laymen—good men, good women, and affectionate spirits—who desire that all men may be saved and come unto the knowledge of the truth—*such* should, and *only can*, compose this Christ-like band of brothers. Let there be no arbitrary laws of organization, no specific plans for searching out and investigating apparent and *sequestered* instances of poverty and vice; but let *one impulse* dilate their hearts, and energize their movements, and the Spirit of Christ and the Angel of Charity will form a matrimonial union.

Let the Moral Police be spiritually remunerated, (which they inevitably would be,) with an internal *consciousness* of doing good, which is a *treasure* in the kingdom of heaven, where moths do not corrupt nor thieves break through and steal. And let their pecuniary remuneration flow from the new streams which would be thrown open, composed of copious contributions to the new movement.

The business of the *moral police* should be to search out all the cases and victims of actual want; all the cases of individual vice, corruption, depravity, inebriety, stealing, gambling, and youthful excesses; all the instances of female degradation and abandonment, and all the causes, and the extent, of those vices which flow from ignorance, and crushed or misplaced affection, from business failures, from moral or mental delinquencies, or deficiencies. In a word, the *moral police* must strive, and work, and pray, for the establishment of the kingdom of Heaven on Earth! And then, whenever the peace and laws of the community are infringed upon or transgressed, and the unfortunate transgressor is arraigned before the City tribunal to answer therefor, *he will have an advocate* somewhere among the moral police; some one among them will be thoroughly acquainted with the causes and extenuating circumstances of the transgression. The Angel of Charity will thus plead his cause, pronounce a just verdict, and suggest ways and adopt means by which to prevent him from doing subsequent harm to himself or to the interests of Society.

The Moral Police will also report every case of actual want to the treasurer of the city organization, and the provisional committee will decide upon the most *permanent* means of relief, which it will take immediate measures to have promptly executed. If only temporary assistance be required, the committee will bestow it; but the *permanent* good of the individual and the various interests of society, must ever be the first and paramount considerations.

To this end, let benevolent societies cease working independently of, and, as they sometimes do, in direct opposition to, one another's objects and interests, and strive to concentrate their spirit, impulse, labor, capital, and talent; and there will not be one single instance of real or pretended poverty in the city, nor in any other place where the same measures are carried out.

And for the sake of general health, refinement, and civilization, —and for the important purpose of supplying *every* applicant with *profitable employment*, calculated to reciprocally benefit the individual and the whole—let the entire city be cleansed and beautified; let little street-sweeping girls be justly remunerated for their labor; and let occupations be so well selected and so well executed as to encourage the laborer, do honor to the executive committee, and make proud the spirit of reformation every where. America is now the great light-house of nations,—I desire her to become their example! She towers above the kingdoms of earth; the clouds of old things are fast passing from her firmament; and her intelligence, and freedom, and generosity, and republicanism, and concentrated impulses to improvement, and her sparkling spirituality, will perpetually send out their gentle influences, which will fall like heavenly dews upon, and bless, the unadvanced multitudes and nations beneath her. But we must strive to overcome evil with good; ignorance with wisdom; and poverty, in all things and every where, with abundancies, and with the inexhaustible productions of the earth, which is Jehovah's footstool, and with the divine treasures of the human heart, which is the vestibule of the kingdom of heaven.

My impressions will not permit me to disguise the fact, that the grand, ulterior *object* of the voluntary organization of a MORAL POLICE, is the re-organization of society. I appeal to clergymen and laymen, as the proper minds to advance such a reformation, because they are, or should be, the followers of Jesus,—followers, in the same sense as he was a *disciple of his own high individual Conscience*—a man who sought the "fishermen"; occupied his time in "teaching" them; fraternally associated with "publicans and sinners," and taught them; had no other "place of worship" but the gorgeous temple of Nature; forgave sinners until seventy times seven; and, in every thing and under nearly all circumstances, proved himself to be a philosophical philanthropist—a child of Nature—a man of the Soul! He considered his conscience superior to law—to custom—to prevailing religion—to prevailing government; for he, *in the name of his conscience and our heavenly Father*, openly denounced the laws, customs, religion, and government of his age and country, just in proportion as they appeared to him to be uncharitable, unjust, irreligious, and despotic. Surely, clergymen should be more like unto their Master,—they should be Teachers, not in words, but deeds!

But before clergymen can properly "teach" the multitudes, they must themselves become acquainted with the imperial laws of conscience; with the nature of the soul; with its impulses, tendencies and dependencies; with the constitution of universal Nature; with the elements and attributes of God; for, without the inspiration flowing from such knowledge and mental development, how can they be of any practical service to mankind? Trammeled with a false education and experience, how can they develop the kingdom of harmony on earth? Chained by false positions and interests, how can they rebuke the laws and religions of their country, when unjust and tyrannical? Without further remark, however, I refer to the chapter which follows.

INDIVIDUAL AND SOCIAL CULTURE.

INDIVIDUAL HARMONY is essential to family harmony; family harmony is essential to social harmony; social harmony is essential to national harmony; and national harmony is essential to universal harmony among the inhabitants of the earth. The whole proceeds from, and depends upon the soul, and perfection of the individual. There is no peace and happiness in a family when its various members have discordant desires, feelings, and impulses; and if families are discordant, society must and will correspond. And so likewise do nations war with one another, if society is conflicting and internally discordant. The whole is a *likeness* of the individual, and the individual is consequently molded into a complete *likeness* of the whole. Individuals, by a combination of their constitutional tendencies and impulses, develop families, societies, nations, and circumstances. These same individuals become the victims of their own developments, and consequently they bear the impress of those circumstances, customs, opinions, and superficialities, which they were instrumental in establishing among men.

The consequence of this is to create two distinct classes in the world. The first, and by far the most numerous class, is composed of those individuals who are born into society, where the circumstances and influences of past generations are strengthened by the present, and of which they become the receptacles and the victims. The second class is composed of those fortunate individuals who are born *superior* to surrounding circumstances in consequence of their favorable physical and mental organizations. Therefore there is a class constitutionally *inferior*, and a class constitutionally ***superior*** to the influences, opinions, and conventionalities of the society, the nation, and the age in which they live. The former are the weak and productive, and the latter are the strong and the consuming class. And in this way individuals not only create and develop, but in their ignorance become the victims of, the conditions of one another.

Unhappy or evil consequences flow primarily from unfortunately *organized* individuals; and secondarily from unfortunately *situated* individuals. Inharmonious minds unfold or develop inharmonious circumstances; and inharmonious circumstances develop inharmonious minds. An inventive but misdirected mind discovered the guillotine and caused it to be erected, in order to intimidate the free-born impulses of the heart, in their thirstings for Liberty, and to summarily punish the foes and transgressors of the principles and restrictions imposed by the prevailing government; but at last the inventor himself suffered by the instrumentality of his own creation. He died by the *same knife* that was made to subdue and destroy his fellow-men. Some nations establish slavery and monarchical domination among themselves, and thereby voluntarily sign an agreement which, strengthened by the rising generation, compels them to be slaves and have their rights usurped according to the caprices of their chieftain. Ignorant and misdirected minds create thus what they can not easily destroy.

Again: Happy and good consequences flow primarily from fortunately *organized* individuals; and secondarily, from fortunately *situated* individuals; and these, being higher and more perfect in the scale of human development, are receptacles of Wisdom and knowledge, which they are capable of communicating, and which it is their duty to impart to those of less fortunate development.

Here, then, is made manifest the origin of social evil and social good; and that, too, without the necessity of referring to, or believing in, the partial or complete depravity of the germ of the human family, or of the human soul. If the physical organization is defective, and the progenitive inclinations are antagonistic to the harmony and composure of the soul, thereby preventing the soul from unfolding and manifesting its fair proportions, it does not follow that the soul itself is *innately* defective and is inclined to evil as the sparks tend to fly upward. If vitiating circumstances are overpowering to the conditions and capacities of the individual, and he becomes their slave and their instrument to evil consequences, it does not follow that the individual is disposed to evil, and is but giving expression to his carnal and depraved propensities. No; theologians have fortunately erred in their opinions and speculations on this point. I say, *fortunately*, because my knowledge that the race was never so united and intelligent as now, and all my hopes and faith that it will continue to unfold into more peaceful and harmonious relations, rest upon the *absolute falseness* of this time-sanctified and cardinal point in popular Theology. This belief, that individual and social evil is referable only to the *inwrought wickedness* and rebellious propensities of the human heart, became confirmed in the minds of men, solely in consequence of the ignorance of theologians—ignorance concerning the structure, tendencies, capacities, and attributes of the human Mind. Modern Theologians, and those who reason and act upon Theological authority, are generally standing upon false and mythological foundations, and are pre-eminently disqualified to reason correctly and consecutively from *Cause* to *Effect*. Hence proceed the numerous insults to man's native goodness and dignity; and hence, too, proceed the almost innumerable erroneous theories concerning the *origin* of evil in society, and how to accomplish its extirpation.

Philosophy, Astronomy, Chemistry, and every thing, in fact, that exists in Nature, has been, and is now, subjected to misconception, misappreciation, and misrepresentation; and, above all, is this the misfortune and historical experience of the Human Mind. Nothing has been more insulted, more misconceived, more misapprehended, and misused, than the native capacities, elements, and attributes of the indwelling Spiritual Principle. Individual Merit is unappreciated or improperly rewarded; and demerit is unjustly magnified and correspondingly punished. Merit and demerit, as existing in the constitutions and actions of men, are generally explained and magnified by Theologians in such a way as to give the impression that they are attended with eternal rewards and eternal punishments. Blame and Praise are frequently as unrighteously bestowed. Theologians have long had possession of the human mind. Their Philosophy of its carnalness and intrinsic depravity has been quite universally received, and has proved quite as universally tyrannical and enslaving to the yearning, thirsting, aspiring Soul. Nothing so trammels the immortal impulses of the Spirit, and nothing so clouds the firmament of Reason, as the mythological and theological hypothesis that all the evil and disunity prevalent in society are developed and strengthened by the perverseness and inborn iniquity of the human heart. And it is solely in consequence of this influence, which the belief in human original contamination almost invariably exerts upon the mind, that the mind has been so long in theological bondage,—incapable of rending asunder the chains that bind, and the sectarian prison that confines it, and walking in the warmth and light of reason, freedom, and independence.

But, as I have already affirmed, this hypothesis, this slavery, this imprisonment of the mind, grows mainly out of these three conspicuous and transparent errors, viz.: 1. the Theological opinion that individual, social, and national evils are the natural and legitimate consequences of innate depravity, instead of defective organizations and corresponding circumstances; 2. the almost unpardonable custom, which is created and perpetuated by religious teachers, of accusing and condemning the *individual* for doing that from which he would refrain, but which, truthfully and philosophically considered, he can not help committing; 3. and the almost universally prevailing ignorance concerning the structure, elements, and attributes of the human spirit.

Inasmuch as national, social, and family harmony *is* dependent upon the essential condition of the soul, and the degree of harmonious perfection to which it has attained, it is indispensable to such general harmony that the natural attractions and powers of the soul are correctly apprehended, and stimulated to cultivation. I say therefore, that the best and natural tendency of every desire, faculty, impulse, sentiment, and attraction of the spiritual principle, must be properly ascertained and properly encouraged to development. But popular Theology shrinks from the belief that the soul can grow. It reluctantly admits that the intellectual faculties are susceptible of growth and culture; but that *the affections* can be taught and strengthened, and unfolded into Wisdom, is a point which Theology manifests no willingness to concede. Theology supposes that the affections can be redeemed from their sinful and perverted condition only by a direct interposition of divine influence, which divine influence is accessible only through the blood and martyrdom of Christ. But at this point, Philosophy appears, and, by its more natural, and consequently more reliable revelations, we are saved from the paralyzing influence of the former opinion, and are lighted to a new path leading to new discoveries.

What is the history of Philosophy?

At first, philosophy was *material*—that is, in its infancy. The impulse to independent and fearless inquiry was developed in the mind, and manifested in itself for the first time, when philosophy came forth, like a free-born child, from the womb of Reason. Nature and the human soul were inviting fields and regions of exploration; but to philosophy both were vast, fearful, enigmatical.

Experience and observation (for material philosophy searches no deeper than the surface) combined to give the impression that throughout all nature, change and transformation were incessant and inevitable, and hence that all men and things must change into other and new forms. Hence incipient philosophy developed the doctrines of metempsychosis, the Mosaical cosmogony, and the Pythagorean theory of the four elements. And experience and *superficial* observation on the desires, enjoyments, and the uncultivated appetites of the physical constitution, gave birth to that somewhat unrestraining and unsystematic philosophy of the Epicurean school. But what the Soul is,—or is capable of doing, being, and unfolding,—are questions which material philosophy could not satisfactorily solve.

Then came a higher form of investigation—the *Analytical* Philosophy. It separated atoms, things, and worlds; but it could not arrange them into one magnificent, comprehensive System. The soul was mapped out into passions and sentiments; but how to cultivate and harmonize them it could not comprehend. Under this form of philosophy are enumerated such sciences, as are calculated to reveal the component parts and elements of bodies and substances. Among these sciences are to be found Chemistry, Anatomy, Physiology, Phrenology and Magnetism. These sciences, or these forms of philosophy, are an introduction to a clearer and more valuable understanding of the intellectual structure. They take apart and analyze the body and its functions, and they develop new and startling powers of the soul. But this Philosophy, being also of an external and superficial character, is quite unable to furnish the important information which is required before the spirit can be properly understood and properly cultivated.

Another form of Philosophy grows out of the analytical, viz., the *Synthetical* philosophy. While the analytical takes apart, the Synthetical puts together. Under this head, also, may be arranged the highest developments of the above mentioned sciences. And in proportion as we take steps in this philosophy do we leave the mythological and unphilosophical teachings of Theology, as Theology is at present apprehended. But the highest form of Philosophy—a form, which embraces all the modifications and perfections of the preceding forms—is the interior or Harmonial *Philosophy*. This philosophy leads the inquirer into the interior and living principle of whatever is presented for investigation. With it, the internal is the superior and supremely important part to understand and cultivate, while the exterior is regarded as inferior to it, inasmuch as the latter depends upon the interior for its existence, nourishment, and beauty.

These Theories and Philosophies have performed and are performing important missions in the field of mental and scientific investigation. It was good that there should exist antagonistic opinions concerning any new discovery, because such antagonisms serve to develop important facts and principles in favor of the advanced discoveries. But notwithstanding these discoveries, I am fully persuaded that the real realities of the indwelling spirit have not been properly recognized and estimated by the Theologian, Philosopher, or Reformer. And I am moreover persuaded that nothing but interior philosophy and simple-mindedness will enable the spirit to receive and comprehend much concerning itself and its eternal destiny. But let us inquire—

What has Phrenology done?

The important discoveries of Phrenology have done a great deal toward making mind acquainted with mind, and toward establishing the belief that mind has material instrumentalities, which subserve the purposes of manifestation and educational development; in other words, that the spirit can be educated through the same mediums and avenues that subserve the purposes of its exercise and exhibition.

And I am still further persuaded, that the conflicting and discordant elements of present society can never be united and harmonized *unless the few individuals who are constitutionally superior to prevailing interests and customs, will approach one another's views and labors more closely, and strive to become themselves what they ask of society.* It is evident that a proper knowledge, and exercise, and refinement of the faculties and attributes of the spirit, is required before any individual is duly qualified to teach and practice the principles of unity and reformation. The *inferior* developed classes look up to, and instinctively depend upon, those who are, and those who profess to be, *superior* in morals and intellectual attainments, just as the hands and feet depend upon the head for direction, and upon the heart for blood. But if the superior class are as disunited and conflicting among themselves, as are the classes beneath them, then the consequence of their neglect and transgression, will be excitement, shame, and disappointment.

Now I would urge upon those who *do*, and upon those who do not, profess to be reformers, and to be reformed, the *absolute* indispensableness of self-knowledge and self-cultivation. But this knowledge and this cultivation depend upon the proper analysis, exposition, and direction of the *actuating* and *governing* principles which are incorporated in the human spirit. This analysis and exposition, I am involuntarily persuaded, have not as yet been wholly presented to the world, notwithstanding the many discoveries and close approximations of modern metaphysics and Phrenology. The good which the analytical science of Phrenology has done, and is doing, and will do to mankind, is embraced in this highly important yet scarcely admitted *truth:* that mind *is matter* in a high state of refinement and organization. Phrenology proves this by demonstrating the fact that the mind employs material instrumentalities to exercise and manifest itself, and that it is susceptible to, and capable of, cultivation and improvement through the same mediums. I esteem this as an invaluable discovery; for it not only strikes a deep and a fatal blow at the foundation roots of pulpit Theology, but it proves that the mind is capable of growth and endless progression—that it can be cultivated like a flower, until its immortal fragrance shall be sweet, and pure, and spiritual. If the mind is capable of being altered, deformed, or improved by self-exertion and circumstantial situations, then it is also capable of *endless* expansion. The finer *matter* becomes the more it expands; the more it expands the more it is enabled to do, contemplate, and enjoy. Such I apprehend to be the legitimate teachings of Phrenology.

But, on the other hand, I feel impressed that Phrenological science is inadequate to that kind and degree of cultivation which is requisite to a complete harmonization of all the indwelling elements. Phrenology has done much for physical improvement, mental, and metaphysical science. It has discovered, designated, classified, and philosophically illustrated, the numerous and different manifestations of the mind. It has divided and subdivided, and supersubdivided the faculties, capacities, sentiments, and impulses of the living principle; but then phrenology is an external, a superficial science—one that conducts the inquirer from appearance to examination, and from examination to faculty, and from faculty or propensity to conclusion, which conclusion, though merely founded upon appearance and external observation, is received as almost unequivocal knowledge concerning the intrinsic worth, talent, disposition and character of the individual. I feel moved to consider Phrenology as defective and inadequate to the wants of individuals and of universal society, because in its deductions and conclusions it does not rest upon the internal elements of the soul. We want such an understanding o. Man's spiritual nature as will enable us to harmonize self with social and universal interests. We want to understand the sympathetic and homogeneous tendencies of our own souls, and how to unite ourselves with the corresponding tendencies existing in our neighbor, brother, or nation. Phrenology supplies us with the principles and local demonstrations of these universal sympathies, and tendencies, and with the intellectual education of which I have spoken; but there is too much complication, and too many divisions in its analysis of the soul, to render it wholly adequate to the formation of a brotherhood, based upon individual sympathy, and to complete harmonization of desires and interests.

In presenting a new and different, because a spiritual, analysis of the human mind, let it not for one moment be supposed that I intend to oppose or in any way depreciate the teachings and general conclusions of Phrenological science; on the contrary, believing Phrenology to be true, but subordinate to the system I feel impressed to suggest, present, and explain in subsequent pages, I am convinced that Phrenology may be harmonized with it to the acquisition of valuable results in favor of harmonial philosophy.

What have Metaphysicians done toward a definition of the Mind?

Among all the metaphysical theories and hypothetical definitions of the mental organization and qualifications of Man, I find none *so closely* allied to truth as those of Charles Fourier. But in making this statement, I know what a vast amount of ignorance and prejudice I shall encounter, and what antagonistic sensations it will create in such minds as are not accustomed to thinking in liberal directions. I am not insensible to the splendid system of juvenile education and discipline developed by A. Bronson Alcott; nor to the highly suggestive and partially practicable principles of scientific cultivation, which are diffused abroad by the brilliant constellation of minds at Edinburgh; nor to the profound disclosures, and the almost innumerable amplifications of mental organization and phenomena, presented by Swedenborg; nor to the general information upon metaphysical subjects, which is so wide-spread and characteristic of the present century, for I am proud of the unintentional contributions to harmonial philosophy, which flow from these prolific sources. But that these minds have not discovered *all the truth*, is evident from the fact that those minds which thoroughly *understand* their theories, are searching still.

What is meant by Harmonial Philosophy?

By Harmonial Philosophy, I mean a process of reasoning which may be more properly denominated an ætiological investigation; or an investigation into the consecutive causes of any thing, which investigation leads the investigator deep into the spiritual origin of all things, or of the thing which he is moved to investigate. It is a philosophy which depends upon immutable principles, upon intuition, upon Wisdom, and outwardly upon Nature for its confirmation to the senses. Appearance and external observation are inferior sources of information; and when reference is made to them it is with the design to address those material and *sensuous* minds who reason and believe wholly from externals. Assisted by interior philosophy, therefore, I shall pen my views concerning the spirit and its culture. And hoping to address simple, truth-loving, and intelligent minds, to the end that self-knowledge, self-improvement, and self-discipline may be promoted,—I will now proceed with the investigation. But first—

What is meant by Simple-mindedness?

By simple-mindedness, I mean, *a state of feeling and judgment which is free from the pride of popular education, popular opinion, or sentiments which the mind has long entertained.* I mean a state of mind which is not reluctant to be taught—which feels, and is willing to acknowledge, that the Universe is filled with various and beautiful truths—which seeks the simplest mediums as their vehicle and for their revelation. By simple-mindedness I mean a state of mind which is *candid, sincere, free to embrace truth, willing to acknowledge a fault, not severe, and never arrogant or boastful*

I mean a state which is sustained by instinct or intuition, which is illuminated by Reason or Wisdom, and which recognizes no authority so sacred and unequivocal as Nature. No mind ever received truth until it divested itself of *Pride*, *arrogance*, and attachment to *human* Authority. Frequently, when the heart is weary and fatigued with doubt, with searching, and with reading, and the mind yields to rest, *truths* flow up from the inward depths and refresh the soul. Yea, truths come up, when and where we least expect them. Gold is often found when not sought; and it is seldom sought for where it is most abundant. I ask, therefore, of every individual, who desires to become acquainted with truth and inward harmony, to put himself in a mental condition which will enable him to exercise his OWN INTUITION, HIS OWN REASON, and the powers of his own personality—because any other condition will necessarily prevent the full reception of truth and the full enjoyment of its attending happiness.

It is necessary to keep this distinction prominently in the mind, that the question about to be considered is, not concerning what *materials* compose the human spirit, but what affectional and rational elements and tendencies does it contain? In dissecting a watch, if I were to speak of the *materials* of which it is made, I should say it is manufactured of steel, brass, silver, gold, and kindred substances; but were I to speak concerning its vitality,—its moving and time-recording power,—I should say it is composed of wheels, springs, chains, pivots, and similar mechanical instrumentalities. This self-evident distinction must be preserved throughout the present inquiry.

The structure of the spirit and its native attractions were presented to my mind while delivering a course of lectures in New York, and my generalizations of them are recorded on page 622 of "Nature's Divine Revelations," a Book which has been for some time before the world. But it now appears to me, that the subject demands more elucidation and amplification. It requires to be systemized and reduced to a practical form—a form, which will make clear and straight the path of spiritual culture and Social harmony. In the generalizations referred to, it is shown that the deep, divine, vitalizing, vivifying, and immortal essence of the Soul, is LOVE; that the passive or *neutral* faculty, is WILL; and that the restraining, governing, dissecting, and harmonizing faculty, is WISDOM. This is a comprehensive explanation and statement of the spirit's inmost contents. But on pursuing the philosophical analysis to the soul's most internal and minute organization, it was found that *Love* and *Wisdom* contain elements and attributes, which arrange themselves in a beautiful progressive order; and which play specific parts in the incessantly changing drama of the spirit's present and future existence. Love is found to be the parent, or residence of all those feelings, and impulses, and sentiments, which characterize the spirit in its threefold external connection with Nature, with society, and with nations. And Wisdom is ascertained to be the parental fount of all that Form and Order, beauty and precision, which environ the intelligent individual, and which are the natural companions of reason and erudition. In this philosophy of the human soul, it is well to remember, that *Will* is considered more as the *effect* of a class of faculties than as a faculty by itself; hence, that it is manifested only when Love, unguided or guided by Wisdom, as the case may be, prompts the individual to action, emotion, or determination of purpose. It will be shown hereafter, that the mental or moral constitution of man does not contain the principles of perfect and unqualified freedom; that individual and social cultivation depend upon a practical recognition of the law, that outer and inner influences and circumstances act upon and mold the individual from the moment he enters upon this stage of being, and through all succeeding stages of spiritual existence; and, consequently, that the manifestation of mind which is termed *Will*, is not a power of choice—of unconditional freedom—but an effect of more interior causes. It may be asked—

What did the Analysis of the Principles of Love and Wisdom furnish?

The analysis furnished, without the least anticipation or preconceived desire in my mind, the following revelations concerning the structure and properties of the human Spirit:

In the LOVE, or ACTUATING PRINCIPLE, are

1. SELF LOVE,	3. PARENTAL LOVE,	5. FILIAL LOVE,
2. CONJUGAL LOVE,	4. FRATERNAL LOVE,	6. UNIVERSAL LOVE.

In the WISDOM, or the GOVERNING PRINCIPLE,

1. USE,	3. POWER,	5. ASPIRATION,
2. JUSTICE,	4. BEAUTY,	6. HARMONY.

Locally, man is allied to external Nature. Physically, man is a likeness of the Universe. Spiritually, man is a likeness of God. And I am, therefore, led to affirm that man possesses in a *finite* degree the elements and attributes of the Infinite. An exposition of the LOVE, or Actuating Principle, is now deemed necessary.

What is the Scientific Definition of Love?

Love has a scientific definition, which definition is employed by men without knowing to what principles it leads in their scientific researches. Love is Life. All that men know of motion, life, attraction, repulsion, gravitation, association; and all that is known concerning the laws of fluids or solids; and all results, in truth, that science and experience have proved as proceeding from motion or life, or from their innumerable and dissimilar modifications in the external and objective world, are alone referable to the principle of Love. Indeed, Love is the *primary cause* of all phenomena in Physical creation. Love is the Soul of the Deity: from His soul was created the outer structure of the Universe. Every thing, according to its capacity, is a receptacle of Love—is moved, sustained, enlivened by Love—and there is nothing which Love does not penetrate. The gross materials which compose the planets in space are distributed, and associated, and vitalized by Love. There is not an element known in chemistry, nor in all physical nature, that has not a more interior essence, so fine and imponderable as invariably to escape the detection of chemical instruments, and the minutest analysis,—an essence which is Love. The mineral or vegetable medicine can not enter and assimilate with the human organization unless it contains life. The visible and *palpable*, or material part of the mineral substance will gravitate to, and associate itself with, corresponding substances in the organism; because man is physically constituted of every thing contained in the constitution of physical Nature. And the invisible and *impalpable*, or the spiritual part of the mineral substance will gravitate to, and assimilate with, a corresponding principle in the spiritual organism; because Man is spiritually constituted of Love and Wisdom, which are attractive to kindred elements, which are to some extent contained in every other form of material organization. There is not a vegetable or animal organization that does not contain more or less of the principle of spiritual life, or Love. You may kill, cut, salt, preserve, and *boil* vegetables and animal substances as much as human invention will permit; and yet, if the stomach will admit and digest them, the life (or Love) principle dwells in them still. Thus the life or love, residing in the meat or vegetable compositions which we eat, contributes to the nourishment and sustenance of *our* life or love; and the material portion goes to nourish and renew the material combinations of which our bodies are organized. Love, therefore, is the life of the Deity; and it is universally disseminated and diffused through all things. The scientific definition of the *Love* principle is expressed in such language as has hitherto been supposed alone applicable to physical nature; while it is by all scientific men acknowledged, that Nature's phenomena of gravitation, attraction, and other manifestations, are strictly referable to internal and unseen impulsions.

What is the Scientific definition of Wisdom?

The Wisdom (or Governing) Principle now requires a few scientific definitions, in order to elucidate its operation in Nature. Wisdom is the Body of the Deity. In other words, the Deity is *Love* and *Wisdom*—Love being his soul or essence, and Wisdom his body, or the spiritual form of His Spiritual organization. And the boundless Universe is His external and corresponding Material Organization: hence, as a generalized statement, the poet's inspiration is true, that—

> "All are but parts of one stupendous whole,
> Whose Body Nature is, and God the Soul."

Wisdom is scientifically recognized as the systematic physical arrangement and distribution of plants, animals, and mankind, upon the earth's surface. The mechanical and unimprovable arrangement of bones, nerves, muscles, organs, and various circulating mediums in the animal or human system, are scientific manifestations of Wisdom. The unchangeableness of universal laws or tendencies, and the progressive development of every thing in visible creation, give scientific impressions of Divine Wisdom. The architectural and mechanical precision with which the firmament is built, and the spontaneous intelligence which is indicated in every thing and every where, are forms and evidences of supernal Wisdom.

In every thing and every where is manifested an indwelling Principle of life and motion, which is Love; and over all things there seems to preside a *Governing* Principle, which is Wisdom. These Principles proceed from the same source, operate to the same end, and in the same manner, yet they sometimes *seem* different and antagonistic; nevertheless they are in harmony one with another, and are nothing more or less than the Divine Elements and Attributes of the Universal Creator which are through and over all created things.

The same statement may here be appropriate, (made in reference to the development and truthfulness of this Theory,) that Sir John Herschel made in the introduction to his treatise on Astronomy He says: "*Almost all its conclusions stand in open contradiction with those of* SUPERFICIAL *and* VULGAR OBSERVATION, *and with what appears to every one, until he has understood and weighed the proofs to the contrary, the most positive evidence of his senses.*" But harmonial philosophy sanctions the practice and propriety of appealing to inferior and external evidences as means of confirmation to inferior, and externally educated, minds. The scientific definitions and indications of Love and Wisdom are derived from their most superficial modes of manifestation. But there is an *intellectual*, a *moral*, and a *spiritual* definition, development, and exercise of the principles of Love and Wisdom, which will be unfolded in my subsequent exposition of the human Spirit.—To this work let us now proceed. Meanwhile, let it be constantly remembered, that I am *first* to consider the progressive development of *a harmonious* mind.

First,—What is Self-Love?

SELF-LOVE is the Germ of all the Divine elements of the human Soul; it is the great central spring or angel of love which unfolds, protects, defines and characterizes the individual.

Self-Love is the germ of the Soul, because it not only contains every other and higher element and attribute undeveloped, but gives life and force to all the minute and various modifications of feeling, and sentiment, and selfish propensities, by which every spirit is more or less characterized and individually distinguished.

In the natural and undeformed development of the Spirit, Self-Love stands first and performs the mission assigned to its position and capacity. At first, or while in its infancy, it inspires a sense of self-hood in the mind. It causes the individual to *feel separate* from others; the feeling is undefined, and extends no further than the circle of self.

From Self-Love proceed various animal wants; a strong love of mere existence; hence the general instinctive impulses to self-preservation, self-protection, and self-gratification. A disposition to self-culture, self-investigation, and self-harmonization, flows legitimately from this central source. The perceptions, conceptions, and dependencies, of the individual as related to this love, seem to extend only to the limited boundaries of self-hood. A strong and powerful tendency is manifested with reference to desires, necessities, and gratifications. The spirit is influenced greatly by desires to gratify the eye, the ear, the taste, the smell, and the sense of touch. The simple instinct of appropriating every visible thing to self-preservation, and self-gratification, seems the first and earliest manifestation and effort of mind. The individual is in search of individual happiness; and in the *natural* development of the spiritual elements, these searchings, and efforts, and exertions, are generally confined to the discharge of personal duties and to the gratification of personal desires.

The eye, the ear, the taste, the smell, have almost endless demands upon Nature and human inventions for their gratification. Self-Love, left to its own promptings and impetuosities, would urge the individual into many dangerous and destructive excesses. Love, without Wisdom, is blind. But the rudimental condition,—the infant stage of spiritual development,—is ever characterized by selfish, limited, and impulsive desires, conceptions, pleasures, and demands. The selfishness and limitedness of these love-promptings, however, render their incipient efforts and gratifications quite easy, and quite as ephemeral. Soon, however, self-exertions are found to be but half-exertions; and self-happiness is but half-happiness. The circle of *mere* self-love and education is soon completed or filled, at which moment its incompleteness and emptiness are rendered more strikingly apparent, and the individual experiences, (probably for the first time,) a deep consciousness of half-existence, of incompleteness, of a want of *something* beyond the mere sphere of self-hood and self-efforts. At this point, then, Self-Love widens and elevates itself into another form—into Conjugal-Love.

Second,—What is Conjugal-Love?

CONJUGAL-LOVE is the refinement and expansion of the Self-love element; it is the angel of love which spontaneously reveals the internal affinities and natural relations which subsist between the male and female principles, universally. The union of spirit to spirit—a *true* marriage—is the first and earliest desire of Conjugal-Love.* Self must be completed, and supported, and absorbed, as it were, by its union with another and corresponding self. Reciprocal attachments, dependencies, gratification, assistance, and companionship, are the deep thirstings and powerful demands of the connubial element. This love moves the spirit to seek a marriage in all things. It is not limited merely to sexual unions, but desires relation and marriage to any and every thing which seems to promise congeniality and happiness. Self-Love has now grown to Conjugal-Love, or to the full conviction that self-efforts and self-happiness are nothing compared with what a unity of spirits and efforts can accomplish for the gratification, protection, preservation, and happiness of one another. The marriage of love with love, or angel with angel, or truth with truth, or impulse with impulse, and the spirit with higher good and happiness, is the marriage which Conjugal-Love prompts the individual to consummate.

But this Love—if unguided and not restrained by the positive

* See Philosophy of True Marriage, in this volume.

influence and admonitions of Wisdom—will run into many extremes and unhappy consequences. It is termed the "*angel of love*," because it is, as well as all other loves, the actuating or *female* element, to which Wisdom is a protection and a guardian angel. Love is the female, and Wisdom is the male, Principle in the Soul. But the natural development of Conjugal-Love is *complete* when it finds itself united to a corresponding love, at which point it again feels *incomplete* unless it has living types and representatives of the advanced or expanded self-hood. For, be it remembered, that the generations and prolifications of the *oneness* ultimate in self-extension, self-multiplication, and self-representation—in other words, Conjugal-Love widens and develops itself into another form—into Parental-Love.

Third,—What is Parental-Love?

Parental-Love is the refinement and expansion of the conjugal element; it is the Angel of Love which prompts the individual to embody or represent its peculiar characteristics in the form, life, and deeds of another. A love of offspring is the next in order. Still the circle of self expands, and new self-hoods are the consequences of its expansion. Children are, therefore, the evidences and results of the extension of the individual's physical and spiritual possessions. Parental-Love is not satisfied with the mere acquirement of children, but it reaches far into moral and spiritual things. Facts, doctrines, opinions, sentiments, poetry, truth, ideas, and every thing which the mind is capable of bringing forth, or giving birth to, are vitalized and fostered tenderly by the parental element. Every thing the spirit can produce is fondly caressed and considered its child or offpring. This element of the spirit will naturally embrace the phrenological organs, or selfish propensities, termed philoprogenitiveness and acquisitiveness; for the influence and capacities of these faculties are exerted and manifested by the internal and external operations of the Parental-Love.

The individual also sees, hears, feels, and conceives more than before; for this is the age of VIRILITY; the age of ADOLESCENCE and INFANCY being already past. Efforts, exertions, desires, and happiness, are much dependent upon companionship, co-operation, and expansion of personal capacity. The spiritual *oneness* requires the sympathy and assistance of social combinations. It is now discovered that Self-Love depends, not only on Conjugal-Love, and Conjugal-Love on Parental-Love, for happiness and development, but they all—the oneness, the triune—are dependent upon a still greater circle of being and development—upon Fraternal-Love.

Fourth,—What is Fraternal-Love?

FRATERNAL-LOVE is the refinement and expansion of the Parental element; it is the Angel of Love which prompts the individual to preserve his individuality, protect his interests, and perfect his happiness, by preserving the individuality, protecting the interests, and perfecting the happiness of his Neighbors. A love of Society is next in order. Friendships are conceived in the spirit, and promiscuous associates are sought and cherished. The welfare of other spirits, and how to render individuals contented and happy, are inquiries which are prompted by Fraternal-Love. Gentleness, kindness, tenderness, charitableness, religious solicitude, and political movements, are the characteristics of the fraternal element. Interests and feelings are respected and protected. This element of love is ardent and impetuous—it zealously pervades and embraces the social, political, national, intellectual, spiritual, and eternal interests of friends and society. It impresses the individual with the dependence and assistance which one spirit feels upon and requires of another. It opens the avenues of sympathy in the soul, and manifests great earnestness of purpose in the individual, respecting the relations and general interests of every friend and other individual who contributes to the formation of society.

Fraternal-Love is impulsive, and when unguided by Wisdom,

will create, in her unbounded affection for, and exertions to benefit, others, many excesses and inequalities. Outward society is not alone the object of fraternal desire. Doctrines, principles, ideas, sciences, philosophy, congenial books, employments, and amusements, are the social companions of this Love. All inspiration from men or angels, is sought after and fondly cherished by the Fraternal-Love. The manifestation of mind, designated by phrenological writers as inhabitiveness, adhesiveness, and benevolence, are legitimately developed by the Fraternal-Love; and all we know of Social and Domestic propensities is exhibited by this element of affection, whether its exhibition be confined to the society of individuals, or to the society of principles, employments, and divine things. But this spiritual affection is completely unfolded—

> "When the bright chain of Love, that God hath given,
> Shall extend from heart to heart, and thence to heaven."

For fraternal affection is naturally confined to friendship and attachments; and should any other form of Love appear it is referable to another Love or a higher development of the indwelling spirit. But now is unfolded another form—which is Filial-Love.

Fifth,—What is Filial-Love?

Filial-Love is the refinement and expansion of the Fraternal element; it is the Angel of Love which prompts the individual to fix his attention and bestow his affections upon the Positive and Superior in every thing and every where—to place them upon the good or great, upon the Majestic, the Spiritual, the Supreme, upon the Divine and the Deity. (It should be borne in mind that I am now considering the *actuating* loves or elements of the spirit in their true, *unperverted* form of development and mode of manifestation.) Filial-Love is a love of physical fathers, social fathers, national fathers, religious fathers, and patriarchs. It is the source of every religious sentiment or spiritual prompting. It gives rise to a love of truth for truth's sake, good for good's sake, and to all noble aspirations. It is a high and holy Love; for it sees divinity, goodness, majesty, spirituality, and God in all things and every where. The tendency to seek for, and believe in, spiritual influences and existences, which mankind universally manifest, is phrenologically termed Marvelousness,—which is the name of an organ among the moral or religious sentiments. But it will appear reasonable, I think, that Marvelousness as well as Sublimity, Ideality, and Veneration, are terms, significant of certain manifestations of mind, which naturally arrange themselves under the embracing title of Filial-Love.

Filial-Love is an angel, because it is the prompting and vitalizing cause of every high and noble sentiment; it teaches the spirit of God, and conveys the soul to heavenly joys and spheres of immortal duration. Worship of Authority, of Truth, and Good, and Deity, is the natural tendency of the Filial element. But even while the spirit is delighting and refreshing itself with the unfoldings of this powerful Love, it is not perfectly satisfied. Something more is required. The Soul feels the separateness or difference between each Love or Desire, and its gratification. Self-Love is measured by Self; Conjugal is measured by Conjugal; Parental by Parental; Fraternal by Fraternal; and Filial by Filial-Love; and each has a circle of action and desire wherein it finds its gratification; but there is some wider circle, there is still more room for expansion, and this is the *final desire* of the spirit—the desire for perfect Liberty. Filial-Love is therefore unfolded into another form—into Universal-Love.

Sixth,—What is Universal-Love?

Universal-Love is the refinement and expansion of the Filial element; it is the Angel of Love which reveals a universal sympathy, a universal dependence, a universal liberty, and a universal relationship. A love of liberty is the next in order. Universal-Love expands the ideal and real Self-Love, Conjugal-Love, Parental-Love,

Fraternal-Love, and Filial-Love, to its utmost capacity. Every thing is comprehensively admired; every thing is generalized, every thing universalized. The Universal moral faculties, sentiments, aspirations, and attractions of the spirit are developed and permitted their full, unrestricted action in the Temple of this Love. Liberty! unbounded, undefined, unspeakable liberty, is the positive demand of this indwelling element. This love is the main spring of eternal progression. And this love is an Angel because it teaches the spirit to Individually, Conjugally, Parentally, Fraternally, and Filially behold, acknowledge, and cherish the universal dependence and ONENESS of all things. Universal-Love, *being naturally developed from Filial-Love*, is the highest, holiest, divinest element in the human spirit.

I have now considered the Loves in reference to their order of position in the mental structure of Man, and also in reference to their legitimate or harmonious development and action. But much requires to be said upon the *wrong development* and the *wrong action* of these loves; for there are many *evils* in families and societies which have their origin in no way revealed or explained in the *true* analysis or growth of the soul. I will, therefore, state in advance of the main considerations on this interesting and important point, that the human Loves—or, more truthfully speaking, the Divine Loves in the human form, have three modes of action—two are wrong, and one is right. They have an INVERTED ACTION—A NATURAL OR RIGHT ACTION—AND AN EXTREME ACTION. The wrong actions, or modes of the manifestation of the divine loves in man, are owing to a single cause or a combination of causes, not one of which is justly imputable to the self-will or desire of the individual.* But of this I will speak in another place. It is now necessary to direct the attention to the correct development of Wisdom. And

* See Philosophy of Moral Freedom, in this volume.

here let it be understood, that Love is the spring, and Wisdom is the balance wheel; or Love is the motive power, and Wisdom is the graduating and justice distributing faculty of the human mind. Wisdom is not impetuous, and never has an *inverted or extreme* action; but it has different modes or stages of expression in different spirits,—different only in its progressive degrees of development in the *right* and Divine direction. Let us consider Wisdom's first attribute, which is Use.

First,—What is the attribute of Use?

USE is the central and foundation attribute of WISDOM in the human soul; it is the Guardian Angel of Self-Love; and his mission is to preside over the sphere of Utility, and to employ *every thing* in reference to universal good and according to its original design. Use is the central and foundation attribute, because it brings the individual in direct communication with the outward, physical world. It watches over the wants and promptings of Self-Love, as the parent watches the impetuous child. Use enables the mind to place a true estimation on every thing; to properly discriminate the utility and practicability of every thing; and to form correct ideas of the Individuality, the Structure, the Size, and the quantity or number of any and every thing presented to it in the physical world. Use teaches us *how* to supply physical wants; and teaches *for what purposes* the supply is internally demanded and externally bestowed. The physical organization requires nourishment, and Use teaches the individual to cultivate the earth. It teaches how to make fruit, grain, grass, and animals, grow. It suggests, and presides over the invention of, agricultural implements. It teaches *how* to systematically reap, gather, and chemically prepare grains, and other nourishing substances, for the supply of the physical wants and necessities. Self-Love *desires* the excessive gratification of *Taste*, and prompts the individual to eat much, and frequently; but *Use restrains* and teaches the natural qualities and proper arrangement of *flavors*, and admonishes *when* to take them, and in *what* quantities.

While Self-Love impatiently demands, and blindly searches every place and thing for, *Odors* to gratify the Smell, Use leads the individual forth into the fields of Nature, and teaches him what perfumes can be extracted, and how to extract them; and then explains the innumerable advantages which may arise from the proper gratification of this sense, and how to permanently secure them to the individual. The sense of hearing, or the *ear*, desires gratification; and, while Self-Love is blind, and wildly appropriates every sweet *sound* and accent without reference to time or order, Use invents the truest instruments and teaches their truest application. And so with the desire to gratify the eye,—Use presides over the sphere of *color*, and directs the individual with reference to dress, and colors, and lights, and shades, and how to arrange them with reference to the cultivation of that sense and of all the senses equally. Thus it is seen that Self-Love *desires* gratification, *merely because* it delights; and that Use gratifies, *because* such gratification cultivates the individual and renders happiness pure and unalloyed.

To my mind *the science of taste* is the first development or manifestation of Wisdom; and *whatever direction or impetus* the spirit receives from the impulsions of Self-Love and the admonitions of Wisdom in the beginning of its present existence, such *impetus* and *admonitions* will most assuredly continue to operate, more or less visibly, upon the individual life thereafter,—just as hereditary bias will manifest itself upon the physical and spiritual organization. Thus it is evident that primary *organization*, *direction*, and *education*, are the *three* essential particulars which require the combined attention of Parents and Reformers. The science of taste,—or the perception and development of the beautiful,—lies at the foundation of physical wants, and of Wisdom in the Spirit. The Esthetic Philosophy of Schiller is based wholly upon Utility; and the sublimest philosophy, with which the world was ever made acquainted, takes Use for its center and foundation.

The spiritual attribute of Use embraces, or contains undeveloped, every other and higher principle of internal direction. According to phrenological definitions, the Intellectual or observing faculties, termed Individuality, Form, Size, Language, and Calculation, are simply subdivisions of the attribute of Use. As Self-Love runs through and gives certain inclinations to all the elements of Love, so does Use run through and give to every attribute of Wisdom, a personality, and a corresponding influence upon the physical and moral world. The mission of Use evidently is to lead and teach the Self-Love and the individual how and when to employ the provisions of Nature and Deity to the end that gratification and happiness may be permanently secured to the spirit. *All sciences grow out of this attribute.* In truth, it may be said, that *science* is but a correct cognizance and classification of material conditions, qualities, individualities, configurations, magnitudes, colors, phenomena, and quantities; and this recognition and classification are legitimately the works of *Use*, as this attribute is defined in the foregoing analysis of Man's spiritual structure. In every thing, Use is a matter-of-fact principle—it is very laconic, very simple, and is very easily perceived when predominating over other faculties; and, in every thing, it proves itself the particular guardian of Self-Love and self-approbation. From Use is unfolded Justice.

Second,—What is the attribute of Justice?

JUSTICE is a more perfect form and a greater manifestation of the attribute of Use; it is the guardian angel of Conjugal-Love; and his mission is to *weigh* and *balance* all spontaneous attachments, fix natural relations, and preserve the equilibrium of things. Justice brings the spirit into direct communication with relations, unions and reciprocations. Justice presides over Conjugal-Love, and instructs that female principle of the Soul to find and unite itself with another, whose physical wants, internal inclinations, primary education, and general conformation, are in every way *absolutely* agreeable and congenial. Justice will not permit Self-Love, or Conjugal-Love, to infringe upon, or in any possible manner to retard, the development of truth and its happy consequences. The mission of the attribute of Justice is such as to urge the individual into an internal investigation of the physical creation. The phrenological faculties of *Causality*, *Locality*, *Weight*, *Time*, *Tune*, *Comparison, and Conscientiousness*, naturally arrange themselves under the comprehensive attribute of Justice. The right, the truthful, the equal relation and dependence of one thing, and Soul, upon another, are embraced in the instructions of this attribute of Wisdom. Justice is what teaches the Spirit to judge of relative positions, congenial associations, causes and effects, universal analogies or correspondences, and principles or Laws of universal movements, and how to judge, with intuitive discrimination and correctness, between the seeming and the actual, the visible and the eternal. The beautiful accuracy of Geography, Geometry, Mathematics, and Arithmetical calculation, are alone dependent upon the attribute of Justice for existence and true appreciation. In the spiritual world, Justice is the guardian angel of all attachments, and reigns over all the spirit can comprehend of moral righteousness. With the Deity, *Justice* is both means and end in the elaboration of the material and spiritual Universe—the whole is *weighed* and *balanced* by this internal attribute. Justice teaches the spirit to comprehend what is Truth, and Light, and Freedom, and teaches it how to avoid infringement upon the Laws and principles which operate with a *just* and undeviating precision in the material, intellectual, and spiritual, constitution of things. This attribute is so Divine and all-comprehensive that it supplies the soul with every desirable conception of religious equity and perfection. It demonstrates true religion to consist in Self-justice, Fraternal-justice, and Universal-justice.* In law, in politics, in philosophy, and in religion, this attribute is the standard Authority of the well developed Soul. From Justice proceeds Power.

Third,—What is the attribute of Power?

POWER is a more perfect form and a greater manifestation of *Justice;* it is the guardian angel of Parental-Love; and his mission is to impart serene strength and energy to every affection—to elaborate, to enlarge, and execute the designs of Use and Right—and to expand into the sublime silence of omnipotency. This attribute brings the spirit into direct communication with the moving, changing, and reproductive World. It teaches the spirit to take useful and just cognizance of motive-forces; how to guide the Parental-Love in its various modes of manifestation; how to generate and concentrate influence and strength; and how to employ the great variety of motions which Nature unfolds to human understanding. All mechanical powers are recognized and appreciated only by this internal attribute; the screw, the lever, the weight, the centripetal, and centrifugal forces, are its instrumentalities in the outer expression of internal designs. USE informs of Utility; JUSTICE informs of Right; and POWER executes their united Designs. The sphere of Power is measured by the circle in which Parental-Love is found to lead the Spirit. Every thought and affection is energized by Power. It directs the Loves beneath, and renders them capable of penetrating the darkest recesses in Nature and Man, and empowers them to overcome every thing in the physical and moral world which mars or disturbs the progressing and developing soul.

USE directs the artist, how and where to procure proper material for the elaboration of whatever his Parental-Love prompts him to unfold; Justice directs him how to arrange and combine colors, how to individualize and properly to impress the lights and shades

* See "Philosophy of Spiritual Intercourse," p. 70.

upon his creation; and POWER fills him with serene assurance. By it he gives an expression, an attitude, an influence to his internal conception which rivet the attention of the beholder, and fill him with admiration.

Inspired with Use and Justice, and having every love-spring thereby guided and in subordination, what vast work can not the mechanic cause to be accomplished by the attribute of Power? No delicate invention or stupendous mountain, is too intricate or powerful for him—he feels himself endowed with *power* to make the rough places smooth, and the crooked straight.

The spirit is capable, by its Power, of subduing itself and the various creations beneath it in nature. A magnetic influence proceeds from the human spirit, which is adequate to the fulfillment of every design instituted by the preceding attributes. Its power ramifies and intensifies infinitely; and spreads out into such boundless waves as to blend with, or lose itself in, the sublime omnipotence of the Divine Mind. From the attribute of power comes Beauty.

Fourth,—What is the attribute of Beauty?

BEAUTY is a more perfect form and a greater manifestation of *Power;* it is the guardian angel of Fraternal-Love; and his mission is to teach Harmony, appropriateness, symmetry, and the dependence of parts or persons upon one another—to make every thing an embodiment of USE, JUSTICE, and POWER. This is the attribute which takes cognizance of the fitness and just relations of forms, colors, size, weight, and influences of any and every thing presented to the spirit. Beauty is a condition, but it can only be recognized and appreciated by a corresponding internal state or attribute in the individual. In proportion as the Wisdom faculties become unfolded, does the spirit perceive and estimate the proper relation of one thing, or part, to another, and the *whole* to the end for which it was designed.

Fraternal-Love is the companion—the *conjugal* companion, of the attribute of Beauty. This love inspires, and Beauty is her manifestation. The just relation of members to the family circle, the just relation of families to the social circle, the just relation of societies to the national circle or union, are subjects of the cognizance of this internal attribute. The sphere of Beauty is measured by the sphere in which Fraternal-Love moves and leads the expanding and searching spirit. Beauty is manifested in its guardianship over the impetuosities and impatient demands of Fraternal-Love. Instead of allowing this love to run into various extremes and local excesses, Beauty guides it into a path of progressive developments; and thereby renders it intensely *useful*, *just*, *powerful* and *Beautiful.*

Guided by the male or positive principle of Beauty, Fraternal-Love expands far and wide; and thus—through the influence and instrumentality of this attribute,—

> "Each virtuous mind will wake,
> As the small pebble stirs the peaceful lake;
> The center moved, a *circle* straight succeeds,
> Another still, and still another spreads:
> *Friend, kindred, neighbor*, first it will embrace,
> His *country* next, and next *all human race.*"

In the scientific, philosophical, moral, social, national, and spiritual spheres of companionship and human interest, the presiding judge is the sublime attribute of Beauty. Its mission is to make every thing an embodiment of Use, Justice, and Power,—every thing Beautiful, because it is locally and generally *useful*, just, and powerful. From this attribute comes Aspiration.

Fifth,— What is the attribute of Aspiration?

Aspiration is a more perfect form and a higher manifestation of Beauty; it is the guardian angel of Filial-Love; and his mission is to impart a definite form, position, and importance to every thing—to teach the pre-eminency of intrinsic worth and merit—and to establish the predomination of Mind over Matter. This attribute brings the spirit into direct communication with the metaphysical world. It teaches the spirit that to be worthy it must aspire worthily, to be good it must aspire to goodness, to be God-like, it must aspire to God. It dignifies, and elevates, and gives a perfect form to whatever Filial-Love prompts under the combined influence ot the preceding attributes. Aspiration is the true basis of every true idea concerning goodness, greatness and Deity. Self-dignity,—self-esteem,—self-reliance,—self-possession,—are the legitimate fruits of this noble portion of Reason. Filial-Love inspires the spirit to veneration; and *Aspiration* humanizes, spiritualizes, and nobly defines every modification and tendency of that internal Promethean fire, which ever burns in the soul. This attribute defines the principles of eternal progress, and convinces the understanding that refinement and expansion have no limitation. It informs the spirit of its innate goodness and magnanimity; it points out the means by which to develop them, and teaches the spirit that,—

> "God loves from whole to parts; BUT HUMAN SOUL
> MUST RISE FROM INDIVIDUAL TO THE WHOLE."

Indeed the attribute of Aspiration is the fertile source of energy, enterprise, emulation, and of all human efforts to good, and yearnings for communion with God. Filial-Love gives *life* and *soul* to these efforts, but Aspiration gives them their *form*, *position*, and *importance;* and embracing within itself the concentration of *use*, *justice*, *power*, and *beauty*, it employs universal instrumentalities to the end that such efforts and enterprises may be fully accomplished. Personal dignity and actual greatness must necessarily be proportionate to the degree of development to which this high attribute of reason has attained. If it is in its incipient stage,—as in the savage,—its efforts and enterprizes will manifest the ignorance of savagism. If in the barbarian stage of growth, its manifestations will testify of barbarism. But in the well-developed spirit, its noble form and wise deportment will testify of harmony, which is the next attribute in order.

Sixth,—What is the attribute of Harmony?

HARMONY is the most perfect form, and the highest manifestation of all the attributes of Wisdom; it is the guardian angel of Universal-Love; and his mission is to teach that proper organization, cultivation, and direction of the innate elements of the Soul, which will result in the unfolding of a *Useful*, a *Just*, a *Powerful*, a *Beautiful*, an *Aspiring*, AND A HARMONIOUS INDIVIDUAL.

I have elsewhere said that, it requires a Shakespeare to fully comprehend and sympathize with a Shakespeare; it requires a Christ to understand a Christ; so does it require Harmony in the spirit to appreciate and explain Harmony. This is the highest attribute of the mental organization. It contains and pervades all the faculties and elements of the spirit. It is the ultimate form of the Soul—the Image of its Creator. Concerning Universal-Love,—of which Harmony is the especial companion and guardian, it may be truthfully said, that it—

"Warms in the sun, refreshes in the breeze,
Glows in the stars, and blossoms in the trees;
Lives through all life, extends through all extent,
Spreads undivided, and operates unspent."

Concerning the attribute of Harmony—whose sphere of *action* is as expansive as Universal Love—it may be said that it—

"Breathes in our Soul, informs our mortal part,
As full, as perfect, in a hair as heart;
To him, no high, no low, no great, no small,
He fills, he bounds, connects, and equals all."

That is to say, Wisdom (or Harmony) is universally manifested in God's Great Temple,—that it is stamped upon every thing, and every where. In these elements and attributes, Man images and imitates the Divine Mind.

The Angel of Universal-Love, which is the spirit of Harmony gives the mind of man its boundless desires and its sublime individuality. The former contain every internal spring of action, passion, or impulse; and the latter contains every principle of direction, protection, and guidance. Harmony, in the perfectly developed mind, presides over every suggestion of Self-Love and Use, over Justice, Power, Beauty, and Aspiration; and in a mind fully and properly developed, every prompting of Love and sanction of Wisdom is subjected to the influence and direction of Harmony and the internal and supreme ruler. Harmony presides over flavors, odors, sounds, colors, objects, and sensations of every kind, which the soul desires and demands. It presides over the entire Soul; over families, over societies, over nations, and over the Universe. The spirit is taught law and order by this attribute. Self-Love and Use have, comparatively, no Law or rule of action; but Justice reveals to the spirit a law of fitness and congeniality; Power reveals a law of executiveness and enforcement; Beauty reveals a law of exactness and symmetry; Aspiration reveals a law of progression and endless expansion; and Harmony reveals the laws of individual dependence, individual reciprocation, individual position, abilities, occupation, Destiny, and Happiness.

If the individual is unfolded into Harmony with himself, he has grown into immediate connection with the spiritual World; thus the human spirit grows into communication with its Maker. Harmony proceeds from God into the Universe, and the individual unfolds into Harmony. Thus the animal becomes human; the human becomes Divine; and then God and Man unite, complete the chain of sympathy, and develop one harmonious Whole.

The analysis of the mind is now presented. It will be perceived that Love is the *female*, and Wisdom the *male*, principle; and that, internal prolification and the consequent development of fruits, are the natural mechanism of the human mind, and of the positive and negative principles upon which it is constructed. In truth, each affection is conjugally united to its superior self, which is an attribute of reason. Thus *Self-Love* is united to *Use*, *Conjugal-Love* to *Justice*, *Parental-Love* to *Power*, &c., and each has relative duties, energies, and legitimate fruits—all tending to one object, which is the universal *want* and the universal *theme* among men, viz.,—universal Happiness and Progression. But let us inquire—

What are the fruits of a Harmonious Mind?

The harmonious development of the human mind may be properly compared to a tree—a tree of righteousness. The *germ* of this tree has qualities which unfold a *body*, and corresponding *fruits*. Perhaps, the subjoined table will render this comparison more clear and forcible.

THE HARMONIOUS MIND.

1. Germ.	2. Form.	3. Fruits.
Self-Love, ...	Use, ...	Individuality,
Conjugal-Love, . . .	Justice, ...	Marriage,
Parental-Love, . . .	Power, ...	Offspring,
Fraternal-Love, . . .	Beauty, ...	Socialism,
Filial-Love, ...	Aspiration, ...	Elevation,
Universal-Love, . . .	Harmony, ...	Happiness.

Let me be still more explicit. The foregoing description is referable only to a harmoniously developed mind. The natural (I may say *divine*) tendency of Self-Love is toward Use; and the legitimate *fruit* of *self-love* and *use*, combined, is Individualism; and so the proper fruit of *conjugal-love* and *justice*, is Marriage; the *fruit* of *parental-love* and *power*, is Offspring; the *fruit* of *fraternal-love* and *beauty*, is Socialism; the *fruit* of *filial-love* and *aspiration*, is Elevation; and the legitimate *fruit* of *universal-love* and *harmony*, is Happiness. This definition fully discloses what man *internally possesses;* and what, in a proper state of individual and social culture, he is *capable of being;* and what, in the Spiritual World, HE WILL BE!

What will modern Theologians do with this analysis and classification of the spirit's constituents? Will they treat it with that contempt and skepticism which characterized their treatment of Geology, and of every other science and discovery that has militated against their doctrinal education? The policy, proverbial of theologians,—as indicated upon the pages of the past,—affords a sufficient answer to these questions. But here it may be asked—

If the human soul is not in itself sinful, how did evil originate?

By looking into the human spirit, and analyzing its powers, I find no innate tendencies to wickedness,—no laboratory of vice and corruption,—such as modern religious teachers locate there. No; but on the contrary, I discover therein the elements of righteousness and the kingdom of heaven—the richest *soil*, capable of the highest cultivation; and the richest *germs*, capable of immortal progression and development.

I have revealed *the structure and inclinations of a perfect spirit;* but now I proceed to consider the various obstructions and evils with which the spirit comes in contact in its emergement from the womb of Nature, and in its growth into an eternal individuality. I have said that there is *a class constitutionally inferior*, and *a class constitutionally superior* to surrounding influences, circumstances, and education: and that individuals develop society, and that society develops the individual. The truthfulness of this statement will more distinctly appear in subsequent pages.

But with reference to the origin of evil, and in order to elucidate its causes and consequences, I am moved to detail briefly the following—

COMPREHENSIVE VISION.

I read in one of the Boston papers an account of an aggravated and most soul-chilling murder, committed, as the paper stated, by a detested wretch, long a burden to himself and society. I read also concerning his execution, which account was accompanied with a few remarks upon the punishment he would probably receive in the other world. The relation of this horrible occurrence weighed my spirit down. The position from which I viewed and contemplated the deed, was identical with that educationally occupied by almost every political, legal, and clerical teacher in the land. I viewed it as to its *external* aspect, and was driven to the unreasonable conclusion that man is, in reality, a depraved creature at heart! Oh, how I trembled at this! "But no man," reasoned I, "could do such an evil to his fellow-man, without being evil in the very elements of his being; and if this is an individual truth, it must be a universal one." Yes, only twenty days ago I was filled with sorrow concerning this demonstration of innate sin, of perverted and evil affection, of a voluntary love for, and doing of, evil—voluntary, because growing out of, and being allied to, the Soul's Life. I prayed, constantly, to know the truth, and to view the occurrence, and its causes, from an interior and spiritual position. At length, one day, I felt moved to visit the village grave-yard, that I might be free from outer disturbances. I obeyed the internal impulse. I sought a retired spot, folded my head in my garments, shut myself from sense and outer impressions, and meditated on the subject of my thoughts. Instantly my understanding was opened, and the birth, and life, and character, and the various circumstances which constituted that murderer's experience, were manifested to me in their regular order of succession.

In a small, unclean, unfurnished room, in a cradle, I saw a child. It was physically deformed, especially in the cerebral region. I saw that the cause of this malformation was referable to the ignorance of its parents—they had violated the laws of reproduction and utero-gestation. It was plain to be seen that this infringement and disobedience was faithfully recorded on the person of the child.

In five years more, that child manifested in its plays and conversations the angular and impulsive promptings of love unguided by wisdom, which latter it had not, because of youth and incapacity, and which its parents could not have communicated because of their ignorance from birth.

In five years more, I saw that child the companion of those of equal growth and like hereditary misdirection,—of those who were *born* foes to the interests of society,—those who were *victims* of circumstances, such as surround and influence all persons and families forming the lower strata of civilization.

In five years more, that child was a perverse and wicked youth—was the leader of card-playing and gambling-tricks without the city—and was the chief of mobs and riots within; was chewing tobacco, smoking cigars, drinking liquor. His parents were poor. At first they could not send him to school, at last he would not go. He stood as a representative of inferior situations and circumstances.

In five years more, I saw that youth a man in stature, but not in development of body nor elevation of mind. And in an old, dilapidated dwelling, like the Brewery in New York city, containing about twenty families, I saw his wife—for he was married.

Two years more, and I saw his child. That mother's child was left in the care of a sympathizing but no better situated neighbor, while she, worn out and emaciated, was peddling strawberries in the streets of Boston. I saw her return at night, with food for herself and her little one, and money to procure bread for breakfast; but that cruel man, intoxicated husband, and misdirected father, abruptly and insultingly demanded her little saving, and appropriated it to his own use—to buy rum, whereby to drown the rising feelings of goodness and sympathy within, that his obscured and misdirected soul might not perceive the body's corruption and depravity.

In six months more, I saw him when alone, weeping; but, when seen by others, he was gross, unclean, and disgusting. Feeling that others disliked and despised him, he disliked and despised himself. A whole garment was not in his possession. One by one they had been sacrificed to gratify his over-mastering desire. Indeed, he was a slave—rum was his master. A slave can not do as he will, but only as the master prompts, and sanctions, and commands!

Three nights afterward, he was destitute of liquor, food, friendship, clothes and money. Society had neglected its legitimate child. Nature's universal provisions were withholden, and the husband was urged to violent plans. At this moment he saw a well-dressed and apparently wealthy gentleman, step into quite an inferior oyster-house. The husband hurried on and entered it. He obtained a seat with an air of carelessness, and unobserved. The gentleman was a stranger, was inquiring the most convenient route to a village ten miles from the city. When he paid for his oysters, he unfortunately revealed a well-supplied pocket-book. The temptation was too powerful. The husband saw the magnitude of destitution and starvation compared with the act of assassination—compared with the former the latter seemed justice, to exercise which he at once resolved. He had heard the directions given the stranger, and without a moment's hesitation hastened on the way. After proceeding nearly half the distance, he secreted himself by the roadside and awaited the traveler's approach.

"I don't want to kill him," said the husband: "I will only stun him and get his shiners. The world owes me a living; it don't give it to me; I am resolved to take it. God knows this is justice. I am hungry, and must have something now or I shall die." Now I saw him weep. A sound of footsteps close by announced the traveler's approach. Out he leaped and grasped the stranger by the throat, and sternly demanded his money. The man knocked him down. This unexpected blow fired him with vengeance and determination. He instantly arose and shot the man, and stabbed him hurriedly in many places—mangled him in the most horrible

14*

manner—searched his pockets, robbed him of all he had, threw the body over the fence, and went into Boston to drown sorrow with a flood of rum, which he then could purchase.

I saw him arrested, tried, condemned, imprisoned, abused, sneered at, and formally executed—executed as an example. I saw all this. And I can only say, beware of such justice—it is human, not Divine!

I continued in that illuminated condition nearly an hour after the above vision, reflecting upon its importance and signification, when my perceptions enlarged, and it was given me to follow his spirit.

In the first Society of the second sphere of human existence—where the inferior types of the race are, and where they gravitate for refinement and reformation,—*I mean the Negroes, Indians, and Weak, and Idiotic, and the Misdirected individuals and classes of every community and nation,*—there, I saw that dark spirit. He was small, and weak, and ungrown; he was clothed with all possible conflicting colors, and was disagreeable to behold.* As a coating upon his faint spirit was impressed, or induced, or recorded, every unfavorable influence and evil circumstance that had surrounded and actuated him from his birth to the grave. The malformation had rendered his body inadequate to a regular unfolding of his spiritual elements and attributes; and outer conditions and opposing influences prevented his finding his true position, or making a pleasant and happy journey through this rudimental sphere. The most lovely rose can not grow, if planted in an iron vase, and breathed upon by the chilling winds of Iceland; nor can a pure spirit grow into a love of goodness and truth, if confined within the walls of an ill-formed body, and breathed upon by the freezing atmosphere of uncongenial conditions and circumstances.

* See "Philosophy of Spiritual Intercourse."

But now, higher influences pervaded him—penetrated that superficial coating; it grew thinner and more thin; it became transparent; it dissolved and crumbled into nothing, and lo! the white-robed angel was there! The germ of the spirit sparkled like the crystal in the granite rock. I saw that, from the first, it was pure within, though evil without; the pure soul indigenous to heaven, the outer life to the imperfections and misdirections of earth. I followed him through the first society, and, as he ascended to the second, I could not see the least vestige of that evil garment; but he was a rightly-directed and comparatively perfect being of the inner life. I was overjoyed. The vision ended, and I returned to the outer world with different feelings. I would not call that evil which is good in its way and state of being. What, think you, was the legitimate impression of this vision? I will relate.

1. That there are three sources of evil. First, *progenitive or hereditary misdirection*; secondly, *educational or sympathetic misdirection*; thirdly, *circumstantial or social misdirection.*

2. That the disunity prevalent in the earth is rather the result of those conditions and circumstances which *make* affections evil, than of evil affections, as Swedenborg teaches and Christians believe.

3. That all things and spirits are receptacles of the grand element of the Love of God, which, diffused through nature, as the Soul is through the body, unfolds itself into Wisdom.

4. That man is an incarnated divinity, and therefore that he is not *intrinsically* evil himself, and can not love any thing "intrinsically evil," though he may be bent or misdirected while in the twig-state, and grow up crooked, and despised by sensuous observers, and by the unphilosophically charitable, through this sphere of his existence and development.

5. That as God lives in all things and every where, there are no local or especial Incarnations of this essence. This is the true ground of the grand doctrine of the Incarnation, the highest dem-

onstrations of which are visible in the life and teachings of Christ, and in the profound revealments of Swedenborg.

6. That every human being has an important mission to fulfill, or three uses to subserve. The individual is designed to reproduce its type, to properly direct the heavenly germ in it deposited, and to live here in reference to the principles of Nature and another life.

7. That a knowledge of Nature, and of her laws, is indispensable to the just performance of the *three* uses just specified, constituting man's mission; and that, to cure the evil and disunity prevalent in Society, we must ascertain our inner and outer relations to each other, as members of one body, and our relations to the Material and Spiritual Worlds. In this way, man's moral nature may be elevated from its sensual plane, and a conjunction be established between the human and divine. The teachings of all good spirits, (especially the great reformers, Christ and Swedenborg,) tend to the full discovery and just application of those truths which will constitute a spiritual sphere of attraction, and which will attract and elevate the race to a closer relation among its parts, with the principles of Divine order and harmony, and with the chastening influences of higher spheres.

Such, I am impressed, is the origin of evil, as manifested in the actions of the individual; and its cure can only be accomplished *by removing the three causes* of human misdirection.

The spiritual forces in the soul,—like the natural forces in Nature,—will, when *properly* directed and *properly* applied, develop harmonious and universally beneficial consequences; but these same forces will, if *improperly* directed and *improperly* applied, develop the most disastrous consequences to the interests of the individual and the interests of society. For example,—mechanical forces properly applied to a vessel will urge it safely on its course; but *im-*

properly applied, the same forces will drive it upon rocks and sand-bars and rend it into pieces. Fire, water, air, and other elements in Nature, when employed *out* of their proper sphere, are exceedingly dangerous and destructive—indeed they produce positive evils; but used in their proper spheres, which are prescribed by science, these elements are pregnant with immense and universal blessings to mankind. Thus it is with the passions and elements of the human spirit.

By the preceding analysis it is plain that the indwelling forces of the mind are pure and perfect in germ, and, in their proper direction and development, give birth to corresponding consequences; but when a defective *organization*, a defective *situation*, or a defective *education*, urges one or all of the passional-forces into an EXTREME STATE, OF STATE OF INVERSION, then are developed those numerous evils with which Reformers contend and individuals struggle. Therefore, to ascertain the origin of evil, and why every member of the human family is not harmoniously developed, these statements must be considered with more philosophical minuteness. Let us now proceed to this consideration.

The primary source of evil is hereditary organization. By progenitive influence, arising from parental transgression, the Body and Mind of the infant may be deformed, and in every way disproportioned. The cerebral structure may be inadequate to the spirit's proper growth and manifestation. Or the spirit may be enfeebled, and inclined to an angular development even from its earliest embryotic condition. Progenitive bias,—or constitutional pre-disposition,—has an influence upon the individual from its birth upward, which few can perceive and few understand. The features of parents are visible in the child; and so are their mental deficiencies, peculiarities, and characteristics felt and manifested by the child through its rudimental existence. And here we find the foundation of evil—its origin. Who shall receive the blame? Who deserves it? The parents?—They were, perhaps, born with similar defects of physical organization and character. Shall the evil be imputed to previous generations? Perhaps they were no less perfect. So questions may be asked as to the proper subjects of blame or praise, until we lose ourselves in the animal kingdom—and still echo responds, WHO?

I ask serious attention to this point. Reformation is not merely confined to the emancipation of slaves; to the abolition of capital punishment; to the organization of labor, capital, and talent; to the distribution of the public lands to the poor; or to religion and politics,—but it extends *primarily* to the organization of the Soul and Body, or, if it does not extend so *far* and *deep* now, the time has arrived when it should. Reformers and Teachers should direct not only their attention, but the attention of others, to the numerous constitutional evils which flow from a transgression of the physical and moral laws which govern reproduction.

A wrong organization of the body and mind will prevent the development of wisdom; and the lower or passional-forces will flow into whatever direction surrounding influences in society may incline them: and this is the first formidable obstruction to a proper growth of the spirit. An individual thus organized will develop corresponding influences and situations in society. He will not only be the victim of these situations himself, but will so help to strengthen and establish them as to render them *master* of those who are born with better organizations amid them. Thus deformed minds develop deforming situations, into which hundreds are placed and correspondingly molded. From these vitiating situations will proceed doctrines and teachers which the multitude will receive and support; and the consequence is that a wrong *education* is bestowed upon the individual. Therefore a class of *inferiorly organized* individuals will develop *inferior situations*, which give rise to *inferior* systems of *education*. Wisdom can not unfold in a spirit which is badly organized, and situated, and educated. And hence I say that all evils flow from these three sources. It may be asked—

What are the Evils of an Extreme action of Self-Love?

The *extreme* action of SELF-LOVE gives rise to numerous excesses and transgressions. Individual wants and desires transcend all bounds prescribed by wisdom and natural laws, and their superabundant supplies and gratifications engender disease and unhappiness. The individual manifests great sensitiveness about MINE AND THINE, and feels persuaded that the world and every thing was made for his personal pleasure and appropriation. An excessive gratification of the senses, of the appetites, and every desire connected with self-interest, is a symptom of *extreme* Self-Love, unguided by wisdom.

What are the Evils of an Invertion of Self-Love?

The *inverted* action of Self-Love gives rise to many evils. It urges the individual to dishonesty, penuriousness, and covetousness, and into money-worship, even while his larder and store-houses are abundantly supplied with provisions, and his coffers are filled. To see inverted Self-Love fully exemplified, behold the sloth that produces nothing, but hangs himself upon a tree until he absorbs its life and beauty. So inverted Self-Love makes a man *a sponge* which draws in every available substance, and, when pressed or urged to action, gives out a muddy mixture, both repulsive and infectious. When the passional-forces are pressed by the single or combined influence of a deformed *organization*, a deformed *situation*, or a deformed *education*, into such a *deformity* as an *extreme* or *inverted* state of action and desire, then the individual's influence in society will be correspondingly deforming. An *extreme* state is the hot, the feverish, the exaggerated state; and the *inverted* state is the cold, the repulsive, and the miserly state of feeling and existence.

What are the Evils of an Extreme action of Conjugal-Love?

Conjugal-Love pressed to an *extreme* state is productive of unhappy marriages, and of those numerous evils which result from improper sexual desires and attachments. Profligacy, debauchery, and lasciviousness, flow from this state of the Conjugal-Love. The individual experiences no particular attraction or repulsion, so far as individuals of the opposite sex are concerned, but feels a general inclination to them all. In this respect, the individual is like many animals, which disregard every thing like perfect union, devotion, and fidelity. In other directions, the perpetual love will urge the individual to espouse new doctrines and principles; to adopt new systems, and to marry himself to almost any novel thing presented to public or private attention.

What are the Evils of an Invertion of Conjugal-Love?

Inverted Conjugal-Love is a cold, foreign, uncompanionable state of feeling and action. A hatred of the opposite sex, a general secretiveness of character, and a lonely disposition, are the consequences. In all things the individual is unsocial and grossly unkind—is sometimes bestial.

What are the Evils of an Extreme action of Parental-Love?

Parental-Love in an *extreme* state will manifest itself in great fondness for children, regardless of their color, fortune or parentage. Not only for children, but for every species of invention and ingenuity, will this perverted love manifest its blind fondness and impetuosity. No restraint is felt or allowed to be exercised; and Parental-Love, unguided by the wisdom principle, is dangerous to the welfare of whatever administers to its gratification.

What are the Evils of an Inverted action of Parental-Love?

Inverted, this love urges the individual to dislike children, and to disregard their wants and mission in the world. It will drive some persons to infanticide—and into many inventions whereby children, and every thing which comes under the head of physical or mental production, are tortured and almost constantly tormented and punished. Cruelty to animals is a symptom of inverted Parental-Love.

What are the Evils of an Extreme action of Fraternal-Love?

FRATERNAL-LOVE pressed into an *extreme* state, will embrace any body and any thing as a companion. Indiscriminate association and commingling are symptoms of this passional state.

What are the Evils of an Inversion of the Fraternal-Love?

The *inverted* state of Fraternal-Love engenders war, and cannibalism. It makes the individual *hate* his neighbor and his country. It causes murder and retaliation. An eye for an eye, life for life, war for war, are the indications of this passion's misdirection. The dislike, and jealousy, and hatred, which some individuals entertain toward their relatives, neighbors, and nation, are other symptoms of its inversion. It drives the individual involuntarily across his friend's feelings and interests; and makes him a hermit or anchorite. A disregard of personal feelings, or interests, or desires, or of existence, and a love of tyranny and despotism, are proofs that the pure and beautiful Fraternal-Love of the spirit has been misdirected and turned into evil promptings.

What are the Evils of an Extreme action of Filial-Love?

FILIAL-LOVE pressed into an *extreme* state urges the spirit into unjust estimations of the great and superior, whether in position, age, authority, or talents. It begets boundless confidence, and idolatry. It magnifies, and elevates, and adores, without reference to their intrinsic worthiness. It will run into falsehoods and misrepresentations in favor of whatever pleases its feelings.

What are the Evils of an Inversion of the Filial-Love?

Inverted, this beautiful love gives rise to disrespect, and skepticism. It causes the individual to think but little of age or superiority. Coarse, uncouth manners, and a constant manifestation of dislike to any thing like deference and veneration, are this love's perverted language. An infidel to Nature's laws, to fraternal or conjugal obligations, to religious promptings, to *one's self*, and a cold indifference to any thing calculated to inform one of a Supreme Being, are still stronger indications of inverted Filial-Love.

What are the Evils of an Extreme action of Universal-Love?

UNIVERSAL-LOVE, when thrown into an *extreme* state, is anxious to embrace every thing—even the Universe. It renders the individual impatient if in any way restrained; he is quite unwilling to view the minutiæ of relations, desires, or gratifications. It causes the spirit to be hasty, impetuous, precipitate, and powerful. Nothing seems too vast or great for its desires and capacity; but every thing seems removed and inaccessible.

What are the Evils of an Inversion of Universal-Love?

Universal-Love *inverted*, causes the individual to dislike and despise himself and every body and every thing. It causes him to be skeptical, murderous, cruel, unsocial and grossly selfish. This is the greatest, and holiest, and most powerful love-force in the human spirit; but when *inverted*, it is the mightiest power and influence to evil deeds. Fortunately for the world, hereditary organization, social situation, and circumstantial education, seldom influence this powerful element into wrong directions. This is owing to the fact that but *one* or *two* of the passional-forces can be driven out of their proper channels, and at the same time preserve an individuality of action. But if *Universal-Love* should flow back into other loves, then such loves will be empowered to accomplish mighty evils under *their* respective forms of manifestation.

How do Individuals develop Society?

I have frequently affirmed that all the evils in the Individual are traceable to one or all of these three causes—viz., an *improper organization*, an *improper situation*, and an *improper education.* This we will reconsider in future pages.

Man is a "harp of a thousand strings," which, when properly tuned and played upon, gives forth the most sweet and delightful harmony; but should the instrument be intrusted to ignorant management, and should its delicate chords be harshly or inappropriately stricken, the most frightful inharmonies will issue therefrom.* An engine, well constructed and well managed, will do a mighty and beautiful work; but, improperly managed and applied, the same engine is capable of destroying every individual on the face of the earth.

The affirmation that the individual develops society and that society develops the individual, and that one is invariably and necessarily a likeness of the other, will more distinctly appear as truthful by the following diagram:

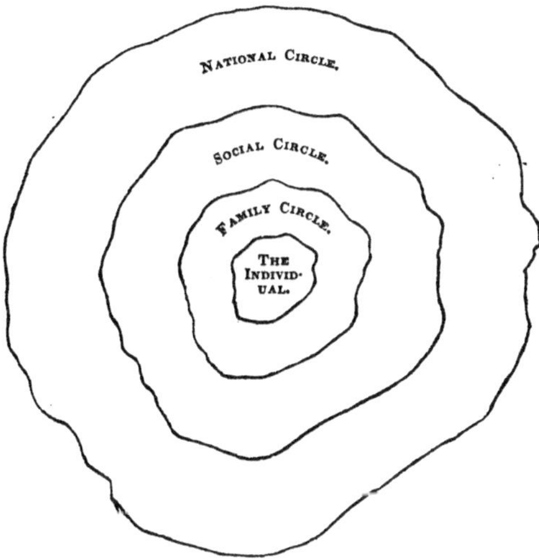

In this diagram the individual is represented as being born in the center. Owing to a *wrong* organization or a *wrong* situation the spirit is incapable of symmetrical development. The passional-forces predominate over the attributes of Wisdom, are flowing in

* See "Philosophy of Moral Freedom," in this volume.

wrong channels, and developing inharmonious consequences. All the inequalities and defects of the individual are reflected and impressed upon the family circle; the family discords and inequalities are impressed upon the social circle; and the social irregularities are impressed upon the national circle. Thus it is plain that individual harmony is essential to family harmony; family harmony to social harmony; and social harmony to the harmony of nations. The national form is but the most external form of the individual spirit. The one will be characteristic of the other.

Concerning the Love elements, it is well to remark, That some individuals grow directly into a proper exercise of Self-Love and Conjugal-Love, while others go on to the higher forms of the vitalizing essence, but manifest great ignorance in their exercise. Thus some persons will incautiously expose themselves to imminent danger and loss of life for fraternal interests, for extreme filial love, or for universal love, when the ends of wisdom might be accomplished in a quiet and gentle manner. Generally, however, the human mind does not attain a growth beyond the circle of *Self-Love* and *Use*, owing to the antagonistic interests of past and present society into which the spirit is ushered and consequently educated.

This proposition is self-evident, as truth always is; and it is time to consider it in all its diversified applications to the human species. The doctrine that 'one member can not suffer without the other members suffering with it,' lies at the foundation of social reformation. It is undeniable that the present antagonistic state of the trades and professions, do rapidly generate and perpetuate hatreds and animosities among individuals; and, it is likewise undeniable, that the teachers in modern theological institutions of the earth do very much toward discouraging social and individual reformation, by instilling into the present and rising generations the baneful conviction that this world is all "a vale of tears," under the Adamic "curse," suffering the penalty of the "original sin," and, hence, that reformation, independent of the church, is impossible, and the thought impious.

If each reader will deeply consider and fully amplify the classification and *proper* manifestation of every element of Love and of every attribute of Wisdom which I have but imperfectly set forth, and also their *improper* manifestation, and the causes thereof, I am fully persuaded that the whole will appear truthful and beneficial.

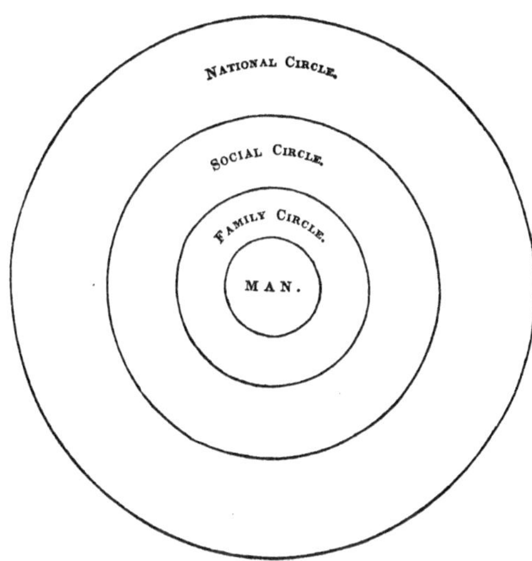

By the above diagram it will be seen that the harmonious individual—one, whose passional-forces are under the perpetual influence and government of Wisdom—develops a harmonious family; that harmonious families develop harmonious societies; that harmonious societies develop harmonious nations; and harmonious nations develop the kingdom of heaven on earth. Thus the constitutionally superior human spirit is a center around which congenial spirits congregate, condense their interests, and form a little world within themselves; and thus—

> "The center moved, a *circle* straight succeeds,
> Another still, and still another spreads:
> Friend, kindred, neighbor, first it will embrace,
> His country next, and next all human race."

The kind reader may inquire—

Is it possible to render the human spirit Harmonious?

Yes,—and what I say on this subject I know from experience to be true and practicable. First let me remark, that the hereditary defects of organization can not be entirely removed by education or favorable social situations. This is true, because organization is before situation or culture. But those defects of character which grow out of vitiating situations or education *can* be overcome and removed by natural and spiritual agencies, even as diseases are cured in the physical system. Happiness is the end of all human desire and endeavor, and spiritual culture is the agency by which it may be attained. To these objects, then, let us direct our whole attention. The following rules are all-important.

1. *In the morning arise, resolved to do nothing against, but every thing for, the Kingdom of Heaven on Earth.*

2. *Happiness being the object, let every action during the day be preceded by such well conceived and well developed thoughts as tend to its attainment.*

3. *At night retire—at peace with yourself—at peace with all the world.*

Draw these axioms into your soul—I know them to be the *first* steps toward happiness and culture. If you fail to take *these* properly, quietness and development are beyond your attainment. See well to this admonition. It is the language of no theory—it is the voice of Truth. The law and method of spiritual culture require also the following directions:

1. *Be contented with the Past, and with all it has brought you.*

2. *Be thankful for the Present, and for all you have.*

3. *Be patient for the Future, and for all it promises to bring you.*

These rules you should study. You should not read them and carelessly pass on. I desire you to stop here and write them down in your daily register, so that your eyes may see them; and write them down on your memory, so that your spirit may see them, and *resolve now!* It may cause many conflicts, and efforts, and struggles, but *resolve that from this moment you will live harmoniously.* Every day will strengthen your resolution. And finally, it will be more difficult to go counter to it than to obey its incessantly unfolding laws of nature. Live thus, and every morning the spirit will feel as new and as pure as an infant. It will feel just born. Live thus, and your companions will grow into your likeness, and discord will not enter your midst. If discord comes in, do not speak or act impetuously. *Be simple minded, willing to be taught, willing to forgive.* Fail not to record these rules of action in your journal and your memory. Do not fail to practice them from this moment. Pages might be written in exhorting you to be simple in spirit, gentle, and forgiving; but brief suggestions will not escape your attention; and may every good spirit assist you to follow out their every manifestation. Remember, these laws lie at the foundation of all spiritual culture—to fail to obey them is failing to obtain individual happiness, and to create Universal Harmony.

What are the Outward Means of Spirit-Culture?

THE OUTWARD MEANS OF SPIRIT-CULTURE are :—

1. Studying the exact or physical sciences.
2. Studying the laws of the body and laws of the spirit.
3. Proper gratification of the external senses.
4. Walking, playing, dancing, and various amusements.

5. Reading, writing essays, keeping journals, and associating with good and ornamentally educated minds.

6. In all things practicing self-discipline and obeying the principles of Wisdom.

Concerning the *outward means* of spirit-culture, let me remark:

First, that, by *studying the sciences*, I mean those particular sciences which relate to the organization—viz.: the science of anatomy, of physiology, chemistry, and of reproduction.

Second, by the study of physical and mental *laws*, is intended the principles of anatomical motion, of physiological functions and measurement of power, and the principles of mental action and predisposition. These sciences and laws should be particularly studied. The infant should be instructed according to their decisions, and parents should be qualified to impart this instruction. *No child should be sent to school before it has attained an age of eight years*, and generally not before its tenth year, because premature education is burdensome and paralyzing to the faculties and passions. Precocious youths are seldom strong and powerful men. They spring into life, and leave it, before the period in which the natural mind is allowed to develop and mature.

Third, by a proper gratification of the senses is intended whatever the preceding sciences and principles will teach and permit as essential to health and cultivation. And what is said further of the outward means is applicable to children, students, and every individual who desires harmony in body and in mind.

What are the Inward Means of Spirit-Culture?

THE INWARD MEANS OF SPIRIT-CULTURE are:—

1. Self-analysis, self-discipline, self-confession of faults, and self-harmonization.

2. Studying spiritual or psychological sciences, the science of analogy, and picturesque geography.

3. Studying painting and music.

4. Occasional meditation.

5. Poetical contemplations.

6. Conversations.

7. Mutual assistance, and mutual manipulations of spirit.—Communion with higher spheres of spiritual life.

Concerning the *inward means* of spirit-culture, let me remark:

First, that *self-analysis* is indispensable to spiritual progress. Let me urge this upon you—*practice it from this hour!* It will teach you how perfect and how imperfect you are—how to exercise kindness toward yourself and toward others. Self-discipline, self-confession of faults, and self-harmonization, will flow out of the *analysis*, as streams flow from the fountain.

Second, *studying spiritual and psychological sciences* is necessary to an extensive understanding of the human spirit, and also to inform the spirit how to meet, treat, and associate with other spirits of different constitutions and impulses. And the science of analogy, and picturesque geography, are beneficial to the spirit in the formation of ideas concerning the planets in space, and of the spirit-home to which we are individually progressing.

Third, *studying painting and music* should not be neglected. The former systemizes the thoughts and conceptions, and the latter refines the spirit and teaches it harmony. Occasional meditation, and poetical contemplations, expand the spirit and supply it with sentiments and divine nourishment. Let the good patriarchs David and Isaiah, be your example. These contemplative spirits let the voice of Divinity speak through them. So should you henceforth, and your spirit will unfold like the boundless heavens, and your deeds will shine like stars in the firmament. You wil see the Father every where, and happiness will be your portion.

Fourth, let me remark of *Conversations*, that nothing so cultivates and delights the spirit as spiritual conferences. The endowments and instincts of the soul are awakened, and the indwelling genius is made manifest. Conversation is a powerful means of spirit-culture and harmony. It touches the social chords of sympathy, and inspires the spirit with new sentiments and language. It ennobles the feelings, and beautifies the general deportment. When two or three, or six, or twelve, meet to sympathize and confer upon subjects of Love or Wisdom, the spirit of God will be in their midst, and they will feel an invisible Presence. Conversation gives to sentiments a form, to efforts a purpose, to language power, and to personality an influence. It calls into harmonious play all the elements of Love, all the attributes of Wisdom, and removes much supposed uncongeniality which sometimes individual absence engenders in the bosom of the passions. In conversation upon pleasurable subjects, Wisdom finds serene expression, and passional impulses run into calm channels; and the spirit feels harmonized with, and purified by, the full interconsciousness which binds soul to soul. Socrates exerted an influence wherever he went. He allowed the still small voice of Divinity, or Wisdom, to speak in the drawing-room, in the workshop, in the market-place, and in the sanctuary of his own soul. Subdued, fascinated, and purified by his personal impartation of truth, the multitudes followed and loved him. Every sentiment and idea sought an external expression; and Socrates incarnated much of his spirit in the deeds and institutions of the nation. Christ conversed always when he taught. He did no writing,—perhaps he could not write; but the indwelling Divinity flowed forth in the simplest language, and the congregation of spirits around him were instructed and rendered capable of spiritual perceptions. Learn self-confession from St. Augustine; and the art of conversation by the examples of Socrates, Solon, Plato, and Christ. Learn self-discipline from the good Fenelon; and harmony by the structure and manifestations of Wisdom.

Fifth, concerning *mutual assistance and mutual manipulations of the spirit* much might be said. I mean by this law of spirit-culture, that three, six, nine, or twelve individuals, having truth and happiness in their souls, should come together, and converse upon any thing connected with the elements of Love and the attributes of Wisdom.* In order to unfold the spiritual capacities and exalt the physical sensibilities, the little circle should adopt Wisdom's rules in relation to diet, exercise, industry, amusements, and other means of an *outward* character, and strive to become refined and harmonious. The enjoyments of this world will be greatly enhanced by cultivating the emotional organization of the mind—the nervous medium which connects it with matter and sensuous influences.

Sixth, there are two kinds of Education. One is an acquisition of Knowledge; the other is a development of Wisdom. An individual may be thoroughly versed in science, and language, and philosophy; and he may possess great knowledge; yet, notwithstanding it all, he may not be in the possession of Wisdom. Wisdom grows up from within—out of, and over the internal affections. The influences of individual presence, and conversation, and manipulations, are agencies of spiritual education. Let not these communions be mingled with unholy and vitiating thoughts and actions, though mirthfulness and healthful exercises are not to be avoided. A circle thus formed will grow into one harmonious whole; and its influence will extend far and wide in society. A proper and perpetual concentration of their love and intellectual powers upon the subject of spirit-growth and purification, will bring them into conjunction with the internal world and the Divine Being.

Seventh, concerning *communion with higher spheres of spiritual life* pages might be written. But let me remark that this is the highest means within the grasp of man whereby to unfold his spirit like a flower, and to enjoy more of this world and the next. This

* See "Philosophy of Spiritual Intercourse," concerning the formation of circles.

communion is possible only in two ways, viz.: 1. By becoming personally refined and harmonized, and turning the feelings frequently toward divine things. 2. By employing some reliable individual, as a medium, whose interior senses are opened, whose communications are truthful, and whose natural, normal disposition is altogether amiable, gentle, sympathetic, and generally meditative.

In conclusion, I feel moved to remark, that those who are constitutionally superior in body and spirit to the masses beneath and around them, should form themselves into circles of Love and Wisdom. It is plain, that popular theology or popular education are insufficient to supply the spirit with its proper nourishment and encouragement to an easy, natural progression. Theology is inadequate to the reconstruction of society; and *popular education*, which is saturated with this theology, is inadequate to the proper direction and cultivation of the spirit. It requires but little time to learn what *is useful*, to learn what *is just*, to learn what *is power*;—and *Beauty*, *Aspiration*, and HARMONY, are familiarly explained in the fields of universal Nature and Humanity. To understand what harmony is, the spirit must become harmonious. A harmonious individual is a revelation of the Divine Mind. The science, the chemistry, and mechanism of Divine Creation, are represented in the human form; and the holy elements and attributes of God are incarnated in every human spirit. To be like heaven let us aspire to heaven; to be like God let us aspire to God. Harmony must begin with the individual; it will thence spread over families, societies, and nations; and then the Whole will represent the Individual, and the individual will represent the Whole; and God will be **ALL IN ALL.**

THE RIGHTS AND MISSION OF WOMAN.

In relating my impressions upon this long-neglected and vitally-interesting subject, as also upon other subjects, the reader is requested to consider me as giving utterance to sentiments and convictions, which are wholly *free* from educational predilections or prejudices, either *for* or *against* any Age, Country, Position, Complexion, or Sex—for I constantly realize my general relationship to the great Body of humanity—a sojourner on the earth, confined by prejudice to no particular or favored spot—acknowledging a universal country and a universal brotherhood.

Much has been well spoken and written upon the "Rights of Woman," and many valuable suggestions for her improvement and elevation have occasionally been developed; but I feel deeply impressed with the conviction, that the relation of the sexes, and their reciprocal dependence and claims upon, and duties to, one another, are but little understood and acknowledged. This fact can be accounted for, only by admitting the hypothesis that there is a great destitution of correct thinking and acting in the world, and a surprising misapprehension of the true springs of society and government. The stronger sex, that class of individuals too frequently misnamed *man*, would certainly proceed immediately to unfeigned repentance and humiliation, could they but once behold the vast amount of vice and unhappiness they have caused to befall such a mass of the weaker portion of humanity. Man has depressed, deceived, degraded, betrayed, and enslaved Woman to an extent almost beyond expression. Because woman, in her unsuspecting and undeveloped state of mind, has manifested a fondness for display and attention, man has frequently taken advantage of this affection; and, instead of regarding it as an incipient manifestation and prophecy of latent female excellence and beauty, he has bestowed flattery, instead of a refining admiration; and a fawning gallantry, instead of that honest counsel and faithful protection which gladdens and elevates the dependent Soul.

I can not but deplore the structure or education of that mind, which can, contemptuously and arrogantly, pronounce woman as only the fit companion of children; for such a mind always shrinks from the attempt to place the female element in a circle of usefulness, wider and higher than her present narrow inclosures, known as the kitchen, the bedchamber, and the nursery. The perpetual perplexities, and unbroken monotony of these departments, are too depressing and fatiguing to be endured; and women, especially among the higher or wealthy classes, are beginning to despise and shun these confining and enslaving duties, on the ground that they are unpleasant, degrading, and unfashionable. It can not well be denied, nor disguised, that woman is sometimes moved to rebel against what are considered to be her respective duties, and that she runs into numerous vices, follies, and extravagances, simply because she is not properly placed in society; and because, also, those who govern States and Nations are profoundly ignorant of the interior attractions which are natural to the female character, and of the sublime influence her spiritual organization qualifies her to exert upon the race universally.

A misunderstanding or misappreciation of the rights and mission of woman has been, and is now, the cause why man usually regards the various impulses and attractions of females as weak and childish. It is said that you can not reason with a woman, and consequently, that it is the province of man to think, decide, and legislate for her; but, I think, it will be seen that there are two causes why woman does not generally manifest an equal tendency and strength to exercise judgment; one is because she is deprived of her natural liberty and ability to do so; and the other is because, except in a few cases, man treats her, not as a reasonable being, but as a mere child; not as a companion worthy of honor, but as a slave.

In the rudimental development of mankind—in the savage state of human progress—women are esteemed as slaves and domestic chattels. Cows, mules, horses, and women, are valuable and conspicuous items in the domestic and agricultural inventory. In the eastern countries—in upper Europe and Asia—women are not unfrequently compelled to perform the labor of *oxen* or *mules;* they are obliged to tread the rough fields, and gather in the harvests, while their husbands are luxuriating in idleness and smoking their pipes. Nor is it necessary to cross the Atlantic to "pluck the mote from our neighbor's eye"; because there are numerous instances among us, where husbands owe all the comforts, delicacies, and refinements which they possess, to the ceaseless industry, studied frugality, and to the constitutional modesty of their companions. And there are men—fathers—who, in the attempt to maintain their supposed entailed power and superiority over women, will frighten mothers into the paying of tribute, by threatening to deprive them of their children. Sometimes the husband is an inebriate, and will take the children into the midst of depraving influences. And there are husbands, also, who, in order to support and defend the position of being at the "*head of the family*," will proceed to angry contentions and useless discussions before their children—sometimes at the expense of damping or perverting the natural affection of those young hearts, and of extinguishing within their own soul what little love may yet linger around the memory of former attachment for the now disregarded companion. These are sad pictures to gaze upon! Yea, in our own country—in the sunny South—there is even now *a class of females* (and males also) *compelled, or condemned, to live and labor, and to be sold like cattle; being regarded simply as machines, capable of locomotion, and of producing like machines.* Thus, even in this civilized land, the cruelties and despotisms of savagism are yet in existence.

In the patriarchal development of humanity, are also visible the assumptions of masculine superiority to the feminine. By patriarchal development, I mean that state of human progress which hereditarily and legally imparts to the male the right to hold property, and to guide the reins of government, to the exclusion of female ownership and influence. Primogeniture is a bequeathment of the patriarchal age, whereby women are deprived of the power to possess property, and are thus made dependent on their husbands, or others, for subsistence and privileges. This law establishes a system of usurpation on the one hand, and a system of servitude on the other, between the sexes, which can not but operate unfavorably upon the natural and moral inclinations of the female. Woman has desires and impulses which man, because of his dissimilar constitution and impulses, does not and can not perfectly understand; and, sometimes, to gratify her desires, being impatient of restraint, she is moved to break away from her allotted sphere, and, not being properly guided, to rush into extremes of habit and passion, greatly to the disfiguration of her naturally beautiful and pure character. Among the civilized nations it is said, and generally believed, that woman is so constituted as to render her incapable of moving harmoniously in any other sphere than the one at present apportioned her by civilism—where, instead of being regarded as a mere chattel, or a domestic slave, she has been promoted to a position in which she subserves the purposes of a drawing-room adornment, a parlor picture, or a walking ornament—and she is considered and treated as a passionate, a sentient, and a reasonable being. But, I think, it will be acknowledged that, even in *Christian* Europe and America, woman is generally esteemed not as a companion—not as a gentle and regenerating principle, acting an important part in the humanitarian drama, and exerting there an influence as great as, if not superior to, that which is therein exercised by man. Even in these, the most enlightened portions of the world, the expressed opinion is, "*Woman was made for Man*"—thus implying a kind of servitude of female elements to masculine attributes. To acquire a "finished education"—to "get married"—to "have children"—to "remain at home"—or to "go when and where" her husband goes, (as he desires,) is a synopsis of "Woman's Rights" and mission, as they are generally apprehended, in the most enlightened and civilized parts of the world.

It is easy to understand why woman is frequently found to manifest weakness and impetuosity in her judgment, desires, and impulses; nor is it strange that female prostitution should, in various forms and modifications, exist in the sequestered and public portions of society. I affirm that, should any being, possessing the qualities and spiritual desires of the female character, be situated in the midst of *flattery*, *deception*, and *slavery*; and, should that being become accustomed to just that kind of evanescent attention, which is characteristic of the deference which acknowledged superiors manifest toward idolized inferiors, or to choice ornaments, it is positively certain that *infidelity*, *vice*, *alienation*, and *wretchedness*, would be the legitimate fruits developed.

As are a country's institutions so are the people, and, *vice versa*, as are the people so are the institutions; they reciprocally affect each other's character and development. Action and re-action are inevitable; and, therefore, just that influence which *man* (as a governing principle) exerts upon the position and character of woman, the latter will, and must, necessarily exert upon the world in return. There are, in the world, a few enlightened minds who know *how* dependent society is upon the morals and refinement of the female character; and such know that woman is, and must be, what man and society make her. The female character has a threefold, and, at the same time, a fundamental and a vital influence upon the world, viz.: It builds the foundation of society and of nations by moving in, and presiding over, the *sphere of childhood*, the *sphere of the family*, (or the home,) and the *social sphere.* According to surrounding circumstances, and according to the quality of the materials which she is compelled to employ, will be the foundation-elements which woman furnishes, whereupon to erect the mighty superstructure of nations and the world.

A synopsis of her influence is this: Through the medium of *childhood* she *molds* the *individual*—through the family medium, she *influences* and refines the husband—and, through the social medium, she influences and *spiritualizes* legislation and government.

Female elevation, and consequent liberty, are the inevitable results of social re-organization, and a true republican government. The female spirit is a beautiful combination of immortal springs and affections; but if the sphere of its movements is, in any respect, limited or circumscribed, so as to cramp its infinite expansion and improvement, then will dissatisfaction, and, perhaps, dissipation, be developed. Philosophers and legislators have not bestowed sufficient thought upon the variety and importance of female influences; nor have they been sufficiently minute in their investigations into the secret springs of human action, misdirection, or improvement; and hence there are many discoveries yet to be made and disclosed, which will conspire greatly to the development of harmony among nations.

The extent of female influence is as little understood by the sex, themselves, as it is by the world of minds in general. For, upon investigation I learn, with as much pleasure as astonishment, that woman exerts *three-fifths* of *that* influence which moves the human world. The internal and spiritual circles are spheres in which she, particularly, performs her *mission.* 1. The first circle is the *childhood sphere.* 2. The second circle is the *family sphere.* 3. The third circle is the *social sphere.* And on these fundamental spheres the female element should be completely incorporated, and allowed its legitimate action; it desires no wider or higher scope, nor could it feel harmonious in different spheres of action and movement. Woman will act in these three circles, and *it is not* possible to prevent her; but *it is* possible to surround her with deforming circumstances, and to put her in the possession of heterogeneous materials, and thus cause her works to be imperfect and unprofitable to the race. For instance, the female gives (*directly*) constitution and character to the individual through the mediums of childhood, domestic example, and social intercourse; but she is only an instrument and dispenser of those personal and several influences, those home conditions, and those social tendencies, with which her husband and the world's customs have surrounded her, and the individual which she is instrumental in developing. Woman will inevitably develop the world; but by way of compensation to her, and for its own interests, the world should supply her with good matrimonial relations, with pleasant home advantages, with ennobling social institutions, all so complete and harmonious within themselves, as to make it easy and natural for her to furnish society with noble minds.

All the heroes, poets, artists, philosophers, and theologians, that ever moved upon the earth, were put in possession of their various maxims and attributes, mainly, by woman. She exerts a positive influence upon the constitution and character of the individual until the *national sphere* is reached, when, compared with the influence of the male, the female power is negative; and now the wisdom principle pervades the individual, for the purpose of modifying, harmonizing, and further developing the mind. Properly, and naturally, man has but *two* circles of action,—he moves harmoniously, first in the *national sphere*, and second in the *universal sphere*—because these are the circles of government and harmony. Woman can not produce harmony of herself, but she can furnish the proper *elements* for its elaboration and establishment; and man can not produce these elements, but he can discover, furnish, and enforce the principles of *discipline*, or the natural laws of government.

Thus, the *childhood sphere*, the *family sphere*, and the *social sphere*, are spheres or circles of love; and the *national* and *universal spheres* are circles of wisdom. The former are properly the arena of female action and influence, and the latter are properly the spheres of intellectual government. And therefore, as it has been explained, the female influence is positive and powerful upon individual constitution and character, until the point or verge is approached, where discipline and government are natural and necessary, when it becomes negative, and acts, thereafter, as a balance-wheel to the higher portions of humanity's governmental and constitutional arrangements.

I come, now, to consider woman in her first sphere of action, viz.—in the *childhood sphere*. According to the situation and education of the female, will be the constitution and inclinations of her offspring. The truthfulness of this proposition is beginning to be recognized by pathological and physiological inquirers, and especially among the self-subordinating and profound students of scientific medicine in Germany; but, notwithstanding the vast amount ot ignorance and skepticism which exists upon this subject, I am perfectly aware that human reformation must begin at this point; and, consequently, with the elevation and education of the female character. The impressions and hereditary predispositions of the body and mind, are alike imparted by the parents to the child. Progeni tory influence is inevitable and irresistible; hence, the attention ot philanthropists and philosophers should be directed to this point, to investigate and remove the origin of human weaknesses and misdirection.

If parents are engaged in pursuits and occupations, calculated *only* to develop their social and animal nature, the child will be an exact representative of the peculiar characteristics and situations of its progenitors, and, also, of the various influential circumstances by which they are continually surrounded; therefore, the child will, most likely, grow into maturity with an inferior moral and intellectual development; and will experience many social temptations, and animal attractions, over which the moral and intellectual faculties can have no absolute control.

Again: If one or both of the parents have an inordinate desire to accumulate property, and acquire riches; and in the gratification of which pursuit, they employ their intellectual faculties, combined with the inferior faculties of self-esteem, firmness, combativeness, and destructiveness; the child will almost *inevitably* be born with a similar organization, and will, almost as inevitably, exercise throughout the whole of its life on earth, the same faculties in the attempt to gratify the same desire.

Again: If one or both of the parents have a selfish, arrogant, combative, and impetuous disposition, with a considerable weight of character, the child will be born, and grow up with a similar disposition, and ability to make itself, and many other individuals, very unhappy.

And, again: If there be a disposition on the part of the parents to mental derangement, the child will experience, and perhaps manifest, an under-current of the same constitutional defect. These are a few cases illustrative of the many influences which are constantly at work, impeding the progressive beauty and elevation of the race.

The influence of the mother upon the child is almost incalculable. She associates with it continually; whereas, the father sees it only now and then. The mother is familiar with its powers, its passions, and its impulses; whilst the father sees them but partially, and even when he witnesses their exhibition, he does not understand their origin and true mode of treatment. The mother can sympathize with all its little movements, and spontaneous attractions; she can understand the secret cause of its impetuosity and uneasiness; she can forgive, and subdue, and impress maxims of action; but the father is disqualified to understand those childish impulses, and still less is he capable of "hushing" the youthful tempest into sweet repose.

If troubles arise—if violent and quick disputes, and altercations, are developed in the nursery, the Mother knows in what way to approach each child—how to still this little one—how to admonish that one—and how to gently discipline the other; but the Father naturally knows nothing of these secrets—he can frown and stamp down infant passion—can coercively and peremptorily establish a superficial obedience and harmony among children; but he can not magnetically soothe, as the Mother can, the disturbed bosom into dreamless slumber.

The child is naturally attracted to its Mother's heart, into the sanctuary of its Mother's soul;—but there are mothers who repel and abuse the tender spirits, who thus seek their native home within the parent-bosom. Alas! that they should ever be once repelled, or chilled in their natal atmosphere.

When the child is injured,—or when it has wrought injuries,—it spontaneously and instinctively discloses to its Mother, the things whereof she interrogates. In the still evening, and in the quiet hours, the child will gaze upon its Mother's face—will look into her heart—will hush, to listen to her spirit—and thus draw into its inmost soul, impressions of parental nearness and loveliness And in such moments, the Mother can—she has, in truth, often in one comprehensive sentence, impressed a thought, or developed an impulse, in the youthful mind, which, forming there a channel, has given direction to its every subsequent desire and enterprize.

The Mother daguerreotypes her constitution and habits upon the child; and, although subsequent education and the circumstances of its intercourse with the world, may modify and obscure, in a great measure, its early impressions, yet there are times when *nature* and *intuition* transcend superficial culture and custom, and the spirit can not but internally *hear* and *obey* the whispering ad monitions of the maternal heart,—its sweet, low breathings echoed by memory; and the weary mind unrolls its pages, and on the first unblotted sheets, reads what the Mother's hand had traced.

The noblest philosophers of Greece could not resist the impulse to quote, from the nursery-vocabulary, many axioms and principles of life, the outlines and back-ground of which, were drawn by sympathizing Mothers, on their spirits in childhood.

The rudest and most indomitable tar, rough though he may seem, and bold, while laboring to save the sinking ship, will drop a tear—not because of the fearful danger and awful catastrophe which await him, but—at the *remembrance* of his Mother!

The great and powerful legislator of France, Lamartine, though intellectualized by studying the profoundly sublime disclosures of poets and philosophers, could not but revert to the impressions of his childhood, in his appeals to the people; they were indelibly written on the first pages of his mind, and they added, not a little, to his influence, which consisted in a straight-forward, simple announcement of natural and mighty truths.

The influence of Mothers upon their children, and the unspeakable importance of their position in the formation and reformation of society, and the world, is unconsciously and instinctively acknowledged by the Roman Catholic and Protestant systems of religion. Their regard, not for the husband of Mary, but for Mary as the *Mother* of Jesus, amounts, not only to positive idolatry, but to an important acknowledgment of the absolute inseparableness of her existence and constitution, with the mission and destiny of Jesus.

It is wise and good for man to acknowledge his dependence upon the world—to understand and confess that Woman builds the very foundations of national institutions and governments; and it is not wise or righteous to attempt to disguise or escape these conclusions, for the harmonious proportions of humanity's future structure will depend entirely upon the education and elevation of the female master-builders.

The sphere of childhood is a garden; and its cultivation depends almost exclusively upon Woman. In this garden, the love-principle (the female) is at home; the immortal germs of individual constitution and character are deposited in the soul's rich soil; the tenderest buds of affection spring forth; and the gentle horticulturist watches and protects them day and night. The Mother understands, *how*, *when*, and *where*, the youthful bud bursts forth; she understands the causes and locality of every thorn, that the unfolding flower of the spirit has developed in the process of its blooming; and there is no hand so beautifully calculated to keep those thorns from injuring the surrounding and clustering blossoms, as the hand of the gentle Mother. With tenderness, she removes and destroys the weeds, (or errors,) which may be found in the wide-spread garden she so carefully tends; she supports and defends the weak plant from the storms and tempests of passion and society—and her field of labor breathes forth the delightful fragrance of tenderness and affection. The tender Mother employs the choicest instrumentalities in developing each individual, and her garden bears no evidence of violence, no traces of impetuosity. But the less gentle and stern Father would trample upon the tender plants, violently pluck the thorns away, and employ heavy and unsuitable implements in cultivating the youthful mind; and then, in the place of gentleness, tenderness, and affection, there would be developed combativeness, resistance, and grossness—and the young plant would grow up rank and unbeautiful.

But it is said, that Woman is too tender, too forgiving, too weak and undecisive, to impart to children correct habits of thought, desire, and action. It is asserted that Woman spoils children, and causes them to out-grow the bounds of correct discipline, and I must acknowledge that this is sometimes true; but how clouded must be those perceptions which can not recognize the causes of this weakness in female family government! Elsewhere, I have said that Woman does not understand herself any more than she is comprehended by Man. There are Rights of Woman which she does not claim of Man, because she is generally ignorant of her natural attractions, mission, and demands; but I am impressed to inform her of her just claims upon society, and assist her to procure them.

First: Woman builds the foundation-walls of society—this, her position and her organization impel and compel her to do—and, therefore, she needs to be educated in the peculiarities of her position; she needs to be informed that, naturally and philosophically considered, the female element is constituted wholly of divine Love—that she is an embodiment of the Love Principle;—she needs to be informed that True Marriage is the most divine, sacred, and eternal of all relations into which the human and immortal Soul enters;—she needs to be informed that True Marriage consists in, and is developed, not by flattery, passion, personal charms, age, wealth, education or perpetual deception,—but that a *true* union, a *true* oneness of Soul, is developed by an internal affinity, by the interior and eternal Law of Association;—she needs to be informed that the consequences of True Marriage are of everlasting duration—that every Spirit receives an immortal organization from birth, perfect or imperfect according to the direction and structure originally imparted to the body and mind; and she needs to be educated in these things,—not by stratagem, by intrigue, or by a sacrifice of *natural* and *true* modesty,—but she should be enlightened in them by some paternal companion, or congenial Teacher, who is sound in pure philosophy and true religion.

Let the rising generation be thus instructed, and those females who receive, and act upon this philosophy of human improvement, will impart it to their offspring; and, at least, such, among Women, would no more be accused of "spoiling children,"—nor complained of, as wanting in energetic culture of the gardens of childhood, or of being too lenient in their watchful care of the tender plants and beautiful flowers.

I come now to consider Woman in her second sphere of action, viz.—in the Family Sphere. According to the organization and education of the female spirit will be the *home* she presents to her husband and children; and I think it will not be denied that a Man is generally a representative of the kind of home he calls his own. The female presence *there*, is the Spirit of his life—the central spring of his joys and intellectual actions—and without her, Man is unrefined, wanting in gentleness and majesty. She displays a grace and ease in the several departments of her vocation, and breathes forth from her boundless love an atmosphere, to inhale which, is purity, refinement and happiness. She manifests her heart in her works; and its gentle and varied pulsations are felt throughout the veins and arteries of her household. Harmony in the family regulations develops harmony in each Individual; because action and re-action are the inevitable results of life and animation. *Home* is a reality; and the reality has developed the *word* which is wreathed with affections, potentialized by internal attractions—the sweet word *Home*, which is next to Mother, on every tongue, and in every heart.

The husband, after discharging the duties of the day, hastens to receive the fond welcome, and meet the ready smile which beams upon the countenance, of his eternal companion,—joyfully returning to the refreshing scenes, and peaceful rest, of the well developed *home*.

The Child, become a Youth, desires to explore regions beyond the sphere of the sacred household attractions; he would travel,—the voyage is undertaken; and after he has "encompassed Sea and Land" to gratify the innate desire for the new, and the beautiful, there is not a word in human language, not an impression upon his spirit, so dear and omnipotent as the *word* and *thought* of *home*.

Going from *home* is productive of sadness; returning *home* is delight and joy. Happy are they who, because of their harmony and freedom of Soul, can not *depart* from home, always carrying it with them, being, in themselves, the very essence and elements of its constitution.

The Poet, the Philosopher, the Artisan, and the Legislator, are alike dependent upon the beauties and harmonies of *home* for inspiration and power. The works and influences of these minds, are *linked* and *measured* by the blessings and spiritualizing influences which the female breathes forth in their Home.

Woman is a spirit of Love,—she is a Revelation of refinement, of grace, and of beauty. She possesses the power of rendering the local habitation of her husband and children a representation of paradise, and of illustrating to the world a beautiful Heaven upon earth.

But it is said that Woman is obstinate in her firmness, self-willed, determined to have her own way—that she breeds discord and disturbance in every part of the house—that she makes home, and all its constituents, unbeautiful and unhappy, and I must confess that, in too many cases, this is true; but there are causes for these anomalies and contradictions which the Rulers of society would do well to heed. Woman has Rights which she should demand of society, because the family over which she presides is the foundation of the Social Structure, and she therefore needs, and may claim, to be educated in the duties of life, or rather in the nature and extent of the Mission which Deity designed her to perform; she needs to be disabused of the enslaving conviction that merely "keeping house" and "bringing up children," are duties which the law compels her to, according to the letter of the "marriage contract;" she needs to be informed that her Mission is a sublime and universal one—that she is to people, not only the Earth, but all the Spiritual Spheres and Heavens; she needs to be informed that *firmness* and *determination* are indispensable to the prompt and faithful discharge of her duties—that harmony may be established in the Childhood Sphere and in the Home, so that the husband and the children may reciprocate the same, to her Soul and to Society; she needs to be in the possession of a permanent, and Spirit-inspiring residence, and to be situated in the midst of good and elevating scenery; she needs, and may claim, to be enlightened upon these subjects, and to be well and happily situated in her marriage, in her maternal, and in her domestic relations;—let this justice be done her, and then Woman will no longer be accused of the disposition to create disturbance; nor will she be considered deficient in any of those spiritualizing and irresistible influences, which should constitute and pervade every department of the sacred household sphere, and cast a halo over the holiness of *home.*

I come now to consider Woman in the third Sphere of action, viz.—in the Social Sphere. According to the organization, education, and situation of the Family, will be the structure and characteristics of Society; for Society is the highest, and widest circle of human life, in which the Love or female Principle is constitutionally qualified to move, and exert a positive influence. It must not be disremembered that Woman builds Society by building the foundation-walls of Childhood, (which makes the individual,)—and also of the *home*, (which makes the husband;) and thus it is that Society is the foundation of the National Superstructure, into which the female Principle can not naturally and gracefully enter. But Society is the *great* Fort of female action and influence. There she breathes forth an atmosphere of fraternal love, and modifies the quality of that heavy and oppressive influence which ordinarily circulates among Men. The Tradesman, the Banker, the Commercial Changer, are kind, prompt, and courteous to each other, because of the indwelling Spirit of Fraternal-Love and refinement, which the Wife, the Mother, or the Sister, unconsciously and spontaneously impress upon the sterner Sex.

Woman naturally sheds abroad upon the world of Mind, a warmth of Spirit which soothes, enlivens and develops the better nature in the soul of the strayed wanderer, and in the darkened heart of the midnight assassin; and the boldest and most courageous Warrior, or Highwayman, will sheathe his blood-red saber at the gentle signal of the female Spirit. Her gentleness and tenderness enchant; and her hand acts like a magic wand upon the Spirit of the strong Man and the Barbarian. She imparts, from the inmost recesses of her love, a spiritualizing and beautifying magnetic influence, which alike subdues and captivates the mind. The noble *Pocohontas* defended the fallen guest, by standing between him and the ferocious Savages; she sent forth into their enraged souls a volume of *love* and sympathy, which calmed the storm of passion, and charmed enmity into friendship. The gentle power of Woman over man is beautifully illimitable and incalculable. The primitive history contains many numerous illustrations of this truth. The beautiful Delilah was the *only power* the Philistines could employ by which to overcome their direful and mighty enemy. Samson would yield to no one but Delilah. And Holofernes could be subdued only by his fair and captivating visitor,—the firm and determined Judith.

National histories have immortalized the names of several females, whose internal power and pure accomplishments, have performed almost miracles upon the minds of Heroes and Barbarians.

A constant association with pure and cultivated Woman is one of the most powerful causes of the development of sympathy, morality and religion. Religious denominations consider the female character an indispensable element in their combinations; the clergymen influence men by first incorporating the female principle into their church organizations. Two-thirds of the Men, great and small, are led to that church which the female prefers; and, for various reasons, there are but few who would like to venture to pursue a different course.

There are emanations of warmth and purity from Woman's soul, which penetrate, more or less, every heart in being; and where these emanations are felt, and this penetration experienced, there dwells something of that sublime influence which Angels impart to one another in higher spheres. The beautiful accomplishments ot the female mind act correspondingly upon the opposite Sex; the natural and innate tendency of the female spirit to cultivate the arts, to beautify the person, to augment the power of fascination, to awaken music, to dance, and to adorn the power of motion by melting her grace into poetry,—all this acts correspondingly upon the masculine Spirit, and thus Society is, or might be, rendered one vast circle of flowers and ornaments.

But it is said that Woman is disposed to disturb the harmony of Society by petty contentions,—that whole neighborhoods are confused and disconcerted by the pusillanimity and cupidity of Women,—that they will defame each other's character, and generate ill-will and jealousies, whenever and wherever they can,—that they will dress their persons, and superficially ornament their minds, in order to deceive and debase the youthful and weak members of Society;—thus Solomon admonishes the reader " not to enter the house of the strange Woman;" and it is asserted that, from the "beauteous Eve," to the boarding-school miss of the present century, Woman has caused war, dissensions, and disturbances, both Social and National; and that she is, in fact, the most uncontrollable creature with which man is compelled to contend.

This statement is partially true; but there are causes for all this feminine deformity and imperfection, which it would be well for Reformers, and Legislators, to understand and remove. Woman has Rights to demand; she needs to be instructed that her Mission extends to the threshold of National Government; for that government will be a representative of her situation and influence; she should be informed that she is not an inferior ingredient in the Constitution of humanity; she should be taught that her angelic endowments, and immortal qualifications, were not given to her as toys are to children; that she is not to be insulted with flattery, deceived by false attention, enslaved by heartless promises; that she is no man's superior, nor his inferior, or slave—but that she is his eternal Companion—the Spirit of God in the majestic form; she needs to be informed that upon her Constitution—Education—Situation, depend the harmony of the Individual, the harmony of the Family, the harmony of Society,—and, consequently, the harmony of Nations universally; she needs to be informed that the destiny of the Race is in her hand, and that the Sympathy, the Virtue, the Refinement, and the Elevation of every individual is dependent upon her heart, her mind, her philosophy, her actions. But that she may accomplish her mission, Woman must claim her Rights, and demand of man the following:

1. A *just* representation of her interests.
2. A *good* matrimonial relation.
3. A *complete* education.
4. A *harmonious* local and social situation.
5. Counsel, not commands; admiration, not flattery.

6. Honor, not patronage; pure wisdom, not its semblance or counterfeit.

It is not consistent with the question under consideration, to suggest the *ways* and *means* whereby these *Rights* can be secured to Woman; but, I think, the enlightened and accomplished Lady, and the true and intelligent Gentleman, can not but perceive that, inasmuch as Woman is the builder of the foundation of Nations, she should be furnished with sound and pure materials as a kind of compensation for the work she performs in the hearts of men, and in the gardens of God.

The progressive state and estimation of Woman in the world may be seen in the following synopsis:

In Savagism, she is an idolized slave;

In Barbarism, she is regarded as a domestic Chattel;

In Patriarchalism, she is an acknowledged Influence;

In Civilism, she is a reasoning Ornament;

In Republicanism, she is a principle of Love.

To the harmonious individual, the Age of Republicanism has already arrived; but, when he looks *without himself*, upon Society and the World, he sees Man and Woman in every possible situation and stage of development, on their way up the mount of human progress, like scattered monuments in the path, marking the distance. Some are just emerging from Savagism, some from Barbarism, some from Patriarchalism; but only a few have reached the summit of Civilization, which is the *vestibule* of Republicanism!

Let this truth be impressed, and remembered, that Female Elevation, and consequent Liberty, are the natural *concomitants*, and the inevitable *results*, of social re-organization, and of a *universal Republican Government.*

THE PHILOSOPHY OF TRUE MARRIAGE.

The principles of matrimonial association are universal and eternal. The Law of association or affinities develops the *true* relation which subsists between one atom or individual and another; and the corresponding association of the particles or spirits thus drawn together, is an outward expression of true marriage.

The Law of Conjugal Union is first represented in the structure of the Divine Mind; next in his inconceivable relations to the Universe. The essential elements of the Divine Mind are embodied in the form of Love, and his Celestial attributes are embodied in the form of Wisdom. As I have elsewhere said, *Love* is a *female*, and *Wisdom* is a *male*, principle; these in their divine relation and unity, generate the whole universe of matter and mind. The subsequent manifestations of this divine matrimonial relation are less sublimely grand and perfect, but not less demonstrative and unmistakeable. In the natural elements are corresponding exhibitions of true marriage. Electricity indicates positive and negative relations; magnetism is the *male* or positive principle, and electricity is the *female* or negative principle. The atmosphere is constructed upon the same principles: Oxygen is the *female*, and Nitrogen the *male*. Water, also, is thus made; Oxygen is the *female*, and Hydrogen the *male;* and between them life, nourishment, atmosphere, an kindred elements, are generated and evolved.

There is a beautiful matrimony between particles in chemical compositions;—they seek out and ultimately associate with one another. Plants are congenial in the same manner; and so are the various classes and species of organizations in the animal kingdom. To the outward searcher after truth, I would recommend an investigation into the marvelous revealments of the sciences of Chemistry, Botany, Zoology, and Ornithology; because these various departments of inquiry furnish incalculable examples and confirmations of the beauties of true marriage.

As is the Divine Mind, so are the ultimate productions of Naure—his children!

Every individual, *abstractly* considered, is an embodiment and representation of Love and Wisdom. The elements of the human soul are organized into an image of Love or Life, and the attributes of intelligence are unfolded into an image of Wisdom, or Guardian Power. Therefore every human soul is constructed upon male and female principles; the *male* is positive, and the *female* is negative.

But each and every individual, considered *relatively*, is not Love and Wisdom alone and complete within himself or herself, but is only one of these principles, and hence experiences an affinity for its apparently opposite or dissimilar self. It is when, and *only* when, an individual realizes its dependence upon another individual, that sensations of loneliness, dissatisfaction, discontent, and incompleteness unfold themselves in the spirit. Congenial association is now loudly and imperatively demanded by the isolated and seeking heart. Heart calls to heart. The *female* is alone without her *true* companion; and the *male* is alone without the female; the female is seeking for its Wisdom principle; and the male is seeking for its principle of Love.

There is no happiness separate from true conjugal association. One spirit can not resist the attraction to another spirit; it is simply Wisdom searching for Love, or Love for Wisdom. It is not strange that the heart seeks its *true* associate; because when we comprehend and realize the truth that the Deity, his universe, and the human soul, are constructed and subsisting upon the principles of male and female,—positive and negative,—or Love and Wisdom, it is easy and natural to understand the attraction which the dependent Soul feels toward its true companion. It is Soul seeking for Soul,—Life for Life,—Love for Wisdom,—Spirit for Happiness. Yes, it is when the soul realizes its relation to, or dependence upon others, and especially its particular dependence on *one*, that it begins to seek for itself.

Conjugal-Love must be responded to by Conjugal-Love; else the Spirit will be unhappy. The properly unfolded *female* character is an embodiment of Love; and the *male* character, when properly unfolded, is an embodiment of Wisdom. The female, being Love, possesses within her soul the immortal springs of beauty and loveliness; but if she is, by means of uncontrollable circumstances and legal enactments, associated with a companion whose powers and attributes are not sufficiently great and noble, or kind and generous, to extract from her sentiments of continual respect and admiration, then will she most certainly manifest uneasiness and generate discord. It is depressing to scan the multitude of marriages which have resulted from no higher causes than the infatuations of passion and evanescent personal charms,—of popularity, of individual position, the superficial accomplishments of education, the advantages of wealth and convenience,—or from the so frequent coercion or incitement of accidental outer circumstances. In the world, every where are visible these superficial and ephemeral marriages,—marriages! did I say?—No, not marriages, but worldly legalized attachments—legalized adulteries and bigamies; which not only distract and deform, but *arrest* the development of beauty and happiness in, the thus enslaved Soul.

True marriages are natural, inevitable, harmonious and eternal! By the assistance of interior perception and comprehension, I was enabled to ascertain the glorious and consoling truth that every spirit is *born* married! When I gaze upon an infant, a youth, a lonely individual, the voice of intuition and true philosophy says—"that infant, that youth, that lonely individual, has some where an eternal companion!" Therefore I perceive and understand that a meeting, and, in the present state of society, a legal recognition of such companions are an outward expression of true marriage. And yet, no ceremony, no promise, no written or legalized agreement, can *unite* that which is *internally* and *eternally* joined; nor can these solemnities *unite* that which is *internally* and *eternally* separated. If two are legally married, and if this outer expression of *unity* has no other primary cause than the fascinations of feature, the advantages of position or wealth, or the accident of circumstances, then is the female unconsciously living with another Spirit's companion; and so also is the male living in perpetual violation of the law of Conjugal Association; and consequently both are rendered dissatisfied and unhappy.

The best evidence that two individuals *are not* naturally and eternally married, is that, by dwelling together, they generate discord, discontent, disrespect, and unhappiness; and the best evidence that two *are* internally and eternally married, is that, by dwelling together, they generate harmony, respect, admiration, and contentment. The laws of Nature, or God's laws, are superior to human enactments and jurisprudential proceedings; yet, until mankind are more refined and acquainted with the laws of mind and matter, we must submit to human legislation, and human laws must be permitted and obeyed; but herein is a great, and, at present, necessary evil which *all* should strive to understand and overcome; that human laws may be made no other than Divine; and then, notwithstanding the misapprehensions and local transgressions of them which might sometimes occur, there would not exist one-tenth of the discord, licentiousness, and unhappiness that now mar the face of humanity.

Every individual is born married; every male and female,—every

Love and Wisdom,—has a *true* and *eternal* companion. This marriage is solemnized by Supreme sanction, and is sanctified by Angelic harmony. It depends not upon personal beauty, or education; neither upon wealth, position, situation, time, age, or circumstance; it is the spontaneous and inseparable conjunction of affinity with affinity, principle with principle, and spirit with spirit.

In reply to the question—"Will *all* the individuals married in this life, continue to live together in the Spirit-World?" I received the following vision: In England, in the city of London, I saw a gentleman undergoing the metamorphosis called death. He had been for several years married to an uncongenial companion; they had frequently and severely injured and insulted each other; and were quite dissimilar in their temperaments, habits, attractions, and desires. From the scene of this departure, my perceptions were directed to a dying Turkish lady, in Constantinople, who, according to the Eastern custom of polygamy, had been a favorite wife of the Sultan. The two deaths, or transformations, occurred at the same moment; and when the two spirits were emancipated from the body, and from the superficial restrictions of society, they ascended—and by the irresistible attraction of conjugal or spiritual affinity, and in accordance with the law of perfect spiritual adaptation,—they approached each other—and, rapturously embracing, manifested the fullest realization of the beautiful fact that they were eternally ONE.

It is consoling to the enlightened philanthropist to imbibe and comprehend the truth, that a *true* conjunction of souls is the invariable and inevitable consequence of a residence in the second Sphere, where deformities and injustices are overcome and forever exterminated. *There is but one only and true marriage;* and it is highly possible that the unfortunate individual who may have had several companions on earth, has not yet met with the real sharer and associate of the spirit's eternal joys and peregrinations.

That Spirit which is still seeking and praying for congenial companionship, should rest perfectly assured that it has somewhere a mate—somewhere an eternal associate! Life will not always be incomplete. Let the seeker remember this; and, being already in principle joined to some true and faithful one, let the heart be glad; and let it realize, by means of anticipation, the final meeting, which, if circumstances and earnest desire do not consummate it on earth, will be inevitably developed, perfected, and confirmed in the higher country. And those who are unfortunately situated in their world-ly-legalized marriage relations—they should, also, rest in the sublime and unfailing assurance of eternal principles, that a due separation is in the future, and that a due *meeting* will be the issue of an introduction into the Spirit-home. Perhaps the true companion has already gone before; if this be so, it is altogether probable that the spirit remaining here will feel drawn toward the higher world, when searching for its companion. There is a holiness in this natural and true marriage—*which is a consequence of our being—an inevitable result of our own existence*—that, when once conceived of by the heart and understanding, must make every spirit on earth rejoice; and insure purity and faithfulness in that soul which would live for the *one* whom God hath given, and "keep itself unspotted from the world."

Where the *true union* is enjoyed, there can not exist the slightest cause of jealousy, of coldness, of estrangement, of disrespect, or alienation; for perfect and entire confidence wreathes every thought which the one entertaineth of the other; and by a commingling of their mutual love, the truly joined—the God-made ONE—can consume every unfriendly and discordant impulse which might arise in their undeveloped bosom. The Love-principle, or the female, is the actuating, the prompting, the life-giving portion of the eternal ONENESS; and the Wisdom-principle, or the male, is the governing, the guiding, and harmonizing portion; and thus the twain are ONE in essence and organization. Love, or the female,—with her immortal and impetuous springs of life, beauty, and animation,—is, if unguided and unassociated with Wisdom, unspeakably lonely, and very liable to misdirection; on the other hand, Wisdom,—or the male, with his immortal attribute of harmony and government,—is, if unassociated with, and deprived of, the life-giving elements of Love, a mere iceberg, a mere isolated oak, cold and unbeautiful. But these reflections are more properly connected with the consideration of the *mission* and *influence* of the male and female principle, or the sexes, which consideration may be found in the previous chapter.

The reader should be impressed with the conviction that the Law of Association, which moves alike the universe and the human soul, will determine and proclaim who is his, or her, true companion. No clergyman, no testimony, no legalized contract, or record in Church or State, can determine upon the proper conjugal associate, nor develop the everlasting affection which the spirit demands. The evidence is within. Search yourselves. If ye are truthfully married, then will ye have mutual or parallel attractions, corresponding desires, and similar constitutional tendencies; and where the one goes, the other will go; and on earth, as in the higher spheres of existence, ye will have *one home*, *one purpose*, *one destiny*, *one God*, *and one religion.*

Where a union is perfect, there is no conflict; when Wisdom decides, love will respond. If a wife loves her companion, she will involuntarily keep his commandments, which to her are wisdom's ways; and if a husband loves his companion, he will treat her *not* as an inferior, not as a superior, not as one incapable of exercising reason; but he will honor and protect, and guide, and develop her indestructible sensibilities, and be to her a haven of rest.

Every heart prays and pines for that holy and protecting love which will not change, however varying may be the vicissitudes of human life, but which strengthens ever, in sickness and in health, in youth and in maturity, in prosperity and in adversity, and which, while it strengthens, fails not to represent those noble and beautiful qualities of the soul which distinguish the sexes and characterize the stronger Man, and gentler Woman; and this distinction must be marked and perpetual in order to experience the blessings consequent upon the existence of perpetual love and honor, one toward the other.

The true marriage is first Natural, then Spiritual, then Celestial, in its progressive growth. And the eternally conjoined have an unfailing evidence of their destiny by experiencing a continually unfolding love for one another, which grows stronger and stronger as they pursue life's path and near the Spirit-Home. But here let it be impressed, that with some on the earth, *misunderstandings* may occur, and, by their fearful and invidious influence, even the truly married may be moved to separate on the way, until they arrive *where* misunderstandings can not exist. These misapprehensions may proceed from the dissimilarity of individual education, or from habit and acquired superficial desires; but from whatever outer cause they may arise, search ye within; and, if ye are conscious of entertaining a living and growing affection for the offending spirit, strive to extinguish all differences and unfriendliness instantaneously by a mutual flash of that love which is immortal.

The human Soul is capable of inconceivable expansion; its sensibilities are pure and almost immeasurable. The female Spirit feels a boundless, undiminishable love; the male is conscious of a high and insurmountable wisdom; and these embodied principles irresistibly seek and implore the presence of one another. To every individual, its counterpart—the one most loved—is the purest, the greatest, and the most beautiful, of all human beings; others may be beautiful and attractive, and may possess in reality many more accomplishments; but *to the lover*, the *one beloved* is the most beautiful; because there is *felt* an inwrought adaptation of desire to desire, impulse to impulse, organization to organization, Soul to Soul! This philosophy of marriage is that which angels know—the only true marriage, which originated with the Divine Mind; which is sometimes prophetically or incipiently indicated on the earth; which is enjoyed in all spheres of angelic and seraphic life; and which is spontaneously established by the sublime Law of Association that conjugally unites Atom to Atom, Spirit to Spirit, Angel to Seraph, and God to the Universe!

These principles of matrimonial association are, to the spiritually enlightened, altogether self-evident, chaste, and exalting; and it seems almost like "an act of supererogation," to venture the addition of a single thought with reference to the daily application of these principles to mankind. Nevertheless, upon reflection, a practical application of these truths is greatly to be desired, and a few suggestions concerning it are here deemed wisdom.

In the first place: a female, in seeking her congenial associate, should, particularly and especially, desire a companion with social, moral, and intellectual qualifications adequate to the position of friend, counselor, protector, lover, and governor. Her affections should not be purchased with gold and glittering ornaments; she should not fix her thoughts upon personal beauty, and her affections upon rich possessions, that fade away in the "trial hour;" but let the purity and permanency of mind—the fullness and congeniality of soul—be the foundation of her attachment, and she will never repent the "hour of marriage," as too many are compelled to do after having yielded themselves up to some external fascination or excitement, and thus secured to themselves a rudimental life-time of sadness and misery.

And it is very wrong to enter upon the marriage state early in life. This is a sad error of American women. The joy, beauty, and perfections of the female character are naturally developed in maturer years; but, owing to the general encouragements to precocious development and the unchaste and improper marriages which result from such encouragements, the female is usually *depressed, perplexed, and loaded with maternal cares*, at a period when youth should be allowed its full and perfect development.

It is my impression that a physiological law will be unfolded to man, calculated to suggest and regulate the period when marriage is alone chaste and righteous. I anxiously await the discovery and application of this principle. Meanwhile, the male should seek the female with the most pure and unselfish motives—the principle of an *internal* affinity should alone actuate him in his desires for a conjugal companion. There is no security, no probability of happiness, separate from principle. The indwelling consciousness of right, in every mind, can not be violated with impunity. Insensibility may be induced with opiates or alcohol, and the dictates of conscience may be silenced with a succession of physical excitements; but when the body will no longer yield to opiates or diversion, then comes the "tug of war" in the soul. The slightest impression of wrong doing comes boldly up before the imperial court of conscience, every unholy thought is a prisoner before the reason, and thus every man experiences the legitimate consequences of his sins against the Holy Ghost, which can not be forgiven by any person or principle, but only *outlived* by a righteous life.

THE PHILOSOPHY OF MORAL FREEDOM.

Is Man a Free Agent?

It is impossible to calculate the innumerable evil consequences which have proceeded from an *affirmative*, or the good that may flow from a *negative*, decision of the question under present consideration. It lies at the foundations of social re-organization. It is a fundamental and indispensable question in theology; and I am perfectly aware that the whole Christian superstructure is suspended or sustained by the confidently asserted and supposed truth that *man is a free agent.* It is maintained, by the so styled orthodox portion of Christendom, that original sin is a consequence of man's personal freedom; hence the great sustaining pillars of the Christian religion—Original sin, Atonement, Faith, and Regeneration—stand upon the alleged truth of man's individual and moral freedom.

Acknowledging the truthfulness of this theological hypothesis, clergymen teach their congregations that each individual possesses the power to decide upon, and eternally fix, his future position and character; that he can choose between good and evil; follow God or Baal; tread the broad road or narrow path; and secure to himself a permanent residence in hell or in heaven, as he wills. Upon the foundation of individual free agency, also, rests the entire system of past and present jurisprudence—the system of merit and demerit—praise and blame—rewards and punishments. Impanneled juries render their verdicts; statesmen legislate their rules of government; and kings command their subjects upon the supposed truth of the freedom of the human will. Thus it is evident that a vast variety of relations and proceedings have their support and justification only on the assumption that the Human Will is unqualifiedly free and unrestrained.

The profoundest and most spiritually illuminated minds have gravely affirmed and argumentatively defended this question. It is astonishing to trace through human history the mighty phalanx of intellects which have rallied their forces in defense of what they conceived to be the truth of individual freedom. But notwithstanding this formidable array of oriental authorities, and of scholastic disquisitions and decisions, upon this cardinal question in canonical theology, I am nevertheless impressed to enter the field against them, and demonstrate the fallacy of their decisions, by proving (as far as a negative is susceptible of proof) that man is, in every possible sense, a being of necessity—a depending and necessary part of the universal Whole.

Man enjoys a twofold relation to the universe; there exists a *physical* and a *spiritual* relation; the physical relation is the connection which subsists between the *body* and *external* nature, to elements and objects, time and space; and the spiritual relation is the conjunction which subsists between the *mind* and *internal* Nature—or to purity, to truth, to justice and to Deity.

We will now examine the question, *Is man physically a Free Agent?* more minutely.

Unconsulted, unsolicited, and unable to change or improve itself, the human organization is introduced to physical nature; and by the provisions of parental love it is nourished and developed; but without food, air, light, heat, and exercise, the individual would disorganize and cease to exist as a physical being. This statement is self-evidently true and incontrovertible.

The question under investigation commences at this point. I presume it is distinctly evident to every philosophical intellect, that if the individual is a *free agent*, his freedom would exist prior to his natural birth. If the mind is intrinsically free—if it is totally independent, unrestrained, uninfluenced, untrammeled by any object, element, or circumstance in physical nature,—then would the individual be qualified to select, from the vast system of Nature, his own anatomy, his own cerebral structure, his own temperament and organic powers. But is this a truth? Nay; there is an infinite contrariety of physical organizations, each representing the various elements, objects, and influences which have acted *upon*, or entered *into*, and diversified, the respective constitutions of their immediate progenitors. I think it will be conceded that no being is possessed of the ability or liberty to direct the formation of his own body, and consequently that, at least in this respect, *man is a creature of necessity.*

The beautiful and acknowledged sciences of anatomy, physiology, and phrenology, demonstrate the absolute *dependence* of the body upon surrounding elements and circumstances. If man is physically in a state of freedom, it would be absurd for any individual to remain with a black skin, with a defective cranium, with a weak physiological structure; because he could, and probably would, change and improve these peculiarities of his organization, when and as he desired; and he would not, supposing him to be in a state of physical freedom, be under the necessity of breathing the air to sustain life, of eating material substances to preserve bodily strength, of reposing to refresh and restore organic and muscular vigor; but he could, by simply willing to do so, exist without breathing, eating, or sleeping. Surely, all this is plain truth and simple.

Probably, the impression that *man* exists in a state of *freedom* has arisen from a highly superficial and unphilosophical view of his *apparent* independence of nature; and, also, from the incontrovertible fact that he is very superior to every other organization which is related to the subordinate kingdoms in the material creation. With regard to man's independence of nature, I feel impressed to remark, that he is as much, but no more, independent of the vast organization of matter and mind, which constitutes Nature, as are the birds in the air, the fish in the sea, the animals on the earth, and the electrical elements of the universe, which *seemingly* play *at will* in the firmament. The discerning mind can not but acknowledge, that the four temperaments—the nervous, bilious, sanguine, and lymphatic—give to different individuals various and distinctive peculiarities; and that some organizations are influenced pleasurably by heat, others unpleasantly; some persons are strengthened and gladdened by cold, while others are, by the same influence, physically debilitated and mentally depressed. In truth, when considered with reference to his physical relations to universal Nature, it is impossible to escape the conviction, that man is constantly subjected to material influences over which he can exercise no absolute control. Hence the conclusion is legitimate and inevitable, that man is *dependent* upon all nature for his subsistence and existence; and that he is perpetually and reciprocally, so to speak, both the *subject* and *master* of the various objects, elements, and causes by which he is constantly surrounded.

There is a kind of independence, based upon, or growing out of, human individuality; and, in this sense (which is at best abstract) every thing—atom, flower, man, and nature—enjoys a species of personality and independence; but abstract reasoning and observation are quite unwarrantable, because they are not in accordance with the views which nature every where presents. Nature never presents one thing as independent of all other things. No; there is not a pebble, a plant, an animal, nor a human being, which has not had *parents* and relations. Nature represents herself as *one great inseparable whole;* which whole is composed of innumerable parts and particulars; which parts are essential to, and dependent upon, one another—and throughout this stupendous, inseparable whole, there is no absolute independence. Yet the *parts* give rise to what we term *individuality*—first, from their peculiar constitution; secondly, from the quality and magnitude of the influence they are discovered to exert upon other parts and personalities. For instance,—there is a manifest *individuality* and apparent *independence* in the male and female structure—the dissimilarity between the two structures is the cause of the personality; and their personality is determined by their different actions and influence; but they can not exist independent of one another, nor of the innumerable elements and means of nourishment which surround them in nature.

The law of gravitation, of attraction, of cohesion, will never change; and, notwithstanding the alleged freedom of the human will, a man or an apple *will alike fall* should they be suddenly disengaged from any elevated position above the earth's surface. And it is coming to be seen and acknowledged that, that which is *physically and scientifically true* can not be morally and theologically false; that is to say, in Truth there is no antagonism, for God *is* Truth and unchangeable! But there proceeds from the *individuality* and *influence* of every thing existing, a kind of responsibility or *expectation;* and this responsibility, or expectation, is summed up in the simple statement, that we expect or require of every thing a continual manifestation or representation of its characteristic power and abilities. Thus, we expect (and, therefore, *require*) certain odors from the violet, the rose, the strawberry, and the peach; and this is the kind of responsibility which all individualities should be expected to sustain; but when we come to man, we are seldom disposed to manifest the same degree of rationality and justice.

Owing to the erroneous assumptions of theologians, on the freedom of man, the Church and the State hold every individual almost equally responsible for his actions. In order to illustrate the different degrees of physical freedom, and consequent responsibility, I desire to direct the reader's attention to the simple measurement of physical strength, as illustrative of the great dissimilarity of personal power and capacity.

JOHN, in consequence of a defective arrangement in his temperamental and organic systems, can raise from the earth only *fifty vounds;* and should he *will* to raise more than the above weight, it nevertheless would be impossible for him to do so.

JAMES, in consequence of having inherited the possession of a more perfect muscular and organic system, can raise from the earth *one hundred* pounds.

JOSEPH, having received from his progenitors a still more perfect organization, can raise *two hundred* pounds; and

HENRY, in consequence of his more harmonious constitutional powers, can raise *three hundred* pounds.

But neither of these individuals are capable of raising a greater weight, though they should strive to exercise what the unphilosophical class of minds term *Free Will.* The discerning intellect will readily perceive, that John deserves no more *blame* for having a weak body, than does Henry deserve *praise* for the possession of a strong one. They neither directed the formation of their own organizations, nor the bestowment of that physical strength, the measure of which is thus determined. Hence, we should *expect* from each one just that which is ascertained to be his constitutional power; and nothing more on the fallacious supposition that the mind is endowed with a perfectly free will.

The truth is simply this: Man did not make his own organization, temperament, nor vital powers; and consequently, in this relation, at least, I think it will be conceded, that man is not a *creator*, but a *creature*—that he is not a *master*, but a *circumstance.* Therefore, just in proportion to man's constitutional powers and qualifications, is he capable of thinking, acting, and influencing; and I think the generous and expansive intellect will perceive and acknowledge, that Man naturally and spontaneously *requires* of Nature what she seems to *expect* from him—thus making their dependence and *responsibility* equally a matter of unqualified necessity. For instance, John can lift from the earth no more than *fifty* pounds, which describes and measures his sphere or circle of comparative freedom, and hence he *requires* of Nature a continual contribution of air, water, heat, nourishment, &c., just in proportion to his constitutional ability to reciprocate the favor. On the other hand, Henry can raise from the earth *three hundred* pounds, which also describes and measures his sphere or circle of comparative free agency, and he also requires of Nature a corresponding supply of air, nourishment, and other means of subsistence. In still plainer language, every man should be *expected* to fill the measure of *his own* capacity; and every man should give to, and require of, Nature (and mankind is a part of Nature) physical support in proportion to his constitutional wants and powers. It will be seen that Henry can perform more than John, and consequently the former *requires* more in return; but both individuals are equally *creatures, causes,* and *circumstances;* and there will ever be a correspondence between the effects, which intrinsic and extrinsic causes produce upon them, and the effects which they develop upon and among the individuals and circumstances by which they are surrounded.

I come now to consider the "free agency" of the human mind in its superior relations—that is, as I have already said, its relations to Purity, Truth, Justice, and Deity.

It has been shown that man, as a physical being, has no absolute and unconditional freedom in his will or movements; and I am fully persuaded that the philosophical understanding will readily and cheerfully concede the proposition, that *that which is physically and scientifically true, can not be spiritually and theologically false;* for the universe is one inseparable *whole*, without antagonisms, without contradiction, and without the least possible shade of actual inconsistency.

Concerning the terms, "Free Agent," a few remarks are deemed necessary. On reflection, I think it will appear evident to the reader's mind, that the terms involve a positive contradiction. According to the highest and most popular authorities in philological research,—whose definitions of words are usually received as correct,—the term "Agency," can not be employed consistently, in connection with the word "Free," as these terms are used by theologians. Sir William Blackstone understands the term "Agency," as appropriate to the position of any individual who acts, or performs business, for another;-hence, it is proper to apply this term to the occupation of a factor, a deputy, a minister, or to the business of an attorney; but it is a positive absurdity to employ the term "Free," in the same connection. If an individual is an *agent* —if he holds an *agency*—he is necessarily transacting business for another; and it certainly will appear evident, that, should a man be thus engaged, he is not a free, but a *bound* agent; such a man is acting for another, and not for himself. Inasmuch, therefore, as these terms are inconsistent with an understanding and solution of the question under present examination, it is proper to investigate and analyze the proposition in a new and more philosophical form, viz., *Is it true that man has absolute freedom of the will?*

By *freedom of the will*, theologians, and all who are devoted to the mythological theology of modern days, understand that an individual has, from the moment he arrives at the age of discretion and responsibility, concentrated in himself a power whereby he can become the supreme ruler of his own instincts, propensities, impulses, and movements; that he can *love* or *hate*, *act* or *rest*, *preserve* and *destroy*, just as he internally wills to do; and that he can develop good or evil, truth or falsehood, heaven or hell, as, when, and where he desires. I trust no earnest disciple of mythological theology, (such as is proclaimed from popular pulpits throughout Europe and America,) will venture to accuse me of misrepresenting their definition of free agency; because it can not be denied that clergymen suppose the human soul invested with the power of selecting, at any time, whom it will follow—God, or the Devil! I have already said that the supposed truthfulness of the theological assertion, that man has an absolute "free will," is the *thread* by which the whole system of unphilosophical theology is suspended in the sacerdotal atmosphere. In other words, it is the only foundation whereon rests the entire theological superstructure, whose towering, but trembling, turrets are visible in our land, sending their discordant and lifeless proportions high up in the air—shutting out, so to speak, the broad light of heaven from the soul's aspiring gaze. Almost every sect in Christendom admits that the *Atonement* was instituted as a means, whereby mankind might escape the otherwise everlasting effects, consequent upon the commission of the "Original Sin;" and yet, at the same time, this identical *Atonement* was intended by the Divine Being, who, clergymen say, instituted it, to operate as a means of satisfying the infinite demands of eternal justice, which have been infringed by the disobedience of the first human pair.

The intelligent reader—he who does not consult superficial and popular authorities, but the sublime and everlasting teachings of Nature, Reason, and Intuition—such a reader need not be informed, that all these cardinal principles in theology are wholly and unqualifiedly erroneous. Even the doctrine of there having been at any period in the earth's dark and mysterious history, a "first human pair," sounds to the ear of a geologist like the tale of an Egyptian priest. But how transcendently absurd are the suppositions of clergymen, respecting the higher consequences of man's having in his possession a free, untrammeled will! It was the supposed freedom of the *Will* which caused the fabled angel to make war in heaven; and, according to the celebrated Pollok, it is the power, which, by being impiously exercised, peoples the innumerable caverns of Hell. This impressive and orthodox poet affirms that—

> "Each has his conscience, each his reason, will,
> And understanding, for himself to search,
> To choose, reject, believe, consider, act."

This affirmation I am impressed to consider a complete generalization of the belief of nearly all the sects in Christendom.

The opinion entertained by the most advanced believers in oriental mythology, (or popular theology,) and literature, is, that Man is born on a middle ground, being especially inclined to neither goodness nor righteousness; that he occupies an intermediate position between holiness and wickedness—having the bequeathed ability to select his associations, to refuse the evil and choose the good, or, *vice versa*, to reject the good and choose the evil. And by the most advanced believers in oriental mythology, I do not mean the *forty* sects that have arisen from the five hundred different and conflicting versions of the Bible, since the publication of the sacred canon, but I mean the three grand divisions of protestantism, viz., Calvinism, Methodism, and Swedenborgianism. These sects imbibe and advocate the opinion, that man is situated, intermediately, between *good* and *evil;* that he has the power to reject the one or the other; and, that man thus determines his own eternal character, destiny, and situation in the world beyond the grave.

Justified by the impression that there is but a very little pure reasoning among men, I will, without bestowing any more attention upon the speculations of clergymen and sectarians, with regard to this subject, proceed to consider the popular doctrines of "free agency;" and I desire the reader to open his understanding, and be exceedingly watchful as to the legitimacy of the conclusions which I shall develop by the following process of ratiocination. I will commence with the most recent improvements in the doctrine of free agency, and which are adopted by the most advanced believers in mythological theology; hence I begin with this proposition—"*Man is inclined neither to goodness nor wickedness.*"

The absolute falsity of this theological proposition is so self-evident and conspicuous, that, but for the general fear or inability to reason on these points, which many minds feel, I could pass it by unanalyzed and unexplained. Yet, when I behold the multitude of pernicious errors, and closely combined evils, which have no other origin or foundation than the asserted and received truthfulness of this proposition, I feel strongly moved to attempt its examination.

To begin then:—It has been incontrovertibly demonstrated, that *Man* is the noblest and most perfect work of God; that, to develop his *physical*, and to eternally individualize his *spiritual* organization, all the vast, stupendous and innumerable processes of Nature were instituted; that, in order to unfold the divine image in the human form, the Divine Mind breathed the essential elements of His inmost nature, through nature's innumerable organizations, into the organization of *Man;* and, therefore, demonstrated that man is the ultimate development of universal matter and universal spirit —that he (man) is the most perfect embodiment of matter and mind in the immeasurable universe, except the Divine Mind itself! In consequence of this sublime derivation and organization of the human soul, the assertion that man is inclined neither to good nor evil is rendered totally erroneous. For if it be conceded, and science compels this concession, that man is the highest organization in the stupendous system of nature—that he is a microcosm; that he *lives*, and *moves*, and has a *being* in God's universal spirit—

then, I ask, can he be a *passive* creature when first introduced upon the earth? Can he be born without a spring of action—without an impulse—without an attraction? Is man, when first created, an *empty* vessel—a mere shell—into which flows the spirit of wickedness or holiness, as his uneducated and unexperienced "will" determines?

Surely, all nature and pure reason contradict this theological proposition; because every intelligent individual knows, by the mysterious workings of the elements of his own interior soul, that wants—desires—attractions—and impulses, are born with him; and he knows that *internally*, he is a living Whole. In truth, man inherits *inclinations* from his birth. Those which proceed from his immediate progenitors are temporal, but those which he receives from his Heavenly Father are eternal! Man is not, therefore, situated between *good* and *evil*, or heaven and hell; because, I repeat, he is the *superior* production of God and Nature; because he stands on the summit of creation—a little lower than the angels—requiring simply a constitutional harmony, and a spiritual development, to understand and enjoy their continued association. Nor is man merely a recipient. He is filled with *motion*, *life*, *sensation*, and *intelligence;* he is God manifested in the flesh; he is a son of the Most Glorious and High!

But there is another proposition which may not be wholly unworthy of notice. I allude to the following—"Man, although inclined neither to good nor evil when introduced into this probationary existence, yet possesses the power of choosing between them."

The enlightened intellect will readily perceive, that both of these theological propositions were expressly instituted for the purpose of rendering apparently philosophical, the assertions of the Primitive History, (the Bible,) on this subject,—that is, to render man's moral attitude reasonably consistent with the biblical statements which imply the "free agency" of the soul. But let us examine the last proposition.

Is it philosophical or true to affirm that an individual can discriminate between good and evil, without possessing either an inclination toward them, or an understanding of what is meant by good and evil? It is said that man has no natural inclination toward evil or good, and that he is neither one nor the other, until after he acts or chooses; and that his action and choice are solely the offspring of his moral freedom. But is this statement consistent with truth and pure philosophy? Surely, without *inclination* the soul can not experience any attraction; and without *experience* the human mind can exercise neither freedom nor reason. Hence it is unreasonable to suppose that the spirit will seek good or evil without first having an internal desire for one or the other; and it certainly is still *more* unreasonable to suppose that an individual can exercise a preference for any thing, without *first* having an *understanding* of that thing's nature and influence. I, therefore, feel impressed to affirm, and I know the subject justifies any strength of assertion, that man does not and can not *select* his associations without a personal knowledge of their character and influence; and, that, in order to obtain this knowledge, he is dependent upon surrounding suggestions and interior promptings, both material and spiritual; and, consequently, all these premises being incontrovertibly true, I am led to conclude that man has no absolute freedom of the Will.

According to the oriental fable, which is in some particulars very beautiful and symbolical of truth, the *first* female was informed, upon the highest authority, that the fruits of one tree were good, and that the fruits of the other tree were exceedingly evil. But she did not *know* the truthfulness of this statement, and the consequence of this ignorance on her part, was, that this information inflamed her uneducated mind and desires to such an extent, that she could no longer resist the temptation to acquire a knowledge of this truth, by an actual experiment,—just as a child, unless it receives the experience and testimony of others in all confidence, will try the fire in order to ascertain whether that element is really hot or cold. Here, then—at the alleged beginning of the human race—is manifested the universal truth, that causes will produce corresponding effects; because here it is seen that the temptation or information imparted to Eve, overpowered her inexperienced spirit, and she was moved to act in a corresponding manner upon the spirit of her companion. Now it must certainly be admitted that *reasonable* action or selection depends invariably upon prior experience and understanding. Consequently, the human mind, in order to reasonably choose between good and evil, must first ascertain by actual experience, or by interior perception, what good and evil are. How is it possible, therefore, for an individual to be a free moral agent, without having an infinite ability to discriminate between the seeming and the actual, between the false and true?

To fully comprehend this question, it is essential that we understand the nature and qualifications of the human soul. If we obtain a true knowledge of man, we will proceed forthwith to change our thoughts and actions respecting him. We would change our penal codes, our principles of government, and the character of our religious and moral instructions,—I may add, our whole social structure. For when we once perceive and realize the truth, that man can not control his belief and opinions, nor *all* of his actions and character, our souls will expand with compassion and benevolence; and we will combine our labor, our capital and talents, to improve his social, moral, and spiritual condition.

How unreasonable and deplorable it is to teach a doctrine so dogmatic and despotic as to be under the necessity of enforcing its adoption by threats and denunciations! And yet our religious teachers, the clergymen, do it perpetually. Surely nothing can be more unphilosophical and despotic than the passage—"He that believeth shall be saved, and he that believeth not shall be damned;" because no human soul can either believe or disbelieve without a sufficient preponderation of evidence. The wild savage is not to be damned for not believing in the existence, life, and miracles of Jesus; nor is the Christian to be blessed for believing them; because neither can manufacture his own convictions—can not have absolute control over the promptings and inclinations of his own mind. If the reader desires to test the truth of this assertion, let him try this moment to *hate* a much beloved friend, or to *Love* a very repulsive and disagreeable person—to doubt the existence of any trees, stones, and men on the earth—to *disbelieve* the reality of his own existence.

Swedenborg asserts man's personal and moral freedom, and, at the same time, fixes him in a position *between* two mighty invisible attractions—one Hell, the other Heaven—a class of *good*, and a class of *evil*, spirits on either side, ready to impart whatever *thought*, *doctrine*, *passion*, or *error* the individual feels disposed to entertain! Now, in the face of this statement, the reasonable intellect inquires—How is it possible for man to be "*free*," while pent up between two contending forces—between such positive attractions? Is an object which is *braced* on all sides, in a state of freedom? Reason, the soul's prime minister, replies unequivocally in the negative; because man, materially and spiritually, possesses universal affinities which he did not create, which he can not control, which he can not destroy; but he is compelled to *act as he is acted upon*, and to manifest character according to his constitutional capacity and social situation. Thus, even admitting the affirmations of Swedenborg, that man is introduced into this world between two great eternal antagonisms, Heaven and Hell, it is distinctly obvious tha man would not, because he could not, be in a state of absolute moral freedom. Yet, there really exists a *species* of freedom, liberty, or independence in human thoughts and actions, and which, though comparative, gives rise to many misapprehensions as to the extent of man's accountability, responsibility, or obligations to the HOLY MAGNET of the universe, which is Deity.

The character and extent of this independence, *which is altogether comparative*, I will now proceed to explain.

As is illustrated in the case of the four individuals already mentioned, who were designed to present a measurement of physical capacity and strength, I will consider the relative powers and actions of the same four men—each born of the same parents, and commencing their manhood in a similar social situation—viz., *in extreme poverty!*

JOHN, the first man, is in the possession of a weak and combative mind; his wisdom principle, or reason, has been called into action but very little; his animal powers and propensities have ruled his better attributes, as barbarians once ruled the nations of the earth; he is vain and ambitious; and, contrasting his social situation and prospects in the world, with the plenteousness and advantages of others, he becomes exceedingly nervous and impatient. Yet, notwithstanding this constitutional susceptibility to the slightest causes of uneasiness and dissatisfaction, he endeavors to struggle along, revealing his nervousness and impatience to no one, and disturbing no individual or community. At length, however, this weak-minded, vain, and ambitious man, is unexpectedly thrown out of employment; and the pangs, the mortifications, and the disadvantages of *poverty*, sting and wound his sensitive and weak intellect into an uncontrollable state of despairing passion. A wild, reckless desperation of mind succeeds this passion, just as a fever succeeds a chill; and he forthwith plans the destruction of his employer. But here the reader inquires—"How can one man 'plan' the destruction of another, unless he be both a *sane* and a *free* agent?" The answer is briefly written: there is a Law, universal and eternal in its nature, which flows and governs unchangeably throughout the entire infinitude of matter and mind—and this law is *Order*. Hence in obedience to this universal tendency, there is nothing but that gets into something like order and arrangement. The savage marches his tribes, the birds fly, the fishes swim, the seasons come and go, all representing an order and harmony more or less obvious. The affrighted steed, though dashing madly through the crowded streets, preserves an indwelling *order* in the motion of his heart, his muscles, and in the galvanic actions of his brain. There is no insanity so extreme,—there is no hallucination, no disorder, so nebulous and chaotic,—but that is attended by something resembling a periodicity of movement, and an order of position in the constitution of things. So with *John.* He, like every other man, possesses the *Secretiveness* of the serpent, the *Cautiousness* of the cat, the *Ingenuity* of the beaver, the *Destructiveness* of the tiger, and the *Pride* of the lion. These elements of the human soul, if not tamed and harmoniously exercised by the wisdom principle, may become inflamed and violent as the beasts of the forest; and, yet, there will be in their manifestations of fury, a kind of *order*, which is the indwelling tendency of every thing in being.

Let us not shrink from the legitimate conclusions to which Truth conducts the soul. I am impressed to present no theory; only to write concerning those things which *actually* exist in the constitution of God and Nature; and man is a part of this great living Body. I say, then, that John *plans* the destruction of his employer; he takes advantage of the first opportunity favorable to the accomplishment of this deed; he commits the *murder*, possesses himself of all the available wealth about the person of the fallen man, and hastily leaves the country.

James, the second man, has inherited a similar sensitiveness of mind; is also vain and ambitious; but he is more secretive than combative; he feels more of the disposition of the *serpent* in his nature than that of the *tiger.* Like his brother, the various reflections of indigence upon his character and habits move him to a corresponding uneasiness and discontent. He sees and feels the advantages which more fortunately situated individuals have over him,—that they can enjoy what, and go where, he can not; and, reasoning superficially, perhaps *soundly*, he feels that he is not to blame for all this difference; that he had done nothing to merit the unfortunateness of his situation; that others have done nothing to merit their wealth and luxury; that his neighbor was born rich and he was born poor; and, inasmuch as the fortunate classes do nothing toward reconciling him to his situation—manifesting no disposition to ameliorate his condition, and to divide with him—he does not see but that he is totally justified in the attempt to help himself to the superabundance. But, his combativeness being small, he does not see that he should yield to the slightest impulse to commit murder—in truth, he has never felt any such impulse since his birth,—but, his *secretiveness* being large, he sees that his impulse to plunder, to steal, to appropriate unto himself the property of others, is his immediate and overpowering disposition. He consequently yields, *because the temptation is stronger than his restraining powers*, and becomes a robber!

JOSEPH, the third man, has also inherited a structure of mind analogous to his brothers; he is sensitive, vain, and ambitious; he has small combativeness, small secretiveness, but very *large benevolence.* The same combination of influences and circumstances surround and act upon him, as upon his brothers; and he is wounded and goaded by wants in various forms and degrees of severity. He sees precisely what his brothers see, concerning their own situation, and the social position of others; and feels that there is enough for him in the possession of the rich, even after they have built their splendid mansions and churches; and gratified many of their most extravagant desires. But he does not wish to *injure* the better situated individual, nor to take his property *unasked;* yet, it is clear *to his mind* that the rich man can spare a few pence without inconvenience. Hence, Joseph, having no particular disposition to labor when work could be obtained, nor any success in obtaining an occupation when he had the disposition, yields to his temptation to *beg* for a subsistence.

Henry, the fourth man, possesses an organization vastly superior to his three brothers. He has a full share of energy and self-government. His organs, phrenologically speaking, are harmoniously developed. Combativeness, secretiveness, benevolence, and self-esteem, are full, and in constant subordination to the superior faculties of judgment and understanding. And he, too, is extremely poor; he thinks upon the superior advantages and circumstances of the wealthy; he is very industrious to acquire means of personal subsistence and comfort, and is surrounded and affected by every cause, internal and external, which acted upon his brothers; but, notwithstanding all this, he is neither moved to kill, to steal, nor to solicit alms. He is thrown out of employment—is destitute of food—is overcome by prostration and disease, and at last *dies of starvation.*

Here are presented four cases,—whose parallelisms are discoverable in many portions of France, England, Ireland, and America,—where individual crime is limited to, and measured by, individual capacity. John, being the weakest in his moral constitution, was consequently overcome the quickest; but Henry, having the strongest and most harmonious intellect, was not so affected by those *causes* which moved John, James, and Joseph, to the commission of those crimes and acts, which are termed *murdering*, *robbing*, and *begging.*

Thus, it is seen, that *four* different individuals starting from the same place, were caused to tread *four* distinct paths, and to arrive at *four* distinct terminations. The enlightened mind will perceive that these distinct paths and terminations, were the result, not of "Free Will," but of absolute and unconditional necessity. The first man was a *victim* of an inflamed organ of combativeness—the primary cause of which inflammation was extreme *poverty*. The second man was a *victim* of an inflamed organ of secretiveness; the third man was a *victim* of misdirected benevolence; and the fourth man was a *victim* of unmitigated poverty. Society was the *first cause* of these disastrous terminations, because it permits extreme poverty; and the parents were the *second cause* of these fates, for they imparted the organizations, which, by being so obviously dissimilar, caused the dissimilar terminations of their four sons.

From the foregoing, the conclusion is certainly legitimate, that an individual is accountable according to his capacity; and by accountability or responsibility, I mean, that an individual is to be measured and estimated according to his actual merit and capacity, and, that corresponding *thoughts* and *deeds* are to be expected to flow from him—provided all external conditions and circumstances are not *very* unfavorable to this legitimate manifestation of his character.

Inasmuch as Man is both an *actor* and a *circumstance*—both a *cause* and an *effect*—he should be treated, not as a being having the *will* and *power* to do what he desires, when and where he pleases, but he should be *born*, *educated*, *situated*, rewarded and punished, as a TREE, which is capable of yielding an abundance of *good fruit*, only when it is properly organized, and correspondingly conditioned in a GOOD SOIL!

The doctrine of the free will, or agency, of the soul, is positively contradicted by every thing in nature and man. Every thought, every motive, every deed, and motion that is wrought in the human constitution, arises from the operation of the interior laws and essences, and from the combinations of the physical and mental economy, and these laws of our nature are inevitable and unchangeable. The *comparative* freedom which man seemingly inherits, coevally with his individuality, is *exactly* illustrated by all the independence which a gold fish is perceived to enjoy in the globe of water. The fish *is at liberty* to swim in any direction it desires; nevertheless it is dependent upon the water, this upon the glass globe, this upon the window of the building, this upon the earth, this upon the sun, and thus *there is one unbroken chain of dependencies from the fish to the Deity!* So with man. He is *free*, physically, to move about upon this globe of earth, but he can not live without the perpetual contributions of food, air, light, &c., which flow unto him from Nature; and he is spiritually (or morally) free to move about *within* the circle described by his capacity and degree of development; but beyond this circle he has no more freedom than the fish as above described.

Although Pope, in his "Essay on Man," revealed the true relation which subsists between man and nature, and proved that human Will is subordinate to God's Will, yet he was unfortunately moved to contradict this sublime truth in his "Universal Prayer." I am impressed to regard this as a great departure from the uniform expression of wisdom, visible throughout this author's works. He evidently sacrificed philosophy to theology, when he affirmed that God in—

> "Binding nature fast in fate,
> Left *free* the Human Will."

It would be as consistent and as true for me to affirm that an artisan made a watch *complete* and *united* in all its parts, yet—

> *Left free the middle wheel!*

It is not possible for God to bind nature fast and leave uncircumscribed the freedom of the soul; for Man *is a part* of Nature, and he is designed, ultimately, to move as harmoniously in the great whole, as the heart in the human body. The laws of God we can not alter; and, notwithstanding thousands of clergymen, commentators and magistrates, believe, and teach, and act, and punish, and blame, and praise, upon the *supposed* truth of man's "free moral agency," yet the stupendous panorama of the universe will move on in its sublime and harmonious ORDER, and TRUTH will live unchanged forever!

Verily, the poet was right in affirming that—

> "We will, and act, and talk of liberty,
> And all our wills, and all our doings, both,
> Are [now] limited within this little life;
> *Free Will* is but NECESSITY in play,—
> The chattering of the golden reins which guide
> The *purposes* of Heaven to their goal."

This conception of man's moral state is an unfailing source of consolation and happiness. It removes, at once, all doubts as to the ultimate issue of this life; it satisfies the soul that the 'Lord God Omnipotent reigneth;' it makes the Deity the Great Moral Sovereign Ruler of all human and angelic hosts; and it especially points tó the reconstruction of society, and to new methods of educating and of punishing (rather of reforming) the human race.

In conclusion, let me impress the reader, that this philosophy of human motives and movements, develops the religion of distributive justice—the spirit of compassion—the law of love to man—and the glorious morality of universal benevolence; and I may add, that it may open the reader's love and wisdom to a better and higher perception and appreciation of the nature of man, of the goodness and justice of God, and of the beauties of His material and spiritual universe.

THE PHILOSOPHY OF IMMORTALITY.

Although the uncultivated intuition of the human mind has been sufficient to inspire all men, and races of men, with a desire for, and an undefined belief in, the soul's endless existence; nevertheless, the reader can not but perceive the gradual decay and disappearance of this instinctive and undefined faith as the reason-principle begins to be developed and exercised upon all philosophical and ethical themes of thought. This is a favorable prognostication. It signifies that the clouds and dark forebodings which superstition has thrown over the speculations of the human mind, concerning the probable realities and possessions of the other world, are to be consumed by the sunlight of a free and healthy philosophy of Nature's divine revelations, of the mysterious beauties which pertain to the moral government of God, and of the real possessions of the spiritual Universe. All this, I think, the reader's reason will readily recognize.

But in this place it is necessary to again impress the proposition, That no substance or power of any character, whether physical or intellectual, possesses within itself the power of self-investigation or comprehension. Therefore you can comprehend and trace, analogically and correctly, grosser substances to the formation of yourselves; but you arrive at Mind, Intelligence, *Spirit*,—and though this is the principle which has enabled you to explore and comprehend all below it, you find that this itself is necessarily vague and indefinite to you. And hence there is either too much belief as respects this principle and its composition, or too much *disbelief;* and each is a natural consequence of a principle attempting to investigate *itself.*

Having no means to arrive distinctly and evidently at a knowledge of the essence and principle of Intelligence, you are compelled, so to speak, to let me occupy the superior condition, and thereby reveal what you would willingly and joyously receive, as corresponding to your natural yearnings, and answering your desires for a higher, nobler, and more dignified understanding of your nature and its legitimate offices and ultimate destination.

Perhaps the philosophy of the soul's innate or constitutional Immortality may be more familiarly placed before the reader's mind by presenting the following letter, and the reply, than by any other process of ratiocination.

St. Louis, April 10th, 1848.

Mr. A. J. Davis :—I have read your Book, and am a believer in most that I have read, but am not so well convinced of the immortality of the Soul as I wish to be. I therefore write you, believing you a philanthropist, and that you are willing to increase light, knowledge, and truth. By the immortality of the Soul, I mean the unending duration of the intellectual powers, the faculties of thought—the mind, without ever losing its identity. For if at death such a change occurs as to render the soul totally oblivious or forgetful of the past, so that the memory of our past earthly existence shall be lost to us forever, it would be to *me* equivalent to annihilation. What proofs have we of a continuation of identity at death? I believe the soul or spirit does not lose its identity, but continues progressively increasing in knowledge, wisdom, and happiness. But still I am not as well convinced as I wish to be.

My object in writing you is, simply, as an inquirer after truth and light, to be convinced wherein I am wrong, and to be set right; but more especially to obtain *the proofs* in favor, not only of the immortality of the Soul, but of its perpetual never-ending *identity*, recollections of the past, recognition of friends in the future state, &c.

I hope you will answer this letter, either directly, or cause something of yours on the above subject to appear.

Yours, &c. J. S. F.

Reply.

New York, Sept. 15th, 1848.

Esteemed Inquirer:—Your letter came while I was engaged in a very minute and elaborate anatomical, physiological, and pathological investigation with reference to a design to communicate to the world a simple and higher kind of medical information; and while absorbed in my interior researches, it is both painful and injurious to allow foreign subjects to break in upon them. This will account for, and excuse, my protracted silence concerning the unspeakably important inquiries embodied in your letter.

But before laying the foundation upon which rests the individualization of the elements of the human mind, as well as all true knowledge concerning it, I feel impressed to say a few words in reference to the origin and influence of three kinds of belief therein, which are entertained by many laymen and clergymen, and by individuals in general, viz.: a belief of ignorance, a belief of desire, and a belief of the understanding.

1. *A belief of ignorance* is a faith unaccompanied, and consequently unsupported, by adequate reasons. It is derived from the hereditary inclinations of the mind, or from doctrinal education imparted by the prevailing Theology or influence within the sphere o. which the individual exists.

2. *A belief of desire* is an instinctive or intuitive faith in the endless perpetuation of personal existence. It arises from the central

desire of the human mind, which is unconsciously considered as a living internal prophecy of its eternal destiny. This belief is grounded in no universal principles, nor has it any substantial basis upon which to rest and stand secure, except an inference derived from its own aspirations, and the general tendency of all created things.

3. *A belief of the understanding* is a faith based upon absolute and unequivocal knowledge. It grows out of a complete recognition and thorough understanding of those immutable principles which flow from the bosom of the Divine Cause into the Universe, and by which every thing is governed with an unerring and unchangeable government.

The influence of the first is to generate *Skepticism*, because the believer can neither furnish himself, nor an inquirer after truth and rest, with a tangible and substantial reason, and because, too, he refers the intelligent seeker to historical accounts of supernatural phenomena and occurrences, at once startling, absurd, and incomprehensible. The influence of the second is to cause an *anxiety* in the understanding, because the believer has no ground upon which to rest his faith except internal desires, external inferences, and vague probabilities; and because when he attempts to investigate the basis of his belief (which is seldom ever attempted) he discovers it to be unsound, and consequently unsatisfactory—not sufficiently expansive and strong to cover the whole ground occupied by doubts and objections, and to remove all obstructions to a full confidence in the sublime truths of an immortal personality.

The influence of the third is to promote *happiness*, because the believer can give a reason for the faith and hope within him—because his understanding is convinced beyond the sphere of ignorance, and desire, and inference, and probability—and because he has a divine guaranty in the fact of individual existence; because he is himself a note drawn on the Bank of an eternal life, and signed by an Almighty Hand, payable in such installments as are measured by his entrance into, and departure from, each sphere on his voyage around eternity.

I think you will agree with me when I say that you occupy the second position with regard to a belief in a future state; for you "believe the Soul or Spirit does not lose its identity, but continues progressively increasing in knowledge, wisdom, and happiness." But like thousands of our fellow-men who strive to believe in and hope for immortality—you are not in the third position, else you could not have said, "Still I am not as well convinced as I wish to be." Now that we may obtain and secure a belief of the understanding, which alone communicates internal rest and positive encouragement in the faithful discharge of our duties on earth, I will proceed to place before you "what proofs we have of a continuation of identity at death," or to show why we are immortal.

The foundation of the whole superstructure is the absolute indestructibility of Matter, or of that Universal substance which gives us a tangible individuality, and which constitutes the outer physical organization of the Great Positive Mind. Matter is eternal; and is every where present. It is in all things, and *is* all things, and there is nothing that is not matter or substance. Upon the universality and indestructibility of matter, therefore, rests the all-glorious reality of an eternal life. But now the question spontaneously arises, how does matter constitute an individual, and how, or by what means, is that individual rendered immortal? Let us interrogate Nature. She points up to the eternal Mind, who instituted laws that manifest themselves through her unfoldings, and she bids us consider the principles of Association, Progression, and Development.

Under the powerful and constant direction of these laws, we perceive the unbroken and perpetual tendency of all forms and substances toward unity, perfection, and organization. From the Great Central Mind proceed innumerable elements and substances which form innumerable nuclei. These individually attract those elements and substances that have corresponding individual affinities; and these accumulate, and condense, and purify, and form suns, systems of suns, comets, planets and satellites. Then from the central mass and fertile womb of each planet, rudimental particles ascend, and undergoing a process similar to that by which the planets were made and developed, they ultimate and develop mineral combinations.

Then again, by the incessant action of body upon body, and essence upon essence, and substance upon substance, mineral compositions not only generate vivifying fluids and mediums, such as electricity, magnetism, &c., but actually and constantly lose themselves in vegetable organizations. By a similar action, and a new and higher combination of appropriate particles, the vegetable loses itself in the animal organization, and this emerges into the organization and development of Man.

You will doubtless perceive that *man* never loses his identity in subordinate forms and organizations—that he is not their slave as they are his, nor is he designed to supply them with appropriate nourishment, as they supply him; but that minerals, and vegetables, and animals, all lose their identity in man, for he is the grand concentrated production and union of them all.

Thus in the planet, in the mineral, in the vegetable, and especially in the human body, do we behold unmistakable manifestations of the laws of association, progression, and development; or of the universal and constitutional tendency of all matter toward a state of unity or individualization. This brings us to the contemplation of a conspicuous reality, viz.: that every organization seems more and more complete and perfect in position, and influence, and importance than any previous one, from the mineral up to Man. All forms inferior and subordinate to Man, are but *parts* of him; and in order to fully comprehend why man occupies the highest position, exerts the strongest influence, and is in every way the most important, we must proceed to consider the use for which man was made.

Under this head I will place an extract from my medical work.* Its teachings are not according to the decisions of popular physiologists, but I venture to believe they will be found in accordance with the revealments of Nature and Reason. When speaking concerning the brain, I say, "The brain has three uses or functions. 1 To receive the omnipresent moving essence of the Great Divine Spirit, which resides in and is extracted from all elements and substances in being, especially those which administer to the nourishment of the body, and to the gratification of its various desires and senses. 2. To concentrate, and refine, and elaborate this all-animating essence, and to dispense it to the appropriate part or parts of the dependent system, according to its (the essence's) relative degrees of refinement and progressive plans of manifestation, viz.: as Motion, Life, and Sensation. 3. To give this essence its germinal and *indestructible* organization, and to connect it with elements and substances in the outer world, by which connection the Brain is instrumental in the movement and government of the body—and to enable the interior organization to manifest intelligence in reference to itself and external things."

It is clear, I think, that the physical organism of man is designed to elaborate, and to establish, the eternal individuality of the human mind. Other organisms are less perfect, and consequently inadequate to the same end. But it may be said that many animals possess qualifications identical with, and in some instances superior to man; and that the reason is not sufficiently clear why man can give birth to an immortal spirit, and why the animal can not. I would reply that man is the ultimate organization—that Nature is a perfect, and powerful, and stupendous Machine, constructed upon

* See "Great Harmonia," Vol. I. The Physician.

the Universal Mechanical principles (so to express it) of association, progression and development, by which machine the man is manufactured; and that the explanation is to be found by considering man, in the capacity of individualizing the spirit, as a machine. Animals are but parts of men; they are but portions of the human mechanism. Let us think of an illustration. Suppose you desire to construct a pin machine. In your mind the machine is first created—it stands in all its parts complete in your memory. You proceed to collect and correspondingly perfect the parts with reference to the whole. You adjust the parts, the machine is developed, and its work is admirably performed. The work is to *individualize* or make the pin. Now with the same propriety it might be asked, why can not those parts make a pin as well as the machine, which is a congregation or combination of them all?

It is evident that the *use* of Nature is to individualize Man; that it is the *use* of man to individualize the spirit. But now the question spontaneously arises: how can the spirit exist independent of the body, and how can its personality be preserved? I am taught to reply that the spirit can exist separate and independent of the body on the same ground that the body can exist separate from, or independent of, Nature. For Nature made the body, even as the body made the mind; and, be it remembered, the same unchangeable and eternal principles of creation operate uniformly every where and at all times. And I am further taught that the spirit preserves its identity on the ground that every organization is absolutely different. This fact precludes the possibility of absorption, or amalgamation, or disorganization. The difference in the arrangement of inherent elements establishes the individual in this life, and through all eternity. If spirits were constituted alike they would inevitably and irresistibly gravitate to but one center, would desire to occupy but one position, and to fill but one locality. But being constitutionally dissimilar, they can not, nor do they desire to, be absorbed by, or amalgamated with, other spirits, nor can they lose themselves, as some have been led to suppose, in the universal Spirit, or Great Positive Mind.

There are three evidences, therefore, that the Soul will preserve its identity after the change which is called death. They are these: 1. It is designed that Nature should develop the body. 2. It is designed that the Body should develop the Mind. 3. It is designed that the Mind should develop itself differently from other minds, and to live forever. These are no inferences, no conclusions based upon hypothetical reasons, but they are the universal testimonies and absolute demonstrations of creation—indeed, they are simply Nature's own instructions.* You can readily, I think, believe and comprehend, why there will exist a "recollection of the past, and a recognition of friends," in the other world, by reflecting upon and understanding the ultimate connection which exists between the first and second spheres of human existence. The relation is as intimate as that between youth and maturity, love and wisdom, perception and memory. The experience, character, and progress of an individual in this life is recorded upon, and will be, to a modified extent, manifested by, that individual in the life to come. And the friend or companion who has impressed us with friendship and affection here, will be remembered hereafter.

The passage from this sphere into the next is no more a change to the individual than a journey from America to England, excepting the almost complete emancipation consequent upon the change, from rudimental misdirection and earthly imperfections.

So I am taught concerning the principles upon which rest the sublime and heavenly realities of an eternal life. And so I am taught

* There are two other demonstrations of the Soul's immortality, viz.—The independence of the mind from the bodily organism, as manifested in Clairvoyance; and spiritual communication, through electric vibrations. See "Philosophy of Spiritual Intercourse," by the author.

concerning the transformation known as physical death. And I can assure you that, to the convinced and enlarged understanding, there is no death,—only the most important and delightful change in the mode of personal existence. And as we are immortal, and the memories of this life remain with us until displaced by more profitable and spiritual ones, let us at once resolve to institute and manifest henceforth a well-ordered life, and a godly conversation.

With a willingness to instruct, and to be instructed,

I remain yours, &c.,

A. J. Davis.

From the foregoing process of reasoning, it is distinctly obvious, that the *truth* or principle of immortality is reduced to a science—to a mathematical demonstration. This kind of reasoning is not necessary for all men; because there are but few minds that allow themselves to launch forth upon such a boundless, and hitherto, fathomless sea of intellectual speculation,—they rest upon a belief of the Intuition, and never think of questioning the possibility or impossibility of the spirit's eternal identification. The foregoing letter will, therefore, be of particular service to those, only, who have distressing doubts upon this sublime subject.

CONCERNING THE SPIRIT'S DESTINY.

NATURALLY succeeding the philosophy of the soul's immortality, unfold thoughts and speculations concerning the eternal peregrinations and multiform destinations of that soul, which is thus plainly demonstrated to be constitutionally and intrinsically undying and unchangeable. These thoughts were awakened in the mind of the already introduced interrogator, probably by the reply which I was moved to make to his previous communication. It is my impression that the subject before us can not be treated so familiarly in any other manner, as it is in the following reply. I therefore introduce the letter and the answer as they originally appeared.

ST. LOUIS, MO.

A. J. DAVIS: SIR,—Your letter in answer to mine on the Immortality of the Soul, has given me great consolation; for which, please accept my heartfelt thanks. There is, however, one subject on which I desire more light:—it is this: If the soul, mind, or spirit of man is substance—matter—it appears to me that a time in the future will arrive, when the matter of the earth will all be converted into spirit, or as much of it as shall be capable of becoming spirit. If a part only of the matter composing our earth is capable of being changed into spirit, and will be so changed, to what use will the other part be devoted? If all the matter composing our earth can and will be changed to spirit—that, as it regards our earth, will be the end of inanimate matter. In either case, what and where is the final home, resting-place, or destination of the soul? Lastly, what is the difference or distinction between *Soul, Mind, Spirit and Matter?* If you can give me as much satisfaction on these points as you have already on the immortality of the soul, you will lay me under an obligation that I never can repay; and if it is not asking too much, I would solicit an answer, by which you will oblige many readers who are seeking light and truth.

Your sincere friend,

J. S. F.

Reply.

Esteemed Inquirer:—Your letter came duly to hand; but investigations in a region of thought quite removed from the nature of your inquiries, and outer circumstances over which I had no control, were the causes of the procrastination of my reply. Subsequently to the reception of the above letter, I received another from your hand, containing a repetition of the above inquiries, and a very beautiful Map and View of St. Louis. It is not necessary that I should express my thankfulness and pleasure for the reception of the Map and inquiries, as your knowledge of my mental structure is sufficient to convince you that nothing can afford me more pleasure and satisfaction than expressions of Fraternal Love, and independent investigation after truth. You are, I believe, a representative of a very advanced class of individuals,—the result of toleration and free principles. It must be consoling and encouraging to the progressive class of your citizens, to contrast the cold, restrictive, conservative spirit of the founders of your city, the Jesuits, with the comparatively free and republican principles which permit the erection of any church and the preaching of any religion. And exercising the spirit of the enlarged liberty thus conceded to all, you have instituted inquiries which I am pleased to receive and impressed to answer.

I have interpreted and transposed your questions, in order to render them naturally progressive, in the following manner:

1. Will all matter become spirit?
2. To what end will unspiritualized matter be appropriated?
3. What difference is there between *matter* and spirit?
4. Are soul, spirit, and mind synonymous, or are they not?
5. Where will the spirit reside?

In approaching a subject so vast and sublime, our minds should be almost totally divested of the impressions and influences of birth and education. We must think upon the questions as one would think who had just entered into this world of life and being, with all his intellectual and reasoning faculties in a high state of development. This state of simple-mindedness is necessary to a proper reception and understanding of the truth. In *seeking* the truth we must be like untrammeled and unsophisticated infants; but in *understanding* and *applying* the truth, we must be like free-born and highly enlightened men. In this mental condition we will now proceed.

1. *Will all Matter become Spirit?* Answer: No. Because *matter* and *motion*, or *matter* and *mind*, are eternal. We have no grounds or foundation from which to reason, if we attempt to question this fundamental conviction of truth. We must begin to reason (if we desire to reason) in this manner: God and his Body are eternal. There was nothing prior to Deity by which He could have been created; nor was there ever a period in the depths of time when Matter did not exist. God was not created—matter was not created. Any thing that is created contains within itself the elements of change and disorganization. Any thing uncreated is beyond the sphere of change and destruction. I mean that if any thing was created, as theologians believe that matter was created, out of nothing, then *that thing* would contain within itself the elements of returning to a similar state—it would change back

to nothing. We must admit that Mind (or God) and Matter (or Nature) are uncreated and eternal.

All we know of creation is simply confined to that unceasing and universal change of atoms which is going on in the vast, immeasurable organization of God, called Nature. Creation, in truth, is simply a change in the *form*, *position*, and *influence* of atoms and elements in the Universe in which we reside, and of which we are an important and inseparable portion. A corresponding creation is perpetually going on in our own constitutions. Every element, every fluid, and every substance known in the animal economy, is undergoing some modification or change,—something is, in this sense, constantly being *created* in our bodies.

The food which we eat is analyzed and appropriated by the gastric fluid and the digestive functions; and one portion thereof goes to the formation of bone, another portion to the formation of muscle, another to nerves, another portion creates new veins and arteries; and the most sublimated part goes to the formation or creation of that *spiritual principle* by which the whole system is moved and illuminated. This familiar illustration is sufficient to impress a definite idea of what constitutes creation, and how the atoms, fluids, and elements in universal nature, change and circulate from the center of eternal power to the uttermost manifestations of boundless infinity.

Now, to ask if *all* matter will become spirit, would be admitting into the mind the possibility of that which was *uncreated* ceasing to exist. This question is not consistent with the fundamental grounds of all our reasoning, and therefore the question answers itself in the negative. God is a spirit, and the ultimate of his creation, or the prolification of his spirit in nature, develops corresponding embodiments, which we term human spirits. Spirit will produce spirit, as a flower will produce a flower.

The question moreover implies the possibility of a *final* termination; and I think your mind was impressed with an idea, that a time will arrive in the future when creation will be complete, that matter will all be distilled into spirit, that human souls will reach their "*final* home," and that universal progression will end. All the matter composing our earth will be refined into spirit, and all the matter which we can see in the form of suns and planets in the boundless firmament will ultimately be converted into spirit, but then there still *remains* a universe of matter—a boundless universe of materials—unspiritualized, and material, too, *millions* of times *lower* than the earth in the scale of progress and refinement, or than is the granite rock now beneath the refinement of the human spirit. Therefore, to our very limited capacity of comprehension, *all* matter will become spirit; but to the illimitable capacity of the Central Soul, and compared with the inexhaustible materials composing his physical constitution, a *very little portion* of matter will seem thus converted.

2. *To what end will unspiritualized matter be appropriated?* This question implies the supposition that the process of creation—of progress and development—will ultimately cease, and that *final* arrangements will take place; that every *thing* will have a position and occupation assigned to it, and that eternal fixedness will pervade infinity. But, although this hypothesis is not allowable in our philosophy of everlasting progress, there is an answer to the question. It is this: When the *present* structure of the Universe shall have served, so far as it is capable, the purposes of material refinement and spiritual development, and has converted as much matter into human spirits as its innumerable and immeasurable arrangements will perform, then the *refuse* materials will fall back into that "unimaginable ocean of liquid fire," and a *new* structure will be developed. Before the *present* order of the Universe will change, *more* than what we now term an *Eternity of time* will have passed away. But the change must and will come. And

every re-construction of the Universe will be an *infinite improvement* upon the preceding structure. And the ultimate creations or unfoldings of each succeeding structure, will infinitely transcend the developments of those *Universes* which have disappeared, and will thus sink into the oblivious past. Thus the unspiritualized portion of matter will subserve the purposes of a new creation. And it is thus that the principles of Association, Progression, and Development, exert their united and perpetual influence upon the empire of worlds of which our earth is but a very insignificant portion.

3. *What difference is there between Matter and Spirit?* Almost *all* words which describe the quality of any thing are relative—they have a relative significance. We speak generally from contrast. Indeed, in a Universe like this—so replete with varieties and differences—it is almost impossible to employ any other than relative words to communicate our ideas. The general opinion is, as you are doubtless aware, that spirit is something *entirely* unlike matter. But reason refers us immediately to *this* simple conclusion: that spirit *is* something; and *something* must be substance, or else it will be *no*thing; or else, in plainer language, there could be no such a *thing* as spirit. Receiving reason, then, as our guide to truth, we can not resist the conviction that spirit *is* substance, and in the absence of a better word, we term *that* substance "matter." We must not confound the question under consideration with others of a similar character. The question is not respecting the source from which the spirit proceeded, nor the elements and principles involved in its indestructible constitution, but it is, What *difference* is there between matter and spirit?

I answer,—spirit is a word which signifies, in my mind, an organization of matter in the highest state of advancement, refinement, and perfection. Spirit is an indissoluble *unity* of the finest particles of matter. There is as much difference between spirit and electricity as there is between electricity and the common earth;

.n.t electricity is matter, and so is spirit. If we were above the plane of material development where spiritual organization takes place, then we would be surrounded with illustrations and analogous processes: but as it is, you will readily perceive that a spirit can not investigate and comprehend itself, and hence the *obscurity* which gathers around the investigation after we pass a certain point in the attempt to get above and look down upon the spiritual organization. But the *difference* between the *apple* and the appearance and substance of the *tree* which gave it birth and individuality, or between the wild rose and the rocky and mossy substances which gave that rose its nourishment and beauty, is not less strikingly wonderful than the difference which exists between the *matter we see* and the *spirit we feel.* Detach the apple from the tree, and compare it with the form and substance of that tree, and you have a no less powerful contrast than that which we find when comparing what we *feel* and *know* of spirit with what we can *see* and *handle* of matter. The phenomena of the former are no more understood and appreciated than the phenomena of the latter. Spirit is *organized* and *eternalized* at the highest point to which gross, or what is termed inanimate, matter can ascend. Spirit *is,* therefore, matter in the highest state of refinement and organization; and the *difference* consists simply in this: *matter* is gross, inferior, and external—and *spirit* is refined, superior, and interior. The terms *matter* and *spirit* are thus indicative of the *difference* in the condition, form, and influence of the *same* identical substance, and nothing more.

4. *Are Soul, Spirit, and Mind synonymous, or are they not?* I am thankful for this question, because no opportunity has presented itself, since the delivery of those lectures which compose th "Revelations," when an explanation seemed appropriate. And I have not been insensible to the vast amount of obscurity and contradiction which the diversified employment of these terms has

produced among those who have struggled to become philosophically metaphysical, and even among those who consider themselves already accomplished reasoners.

Some philosophers, and Swedenborg among the number, consider and affirm that the *soul* is the outermost enveloping medium, that the *spirit* is the intermediate or conjunctive medium, and that the *mind* is the seat or center of the thinking Principle. Thus what I denominate *Life* is sometimes termed *Soul;* what I denominate *sensation*, is sometimes termed *Spirit*, and what I denominate *intelligence* is sometimes termed the *Mind*. Theologians, I believe, do not attempt to discriminate between these progressive states of human individuality. I except, of course, the metaphysical portion of that profession. Now in order to prevent misunderstanding hereafter, at least among those inquiring individuals who read what I have produced or may produce, I cheerfully respond to the question.

1. I consider *motion* the *first* manifestation of mind,—an indication of the *Great Mind* which resides back of, and in, Nature; and a *prophetical* indication of the existence of a *corresponding* mind as an *ultimate* or perfection of Nature.

2. I consider *Life* the *first* development of Motion, and the second indication of Intelligence.

3. I consider *Sensation* the *first* development of Life, and the third indication of future or ultimate Intelligence.

4. I consider *Intelligence* the *highest* development of *Motion*, *Life*, and *Sensation*, and a perfect manifestation of the internal living and unchangeable organization. And when I employ the terms *Soul*, *Spirit*, and *Mind*, I mean the *internal and immortal Individual.* When Motion, Life, Sensation, and Intelligence are conjoined and organized, I term that organization a unity of elements and attributes; and these elements and attributes arrange according to their natural order, under the comprehensive terms of

Love and *Wisdom*—terms which are perfectly expressive of the natural characteristics and legitimate manifestations of those internal principles. Therefore, when I use the nouns substantive—*Soul*, *Spirit*, *Mind*, and *Individual*—the thought which suggests their employment is resting *invariably* upon the inward *Homo*, upon the individual *Oneness*, which is constructed upon those principles which elevate that *oneness* above the plane of change and disorganization. Hence the question is answered affirmatively—the terms are unqualifiedly synonymous.

5. *Where will the Spirit reside?* This question was suggested in your mind by admitting the supposition that there will be an *end* to matter in the form of worlds; because, if material worlds cease to exist, the mind can not reasonably imagine any local habitation for the myriads of individual souls which would claim a residence somewhere in the solitudes of immensity. And also it seems that your mind was pervaded with an undefined idea that "*final*" destinations will be gained by all souls and every thing. But as matter is eternal and souls progress forever, according to what has been stated in answer to questions on that head, therefore the present interrogatory demands a different answer.

I have said that the present structure of the Universe will ultimately change, and that a *new* Universe will come forth, and that *new* and *higher* creations will be the inevitable consequence. Now when all worlds of material organization shall have performed their respective missions in the individualization of immortal spirits, and each world shall have disorganized and fallen back into its original vortex of chaos, then where will the Spirit reside? The question comes in naturally here, and here the answer will be best under stood, because it is necessary.

After the individual souls leave this planet (and all planets in universal space which yield such organizations of matter,) they ascend to the *Second* Sphere of existence. Here *all* individuals undergo an angelic discipline, by which every physical and spiritual deformity is removed, and symmetry reigns throughout the immeasurable empire of holy beings. When all spirits shall have progressed to the Second Sphere, the various earths and planets in the Universe, which once swarmed with life and animation, will be depopulated and not a living thing will move upon their surfaces. And so there will be no destruction of life in that period of disrganization, but the earths, and suns, and planets will die—their life will be absorbed by the Divine Spirit. God is Positive—all else is negative. He is the Moving Power—all else is moved. He will expand his inmost capacity and *attract* the glowing elements of His being which permeate the boundless expanse of matter; and all matter, which is not organized into spirit, will die and fall into its original condition. But the inhabitants of the *second* sphere will ultimately advance to the *third*, then to the *fourth*, then to the *fifth*, and lastly into the *sixth;* this sixth sphere is as near the great Positive Mind as spirits can ever locally or physically approach. It is greater than all the others. It encircles infinity. It is in the neighborhood of the divine aroma of the Deity; it is warmed and beautified infinitely by His infinite Love, and it is illuminated and rendered unspeakably magnificent by His all-embracing Wisdom. In this ineffable sphere, in different stages of individual progression, will *all* spirits dwell. They will be held together by the attractive emanations of Deity, like the safe protection of an infinite belt, which will embrace the entire sphere in which will reside incalculable multitudes of created and eternalized souls. The Universal Father will thus gather to himself all the images of his creation—all the diversified members of his household; and thus "the house of many mansions" will be completely occupied by the many members of the ingathered family. This may be considered as the home of the spirit; but still greater missions and blessings will determine the paths in which every conjugally united *oneness* will tread—paths strewed with innumerable and immeasurable worlds of beauty and harmony.

When all spirits arrive at the Sixth Sphere of existence, and the protecting Love and Wisdom of the Great Positive Mind are thrown tenderly around them; and when not a single atom of life is wandering from home in the fields and forests of immensity; then the Deity *contracts* his inmost capacity, and forthwith the boundless vortex is convulsed with a new manifestation of Motion—Motion transcending all our conceptions, and passing to and fro from center to circumference, like mighty tides of Infinite Power. Now the law of Association or *gravitation* exhibits its influence and tendency in the formation of new suns, new planets, and new earths. The law of progression or *refinement* follows next in order, and manifests its unvarying tendency in the production of new forms of life on those planets; and the law of Development follows next in the train, and exhibits its power in the creation of *new* plants, animals, and human spirits upon every earth prepared to receive and nourish them. Thus God will create a new Universe, and will display different and greater elements and energies therein. And thus new spheres of spiritual existences will be opened. These spheres will be *as much* superior to the present unspeakable glories of the sixth sphere, as the *sixth* sphere is *now* above the *second* sphere, which is next superior to the sphere of earth. When the new and superior Universe is completely unfolded, or when the new heavens and the new earths are developed, the spirits in the *sixth* sphere will be again in the second sphere; because the *highest* sphere in the *present* order of the Universe will constitute the *second* sphere in the *new* order which is to be developed. Thus there will be *four* spheres for the spirits and angels at the consummation of the *new* unfolding, to advance through, as there are now *four* between the *second* sphere and the sixth which we have been considering.

There have already been developed more new Universes, in the manner described, than there are atoms in the earth. And I suppose it is scarcely necessary to state that the human mind is incapable of computing the millions of centuries which are required for even those souls that now inhabit the Second Sphere, to progress into the one above it—into the Third Sphere. And it would be still more useless to state that as many millions of such eternities as we can possibly conceive of, will roll into the past *ere we begin* to pproach that change of Universal relations of which I have spoken.

But I have answered the question. The Spirit will have no "final home;" because, to an immortal being, *rest* would be intolerable,—it would be next to annihilation, and greater than the most perfect concentration of all the miseries of the fabled hell. But the spirit will progress eternally! It will always be in harmony with surrounding circumstances, and thus will always reside in heaven. The same differences will exist in future spheres of life as exist in this world,—I mean those differences which are established by the real *intrinsic* perfection of the constitution, education, and harmony of the individual. But the spirit will walk in those shining paths which angels tread, in opening communications between the celestial inhabitants of celestial spheres and those high-born spirits of our earth. Let us, then, live justly, truly, and purely; because by so doing our position will be commanding and glorious in those numberless spheres where the spirit will reside.

In the bonds of faith and friendship,

I remain yours, &c.,

A. J. Davis.

WHAT AND WHERE IS GOD?

EARTH can forge no chains whereby to fetter human thought. The Mind is designed for boundless freedom; its aspirations are unto the beautiful, the glorious, the sublime, and unto the Great Moving Principle of the Universe. There is nothing too free, too stupendous, too magnificent, or *too holy*, for human contemplation. To search, to explore, to analyze, to interrogate, to reveal,—is the attraction and mission of the expanded and illuminated intellect; and there is not, in the expanded earth or unfolded heavens, any thing too minute or insignificant, too incomprehensible or all-embracing, for the untrammeled mind to investigate and breathe into its subtle constitution. The mind seeks eternal things *because* it is itself everlasting and eternal. It strives to comprehend the wide expanse of infinitude, because it is itself a part of an inconceivable Infinite Mind. To say that the human Soul shall not venture the investigation of pure, everlasting, and infinite things,—to attempt the imprisonment of human thought and feeling,—is to say and attempt the most absurd and impossible thing. The mind is incarnated in a physical temple whose dome is measured by inches, yet its thoughts and affections expand forth into apartments of much greater dimensions; and, dissatisfied with the large, well-furnished drawing-room, or bed-chamber, the mind seeks the wide-spread earth, ascertains the location of its restless seas, its numerous mounts and vales, determines its diameter and measures its circumference. And yet the mind sleeps not the slumber of perfect satisfaction. Earth is too limited, too easily comprehended, and its materiality is too obvious for the soul. The firmament invites the aspiring Thought; and the mind seeks the living Orbs that roll far, far away through the dreamy wastes of boundless infinitude.

Star after star is counted; and the various constellations of celestial bodies are told, and mapped out like mile-stones along our familiar roads. And yet the mind goes on! it searches the ineffable mysteries of the siderial heavens, and the magnitude of those invisible worlds of grandeur which revolve beyond the most distant stars. Amazed at the greatness, and grandeur, and harmony, and incomprehensibleness of those things which are visible beneath, around, and above, the soul,—pulsating with joy and with the inexpressible desire to know more,—inquires, "*What and where is God?*"

And this involuntary interrogation of the soul, is not to be hushed by any human power; it is a thought which no dungeon can confine, nor chains fetter; it can only be quieted with knowledge. Untrammeled and uncontrolled—save with the material or bodily senses—the soul has sought this knowledge by throwing open all the accessible labyrinths of nature which promised or appeared to lead to God. The fields of science have been traversed and explored; the beauties of art have been spread out by the human mind for human contemplation; and the religious and theological works of all nations have been searched, to the end that the soul might comprehend and gaze upon the supernal Ruler of the Universe! but he still remains the Great Unknown, the Great Mind—the unseen and uncomprehended Father of all spirits—the Pure, the Holy, the Everlasting, the Infinite!

All nations believe in the existence of an invisible Principle; something resembling a human being, and yet a mighty and powerful Spirit—capable of accomplishing and extinguishing all visible and invisible creation. Among some pagan sects, there is a conception of God which resembles the conviction that prevailed among the early Egyptian sects,—a "Spirit of Nature," which possessed the features and attributes of "Man" to an infinite degree,—a "Great Prince,"—a "King of Kings,"—a "Lord of Lords,"—a being essentially *human*, and yet, sufficiently exalted and supreme in holiness, to be called *Divine* and *Immaculate* in the superlative sense of those terms. Perhaps we can comprehend this subject, more easily and naturally, by allowing ourselves to ask, in all sincerity and simple-mindedness, the following question—

What is the origin of a belief in God?

The filial element or affection in the human soul, as I have heretofore explained, is the residence of a love for superiors. Hence belief in God, or in a superior power, is indigenous to the soul, and consequently to all nations and tribes on the surface of the earth. After the mind has familiarized itself with surrounding objects and scenery, and when these cease to awaken feelings of curiosity and amazement, then the mind goes forth after the Invisible and Superior.

There are innumerable springs of Life and Causation. Outer and visible things proceed from inner and invisible sources. And the young and uncultivated mind is compelled to inquire,—who made all these things? The *conceptions* which the mind will entertain of God will be measured by the prevailing belief of his countrymen; but the idea which the mind will form of God, if it thinks independently and legitimately upon the subject of a superior power, will be an exact revealment and representative of the character of the individual himself. An idea is the *form* or organization of a conception; the latter is the soul of the former.

Overwhelmed with admiration and gratitude, the unsophisticated Indian meditates upon the wonders of the Great Spirit. And many and diversified are the reasons, he thinks, why he should regard, with unspeakable respect and fear, the mighty maker. And to the Indian, almost more than to any other being, are these reasons omnipresent and powerful. Behold the beasts of the fields, the fowls of the air, the fishes of the sea,—how strong! how sublime! how useful! The seasons go and return; the mountains are ladened with fruit and foliage; the fragrant valleys are radiant with flowers; and the Heavens are studded with innumerable lights whereby to guide him on his way.

Ask the Indian of God, and he will describe to you a sublime sachem,—a powerful chieftain of a glorious tribe. If he has thought sufficient to give ideas utterance, he will describe the lakes of fish, the forests of birds and beasts, and the great hunting-grounds, belonging to the mighty sachem of the spirit-land. According to the state of his own individual mind will be the God of the Indian; the difference will consist *not* in character, but in magnitude and power. To disbelieve in a superior chieftain, is to the Indian an impossibility; his own existence is his demonstration. His own character and desires constitute his standard of judgment; and his God *is himself* magnified and refined.

Ask the pagan of God, and he will inquire of you of which one you would learn. He has a God of fire; a God of earth; a God of air; and a God of water; he has a God of the passions—a God of the seasons—a God of the imponderable elements—a God of the planets; and a representative of them all in Fetich, the Idol of the Hindoo and other pagan nations.

The pagan-God is essentially a God of the pagans. His attributes, his government, and his judgments are pagan; and paganism is his religion.

Taught by experience, and confirmed by his position and title, the Patriarch believes in a God of a patriarchal character. Moses conceived it proper and expedient to govern his uncultivated followers by coercive measures; and *his* God governs by the same system. The ten commandments were conceived and written by Moses; consequently they were communicated and sanctioned by the Mosaic-God. The patriarchal God is a magnified and refined Moses; because if you understand Moses' mental organization and disposition,—if you understand his system of social and national government; if you understand his caprices and fickle-mindedness, his advancements and retreats, his experiments and regrets,—then you understand the disposition and government of the patriarchal God.

The God of Joshua was capricious and revengeful. He permitted WAR, and RAPINE, and DEBAUCHERY. The difference between the God of Moses, and the God of Joshua, is the difference between the two individuals. Indeed the fact can not be disguised, that the God of Joshua was different from the God of the ten commandments just in proportion to the difference of opinions and actions which characterize the history and experience of the two chieftains.

The Patriarchal-God is possessed of all the attributes and titles consistent with his position; but the peculiar mode of his manifestations to his dependent children is invariably determined by the peculiar circumstances under which the (so called) revelation is made. For instance: Moses relates how his God drew near Mount Sinai, how thunder and lightning, fire and smoke, indicated his presence. This was the most fearful mode of divine manifestation. Again Moses saw his God manifested in the burning bush; at another time, only the posterior portions of his person were visible—his face being death to the beholder. It however appears from the primitive history that God was frequently "face to face" with Aaron, and with others within the cloud over the tabernacle; and also that he "walked with Noah," and gave him intimations of the Deluge, instructing him how he might be saved, together with two of every kind of reptile, bird, and animal.

The mode in which the God or Gods of any nation or individual are said to have manifested themselves is never to be confounded with their disposition and system of government. I am impressed that all accounts of the various manifestations of Gods that are traditionally and historically preserved, and handed down to us, are stratagems, misapprehensions, or the falsehoods of individuals. Men and kings who go to war aspire after the approbative sanction of their Gods; and, fearing that their armies or followers will lose courage and strength unless approved and justified by some superior power, these Leaders and Kings will take advantage of some already acknowledged God, or will *invent* manifestations of divine approval by performing seemingly marvelous works and supernaturalities. Joshua led the Israelites on to battle; confiscated property; laid cities low; devastated populated regions; murdered his male prisoners, and brutalized the female captives,—all, in the *name* and under the *approval* of his God.

The Persians have regarded, and do still regard, Ormudz as the authority by which they live and govern. The Hindoos regard the Juggernaut-Idol as sufficient authority for all the deeds of cruelty as well as deeds of goodness which they feel called upon to do; and the European and American nations regard the Bible-God (which is the sovereign Idol of the Sacerdotal orders of Christendom) as sufficient authority for *War*, *Monarchy*, *Tyranny*, *Slavery*, and *Murder*. Ask the Christian of God—and you will receive an answer composed of three things—Education, Situation, Conviction. Conviction, however, is the measure and result of the other constituents of the answer; and it (the conviction) may be estimated as an expression of what the individual feels.

Thus, to ascertain what a person's character is, inquire of him concerning the God in which he has faith—and his reply,—if legitimately and honestly stated,—will be a disclosure of *his own* disposition and spiritual or intellectual growth.

It was lately said to a gentleman of acknowledged talents and veracity, that the language used to the Jews and multitude, (attributed to Christ,) "ye serpents, ye generation of vipers, &c.," was ascertained to have been used by another individual; and that such expression was inconsistent with the uniform moral-sweetness, and philosophical forgiveness of Christ's character, and not in the spirit of his words, "Father, forgive them, they know not what they do," uttered, under thrice more painful circumstances, to the same class of individuals;—but the gentleman impatiently exclaimed, in reply,—"Christ *did* say so—I *know* he did—*it was just like Christ!*" But, in fact, it was not like Christ—*it was just like the gentleman.*

The christian God is constituted upon patriarchal principles. His government is of an arbitrary, and monarchical character; and he is not much superior to the caprices, experiments, jealousies, and retaliations of the Mosaic, or the pagan-God. But these defects of character are concealed from observation by the magnificent garment of Justice. His capriciousness is termed justice. His partial gifts and judgments are named justice. His everlasting punishments, and malicious persecutions of the wicked (so styled) are called justice; and, thus, the beautiful term "*Justice*"—which is, (in its true sense,) *the representative of a principle of universal reciprocation of rights and enjoyments*—is employed as a *mask* whereby to conceal the defects of the character of the patriarchal God.

If Christians put to death a murderer, they do it because their God does so. If they go to war: if they enslave the negro: if they support Kings: if they condemn, and crucify, and manifest vengeance toward their enemies; they do it because their God does so. Acting thus upon supposed Divine authority, and confessing openly that their God possesses the savage and patriarchal attributes under the term of *Justice*, Christians prove themselves intellectually and morally undeveloped—they prove themselves deficient in their perceptions of Justice and of a Supreme Being.

Again, I repeat, the God of the human mind is the magnified perception of itself—and sometimes it is a prophecy of its *future* self!

Individuals, or a people, *first* make their God; and then their God makes them—forms their character, and their religion! A madman or an impostor generally becomes the victim of his own madness or imposition; and so, upon the same principle of cause and effect, do the people make Gods: and Gods make the people. Thus an individual is both a Creator and a creature;—thus with nations—thus with centuries.

With the mind injured, insulted, and repelled by the encroachments of inferior or prevailing theology, and with every generous feeling chilled by its uncongenial breath, some individuals leave the popular religious field, and marshall together upon independent grounds. Dissatisfied with every thing heard or written on theological subjects, these minds become skeptical as to the doctrines of the past, and turn from the *old*, to investigate the truths of the New.

If they turn within and think of God,—THE ONE TRUE GOD,—there are *three* ways in which independent thinkers and investigators conceive of his existence, viz.:—Scientifically—Philosophically—and Theologically. These consistent, but *different*, forms of investigation and conception of the mode of the Divine Nature and Existence, give rise to many illegitimate and erroneous conclusions,—especially among those who think without system or ordinary technical discrimination.

If a mind is skeptical—if it is on that barren desert of Ice, known to all pilgrims after truth, as *Atheism*—then, also, does the individual reveal his true disposition and spiritual development. If his God is Nothing—if his God is Chaos, then is he Chaos. With the soul thus deprived of that superior perception of itself, which may be called knowledge, the individual is undecided and unreliable. His confidence in himself or in his neighbor, is like his conceptions of God, merely nothing!

The fact is undeniable, that whether you ask the Savage, the

Barbarian, the Patriarch—or whether you ask Moses, or modern religious leaders, *who is God?* the reply will, invariably, be characteristic of the growth, the government, the disposition, and the qualifications of the person, his Age, and Nation. But to bring the *first* view of Deity before the mind, let us proceed to consider the following question—

What is God scientifically considered?

Knowledge is another name for experience, which the huma mind can only receive through the medium of the senses. I mean, the sensations of pleasure and pain, of cold and heat, of quietude or disturbance which the individual experiences, by coming in contact with the vast contrariety of elements and objects in the material world, which sensations are treasured up in the memory. Indeed, it is more proper to say that all sensations, experienced in a sensuous manner, are recorded upon the living principle; and to the inferior individual, as well as to the spiritually enlightened mind, these records are visible, and serve as guide-boards and living admonitions in the paths of life.

The senses are adapted to the objective world; they are windows through which the soul communicates with external Nature. In truth, the senses establish a connection between the soul and the outer world, or the world of effects. The senses can not, therefore, recognize causes, except they may be of a very external and superficial character, because *causes* reside deep in the bosom of the invisible world.

Those minds which are termed and considered *scientific* are such as are highly educated in the nature and diversification of effects. Science is simply a knowledge of effects, or of external objects, o. elements, of their mode of existence, the nature and extent of their influence, and the principles by which they are individually governed. *Science*, then, is an investigation into the nature of *effects*; and *Philosophy* is an investigation into the nature of *causes*.

Scientific researches are *inferior* to every other species of human inquiry after truth and knowledge; because they do not, in themselves, develop or refine the mind, only inform it of a wider and vaster range of effects and external phenomena than a mere personal existence among them could possibly furnish. But the principal reason why I deem science inferior to other spheres of inquiry is this; when exclusively pursued, it renders the individual only a materialist, a mere believer in external and visible objects and phenomena, and a disbeliever in almost every thing of an invisible and superior character. But yet there is a kind of *compound science* which embraces every thing of a palpable nature, and which leads me,—and many individuals who can only reason and perceive from what they see, hear, taste, and experience,—to the threshold of the question under consideration. And here let me be correctly apprehended. The inquiry is wholly scientific—recognizing that *Facts are Things*, and *Truths are Principles;* and that the present view of God is one which reason recognizes as demonstrated by experience and observation—not depending upon, or seeking for, any other class of proofs which naturally arrange themselves under a philosophical or theological inquiry into the same subject. In all these considerations, I am impressed to be brief and comprehensive.

God, scientifically considered, is the greatest Fact in the universe—He is the greatest Principle—He is the greatest Reality!

God is, in this sense, the Active or Moving Principle, and is different from Nature in this one particular respect, that while God is *Active* and *Moving*, Nature is *Passive* and *Moved*. Contrasted with God, Nature seems inert and lifeless; but positive inertia and lifelessness are not in existence. Inasmuch, therefore, as God is the greatest Fact, and the greatest Reality in being, it follows, from scientific principles, or from principles of scientific induction, that he is a *fixed Fact*, and a *fixed Reality*. In plainer language, God is a being of absolute necessity. It is *possible* for God to exist, to will, to act, to enjoy; but it is *not possible* for him to cease to exist; or to change in his nature, disposition, or in his mode of existence. Hence we have a perfect assurance in the Eternal *Existence* and *Sameness* of God; since from scientific principles it is proved that He is a Principle of Necessity, so far as Constitution and Existence are concerned. And yet it may be said that God is a Principle of Freedom in so far as immutable action, in an infinitely righteous and divine manner, seems to render that action or matter of voluntary but unchangeable *desire*, and voluntary but unchangeable volition. There is in all this only the freedom of an eternal uniformity of life.

Science can only recognize God as a Fact—a Reality—a Principle—a Thing, so to speak, superior to all other things—and a Principle more living than any other principle.

Profoundly philosophical as was, in general, the brilliant intellect of Baron D' Holbach, it is nevertheless true that he obtained a no clearer comprehension of the existence of God than is suggested and sanctioned by the usual principles of scientific inquiry and induction; and it was for the admirable statement of these scientific concessions and conclusions that I have, in a former work, (Nature's Divine Revelations,) recommended his theological writings to the perusal of independent minds.

Vitalizing all things to the universal satisfaction of all things: and substantializing every thing to the universal realization of substances, God dwells in connection with all substances and elements, and individualizes his Motion, his Life, his Sensation, and his Intelligence in them. Being beyond the possibility of self-destruction, he actualizes Himself in the most external, and apparently insignificant, forms of matter, and thus in his outer manifestation he becomes Nature. The scientific statement, therefore, that God is Nature, is a *fact;* and the mind that can not recognize God as Nature, in this sense, is not in a very high state of intellectual cultivation. And here it may be proper to say that many individuals have thus conceived of God, encountering all manner of clerical opposition,—being denounced as *Infidels*, as *Deists*, as *Atheists*, as every thing but what they are—namely, *believers in God scientifically considered.* They are persons accustomed principally to external investigation; and incompetent to consider God in any other light; and, hence, should be esteemed for *what* they strive to be, *not* for what they are.

Inasmuch as God is a Fact, a Reality, a Principle, it is agreeable with science to suppose that He is Substance—is Matter. It may be said that God is a fixed Substance, and this makes him a fixed Reality. He is a fixed and necessary Power—indeed, *He Is, what He Is;* and it is not in his power to be, or to *will* to be other! It will surely be conceded that this statement needs no argument—it is self-evident truth—requiring no discussion.

God is an organization of Elements and Attributes; but the evidences of this proposition are, properly, confined to a philosophical inquiry into the same subject; for science, as already said, deals only in *facts* and *things.* His elements are Motion, Life, and Sensation; his attributes are embraced by the term, Intelligence. In other language, his elements are included under the theological or religious term, Love; and his attributes under the philosophical term, Wisdom.

Being substance in and of Himself, and exerting an active and moving power continually in the Empire of Matter, it is reasonable to conclude that his attributes and elements are also matter or substance, and that they are apprehended, but not acknowledged, *as such* by the superficial observer of objects and phenomena in external nature. Therefore, according to scientific principles, we are led to the legitimate conclusion, that all the life of plants and animals, and all the phenomena of attraction, gravitation, and of the imponderable elements, are referable to the Active and Moving Principle, called God.

Being universally diffused throughout all Nature—and being so unchangeably fixed as to be beyond the slightest possibility of alteration or mutability—God acts, and manifests Himself equally every where, and in the same general manner. The Laws of Nature being thus universally established, and their operation being thus steady and undeviating, the human mind may rest in the very bosom of confidence, and be never disturbed by doubt or distrust. For, inasmuch as God is a fixed reality—and inasmuch as he can neither Desire or Will to change—we are penetrated with that kind of satisfaction, in the ultimate issues of things, which insures perfect composure, because we have an intellectual perception of truth, without which there can be no perfect confidence.

From external experience and observation, the mind becomes accustomed to the uniform movements of Nature; and it is the mission and business of science to reduce those regular but diversified movements to a system of actions, and these actions must be designated with appropriate terms. Amazed and confounded by terms, and by the seeming antagonisms in the world of Effects, in which the scientific thinker is educated, scientific minds have misunderstood and disputed with one another; but seeing, as I am enabled to do, by interior perception, the wide-spread and universal sameness of Nature's processes, I am impressed to institute the following terms as significant of the modes by which God Acts upon and Moves the Universe. God acts upon matter Anatomically, Physiologically, Mechanically, Chemically, Electrically, Magnetically, Spiritually;—but all of these modes of Action may be generalized under the comprehensive and highly appropriate terms—Attraction and Repulsion; and, still more comprehensively and appropriately, may these modes of Action be designated and interpreted by the terms—Association—Progression—and Development. These latter terms equally signify Principles, and their Manifestations—and are terms belonging to, and originating with, the Harmonial Philosophy.

Let it be remembered that, a scientific inquiry into the Nature and Mode of the existence of God, is the *first*, and most *inferior*, effort of human Reason; consequently, all conclusions of the investigation must be of an inferior and external character, and *true so far as they go.*

But the reason why clergymen and their followers—the laity—will mis-state or denounce a scientific view of God, is to be found in this:—they do not think systematically, nor independently. If clergymen did think systematically and independently, the consequence would be that these scientific conclusions would be acknowledged. All Biblical writers speak of God as a Being, as a Fact, as a Reality, as a Principle; but their terms are more adapted to a theological or moral, than to a scientific, view of God; and hence, in hundreds of instances, disputes and dissensions arise between individuals about *Ideas*, when a misunderstanding of *terms* is the only cause of difference. I think it is plain, that, if God is substance he is a fixed substance; and if he is a Reality he is a fixed reality. When the mind puts on scientific spectacles, so to express it, or gazes into the Infinite vortex of Life and Intelligence through a scientific telescope or medium, it is not to be supposed that its conclusions can be other than absolutely scientific and correspondingly rigid. And it makes but little difference whether it be Confucius, or Moses, or David, or Plato, or Paul, or Baron D' Holbach, or Swedenborg— if they view God through purely scientific mediums, their conclusions will and must be identical; and hence the difference between any of these individuals in the views they entertain of God, *when they do employ their reason*, and any of the (so styled) Deists of the present century, consists simply in the different *mediums* through which they view the same subject. By mediums, I mean the *methods* of the contemplation.

But the difference between individuals, when they *do not* employ their Reason, consists in the difference of their dispositions, and state of intellectual culture. The truth of this will be more fully developed in the sequel.

A *belief* in God, I repeat, arises from out of the depths of the soul's Filial affection; but an *understanding* of God arises from out of the Reason. Those who describe merely their educational, hereditary, or affectional belief in God, describe mainly *their own* characters; but they who describe their scientific, philosophical, and theological or religious belief in God, describe the *mediums* or methods, through which they view Him: and also the state of intellectual growth to which they have attained.

Having proceeded thus far in our definition of a scientific conception of the Divine Being, let us take another step forward, and sincerely inquire—

What is God philosophically considered?

Science considers God in reference to Things, Effects, and Phenomena; but Philosophy considers Him in reference to Principles, Causes, and Designs. Let this distinction be remembered.

God, by gazing at him through a philosophical telescope, appears as the Greatest of all Hearts; as the Great Nucleus, around which the infinite expansion of substances gathers into progressive *forms* and *orders;* as the Great Cause, around which infinite and universal effects congregate, and from which infinite effects proceed; and He appears as the Great Central Source of all Life, and Love, of all Order, and Form; and as the Sustainer and Unfolder of all things—the magnificent Universe!

Beholding the Infinite Cause of all existences, in His works, the mind is irresistibly persuaded to believe that God is an Infinite Organization and Intelligence. That He is an intelligent Being is seen by what He does. The proofs are, that all things flow into forms, series, degrees, and progressive organizations.

It might be said that, Nature exists and operates between God and his designs. All things were instituted for some infinite purpose—for some important end or issue. This issue must correspond to the magnitude and majesty of the Inventor of the Universal Machine. For, Nature,—with her infinite number of *levers, springs, wheels, pulleys, and chemical laboratories,*—is evidently constructed upon mechanical and geometrical principles, for the accomplishment of important ends, one of which ends we have heretofore contemplated.

Surrounded by an inconceivable number of forms and organizations,—each one of them occupying a specific and progressive position in Nature,—the human mind can not but perceive that the cause of them must be, Himself, an infinite Cause; that to produce organizations he must be, Himself, *first*, an Organization; that to produce intelligence he must be, Himself, *first*, Intelligent; and that to produce an infinite machine, he must be, Himself, not only organized and intelligent, but he must have had some glorious end or result to accomplish, according to which his Universal Machinery was constructed. Surely, this is plain reasoning.

God, therefore, philosophically considered, is an infinite CAUSE; Nature is an infinite EFFECT; and the *object*, for the accomplishment of which the whole was thus constituted, is the infinite *Use* or *End.*

God is the Great Positive Mind;—all else is Negative.

Contemplate the eternal Vortex or Center from which proceeded the ten thousand million-fold of worlds that swarm the shores of Immensity;—contemplate the rich and inexhaustible materials which roll in boundless waves to the Central Fount;—contemplate the magnificent azure dome which crowns the Holy Residence of Creative Power;—contemplate the inconceivable interchanging, commingling, and interpenetration of Fire, Heat, Light, and Electricity;—contemplate a Presiding, but inseparably individualized, Great Positive Mind, who, while he commands, compels obedience; meanwhile, Himself, obeys! I say, through the sublime telescope of pure philosophy, contemplate all this Grandeur, this Beauty, this Harmony, and reason will readily conceive the proposition that God is Positive, and all else is Negative.

Spirit and Matter must not be confounded, nor must they be separated. Elsewhere I have said, that, in defining what Spirit is, I was compelled to employ the term Matter, in the absence of a better word, because it is expressive of *substance*, and such is Spirit. So also, in pursuing the present inquiry, the Positive Mind must not be confounded with Nature, nor must they be separated. This distinction must be kept prominently in the mind, that God is as distinct and different from Nature, as the germ of a tree is from its fruits; or as the human Soul is different from the human Body; but here let the distinction end. In this respect the analogy is complete and legitimate.

When speaking of God, the mind is involuntarily impressed to employ those terms which convey the idea of a *masculine gender*. It is easy to understand the cause of this employment of terms, and the thought which suggests their use. When the mind thinks of God, a conception is received of a Great Positive Power—of a Being of boundless celestial Life (which is Love,)—of unlimited Will (which is Omnipotence,)—and of unerring Wisdom (which is Order and Form,)—and it is not possible to conceive of a power and of a reproductive energy of such inconceivable magnitude, without employing such legitimate language as will enable the mind to elaborate its conception of God, into something like an adequate idea of His nature and attributes. Much has been thought, and said, and written, by theological and philosophical thinkers upon the subject of God: his nature, his attributes, and mode of existence; but I think it must be acknowledged that they have left the subject much as they found it; except, perhaps, the profound mystery with which they have clothed it, and the educational and mythological belief, by the assistance of which, a phantom, instead of a god, has been made, to the utter confusion of ideas.

Concerning His personality, let us now inquire. In one sense, He is an individual; and, in another sense, He is not an individual. God publishes and declares the peculiarities and distinguishing characteristics of his personality, to the world day by day, and year by year. In every edition of the human type, though that edition be not revised and corrected, is seen a republication of the Deity, as a personality. It is not unprofitable to learn in what this manifestation of the Divine Personality consists: it consists in this—the Spirit, as already shown, contains elements and attributes which, if an individual is properly unfolded from birth, render the spirit harmonious; and behind the senses of the body are the principles or beginnings of senses, which, after death or transformation, constitute the senses of the mind. Thus, for illustration, back of the bodily eyes are principles of perception; back of the ears are principles of hearing; back of the sense of touch is a principle of sensation within itself; and when the spirit or the individual *is out of* the physical organization, these principles will put the individual in the possession of identical senses—different from those we inherit from birth, *only* in refinement, and capabilities of happiness.

Thus it is with God. He has no physical eyes, no physical ears, no physical hands and feet; but he contains the *principles* of Perception, of Hearing, of Feeling, and all other principles,—this constitutes his personality. Therefore, Deity is an Individual in Principles, and yet not separate from or outside of Nature.

The Principles of Nature, or Deity, are unchangeable. Nature is the mediatorial substance between the Cause and the End or Issue of creation; and it is therefore the instrumentality by which an Infinite Intelligence accomplishes infinite results. And, as was stated in a scientific view of God, those Rules, or Laws, or Principles, (which terms I employ synonymously,) by which He *acts upon* and *moves* Matter or Nature, *are only significant of his eternally fixed mode of existence!* And inasmuch as God is fixed in Nature, like the mainspring of a watch, or the heart in a human body, so also is his *mode* of existing and acting, fixedly and unchangeably, determined by *the very fact* of his being in existence; and by the absolutely inevitable and indispensable constitution of things, of which He is the Unfolder, Sustainer, and Co-essential.

We are now prepared to consider the next question in order—

What is God Theologically considered?

Science considers God with reference to Effects and Phenomena; Philosophy considers God with reference to Causes and Principles; and Theology considers God with reference to his Love, his Parentalship, and his Providence. I am here impressed to employ the term "theology" as synonymous with religion.

God, when viewed through the Theological telescope, ceases to be a Potentate, a Chieftain, or a Judge; but he appears as the Infinite Fountain of all life and activity, of all sensation and intelligence. He is the Great Father—Spirit of all spirits—the Great Type of whom all other spirits are but indications, and corresponding organizations. He is the Creator, and Sustainer, and Father of all. The essential qualities and properties of his Infinite Soul penetrate all Nature, all Things, all Spirits; and these *qualities and properties* are essentially Love, and thus God is Love. Thus do we morally and religiously contemplate the Deity.

Contemplate a magnificently grand, bottomless, shoreless, and incessantly active Ocean; contemplate that Ocean replete with the most graceful and beautiful forms of Light and Life; contemplate that Ocean sparkling and radiant with emanations, so rich, and so effulgent, as to extinguish the brilliancy of the most perfect and the most precious diamonds of earth; contemplate that Ocean as rolling in waves of unmeasurable magnitude, and so peacefully still, as to disturb not an atom that rides upon its bosom; contemplate that Ocean with its tides, on their upward and homeward way, those onward tides, which *can never recede;* contemplate that Ocean flowing into numberless founts or Spirits in all Planets and in all Spheres, so pouring in upon them its living waters as to satisfy all desires for life and tranquillity, and causing those founts to "thirst not again"; contemplate that Ocean—Greater than all —Richer than all—Deeper than all. Think of it as the Origin of all Life, all Love, all Youthfulness, all Spiritual beauty and magnificence—and you have *then* taken one step toward a just theological conception of the essential Love of God!

The Theological view of God converts him into a Parent and Creator. He ceases to be a mere Fact, a mere Truth, a mere Principle, a mere Cause. He is "our Father"! and now we think of the celestial sweetness and of the exhaustlessness of his Love; we think of his near and unchangeable relationship to our most interior selves; and we feel continually a kind of *particular* Providence in our existence, and a protection from the multifarious temptations and accidents of life, when we feel that we unrebelliously do his will. And notwithstanding the fact, that every accident, and every temptation, and every circumstance, can be accounted for upon rational or natural grounds,—and that there are in reality no absolutely special providences,—yet the soul loves, in its child-like confidence, to refer every salvation from them to invisible and supernatural agencies. This grows out of a Filial regard for the Deity; for, if the sublime principle of Reason was brought to bear upon the *causes of events* in human life, the (so called) mysterious local Providences of God would be discovered to be but local or particular manifestations of the fulfilling of his unchangeable Laws by which the *whole* as well as the *parts* are governed.

Nor is the purely Theological view completely divested of the mysteriousness of human events and existence. But when this view is resting, as it always should, upon a Scientific and Philosophical foundation, then it will not only be entirely divested of mystery and supernaturalism, but it will be a source of never-failing and forever growing consolation, to the Soul that entertains it. Therefore, a true understanding of God is to be greatly desired. As is our God, so are we. If He is apprehended as an organized principle—organized as the human Soul is in its most interior principles: and if it is received, that He operates according to eternally-established Laws or Rules of action, which being, in themselves, so surpassingly righteous that they produce a kind of *necessary freedom*, or *independence*, and which Rules can not be violated with impunity—then will our Spirits bow with all the pleasure of an intellectual obedience to the Laws or Will of our Father, and feel a beautiful freedom in the *very fact* of moving in harmony with universal Nature. But if it be believed that God is a separate Personality, somewhere outside of Nature, and that he has one set of Laws by which to govern Matter, and another by which to govern Mind, and yet another by which to govern the moral actions and religious sentiments of individuals; and if it be also believed that an individual may escape the consequences of a violation of any of these Laws, by the superior righteousness, or sufferings and vicarious atonement, of *another* individual; and again, if it be believed that God can be moved to sympathy by prayers—or to passion by the taking of his name in vain, (while the profanation can only injure him who utters it,)—if these things are believed in—then, will the thus believing Spirit be dissatisfied with its uncertain destiny, and it will feel almost continually separate from, and out of harmony with, those things which pertain to the Divine and Infinite.

In Christianity, are to be found the clearest evidences of a belief in God in a purely Theological or religious sense, and, with it, an implied belief in his separate personality. But no where do we find evidences of a Scientific and Philosophical view of God, except, incipiently, in the writings of some of the Grecian Philosophers, and now and then in the investigations of modern Thinkers and Theologians.

When the soul is crowned with a proper development of the religious sentiment,—the everlasting beauty of which tints every thought and impulse with purity and peace,—then, is God found to reside within, and above every thing, as the Father and the Friend of ALL! This heavenly truth was realized by the expanded soul and refined intellect of Jesus, of Paul, of Swedenborg, of Fourier, and others; but the more perfect beauty of this important truth is yet to be indicated in the progress and institutions of Humanity! When the human Soul shall have become sufficiently expanded and refined as to be able to *receive* and *realize* the *truth* that God is the unchangeable Father of Spirits, *then* will all *partial* systems of religion, and government, and discipline pass away; then the colleges and institutions of instruction, instead of receiving students and pupils on condition that they will consent to be measured by some theological rule, will teach the truths of Nature and of God, and thus those institutions will also become revelations of the good and true.

View God with scientific eyes, or through scientific mediums, and he is a "Great Fact;" view God through philosophical mediums, and he is a "Great Positive Mind;" and view God through theological mediums, and he is a "Great Spirit Father." That individual who, from the superiority of his mental structure and intellectual developments, can conceive of God in his highest and truest mode of existence and government, is capable of enjoying much harmony and of teaching the sublimest truths; for as is his Heavenly Father—his God—so is he! This is a truth which should be studied to its foundations, because it has much to do with human progress and harmonization.

There can not possibly be any antagonism between true science, true philosophy, and true theology. Science is the parent and foundation of philosophy; and theology, (*true* theology, I mean,) is the ultimate and perfect development or flower of the two combined. Hence, should science affirm the Great Active Power of the Universe to be a Substance, it must not be supposed that true philosophy or theology will affirm any thing to the contrary; but it is righteous to expect and to receive, from the latter, new and higher revelations and confirmations of the first affirmation; because all truth must be in harmony, though seen from different positions by different minds, in different degrees of growth.

In accordance with a previous definition, it is the nature and mission of Science to contemplate and classify effects; it is the mission of Philosophy to contemplate and classify causes; and it is the tendency and mission of Theology to contemplate and classify the innumerable manifestations and diversified ramifications of Love, Will, and Wisdom, as the latter are distributed throughout the organization of Nature and of the human soul. Science is wholly superficial; it is a system based upon external observation and experience, and it is entirely an offspring of the bodily or material perceptions. Philosophy, on the other hand, is based upon reason and intellectual observation; it is an offspring of the understanding—it is both deductive and inductive—and comprehends the nature of causes, beginning with the CAUSE of all causes, and tracing the slightest details to their most impalpable minutia. And Theology is based upon the Love principle of the soul; it is an offspring of feeling, of affection, of religious sentiments,—it is the science of all sentiments and affectional conceptions,—embracing Power, Wisdom, Goodness, Justice, Mercy, and Truth! Hence it is easy to comprehend the causes of the seemingly vast dissimilarity of views entertained by those various minds whose different structure compels them to think of God, some scientifically, some philosophically, and others theologically. Having thus introduced this vast subject, let us proceed to consider it to its foundations.

Mind and matter, or God and his Body, are universal and eternal! There never was a time when nothing existed; nor can there ever be a period when nothing shall exist. It is impossible for the most exalted intellect to imagine such a thing as nothing, because the proposition is self-contradictory, absurd, untrue. The mind can always conceive of truth. It may not indeed be capable of perceiving and comprehending *all* the truth; but in so far as its capacity extends it can conceive of truth and love it most supremely. If therefore the mind rejects the proposition that God created the universe out of *nothing*, it thence may be legitimately inferred that the proposition is false, and hence incapable of entering into harmony with the reasoning principle of the philosophical mind. That *something* always existed—that the universe is an eternal organization of eternal elements and essences—is a statement which even the *instinct* of the barbarian readily acknowledges as altogether undeniable. We will not, therefore, tarry with useless argumentation.

True science declares God to have seven distinct modes of action, viz.: first, the anatomical, which relates to *structure:* second, the physiological, which relates to *function:* third, the mechanical, which relates to *force:* fourth, the chemical, which relates to *decomposition:* fifth, the electrical, which relates to *combination:* sixth, the magnetical, which relates to *harmony:* seventh, the spiritual, which relates to refinement or *attenuation*,—embracing, in its universal sweep, the government of the moral or spiritual universe. These are modes by which God lives in and moves his universe; and which, though the most rudimental manifestations of the Great Positive Mind, will receive particular attention in the present investigation. Such is a generalization of what universal science declares concerning the ways and modes of the Infinite. But Philosophy brings her disclosures into a higher and more concise condition.

She conducts the soul deep into the universal and ever-enlarging tendencies of material nature, and indicates the names of those principles in accordance with which the Great Positive Mind acts in all the innumerable departments of his empire. True Philosophy declares the first or rudimental tendency of all existing things to be ASSOCIATION; which means that every thing is moved and governed by a principle of affinity—that there is nothing in the expanded universe which has not some relationships—that one particle has an indwelling affinity for another particle, which affinity is not changed until, by the process of refinement, a new affinity is developed whereby that particle is moved to seek new and higher relations. And the same law which operates in the atom is also active in the far distant spheres. The field of its operations is illimitable, boundless, infinite! God lives through all things. Hence this Law of *Association* unfolds its sublime workings every where. But the next principle which Philosophy has named, in accordance with its mode of action, is PROGRESSION; that is to say, every thing *grows* and advances in refinement and perfection perceptibly; that all things are progressively acted upon or moved by the Divine Mind to the end that the pure, everlasting, and infinite may be unfolded from the material and apparently impure combinations of nature. And hence Philosophy—(I mean the Harmonial Philosophy)—names this unfolding process, DEVELOPMENT. Development is the last and highest manifestation of matter and mind. It is the flower of all association and progression; it is the grand and divine consummation of all terrestrial and celestial movements; it is the *ultimatum* of all *supernal* endeavor; and hence this law may be regarded as the deepest—the widest—the highest—the most omnipotent—and as the holiest *tendency* of Nature and Deity. There is no limitation to these processes, no termination to the workings of Development; and, yet, by the latter law, it may be said that every distinct system of creation receives its permanent coronation.

True Theology declares that the essential and unchangeable element of the Great Positive Mind, is Love,—unlimited, inexhaustible—impartial—infinite—eternal! A love that—

> "Lives through all life, extends through all extent,
> Spreads undivided, operates unspent."

And there is not an atom, into which it does not flow, in all this boundless universe. Love is the source of all attraction, of all repulsion, of all affection and sentiment. The little vine seeks association with its kindred vine. Birds of corresponding character and plumage consociate, and mingle together their cheerful, melodious song. The flowers exhale their fragrances, and thus give forth their atmospheres to the congenial elements of immensity. The beasts of the fields, whether friendly to man or not, involuntarily yield to this universal Law of Love, and will breathe into each other's nostrils the instinctive sentiments of friendship and affection. And behold the young trees of the forest! they hasten toward the atmospheric space, far above their elder brothers, to receive the light and heat of the sun. The elements of immensity are affectionally conjoined and consociated—thus water, and air, and fire, and heat, and light, and electricity, are made to occupy specific positions, and to perform particular and innumerable functions, in the wide domain of infinite development. Innumerable worlds, like so many cog-wheels, are held by an indwelling attraction, or love, together in ineffable concord; and thus roll around the great central Orb which gave them birth. But the affections of the human soul are more expressive of this universal and eternal law. Like jewels, they decorate the inward sanctuary of the spirit; and blessed is that soul which has never felt the strong hand of enmity or adversity heavily laid on those precious ornaments of life—tearing them from their native places. And in the midst of these numerous affections—affections for science, for philosophy, for music, for architecture, for friends, for children, for conjugal companionship, for immortality, and for happiness—yea, in the midst of this sublime assemblage of loves in the human soul, there stands, towering majestically above all the rest, a holy and everlasting *love*, which draws the heart toward the supernal Mind! Therefore the spirit seeks to gratify its deepest, widest, highest desire, by striving to see and comprehend the Author of its being. Thus, the free-born mind is attracted toward its Maker—as the particle of iron is drawn toward its magnet; for God is the Great Positive Magnet of the universe, and every thing else is negative to its inconceivable and eternal Power!

And true theology, declares also, that the mediatorial or executive element of the great positive Mind, is Will—boundless, unrestrained, incomprehensible, omnipotent! A will that moves the fixed, unchangeable Laws of Nature; governs the myriads of planets which cluster around the realms of infinitude; and determines the modes of Divine being and doing, because it is, itself, a revelation of *what* God is, and *how* he lives in his empire.

But these elements of Divine Love and Divine Will must necessarily have a governing and directing principle; hence true theology affirms that the highest and most inconceivably glorious attribute of the Divine Mind, is Wisdom. The organism of Nature is ladened with demonstrations of the omnipresence of this attribute. Harmony pervades all things, penetrates all things, pulsates through, and in, all things; and the inductive mind, the scientific mind, the philosophic mind, and the theological mind, can not but acknowledge that Wisdom—superior and supreme—is impressed and expressed upon every thing in existence. It is not the individuality of objects, elements, or organisms which manifests the presence and Wisdom of God—but it is the stupendous TOTALITY of things—it is the vast, harmonious, and inimitable ARRANGEMENT of all visible and invisible realities—which amazes and confounds the contemplative mind, by impressing it with the sublime and irresistible conviction, that Wisdom—eternal and infinite—spreads throughout the length and breadth of the Universe; wisdom being, in this sense, the great flower of all conceivable intelligence, and the glorious ultimate development of all that is pure, everlasting, and infinite! Yea, the outer universe is a visible manifestation of the indwelling Divinity. And while every thing is impregnated with life and sensation,—with springs of incessant and eternal motion; with inclinations and disinclinations; with attractions and repulsions; with impulses and sentiments; with tendencies and aspirations; with sympathies and antipathies,—it is elevating and consoling, for the inquiring mind, to know that Divine Wisdom governs all things, and guides them to their proper destinations.

Thus, it is seen that *true Science* directs the human spirit to perceive the Divine Principle as acting anatomically, physiologically, mechanically, chemically, electrically, magnetically and spiritually; that *true Philosophy* directs the spirit to perceive the Laws of Association, Progression and Development, by which the above specified modes are determined and governed; and that *true Theology* points the spirit to behold, in the structure of the Infinite Mind, the celestial elements of Love, Will, and Wisdom. How unrighteous it is, therefore, to blame and condemn the intellect which can conceive of God, only, as a mechanic conceives of *motive power*—of the *main spring* or propelling forces—whereby a machine is made to perform its legitimate duties! Some persons can not think of God except as a "Principle of Life," inherent in the constitution of matter. Such intellects, owing to their peculiar mental structure, can not elevate their conceptions above the doctrine of *chance*. They can not believe in specific creation; nor,—when they view the sin, discord, misery, imbecility, unnecessary imperfection and wretchedness of mankind generally,—can such intellects readily acknowledge a *wise*, *merciful*, *intelligent*, and *just* "First Cause" of existence. Reasoning thus superficially, and, to the majority of minds, demonstratively, this class of persons becomes the victim of much clerical accusation and denunciation. But then, there comes forth the second class of minds who firmly believe in the eternal existence of an intelligent "Great First Cause," yet can not conceive of him as possessing the human form. They think of him as an organized Intelligence—as a living, thinking, and voluntarily acting principle—as a main spring in the universal clock-work of Nature! and this structure of mind is properly termed the philosophical. But the theological class of intellects—those who are affectionate, religious, and sentimental in their temperaments and impulses—can not think of God as an element of life, nor as merely being an intelligent First Cause; but they think of him as children conceive of ancient giant kings. In their thoughts they contemplate God as a large, symmetrically proportioned and inconceivably glorious "King of kings"; as a monarch robed in auroral magnificence; as being seated upon a throne of ineffable grandeur; as holding in his right hand the scepter of universal legislation and sovereignty; as watching every pulsation of the human heart, and as listening to every word which impulse or deliberation have moved human dogmas to utter; and as hearkening to the prayers of the penitent on the earth, and to the eternal and never-changing glorifications of the celestial inhabitants—the redeemed.

Thanks be unto the Being whom we are contemplating, there are shades of *truth* in all these dissimilar conceptions of the Creative Principle. But it is now proper to commence an examination of the demonstrative evidences of God's nature, of his modes of action, and of the position which he occupies in the immeasurable domain of life and realities. As a necessary and indispensable amplification, then, of all that has gone before, I will proceed to express my impressions of the locality and constitution of the Great Mind of the expanded Univercœlum.

Far, far away beyond countless constellations of suns and planets, and deep, deep in the fathomless bosom of the immeasurable Univercœlum, throbs the HEART of all life and animation. Its deep, harmonious pulsations flow through innumerable vessels to the unimaginable circumference of all planetary existence; and there is not an atom, not a flower, not a solitary vine, not a world, not a soul, not an angel, which does not receive, every instant of time, fresh life and vigor from this inexhaustible source of celestial essences! This Heart is God. His life-elements are embraced by the all-comprehensive term, LOVE; his elaborating powers by the term, WILL; and his governing attributes by the term, WISDOM. These elements, powers, and attributes are organized into ONE SOUL—the MIND of the Universe—THE ONE ONLY AND TRUE GOD!

Upon the very threshold of this investigation, the feeble and finite mind of man is overwhelmed and confounded. It tremblingly shrinks from the boundless scene—the contemplation is too magnificent and stupendous for human thought: and the soul faints at the very commencement of its eternal pilgrimage. But this must not be! Go on, thou searcher of the Infinite—go on!—tremble not when the Great Mind of the Universe is presented to thy vision, for "the pure in heart shall see God"; and shall not fear, but love him, with an ineffable joy and undying devotion!

It is only human thought that circumscribes the residence of the Infinite. We can not think without fixing a *form*, *size*, *locality*, and *sphere of movement*, to the object or cause of our meditations. Hence, I am impressed to speak of our Heavenly Father as residing in the *center* of all existences. And when I speak of his elements, powers, and attributes, as being in a state of organization, the impression designed to be conveyed to the reader's mind, is, that God is constructed *like* the human mind. If we will think of a perfectly *pure*, *just*, *benevolent*, *impartial*, *harmonious* human mind, and then conceive of this mind as being *infinite*, *universal*, and *eternal*, we shall have taken the first correct step toward forming an undying conception of the Super-celestial Intelligence that rules the Universe!

Previous to the present structure of the Universe—when the inconceivable realms of immensity were channels through which flowed a boundless ocean of unformed materials—the Infinite Spirit was manifested only as a principle of Motion. Incessant, unrestrained, unchangeable, omnipotent *action* was the first manifestation of Deity. It must not be apprehended that God was not then an organized Intelligence; for he is an eternal and never-changing Principle; but, at the remote period in the history of the present planetary developments of which I now speak, there were no media or materials sufficiently unfolded for a greater and higher manifestation of the creative principle, than Motion. Nor must it be inferred from these propositions that God is subject to the identical Laws of association, progression and development, which proceed from his celestial constitution and operate so unchangeably throughout the vast arcana of material and spiritual unfoldings; but it is highly essential, in order to form a correct conception of the Great Parental Principle of all things, to understand that these Laws, so to speak, are simply expressions of the Creator's *habits*, or of the peculiar constitutional tendencies of his Divine nature, which are displayed throughout the unmeasurable totality of existence. No! the God of the Universe is not a being of development or growth. He is a fixed Fact—a fixed Principle—a fixed Heart—a fixed Flower of perfection and infinite intelligence; but he displays the elements, essences, and attributes of his inexhaustible and incomprehensible constitution in successive and endless series and degrees; and each of these series, and each of these degrees, is unfolded in an order which is pre-eminently progressive and mathematically harmonious. Human progression consists in the eternal variation and advancement of these series and degrees. Hence it is not proper to say that God, himself, is a progressively developing mind; but it is righteous to acknowledge that every thing unequivocally demonstrates that God manifests his immortal essences and attributes in all departments of Nature in proportion to the readiness of things to become the vehicle of the manifestation. Therefore, I repeat, that, in the beginning of the present structure of the Universe, the Infinite Spirit was only manifested as a principle of Motion.

The great vortex of celestial Intelligence,—the great center of eternal Love, the great nucleus of Omnipotence, the immortal flower of Wisdom, which breathe forth the elements of universal Harmony and the fragrance of undying delights,—is the irresistible Magnet which attracts upward the human Soul. Hence to the unimaginable center of all things, the spirit goes to commune with the one only and true God. And while the theology of the earth bids the soul to think of Deity as the child conceives of a great and powerful monarch, or as the poet dreams of the awful shadows of an unseen power—moving like a conscious, all-pervading atmosphere upon the bosom of creation—the *truly* scientific, philosophical, and theological mind beholds God as an organization of unchangeable and celestial principles. Such a mind conceives of something—A SUBSTANCE—a concentrated sublimation of *real* elements and essences; and thus the Deity, being familiarized with our reason and intuition, causes us to realize the truth that He has proportions, tendencies, and principles of action which he can neither change, suspend, transcend, or destroy. Therefore, "with God all things are" *not* "possible." He can not go counter to the eternal principles of Power, Wisdom, Goodness, Justice, Mercy, and Truth, which describe the sublime perfections of his character. He can not change, transcend, or destroy, the anatomical, physiological, mechanical, chemical, electrical, magnetical, or spiritual processes of his universal constitution. He can not suspend or change the associative, progressive and developing modes of his manifestations in Nature. We have, therefore, assurance made doubly sure that God is a fixed, organized Principle in the constitution of the Universe—"without variableness, neither shadow of turning."

How difficult a thing it is for man to change his habits of thinking! Nature may make her accustomed revolutions; the seasons may come and go; the hours may record the deep pulsations of the Infinite Heart; friends may appear on the stage of life, perform their brief parts, and pass away before the soul of man, and yet his educational habits remain almost unchanged. And why is this? It is because the inhabitants of earth have not yet grown to a point of discrimination between the transient and the permanent, between the actual and the seeming. Humanity is just emerging from its youth into manhood; therefore the world is now replete with the fleeting and evanescent doctrines and theologies which characterize childhood and youth—the germs and shadows, perhaps, of stupendous truths and world-reforming principles; but since humanity is about to become a full-grown man, it is wise to expect that it will "put aside childish things" for evermore. Among these repudiated "things" will be thrown the doctrine that God is not a substance, and the proposition that "with him all things are possible;" for it will be soon discovered that falsehood is not an ingredient in that universal combination of Mind and Matter which constitutes the great system of Nature.

It is not my present design to enter into a philosophical argument to demonstrate the existence of a Deity, because human consciousness, intuition, reason, and aspiration are a sufficient demonstration. There is no absolute skepticism in the human Soul with regard to a Great First Cause; but there is existing much doubt as to the personality and separate consciousness of this formative principle; therefore these revealments are designed to dissipate this wide-extending and painful skepticism, by furnishing a philosophical conception of the Infinite, based upon the relation between cause and effect, between the finite and Infinite. And when I speak of the definite location and eternal fixedness of the Infinite Principle, I intend to impart the impression that the *Cerebrum* and *Cerebellum*, or BRAIN of the universe, is established eternally and unchangeably in the Great Center of all existences. If the Deity had no personality of consciousness it would then be positively impossible for him to realize any existence whatever. It is only by contrast and dissimilarity that we know of our own individuality of character. The reader feels his *personal* existence, because he can compare himself,—his habits, feelings, impulses, inclinations, &c.,—with the innumerable dissimilar objects and individualities which surround him in the vast panorama of life and animation. Indeed, were it not for these countless varieties, he could not realize any definite and satisfactory identity of existence. So with the Infinite principle—God: He can not realize any existence unless there exists something finite, something less comprehensive and glorious, by which a positive *contrast* can be drawn and experienced. The focal concentration and phrenological organization (so to speak) of the Great formative and celestial Principle of the Univercœlum, therefore, is an inevitable necessity flowing from the incontestible premises which Nature spontaneously presents to the perceptions of an unclouded reason, and which are amply demonstrated by the uniform testimonies of human consciousness.

To the Great Center of the countless spheres, material and spiritual, every other center must be finite; so also, to the motions—forces—principles and individualities of the Infinite Mind, all other motions—forces—principles—and individualities must of necessity be distributed throughout the endless planes of creation in a regular and harmonious succession of series, degrees, correspondencies, and representations—all being limited, local, finite and imperfect, when contrasted with Him. Therefore, finite or comparative perfection is the inevitable consequence of the existence of an absolutely infinite and perfect PRINCIPLE. If every thing was infinite in extension, eternal in duration, and perfect in constitution, there could not exist but one all-pervading, unparticled, unconscious element; because there would then exist no foundation for action, no aspiration of the imperfect after the perfect—the finite after the infinite—no GREAT, lesser, least; no HIGH, lower, lowest; but an eternal chaos of unimaginable elements would be the all-in-all of existence. Every thing, therefore, can not be infinite, eternal and perfect. There must of necessity be gradations of motion; procession of series; progression of degrees; and a geometrical arrangement of all parts and principles which flow from the Great Central Brain of the universe into all the innumerable ramifications of animation and structure. Moreover, there can be but One infinite, One eternal, and One perfect principle in the constitution of things. There is not space sufficient to permit the existence of an infinite and eternal *Evil Spirit.* God is positive, all else is negative. If there exists an Evil principle, would not that principle be an integral element in the constitution of the Divine Mind? If there exists any where, in the realms of infinitude, an empire of sin, misery, and endless wretchedness—"a lake of fire prepared for the Devil and his angels"—would not God be also there? God is *all-in-all;*—would he not, therefore, be in the evil principle? God is *omnipresent;*—would he not, therefore, be as much in Hell as in the regions of the sinless and blessed? There is no principle, antagonistic to God; no empire at war with Heaven! it can not be said that God "permits" sin and wretchedness; because he has eternally fixed habits or laws of right. He can not "permit" the great processes of Nature to cease, nor the laws of planetary motion to remain suspended; because these processes and laws are the involuntary and uncontrollable physiological, mechanical, chemical, electrical, and magnetical processions of his uncreated constitution. He did not create these laws and processes—hence he can not suspend, alter, or control them. He can not any more change his eternally established modes of manifestation, than can man will his pulse to continuous stillness or his mind to suspend thought. It is not righteous, however, to think that God is as much in the mineral compound as in the human Soul, that he is—

"As full, as perfect in a hair as heart;"

but it is righteous to believe that He possesses a cerebral organization partially analogous to the human mental structure, and that his celestial and superlatively perfect qualities, essences, and principles flow from the mighty Center of his own existence to the unimaginable and immeasurable circumference of infinite space. God's spirit lives, therefore, in and through all material and spiritual existences—just as the spirit of man permeates and pervades every bone, muscle, nerve, membrane, tissue, fluid, element, &c., which enter into the organism of his material system. Yet every man feels himself more in his head than in his hands or feet; so with Deity. Although he is conscious of living in the universal compound, in the plant, in the animal, in the human soul, in the innumerable suns of immensity, and in the countless spheres of seraphic grandeur and ineffable perfection, yet he realizes a local personal consciousness—in the great encephalon of the boundless Univercœlum.

It is not right to suppose that God is constituted anatomically and physiologically as man is organized; but it is right to believe that he possesses inherently and essentially those *seven* great principles which flow from his constitution into all the multifarious and manifold forms and ultimates of matter which the organism of Nature unfolds to the senses and soul of man. In accordance with the rules of analogical or correspondential reasoning and argumentation, it is easy to comprehend what God is, and where, and how, he lives in the universe. He is the superlative sublimation of all *substantial* qualities—all essences—all elements—all principles —(both those which are known and those which are unknown to man)—in the highest possible concentration of unity; being the very crystalization of all that is refined, pure, everlasting, infinite, unspeakably celestial, eternally bright, grand and harmonious! He resides *particularly* in the mighty vortical encephalon, or cerebrum, of the inconceivable universe; and generally, he

> "Lives through all life, extends through all extent,
> Spreads undivided, operates unspent."

The analogy, therefore, which exists between the Divine Mind and the universe and the human mind and the human body is perfectly and legitimately established. For *as* the human mind is organized on a *finite* plane, *so* is the Divine Mind organized on an *infinite* plane;—just as the seat of human sensation, affection, sentiment, voluntary power, and intelligence, is felt and known to be in the brain,—so are the qualities, essences, principles, omnipotent power, and eternal omniscience, deposited in the great vortical *sensorium* of the universe!

The great and incontestible truth, that all things natural or supernatural, material or spiritual, are locked together in one grand harmonious system of Cause and Effect, is perceived by the consciousness of every rational mind; it is acknowledged and acted upon by the philosophical intellect; but yet there are many minds who can not separate matter from the moving principles of causation which lie within its bosom,—who can not perceive the contradistinguishing characteristics of Nature and God, and the harmonious differences which really subsist between them. With the intention, therefore, of elucidating to such intellects the relations of God and Nature, and the contradistinguishable differences between them, I will proceed to say, that the Divine Mind is POSITIVE and Nature is NEGATIVE—this is all the difference which language can describe. But the idea which these terms are designed to convey may be differently developed. Thus:—God is a positive and moving principle, but Nature is negative and moved. Nature is the body, God is the soul. God is *active*, but Nature is *passive*. God is a celestial and superlatively perfect organization of pure, everlasting and infinite elements and essences, but Nature is an organization of terrestrial materials. God is the eternal flower of all developments, but Nature is the dormitory of all that exists unfolded in the Great Sensorium. God is the Cause, Nature is the Effect. God is the everlastingly *spiritual*, Nature is the everlastingly *material*. Nature is *finite*, God is *Infinite*. Thus, how vast is the difference between the *lowest* atom in Nature and the *highest* principle of the Supernal Power! Yet the two are joined indissolubly and harmoniously—matrimonially, so to speak—and they can never fall asunder; nor can there exist any opposition or positive antagonism among, or in, the innumerable elements which constitute the mighty whole; because God is intimately related to every thing—great or small, material or spiritual, perfect or imperfect—that exists and subsists any where in the boundless empire of his own existence.

The highest conception which the human mind can obtain of the Infinite is essentially theological; but the relations which the Infinite sustains to the finite, which God sustains to Nature, can be comprehended only by a philosophical intellect; and hence, while one reader will understand readily what is meant by the terms "our Heavenly Father" and "Great First Cause," another reader, or, perhaps, the same one, will wonder in his mind what is meant by the terms "Organized Principle" and "Great Sensorium of the Universe." It is not to be expected that all minds will see and understand alike; yet it is well to develop an idea into as many forms and proportions as its nature and scope will permit, to the end that all rational and inquiring minds may perceive and comprehend its applicability to life. To this end, I am impressed to indicate the relations of the celestial elements, which, in a state of perfect, immutable and eternal organization, constitute the Great Positive Mind; also the relation of this Mind to Nature; and the three great Laws which flow from God into the stupendous organism of the Universe. The following statements indicate those relationships:—

1. GOD.	2. NATURE.	3. LAW.
Love.	Substance.	Association.
Will.	Aggregation.	Progression.
Wisdom.	Universe.	Development.

It is seen by the above that God is separate from Nature in the sense that He is *first*, Nature is *second*, and Law is *third*, in the great trinity of organization and development. Hence it is proper to say that,—First, God is the *Active and Moving Principle*—Second, Nature is the *Passive and Moved Principle*—Third, Law is the *Habitual and Elaborating Principle*. It should, however, be distinctly understood that law is not, in and of itself, an "Elaborating Principle," but it is an outer manifestation of the modes or habits of the Infinite Mind as he lives in, and unfolds the innumerable upon innumerable worlds and universes that roll around the Great Center of centers—the Vortical Sensorium of all Intelligence!

For a true and faithful comprehension of the superlatively perfect *qualities* and *attributes* contained in the Great Fountain of Causation and Beginning Principles, it can not be inappropriate to appeal to visible and invisible facts and truths in nature and human experience. Every effect presented to the rational, well-organized mind, presupposes the existence of an adequate cause. All inductive sciences and philosophy, and all contemplation of outer and external Nature, refer the mind to the great creative principles—to the Great Positive Cause of all things. And now these soul-overwhelming questions arise unbidden and spontaneously in the investigating mind—What caused this Great First Cause? What was the origin of the Eternal Source of all causation and unchangeability? What structure did the First Cause originally and eternally assume? If the Eternal Mind ever existed without form and organization, is it not a logical conclusion that He will again be resolved back into his original condition? From these interrogatories, the mind involuntarily shrinks, even while it seeks to comprehend the great beginning principles of all effects, ends and uses. It desires to appreciate the deep, wondrous *motives* which first moved the Eternal Mind to the elaboration of the innumerable forms and structures which swarm the boundless ocean of organic life. It contemplates the brilliant worlds which constitute the glorious stellar system; the silent, easy, natural, harmonious movement of the countless bodies which the cloudless night unfolds to the material senses—bodies which adorn and animate the expanded firmament; and yet these questions remain unanswered. All things pour forth an irresistibly impressive light—an incontestible demonstration—that there dwells somewhere a powerful, intelligent, eternal CAUSE; but when did it begin to exist? and how? and where? These interrogatories are ever flowing, welling up from the troubled depths of the philosophical mind. The contemplative and logically inductive intellect can not conceive that from *nothing*, *something* could have been organized and developed; that effects could exist without adequate causes; that a plurality of causes could exist without a GREAT FOUNDATION CAUSE; and, therefore, his reason and experience surrender. The mind is captured by the universal demonstrations of Nature; and his contemplations and inductive philosophy point to the Eternal Mind as the grand and inexhaustible Fountain of life, support, causation, blessing, and truth!

Inasmuch as a proper comprehension of the habits or *modes* of the Divine Existence can not be obtained by the human mind, in its present sphere of being, except by direct appeals to the visible and invisible truths of Nature and the Soul, I am, therefore, impressed to unfold, through the multifarious stages of material progression and development, the legitimate operations of the various principles of Creation and Divine subsistence. These principles I will progressively put into the propositional form of statement, and proceed directly to their examination. The proposition now presented to the mind is the following:—

First, GOD ACTS UPON THE UNIVERSE ANATOMICALLY.

The well developed mind, I repeat, can not but cheerfully acknowledge that all effects must have parent-causes; and that there must necessarily exist a correspondence or analogy between the causes and the various effects which those causes are instrumental in developing. Yea, the mind can not think without admitting causes into its thoughts; it must, of necessity, have a fixed foundation upon which to base its contemplations and reasonings. And this foundation must be an unqualified admission of the existence and personality of the Great First Cause. Therefore, the conclusion is irresistible, that God contained in the very elements of his eternal constitution the *anatomical* principle, the manifestations of which are every where visible. There certainly could be no structural developments unless the *Cause* of all unfoldings contained the structural law in his own nature. The latter conclusion is as beautiful as irresistible. But to what does it lead the contemplative mind? It conducts such an intellect to the meditation, and comprehension, of the Deity in the primary unfoldings of his eternal essence. The primitive manifestations of God were essentially anatomical or structural.

Accompanying the great expansion of Motion throughout the boundless universe, was the formative principle—the law, which governed the original arrangements of particles, or atoms, and determined the innumerable forms and stupendous structures of immensity. Circle after circle of *suns* were rolled forth; and suns gave birth to numberless *planets;* and planets gave birth to *satellites;*

and satellites moved off to proper and congenial positions, in the immeasurable fields of Infinitude, and gave birth to *asteroids;* and all this was accomplished by the direct operation and superintendence (so to speak) of the great anatomical law of the Divine Mind,—the pure and the infinite!

The structures of immensity are too vast and numerous for human conception; yet the mind will explore and contemplate the architectural grandeur and magnificence of the siderial heavens; and, while lost in the interminable labyrinths of planetary formation and splendor, it will raise its tiny voice, and ask,—What made these structures so ineffably harmonious and beautiful? What law develops these numberless firmaments? and the interrogatories fly, with lightning speed, from orb to orb, from sphere to sphere; and the Deity, hearing the earnest prayer of the aspiring soul, writes the answer on the expanded earth and unfolded heavens—on the crystalized substances in the earth, and on the celestial spheres surrounding immensity—and which, being properly interpreted, reads thus gloriously:—"Order and Form are the impressions and expressions of Divine Wisdom—the Framer and Sustainer of all harmony and proportion; but Wisdom has a primary manifestation which is anatomical—a mode whereby all terrestrial and celestial things are unfolded from the Fountain of everlasting and infinite principles!" Such are the responses of Nature and God to the prayers of the philosophical and honest mind. How essential, therefore, that all should strive and learn to read these Scriptures aright,—for he who is spiritually blind may stand in the presence of a beautiful scene upon which the glory and radiance of ten thousand firmaments are perpetually reflected, and yet not perceive or enjoy a single thing that moves before him, nor read a line upon that illuminated page which our Father's hand has traced!

In the structure of the planets,—in the forms of the solar systems, in the shape of the earth upon which we tread,—are manifold indications of the great anatomical law. The construction of trees, plants, flowers, vegetables, and the numberless diversifications of forms which properly belong to the great vegetable kingdom of Nature, furnish demonstrative evidences that this great law of God is primary in the progressions and developments of creation. And this anatomical manifestation is still more obvious and perfect in the ascending kingdoms of Nature. The anatomy of animals and man! what can be more certain indications of the original and eter nal existence of the great structural principle?

Inasmuch as *spirit* is a *substance* superior to matter, which it moves, the conclusion can not be avoided that the Formative principle, or Spirit, which lies back of, and beneath, all visible combinations of matter, must of necessity contain all which the externals of Nature manifest to the senses. Therefore all anatomical developments visible in the foundation of all animal and human organisms, are incontestible demonstrations that, that power, which originally unfolded these structures, existed *prior* to their outer manifestation. God is the cause, Nature is the effect—that is to say, the *primary form* of Nature is caused by the *primary principle* in the Divine Constitution. Contemplation of the qualities and essences originally contained in the GREAT GERM of the illimitable Univercœlum is necessary to a proper comprehension of the multifarious and stupendous structures into which those qualities and essences spontaneously flow. Every thing is an *incarnation* of the Divine Principle; but the series, degrees, associations, and representations of structures manifested in Nature are expressive of the various principles which the ONE GREAT PRINCIPLE contained and contains. And man is a part of Nature. The form, or anatomical construction, of each joint shows the original principle; and the internal and external formation of the bones and other structural assemblages of the human body, demonstrate the intention of combining strength, lightness, symmetry, and beauty, in the smallest amount of material. No human skill can combine, within so small a space, the same combination of powers, the same variety of forces, the same concentration of harmonious development and symmetry, as are presented in the structural possessions of the human form. But what is this inimitable piece of workmanship compared with the wondrous architecture of boundless infinitude? Almost nothing!—nothing, when the spiritual eyes gaze upon the transcendingly glorious "images" of the eternal Mind that tread the flowering paths of the higher spheres. Nothing! when the soul contemplates the mighty circles of suns and planets that move in the ceaseless ocean of immensity; because the greater consumes the lesser—the finite is swallowed up and lost in the Infinite!

Second, GOD ACTS ON THE UNIVERSE PHYSIOLOGICALLY.

Again we are reminded of the sublime conclusion, to which all Nature points the rational mind, that the external manifestations of creation are a reflex of the internal and invisible principles which reside in the constitution of the GREAT MIND of all minds—in the eternal and illimitable CAUSE of all causes. How uniformly do germs reproduce their kinds. The acorn develops an Oak; and so the germinal embodiment of all known forms invariably produces, unless accidentally or otherwise prevented, the highest ultimate development in its own image and likeness. So the Divine Mind begets his image and likeness in the human soul. This grand concentrated ultimation of the formative principle, however, is never accomplished immediately, but mediately—never directly, but indirectly—through the agency of countless instrumentalities. But the theologies of the "footstool"—of the earth—have never consented to this gradual development of the human soul. They have, from the most remote date of their history, asserted the direct and immediate creation of the first human pair; declared that all mankind are descended from the primitive germ; and that we are born defective and depraved in consequence of the alleged transgression of that germinal duality—the first pair—who, the same mythological theology asserts, came pure and perfect from the Creator's hand. From these theological hypotheses it can not but be inferred that the receivers of them are fully persuaded of the anatomical and physiological constructions of the Deity; that they, like Swedenborg, the spiritual geometrician and physiologist, believe the Divine Principle to be a Divine Man—in the possession of those anatomical and physiological proportions which, in a finite and extremely subordinate degree, are represented in the human form. Else wherefore pray, that the ever-hearkening *Ear* may vibrate with the sound of thy voice, and the Great Mind comprehend thy meaning? wherefore say that "the first human pair came pure from the Creator's *hand*"—and that "the all-seeing eye" watches our every thought, "our comings in, and our goings out?" Is not all this equivalent to asserting your belief in the divine human form of God? Is it not acknowledging most unequivocally, that God possesses to an inconceivable and incomprehensible degree of perfection, the organs of *hearing*, *seeing*, &c., together with *hands* and *feet?* Yea, it is virtually acknowledging Him to be in fact a great "King of kings, and Lord of lords." But the explanation of these conceptions is exceedingly simple—it is that mankind conceive *theologically* thus of God,—viewing him as a great Ruler among the armies of heaven and the inhabitants of earth; as an uncreated, unrestricted, uncontrolled Monarch of the Universe; as a mighty Jehovah, King, Lord, Maker, Sovereign, and Father. And, thus, will the religious sentiments of the human soul ever think of, aspire to, and address, the Great Principle of causation, animation and life, which resides within and moves the stupendous universe. But the harmonial philosophy explains the existence of the senses of hearing, seeing, &c., in man, together with the other structural possessions of his organism, by referring the mind to the fact that *germs* contain, embosomed in themselves, the beginning and ultimate essences and principles which the form, structure, and functions of their final development openly manifest. The externals of Nature, therefore, mirror forth the essences and principles of the great Internal and Eternal Mind. God possesses the *principles* of hearing, of seeing, of voluntary and involuntary motion, of anatomy, of physiology, &c., in the inexhaustible depths of his own constitution; and hence these principles flow progressively and harmoniously forth into material organisms —just as the acorn flows into an oak, or as the azure element among flowers begets itself in the violet. The *principle of hearing* is in God; it thence flows forth through countless avenues and instrumentalities, and amplifies throughout infinitude; and having unfolded itself into series and degrees of forms, to the end that its innumerable diversifications might suit all degrees of material and spiritual perfection, it finally incarnates itself in the physical organ of hearing in man's possession. So with seeing, and all the other senses natural to the human form. They commence with, or exist primarily in, the constitution of the Divine principle, and then ultimate themselves in man. This is the foundation law of all incarnation. Thus we are again reminded of the truth of that ancient proposition in theology, that "man is made in the image of his Creator;" for God is the cause, Nature is the effect, and man is the end or ultimate. The Spirit of God is ubiquitous—is omniprevalent—and tends to infinitely multiply its seven modes of manifestation. As a germ, which being deposited in the bosom of the earth, expands and unfolds its qualities and essences into manifest forms of like nature, so does the *Great Germ of the Universe* expand and unfold its celestial and immutable principles into mineral, vegetable, and animal forms, and finally, as a concentrated ultimatum of them all, into the material and spiritual organism of man. Hence, among all earth's developments, man is the highest incarnation of the Divine principle; but when he shall have progressed to the position of spirits, angels, and seraphs, then his face and form will more and more typify the Divine source from which he and all things originally emanated.

Parallel with the manifestations of the great *anatomical* or structural law flowed the great *physiological* or functional law through the immeasurable labyrinths of immensity. The evolution of forms and structures, consequent upon the immutable operations of the anatomical law, was accompanied with a corresponding evolution or appointment (so to speak) of offices or functions which those forms or structures were adapted to occupy and perform. By the incessant action of the original ocean of unformed materials which existed prior to the present structure of the boundless Univercœlum, there were unfolded,—in accordance with the great primary law of *affinity*, or (which is the same thing) association of particles and essences,—all the myriads and myriads of suns and solar systems which even the telescope demonstrates to be revolving in the unimaginable mazes of immensity. And how exalting it is to the contemplative and devotional mind to know, that every sun, and every solar system—even every particle of matter composing them, and every principle of vitality permeating and actuating them—has some specific and important *function* to perform—has an indispensable duty to discharge in the great organism of Deity! Oh, let us not shrink from the contemplation of these stupendous realities—but let the soul expand before the light of these great, undying *truths*, to the end that we may comprehend the indwelling attributes of our own nature, and more of the modes of the Divine Existence!

Yes, the mighty systems of immensity, whose numbers and magnitudes no combination of figures could describe, have each a mission—a function—an end to accomplish, in the great scheme of progression and development. (This mission, function, or end, is described in the division entitled, "*What is man anatomically and physiologically considered?*" to be found in the first volume of the

Great Harmonia.) There are six circles of suns in the present constitution of the Universe; and each circle has vast assemblages of planets and satellites in numbers inconceivable. But only *one* of these circles has planets that are sufficiently advanced and refined in their constitution to develop and support animal and human existence. This circle is the fifth one—enumerating the circles from the great Fountain CENTER, outwardly toward the circumference of all planetary development. And the sun which sheds its genial rays upon the earth; which sends forth its vivifying emanations adapted to all the forms and structures that move upon the earth's surface; which inspires our sensibilities, and animates our every thought—this sun is only *one* belonging to that boundless fraternity of suns which compose the fifth circle. Hence, our Mercury, Venus, Earth, Mars, Jupiter, Saturn, &c., &c., are members of this great brotherhood of suns and planets, which are sufficiently purified and refined to bear such fruit as *vegetables*, *animals*, and *human spirits*. But, it may be asked, what *function* is assigned to the interior circle of suns, whose planets do not yet yield the above specified productions? These are mighty *wheels* in the stupendous mechanism of the Universe,—wheels indispensable to the accomplishment of the end for which the whole was breathed into this form and order of existence.

The physiological principle of the Eternal Mind expresses itself primarily in *functions* thus exalted and sublime. From the inconceivable SUN which constitutes the Center of the vast Universe, and around which revolve all the numberless circles of suns and solar systems of immensity, there are innumerable functions discharged by the various Orbs, including those which we can gaze upon in our own firmament, and extending far, far beyond our powers of recognition through the agency of the most powerful telescope. The circles of suns and cometary bodies, existing between us and the great central SUN of the boundless Univercœlum, are as essential and indispensable to the existence and fruit-bearing functions of our fifth circle of suns and planets, (including our own earth,) as the roots, body, branches, and other appendages of a tree are essentially necessary to its ultimate productions. But the discussion and amplification of this overwhelming subject is deferred to a future volume. In this place it is only necessary that the investigating mind perceives the operations of the physiological Law, which, because of its universal and multifarious manifestations, must be traced and retraced back and deep to the very constitution of the Infinite Principle itself.

Nothing which manifests life and animation, is without functions; and there is nothing which is not impregnated with the Eternal Spirit of all life and vitality. Hence, the apparently inert stone, the mineral composition, the minute plant, the merest insect, and the slightest organizations of motion and life, all have distinct and appropriate functions to perform in the great Body of causation. There can not possibly be any absolute *chance* formations—any mere *accidental* development of form and function—because the universal principle of *cause* and *effect* is infinite and undeviating in its operations. True, the pool of stagnant water will presently swarm with lizards, toads, and fish; and the moistened flour will, if excluded from light and atmosphere, generate the first types of the saurian or reptile kingdom; yet, how faithfully do the anatomical and physiological laws display their presence, exert their influence, and demonstrate their legitimate energies! Some developments in Nature may appear to be the offspring of evanescent and co-accidental circumstances—may seem to be the effects of a system of concentric causes,—wholly fortuitous, uninstigated and undesigned—but this appearance is deceptive; because nothing can occur outside of infinitude—beyond the sphere of the Eternal Cause, whose spiritual and material constitution comprehends and embraces all existences. The simple fact that the human mind can not conceive of creation without admitting the existence of a *Creator*—can not acknowledge effects, without, at the same time, admitting the absolute existence of parental causes—is a sufficient inferential demonstration that *chance*—" a fortuitous concourse of atoms"—is an impossibility; but that there is a great Central, Creative, Omniscient Mind, fixed in the organism of the mighty vortical sensorium of the Universe.

As before said, it is not consistent with the character of this volume to attempt a demonstration of the existence of Deity. If there could possibly be an act of supererogation—of undertaking the most unnecessary and extravagant thing—such an attempted demonstration would very properly be thus denominated. Because it would be striving to demonstrate that of which every thing is a living demonstration. As well might an individual undertake to prove his own entity when his existence is the only proof which he can furnish, and which is an incontestible demonstration. So the forms and functions possessed by the material organisms in Nature are incontestible demonstrations that the Great Motive Power of the Universe contains, within its own constitution, the principles of structure and function; or, in other words, anatomical and physiological laws which, like living souls, ultimate themselves in material and external organizations. But here the question may be suggested, what is the *design* of all these external manifestations? What grand *end* are they calculated to accomplish? The answer is, the Great Positive Mind, as a Cause, develops Nature as an Effect, to produce the human Spirit, as an ultimate. The human spiritual principle is unfolded and eternally individualized through the instrumentality of innumerable suns and planets, and also through the regular progressive development of minerals, vegetables, and animals; all of which man represents and embraces in the energy, strength, symmetry, and structural beauty of his form, organs and functions. Man is the flower of Nature—the prototype of the living God. The great mechanism of the universe is, therefore, adapted to the complete accomplishment of this unspeakably grand and glorious End or ultimate—grand and glorious, because it fixes unchangeably the structure and immortality of the human spirit! The myriads of suns and planets that inhabit the realms of boundless infinitude are all secondary and subordinate, in position and importance, to this sublime consummation in the order of Nature, viz.:—the production and eternalization of the human soul! Again it may be asked, if God is omnipotent and omniscient, why did he not accomplish this apparently simple work in a far less stupendous and complicated manner? It is because God can not act contrary to his eternally fixed habits or modes; and it was not, and is not, possible for the immutable MIND to act otherwise than in accordance with those laws. Therefore, we are forced back to the consoling conclusion, that God is a fixed, unchangeable, eternal CAUSE, whose resting place is the Mighty Sensorium, and whose field of action is the wide-extending, illimitable Univercœlum.

Contemplation of the varied forms and structures of external Nature is expanding to the soul of man; because it is gazing upon the vitalizing qualities and essences, or, rather, upon the *bodies* and *organisms* into which they spontaneously flow. The anatomical principle breathes forth, and clothes, or *incarnates* itself in the countless forms which we behold upon the bosom of Nature, and swimming in the shoreless seas of infinitude; and the physiological principle is in constant association with the former—like an eternal companion—furnishing its elaborations with motions and forces adequate to the discharge of the varied duties for which those forms were made. Gaze upon the earth in the spring time, when the seed, which the husbandman has sown, is expanding and germinating into being; see how it breaks open the earth's surface, and puts forth its tiny tendrils into the warm and glowing atmosphere, which is vitalized by the sun's heat and magnetic elements. And in harmony with the season, the perfect plant is unfolded; not only resembling its parent-germ in form and function, but multiplying itself an hundred-fold. Thus *one* grain of wheat will bear *fifty* grains equal, if not superior, to itself. There must, therefore, be an *attractive* power in the parent-germ sufficiently strong to draw surrounding elements, and contiguous substances into its constitution. These contributions are not voluntary; but the elements and substances are compelled to enter the sphere of the germ by an overmastering force of attraction. Of this, however, I will hereafter speak. The object now is to show how every power and essence tends to a multiplication of its kind. And in conformity with the undeviating operations of this law, the anatomical principle of the Divine Mind *incarnates* itself in innumerable *structures;* at the same time, and on nearly a parallel plane of action, the physiological principle *incarnates* itself in innumerable *functions*—all to the end that the *human soul* should be developed on the summit of Nature, in the full possession of an individualized and eternalized organization!

The Law of *incarnation* is, therefore, universal in its nature and operations. How unreasonable it is, then, to believe—as many of the earth's inhabitants do—that God is local and special in his personal favors and manifestations; that some particular individual on the earth has received, in accordance with Divine permission and appointment, an unusual share of the celestial energy. The eastern nations are impressed with this conviction. They suppose, as do the Christians concerning Jesus, that their leading chieftain has been the recipient of such a favor; and the consequence is a *sacrifice* of self-dependence and reformation upon the altar of a vicarious atonement for their multitudinous sins and transgressions. The laws of Nature, (which are expressive of God's modes of being and doing,) are emphatic in repudiating the doctrine of a local and special *incarnation* of the Divine Mind. But it may be said, that our inward *conscience* and our rational *judgment*, as we are constituted, will not permit the subjugation of this faith—that, because our *con-*

science approves of the doctrine of God in Christ—that Christ was God manifested in the flesh—that we are not, therefore, to question its truth. But I am impressed to speak against the cherishing of this error, first, because it is an error; and, second, because it opens the broad road which leads to the destruction of much virtue, integrity and benevolence among men, and dwarfs their growth in excellence. Thousands who have been taught to seriously believe in the special incarnation of God in Christ, and that repentance at the "eleventh hour" is as good as in the early stages of youth or manhood, that—

> "While the lamp holds out to burn,
> The vilest sinner may return;"

yea, thousands have been led, by such delusive doctrine, to *procrastinate* their attempts and determination to live good and virtuous lives, because they supposed they could, when on their death-beds, escape the eternal consequences of sin by simply placing their faith in the vicarious atonement and relying upon the sufferings of the Lord Jesus Christ. For is man not taught that "he that believeth shall be saved"? and the yielding up of the soul to Christ at the eleventh hour has always appeared to the *commercial christian believer* as safe as living a virtuous life from his childhood, or as, by his own efforts, progressing away from inherited imperfections, to the attainment of nobler qualities. And almost every believer in the special incarnation of Christ is a commercial devotee—is full of expediencies and desires to be "on the safe side" of all probabilities and possibilities; does not wish to "trade" away his soul and gain the whole world; and hence gives all the personal and pecuniary assistance he "possibly can spare" to the building and popularizing of churches, to the support of the clerical profession, to the missionary cause, and to the education of youth. The latter effect should be considered an evidence that in the end all "evil is overruled for good." But the truth can not be disguised that, the impressions which many unfortunately organized minds receive from the doctrines of vicarious atonement, and a special incarnation of the Holy Spirit, are exceedingly pernicious and disastrous to the general welfare of humanity. The ill-conditioned mind, having murder in its thoughts, meditates to himself the *chances* of ultimately escaping the consequences of his act. He thinks he can repent at leisure. And, now behold the barbarous justice which this theology terms divine and eternal. The murderer is arrested and incarcerated. The day of his execution is fixed. He is attended by "spiritual advisers," who strive with him to effect his soul's salvation from the supposed "*wrath* of God" and the endless punishment of Hell. And in most instances the culprit is satisfactorily reconciled to God—has "made peace with his Maker"—and immediately subsequent to the correspondingly barbarous event of strangulation, he glides, from the scaffold, into the celestial courts of heaven! But whilst the murderer is thus disposed of, what becomes of the murdered? Oh, that is uncertain! Wherefore? Because in nine cases out of ten the illegally murdered individual is removed from earth before he has time to "reconcile his soul to God"—he dies an unrepentant and consequently unpardoned sinner. And what is the consequence of this? Why the latter goes to the abodes of everlasting wretchedness, while the former, he who sent him there, is permitted to reside in the world of the blest! Surely such a theology is degrading and demoralizing to the human soul. It unintentionally holds out the most seductive inducements to the individual, whose misdirected inclinations and unfortunate circumstances move him to the adoption of the various vices. It virtually says to the infirm transgressor of social and moral principles that a full and entire repentance will save him from the terrible consequences of his transgressions. It says to the youthful mind that "he who repents, and is baptized shall be saved" with an everlasting salvation. Hence, the individual concludes, within the secret recesses of his own mind, that he will "take his fill of sin"—will eat of the forbidden fruit—will yield to the temptations which surround him; because popular theology informs him, that, "in the day thou eatest thereof thou *shalt not* surely die;" and tells him that his punishment shall be deferred to the great day of judgment and retribution which is to come; which retribution may be escaped altogether by his simply abandoning in his heart all thought of evil, and believing in an individual who was cruelly executed, about two thousand years ago, by the Jewish people who *sincerely* believed him to be a dangerous man in their community—a preacher of heresy and of infidelity to the then existing religion, and the instigator of a sedition and conspiracy against the Roman government. It must be admitted that this theology exerts a kind of *negative* or *restraining* influence upon the exceedingly limited number of refractory minds who are induced to come within its precincts; but it must also be admitted that these theological opinions do not exert a *positive* and *reformatory* influence, as a general thing, upon their advocates and devotees. There is only one powerful restraint upon the "sinner" in their possession, (and this is founded on fear and not on principle,) viz.:—the bare *possibility* of a procrastinated reconciliation of the soul to God, resulting in its passing by "the day of grace," subsequent to which there are no means of salvation. It is evident, therefore, that this theology is demoralizing to man. It does not make punishment a *certain* and inevitable result of any and every species of individual obliquity and transgression. It does not say, in the language of the primitive history, that "in the day thou eatest thereof *thou shalt* surely die." No, but places the day of retribution beyond the grave, in a remote and dreamy future, which, to that class of persons for whom it is particularly designed, is too far away and indefinite to be of much importance. Now, the Harmonial Philosophy regards every transgression against established principles as an unpardonable sin—as a "sin against the Holy Ghost;"

and it demonstrates the inflexibility and inavertibility of Nature's laws; and proves that no person can possibly escape the legitimate procession of those consequences which follow the violation of any *physical*, *social*, *intellectual*, *moral*, or *spiritual* principle, which is in any manner identified with man's present, or future existence. Let us examine more particularly into this philosophy of rewards and punishments, and inspect more minutely its mighty incentives to righteousness and a life of peace and accordance; let us contemplate what is the sin against the Holy Ghost.

The sin against the Holy Ghost, which is generally understood as being the unpardonable sin, is susceptible of a more reasonable interpretation than the learned scholars of early centuries, and the biblical commentators of modern times, have bestowed upon it. This question of the unpardonable sin has agitated many noble and educated minds; and it is not unlikely that it has confounded and frightened many honest and timid minds who have searched the primitive history for truths and everlasting life. But those clergymen and commentators who have inquired concerning the true meaning of this passage in the Bible, have been thoroughly satisfied, I believe, that it was a sin they never had themselves committed. If it ever was committed, they think the sin is certainly chargeable upon some neighbor, or a certain class of individuals.

Athanasius believed it was chargeable upon the Pharisees, for their contempt of Christ and his works, which they maliciously and wickedly imputed to the agency of the Devil, being at the same time fully persuaded that those works were performed in a good spirit; and in this imputation is an implicit disbelief in Christ's divine and supernatural origin; thus constituting, in the mind of a believer in supernatural and mysterious things, a most formidable sin, one too intrinsically evil to be forgiven.

The difference between a sin against the Holy Ghost and a sin of ignorance, of forgetfulness, of neglect, of inadvertency, and other minor sins against positive or negative precepts and customs, consists in the *former* sin being totally unpardonable, and the *latter* sin being possible to forgive until seventy times seven. But, I think it will appear to those who are accustomed to the employment of their reason, that the punishment which is generally affixed to the commission of the unpardonable sin is *entirely* at variance with those fair proportions which always characterize the principles of justice and truth.

The relation between this crime and its punishment is no more consistent, just, or intimate, than burning a member of the body, or sowing seed, in America, and feeling the pain, or reaping the harvest, in England. Nor are we to suppose that an individual, who (compared with the Infinite Creator) is but a finite and almost insignificant creature, can possibly commit a crime which will be attended with eternal consequences. For, let it be thoroughly impressed, that the human mind can no more *break* or *mar* one of the eternal Laws of Nature than it can render the Deity imperfect or unhappy! To believe that God will punish *infinitely* human beings for any *finite* transaction, is to believe that God is *unjust*—yea, even according to human principles of goodness and equity. Any punishment, to be just, must be proportionate to the magnitude of the transgression; and, therefore, the idea of an individual being punished with an everlasting punishment for that sin, which (according to true philosophy) is only an *injury* done to himself, is an idea only suitable to the barren mind of the barbarian.

But the true explanation of the idea of an unpardonable sin, (which idea I am willing should remain clothed in the terms, "sin against the Holy Ghost,") is now deemed necessary.

The terms Holy Ghost are applied, in theology, almost exclusively to the third person in the Godhead, but this furnishes no clue to a proper interpretation of the idea. The idea is simply as follows:—

The Great Positive Mind lives, moves, and governs, in the vast universe of mind and matter, according to certain fixed laws or rules, which constitute the *Holy Ghost*, or *Excellent Laws* that proceed from his Spirit into All things. The term *Holy*, according to this definition, signifies *excellent;* and the term *Ghost* signifies *law* or *laws.* The individual is always under the control of these laws, which laws operate with an undeviating precision in his physical system, in his social relations, and in his moral and spiritual connections, to the world without, and to the world within him. These laws require the individual to be harmonious in his physical organization, harmonious in his social system, and in his mind. Indeed, a perfectly healthy body, and situation, and mind, are absolutely demanded by the Holy Ghost, or Excellent Laws of our being. Inasmuch as we are governed by, and are only happy and harmonious when obeying, the *principles* of our entire existence, it is plain that any deviation from them would result in discord and unhappiness, to an extent always proportionate to the extent of the deviation; and let it be fully and indelibly impressed upon the mind, that *there is no possible way of escaping the legitimate and entire consequences of any infringement upon the operation of these Natural or Divine Laws.* If you violate the laws of digestion, of gravitation, of reproduction, of locomotion, or of any of the functions of the body or mind, or any of the natural relations which subsist between individuals in society, you will receive the *legitimate consequences* of your violation, and there is no other atonement.

The answer to the question under consideration naturally comes in at this point. It is this:

An infringement upon the operation of Nature's Laws *can not be forgiven*, but must be settled by the individual's suffering the consequences of the infringement. In other words, a sin against the Holy Ghost, or against Natural Laws, can not be forgiven—can not be pardoned—can not be mitigated—can not be augmented, but must be settled by a *full* and *complete* experience of consequences, according to the nature and extent of the sin.

It may be supposed that an individual is punished, not according to what he has done, but according to what he intended to do. If this opinion be entertained with reference to the commission of the unpardonable sin, and in justification of the eternal punishment of the individual who commits it, then I would refer such a believer, for a full refutation of his opinion, to those laws by which we are unerringly governed. If an individual intends to burn his whole body, and only burns a finger, he does not suffer for what he *intended* to do, but for what he *did* do, to his physical system. Should an individual intend to murder a neighborhood, but, failing to accomplish his original design, only causes the death of *one* person, then he does not suffer for what he did, but for what he inwardly believes, or feels, to be the intrinsic evil of his intentions. The deed which would make a civilized man unhappy, would render an Indian joyful. A man is punished by the physical laws for what he does, and by the moral laws, for what he conceives to be the real wickedness of his intentions. But when the wicked intention ceases to inhabit the chambers of the mind, then the individual is no longer committing sin, and is, consequently, no longer punished. The punishments consequent upon evil intentions are exclusively experienced by the individual intending evil; and the causes of his suffering are to be found in those inordinate desires or actions which generate discord in his inharmonious nature. Thus, any thing which produces discord in the physical, or social, or moral systems of our being, will cause us to suffer a physical, social, or moral punishment, and such punishment is always in proportion to the extent and character of the disturbance produced. But, inasmuch as the primary causes of these disturbances are hereditary, educational, and circumstantial, it therefore follows that when these causes cease to exist, these disturbances will also cease to exist;

and hence there will not be a perpetuation of effects or punishments throughout the length and breadth of eternity, as clergymen generally affirm. Now what it is well to believe is, that every infringement upon the physical or moral laws of our being will be followed by its appropriate consequences—*and from them there is no escape.* Therefore, such infringements are sins against the Holy Ghost, and should every Christian in existence be executed upon a cross, it would not lessen a single pang, or save the individual from the legitimate effects of such efficient causes.

And still it may be urged that *conscience* and *judgment* unite their declarations against the doctrines herein set forth. Let us then examine what conscience and judgment are—let us ascertain whether they are altogether reliable authorities.

What is meant by Conscience?

Tender in its nature, and uncontaminated, the little child is born, and ushered upon the stage of life; it finds itself in the possession of rich and numerous impulses, and surrounded by many and powerful attractions. Its eyes are captivated by diverse forms and varied colors; its ears are entranced by sweet tones and attractive sounds; its sense of smell is delighted with delicious and diversified odors; and its whole soul is in the midst of attractions and repulsions without system or number.

Attracted *now* by the voice of parental affection, and *then* by the wild excitement of martial music; now by beautiful flowers, then by a strolling menagerie; and enticed into the fields of fashion—the mind soon learns which of the many and varied attractions produce the most pleasurable and lasting results.

Year after year adding experience to the mind, the child, now advanced toward manhood, learns to discriminate between the attractive and repulsive, the supposed true and the false; and if uninfluenced by artificial or superficial desires and impulses, it will tread the straight and beautiful path which leads to happiness and contentment.

But if the child, on its introduction into life and society, is placed between four prison walls of fashionable and prevailing theological discipline, and if its most pure and natural impulses are met at their threshold with a rash or solemn injunction—teaching that *this* and *that* is evil; then will the mind recoil from, and suspect the society in which it dwells; or else it will break the prison door and rush into fearful extremes in its efforts to be free.

The discipline of unbiased experience creates or erects in the mind a true individual standard of right and wrong; but the discipline of artificial education manufactures a superficial sense of right and wrong; which sense is conventionally or theologically called Conscience. Experience is a mode of educating the Mind; but superficial education is a mode of cultivating the Memory.

The education of the Soul into what the unphilosophical class of minds call a sense of right and wrong, will differ in different countries and centuries; and what is theologically termed *Conscience* will necessarily be different in different individuals, just in proportion to the difference in their religious and general education. Hence, there is a Conscience which is a thing of education; it resides in the memory, and haunts the unhappy possessor like a ghostly phantom so long as it prevails over the spontaneous conscience which naturally flows from the Wisdom principle of the Soul.

Thus, the difference between a Conscience of education, and a Conscience of experience, consists in this: the former is a superficial thing, or a theological phantom of the memory; the latter is a testimony of the Soul concerning its own experience of right and wrong, and is a guide-board by which to discriminate between pleasure and pain, discord and harmony.

It is well to inquire—what proofs have we that Conscience is a thing of education? I answer: the Jews believe that Saturday is the true sabbath, but Christians believe that Sunday is the hallowed day; accordingly they worship on different days of the week. Let the children of Jews and Christians meet and play together daily, and it will be found that the *Jewish conscience* deems it wrong to do on Saturday what the *Christian conscience* deems right, and on Sunday the reverse will exist between them.

Educated by innate experience in this its first sphere of being, the human mind is persuaded that exercise, and music, and dancing, and other innocent amusements, on Sunday, are not injurious, but are oftentimes highly beneficial and happifying to the body and mind; but, educated in the prevailing religion of our age and country, the mind can not possess itself of those recreative and refining advantages without being haunted by that artificial specter of the memory, called *Conscience.*

Children, whose constitutions require plenty of air and exercise, are compelled, among many Christians, to conform to certain fixed rules, and to remain in the house on the Sábbath, condemned to learn long bible lessons, scarcely daring to look up from their book, from which they long for diversion—or to keep a silence which they almost fear to break, even to ask for a drink of water, and why?—because their parents have sacrificed their reason to an arbitrary *Conscience* which is said to be consonant with religious requirements. And although their experience and better judgment testify to the absolute falseness of these rules and requirements, yet having been early victims of them, they can not but shrink from the idea of breaking through them, and acting as their native impulses and reason dictate; the Soul struggles for liberty, but if it be not sufficiently developed to reason correctly and powerfully, then the enslaving *Conscience of education* will surely triumph over its efforts, and the Soul will remain imprisoned in the walls of sectarianism.

The Mahommedan believes our Bible to be a falsehood; and we believe his Bible to be a falsehood—his *conscience* approves what, when, and where, our *conscience* disapproves; and so, also, does the

Chinese *conscience* disagree with the imperative dictates of the Christian *conscience;* and, I think, the reader will find as many different *consciences* as there are different complexions, nations, and languages on the face of the earth.

I say that there are two kinds of *Consciences:*—a *Conscience of Experience*, and a *Conscience of Education*—one is innate and natural, and the other is external and arbitrary. The former teaches us to discriminate between pain and pleasure, discord and harmony; the latter teaches us to distinguish the popular rule and to divorce it from the teachings of reason.

But, considered in any sense, Conscience is educational. And the only method by which to make arbitrary Conscience, or a Conscience of the prevailing theology, the general standard of faith and practice—is for clergymen to commence a tirade against the purity of human reason, to denounce independent investigation, and oppose themselves to science; because the feeble taper of their theology can only shine in the absence of the glorious Sunlight of Reason and Philosophy. But let us inquire—

What is meant by Judgment?

Judgment is more a result of education than of development. Wisdom signifies an unfolding of the principle of self-government and discrimination which resides in the Soul; or it is, in other words, a term signifying the embodiment and harmonious manifestation of the indwelling attributes of the Mind. The act of exercising Wisdom may be termed judging; and the decisions of Wisdom may be termed Judgment. Wisdom is the inward Monitor, or Guardian Angel, (to use a figurative expression,) who takes cognizance of our actions, and who approves or disapproves of them according to their nature, extent, and cause.

Wisdom resides within, and if properly developed, governs the body and subordinate portions and impulses of the mind; but, if Wisdom be imperfectly and improperly developed, then will the

Individual imbibe, through the medium of external education, a kind of artificial standard of Judgment and Government, which is called conscience. And Conscience, as it is apprehended by the religious world, or by theological metaphysicians of modern days, is only another name for Reason, Judgment, Wisdom, and Understanding. Here it may be asked—

When is the Age of Responsibility?

It is generally supposed by metaphysicians and others, that an individual has arrived at the period of discretion or responsibility when he can exercise reason or judgment; when he can discriminate properly between right and wrong, and distinguish the true from the false; but, in truth, no individual has reached the period of responsibility, unless he be elevated above the influences of surrounding conditions and circumstances, and is enabled to practice the decisions of Reason. It is not the mere ability to reason correctly, but it is the strong ability to practice what reason dictates, that marks the period of *self-responsibility.*

But what surprising errors do we find in the religious theories on this subject;—which doctrines have fixed upon about the age of eight, ten, or twelve years as the period when the Creator commences an account with the Creature. From that age, thenceforth, the individual is believed to be capable of choosing between good and evil, and of acting agreeably to his choice. And let it be duly impressed, that, by those doctrines, the standard of right and wrong is already erected, and the individual must be measured by it, and pronounced upon, according to the results of that measurement, and thus are his actions determined.

If a Christian should have children under the control of the inhabitants and the religion of Turkey, the whole system of measurement would be reversed, and the second generation would possess a conscience vastly different from the conscience of its Christian grand-parents. In such an instance it would be the height of absurdity to determine upon the period of responsibility; for the pagan child would not feel compunctions and restraints when and where the christian child *would*, and consequently the sense of right and wrong in the individuals would be entirely educational. Thus, to a very great extent, a knowledge of what is termed *right and wrong* is wholly acquired; and the only question is, who, or what class of individuals, is capable of rendering the *best* judgment upon what is true or false, right or wrong?

But in evidence that there is no reliance to be placed upon age, I would point the reader to the numerous instances in every community where a defective organization of body renders some individuals totally unable to do those things which are considered right by the religious in those communities; and there are also innumerable defects of situations in which an individual may be placed, equally disqualifying the person for the performance of those things deemed sacred and holy according to the best system of measuring good and evil—proving, conclusively, that man, in any stage of growth or sphere of life, is merely a *comparative*, and *not* a free agent.

Hence it is agreeable to reason to believe that the *Age of Responsibility* depends not upon Years nor upon Education, but upon *Intrinsic Growth* and *Spirit-Culture.*

From the strength of the foregoing principles, it is perfectly safe to affirm, that the *physiological* modes of Divine Creation and development are not special and local in their incarnations or display; except as speciality and locality are indices of links in the endless concatenation or chain of causes by which the operations of Nature are identified with the universal habits or manifestations of God. There are no particular vegetable, animal, or human *functionaries* in the order of Nature; for all functions, whether unfolded and established on the material or spiritual plains of formation, are the legitimate manifestations of the general workings of the great physiological principle of the Divine Being, in whom there is no partiality, favoritism, variableness, "neither shadow of turning."

Third, God acts on the Universe mechanically.

It is very unsound and unreasonable to say, that mechanical construction can be an *invention* of the human mind. As well might the Maker of a planetarium profess to have *invented* a solar system, with all its harmonious motions and mechanical forces. But he who investigates the principles of motion, of hydraulics, of the screw, the lever, and the various sources of mechanical power and momentum, is a searcher and contemplator of Nature. Such an intellect is learning, from the mighty mechanism of Nature, how the Supreme Artisan is constitutionally constructed and acting in the wide-spread fields of organic existence. All mechanical inventions, therefore, are but imitations of corresponding forces and structures in Nature. It is certainly a self-evident proposition that man can not *create* or *originate* any thing. He can not make a motion or principle of mechanical action wholly dissimilar to those motions and principles which perpetually actuate the forms and organisms of Nature; but he can investigate, and so familiarize his mind with the geometrical and mechanical possessions of the world of life in which he lives, that he can readily acquire a power of combination, which is new, and this is all the *invention* which the human mind is capable of developing. Invention, then, consists in originality of combination. There is a class of dreams, consisting of new persons, new scenery, new and strange forms and images presented to the dreamer's mind, which are manufactured, so to speak, out of the materials with which the mind is supplied. Such dreams are new, not in the materials which enter into their composition, but in the improved or modified texture and combination of those materials which reside in the memory. The proof of this is, that such minds never dream of things, persons, places, or names with which they have not formed some previous acquaintance; yet the mind, during the hours of slumber, is capable of almost involuntarily combining features, colors, forms, sizes, motions, localities, &c., to such an extent as to extinguish, for the time being, all remembrance of ever having any acquaintance with those things, persons, places, or names, during the hours of wakefulness. So with the mechanic. By investigation he acquaints his mind with the powers and processes, with the inherent properties and mechanical laws of Nature, and then learns to combine this force with that motion, this pressure with that momentum, this centripetal with that centrifugal tendency, and so original is his *combination* of Nature's multifarious instrumentalities that we no longer recognize their primary origin and existence, and hence term the new work "man's invention."

To the mechanic's eye, all Nature is a vast, inimitable mechanism—and God is the Great Inventor. If man can combine bands, screws, metallic substances, and crystalized media, in accordance with those mechanical principles upon which the *eye* is constructed, he will then produce a telescope; and through its instrumentality, he can gaze upon other planets, discover their physical formation, and familiarize his mind with their magnitude and motions in the firmament. If the mechanic employs the *spring*, he but imitates the *elasticity* of the atmosphere, and the perfection of the spinal column in man. If he builds an arch, he but *imitates* the mechanism of the human head. If he combines materials into the formation of a suspension bridge, he but *imitates* the construction of the human breast. If he constructs levers, he *imitates* the bones in his body. If pulleys, he *imitates* his tendons and ligaments. If a pump, he will find his *invention* vastly more perfect in the circulation of blood by the heart. In all things—in water, in steam, in the air, in the tendency of fluids, in the revolution of the earth, in the *cog-wheel* movements of the planetary bodies, in the stupendous *clock-work* of Nature, in the sublime workings of the great *mechanism* of the inconceivable Univercœlum—yea in all things, visible and invisible, in those which are seen and in those which are felt, the true mechanic can learn of God. Such a mind can not be irreligious—can not be unmindful of high and supernal realities. Nor can he doubt the existence of the Infinite and Omniscient Architect; for every thing looks him frankly in the face, and impresses on his mind the truth of original design. He is convinced that the Great Mind embodies with itself all human principles of geometrial and mechanical movement. The *true* mechanic can not but carry in the heart of his mind an unspeakable admiration of, and respect for, the Great Motive Power of the Universe,—he can not but be a good man, a man true to Nature's principles. Yet an unfortunate state of society would smother all such legitimate emotions in the laborer's mind. Nature, which he can see and investigate, fills him with joy and religious sentiments; but society, which he is compelled to stand upon, and conform to, displaces that joy, and those sentiments with feelings of depression, skepticism and despair. When investigating the harmonious productions and movements of Nature, he exclaims: "Surely the Lord God Omnipotent reigneth!" but when he looks upon society, and feels its manifold evils and oppressions, he lifts up his voice in dismay, and says: "Surely there is no God!" Hence we may not expect to find many *true* mechanics in this age of the world. And yet there are such at all times—prophecies of the future!

But when the intelligent mechanic interrogates Nature, there flows into his mind an indescribable sensation of joy and veneration. He traces the origin of all motion to the Great Central Motive Power. The origin of all mechanism must be with the CAUSE of all creation. The mighty *Sensorium* must of necessity contain the essential qualities, essences, and beginning principles of all which is manifested in the great organism of material and spiritual things. Every thing is, in a sense, mechanical in its operations. Even thoughts are *levers* which move the world. Friendship and ties of consanguinity have built ships and circumnavigated the earth. Love has sent its messages through the air on the wings of birds. Commerce discharges its intelligence along the magic wire. And thus thoughts, sentiments, and pursuits, incarnate themselves into vehicles or agencies suitable to their restless nature and easy transportation. It is very instructive to contemplate nature thus mechanically.

Matter and motion, it has already been asserted, are co-eternal principles. Motion was the first manifestation of the Great Motive Power,—*first*, not in time, but in order of its progression or relationship to other laws of creation—and matter was motion's suitable vehicle. And these two principles—matter and motion—contained all properties, all essences, all principles, all laws, forms, forces and motions, to produce all other structures and functions which have an existence in the immeasurable realms of infinitude. Hence, to find the germs and ultimates of all that is terrestrial and corporeal, of all that is celestial and heavenly, we must contemplate the Great Central Fountain of all life and animation—the Great Vortex of all that is pure, holy, everlasting and infinite. Originally Cause and Effect were as brothers, then parents, then grand-parents; but now their relationships to things about us, and to ourselves, have become too diversified, numerous, and remote, to be traced by human thought. All that the most comprehensive and generalizing mind can say, or systematically embrace, is simply this : God exists, the universe exists, man exists—and all besides these plain affirmations of the soul must necessarily be relative, secondary, or demonstrative; and mainly inferential, deductive, inductive, probable and possible. Yet there are mighty truths within mighty truths—stupendous facts within facts—principles within principles—propositions within propositions—these are the *pearls* to obtain which the investigating mind plunges deep and fearlessly into the shoreless ocean of creation and infinitude. There, in its researches it finds many truths which it does not seek, and grasps at many too high and all-embracing for human comprehension; nevertheless, it is good for the mind to erect a lofty standard of thought, and make its aspirations infinite.

Among all the voyagers who attempt the exploration of Nature, there is no one more successful in his endeavor than the true mechanic. He analogically sees that from the lowest to the highest arcana of existence there is a constant evolution or development of principles, motions and forces. The centrifugal and centripetal motions and tendencies of a wheel are but an imitation, on a very imperfect scale, of the corresponding motions and tendencies among the planetary bodies. Motion originally contained all other forms and manifestations of motion; and matter contained all forms and modifications of matter. Cause and effect, positive and negative, material and spiritual, terrestrial and celestial, were all embosomed in the great inconceivable vortex of the illimitable universe.

This contained the principle and nature of all other forms: so that from the lowest and intermediate forms up to the highest, could be constantly produced other forms accompanied with, and controlled and acted upon by, the Great Positive Power. Progression of the angular evolved the *circular*. This assumed, not a spherical constitution, but it was a combination of angular and rectilinear plane. Therefore the continuance of the angular to the circular was only a perpetually progressive form, ascending toward the *spiral*. And this developed diameters, axes, and poles, containing the perpetual angular, and progressed to a still higher and more perfect form, that of the *vortical*, properly the celestial.

Thus from the lowest to *this* sphere of progression, there was a constant development of inherent principles and laws, the lower containing the higher, and the perfected comprehending all below it. The perpetual vortical or celestial, was the Spiritual; in which there is nothing but what is refined, pure, and everlastingly infinite, containing unspeakable and celestial glory, brightness, and grandeur. It is the Vortex, the inconceivably perfect and spontaneous substance of the GREAT POSITIVE MIND!

The greater comprehends the lesser, especially that which was first, and yet the greatest is not developed except by order and virtue of degreed progression. And so each state assumed new qualities and involved new developments, until the highest put forth its everlasting brightness, an index of its own origin!

Thus it is seen how every thing begins with, and ends in, the Great Positive Mind. How incontestibly demonstrative is all Nature that the Vital Principle, which moves, actuates, governs, perfects, and unfolds her innumerable properties and essences, contains the anatomical, physiological and mechanical principles in its very constitution! For Nature indicates the modes of the Divine Existence. As the spirit of man acts on his body so does the Spirit of God act upon the Universe; the former is an exact correspondential representative of the latter, which is the First and the Highest of all life and animation. In order to further elucidate and substantiate the proposition, that God acts upon the Universe mechanically, the delicate construction of the ear, the eye, the brain, the nerves, even the human spiritual principle itself, may be examined; and the motion of air, and water, the tides, the vast multitude of mechanical operations going on in all departments of the earth and creation, the laws of tension and extension, of contraction and expansion, may be analyzed; but I am now impressed to leave the reader to tread these interesting paths of examination and analysis in his moments of free thought, and proceed to another proposition in this magnificent theme.

Fourth, GOD ACTS ON THE UNIVERSE CHEMICALLY.

Taught from earliest childhood to institute a system of thinking so discriminating as to separate material from spiritual things, the human mind is scarcely able, in the last half of its earthly existence, to learn to think with a philosophical consistency and systematic order. The educated classes—classes which emanate from our highest academies and colleges, are taught to think with accuracy and precision upon scientific and relative subjects; but when religious themes are introduced—when theological dogmas are presented to theological students for examination and adoption—it is then deplorable to observe the sad inconsistencies and contradictions that emanate from our systems of instruction. In the scientific and legal departments is erected a standard of judgment which perfectly contradicts the standard adopted by the theological departments. That which is demonstrated scientifically true in one branch of education is held to be theologically false in another. Geological and Astronomical sciences prove unquestionably that the earth has passed through a series of changes, while undergoing the process of formation and development, each requiring more than a thousand years; but theology affirms, on the authority of the primitive account, that the earth was made in six days, or in one week according to our system of diurnal calculation. It must be acknowledged, however, that, owing to the plain and incontestible demonstrations of science with reference to the period of the earth's creation, theology has modified some of its principles of scriptural interpretation so that days can be termed eras, or epochs; and hence, in this respect, a degree of consistency has been achieved between the two departments of education; but in almost every other respect the division walls are high and strong. It would not be deemed possible by such thinkers that there could be really no inconsistency between a scientific truth and a truly theological or spiritual truth,—that what is true in the rough, gigantic stratifications of our planet is equally true upon every other planet, and in every other sphere of existence. Hence, the lines of demarkation have been strongly drawn between the affirmations of theology and the demonstrations of science. Man has been taught to never apply a chemical truth to a spiritual problem. No harmony has been permitted to exist between them.

Science proves the principle of perpetual development and progressive perfection—even common experience, acquired through the external sensibilities of our physical nature, demonstrates the growth of trees, plants, animals, &c.,—but theology, although it yields in silence to natural operations, positively affirms that such principles can not apply to the moral and spiritual state of man. In other words, what is true in the animal kingdom is *not* true in the human kingdom; and what is true in the latter on the earth, is false in heaven. There has always been a vast distinction made between the principles of Nature and the principles of Divine Government. The law of gravitation is to be considered scientifically (so theologians are taught to think) just as we look upon stones, plants, &c., but such minds can not conceive that the same law is equally operative in the innumerable empires of spiritual existence. Now I am impressed to apprehend the movements or principles of Nature as indications of the modes of Divine Existence and subsistence; or as rudimental manifestations of those immutable principles which express the constitutional processes of the Infinite, and the character which he will preserve throughout the endless concentric circles of eternity. But these impressions are not sanctioned by the scientific and theological standards of judgment and education which exist in the world. Why not? Because these popular standards do not any more harmonize with the great harmonia of material and spiritual existence than they do with each other; they are opposed to the universal *unity* of truth; that is to say, theology does not erect a grand all-embracing standard which will harmonize science, philosophy, and theology, with the great psychological and spiritual developments which result from the progressive unfoldings of the human mind. Here it may be asked—

Does Truth reside in every thing?

From a germ of good and truth, unfolds every material or spiritual form; but the form will bear the impress of existing conditions and surrounding influences. Those conditions in which the germ is developed, and those immediate influences which actuate its unfolding, are represented in the ultimate formation. A simple and unimportant truth may be deposited in a community of uncultivated minds; it will become magnified with additions and superadditions of error and misconceptions, and finally will be settled as a subject of undoubted truth and profound importance. Entertaining tales of enchantment, though false, will grow to realities in the youthful mind. So supernatural accounts, magnified and sublimated beyond the infant intellect, become sacred realities and magnificent truths to intelligent men. Thus any germ will gather substances around it, perfect or imperfect, according to the attending and developing influences. Consequently men seem to transform truth into error, and then endeavor to conceal its deformity with a protecting garment of possibilities, and then probabilities, and finally by universal consent. This is owing, partially, to the constructive genius of the human mind, its proud and enthusiastic ignorance, and its affections for truth; for error, when firmly fixed and organized in the mind, satisfies the desire for truth as if it were truth itself, and the possessor imagines himself as happy.

To ascertain how much good and truth dwell within, and, by their adhesive power, hold an idea or proposition together, we are compelled to analyze the interior—the germ. From interior examinations we are conducted to the consoling conclusion that almost every theological system, or belief, or proposition, has germinal excellencies and redeeming qualities—which, as with individuals who seem imperfectly constituted, counterbalance many of their imperfections and engage our attention and confidence. The truth which each system or idea contains, and which has unfolded itself amid contaminating influence, is what preserves the manifold deformities and inconsistencies of the system with which it is incorporated. We object not to receive instruction through the medium of a fable nor will we complain if clergymen embody as *much* truth as error in their multitudinous discourses; but if an idea, having a foundation in truth, has grown out of due proportions, by the mental influences which promoted and governed its development, then the good is submerged in error and removed from the mind; and the form of the truth is no longer useful, inasmuch as the error which it combines exerts a deleterious and imperfect influence upon those who proclaim it, and upon those who listen.

No idea *abstractly* considered, is untrue or evil in its tendency; nor are men, thus separately considered, impure or imperfect; but considered in reference to other ideas, and men contrasted with men, their positive qualities and imperfections become, at once, highly conspicuous. But the reader inquires—

How shall we discriminate between Error and Truth?

Individuals, as well as the body of mankind, have a standard of judgment; and men can not exercise judgment without a rule and method. The way we *know* that twelve inches are more than *one*, is by establishing a standard, or adopting a system of measurement, by which we can ascertain the value of one inch, and then the additional inches, or increasing length, is known by contrast. So do we measure *men* and *opinions*. The ignorance of one is rendered conspicuous by the wisdom of another; and the judgment of an individual will invariably correspond to his spiritual growth. The Chinese measure *our* ideas of beauty and morality, and our intellectual advancement, by themselves; and we measure *their* ideas and growth, by those *we* entertain, and from the position which we, as a nation, have attained and at present occupy. By civilization we sound the depth of savagism; the superior form of the one makes us sensible of the inferiority of the other, and we judge of it accordingly.

The flower was once the highest organization of matter on this earth: then came the animal, whose duality of structural arrangements, and harmony of organism, declared it the next highest form in the order of creation. Finally Man came forth and ascended creation's throne; and now, contrasted with Man, all else is inferior and seems imperfect. Thus man is the standard by which we measure the relative perfection of animals, flowers, and the various forms of matter. So of all other things. Before the introduction of steamboats and railroads, the sloop was an expeditious and elegant mode of traveling; but now, contrasted with the higher forms and inventions, the sloop is very imperfect, very slow, and does not serve the purposes of personal transportation.

Now as we judge of the completeness and utility of natural and artificial creations by their highest forms, so should we judge theological systems and ideas. We prefer Moses to those before him, because his legislations were above theirs; and we prefer Christ to Moses, because Christ taught a superior doctrine, and presented a nobler and holier form of truth, the beauty of which is enhanced by the heaven-wide difference between his character and that of Moses. So we measure Catholicism by Protestantism, and, contrasting the former by the latter, we readily choose the highest, or that which is nearest our education and mental growth. If we are indoctrinated in any modified form of Protestantism, *that* form becomes our standard of judgment; and every other system must be measured by what we believe (because unacquainted with more truthful ideas) to be the highest form of truth.

Who, then, shall say what system of theology is the highest? Every man judges according to his educational inclinations, and actual degree of spiritual enlightenment; therefore who shall say what is most true and perfect? For ourselves, we would answer—*that* system which has for its germ and essence, the supreme excellencies of pure philosophy and science; for by them, and in their scale, must every system of theology be judged and weighed. Our standard is Philosophy. "It is coming to be seen," says a theological writer, "*that nothing can be theologically true that is scientifically and philosophically false.*" This is our rule of measurement, our standard of judgment, and our highest form of truth.

We have, therefore, two privileges and duties to exercise and discharge; our privileges are, according to philosophy, to analyze the origin or germ of every theological system, idea, or proposition, and ascertain how much the real good and truth which they contain, are encumbered with the error which has accumulated upon them during the ages: and our duty is, according to science, to determine the quality of existing forms of religious doctrine, and ascertain their influence upon the human character. The contrast will be sufficient to guide us into the paths of righteousness. Every thing must come to this test; and as we exercise judgment upon all subjects, and ideas, and systems, according to what we know of nature and science and philosophy, so should we strive to become highly enlightened in these, to the end that our judgment may be proper and correct.

The mission, so to speak, of the Harmonial Philosophy, is the destruction of all antagonism between science, philosophy, and theology; and the harmonization of the elements and attributes of the human soul, and consequently to accomplish the millennial union of social and natural interests. It contemplates the unity of all Truth. It recognizes the same immutable laws on earth as in heaven; and when the world shall recognize them, then here, as there, shall "our Father's will be done." That principle which proceeds from the Divine Mind into the spiritual spheres, and there determines the relationships or affections, in accordance with the great law of affinity, is acting in a subordinate manner, and on a subordinate plane, in the chemical compounds of Nature. There is, therefore, a unity of action every where in the Universe. That law of Nature which causes harmony in the materials composing our earth, a law which regulates the stratifications of rocks, the distribution of plants and animals, and the geometrical progression of the human species, is also the cause of harmony in the numberless spheres of refinement and perfection, which constitute and indicate man's future habitations.

We are not to contemplate the chemical action of God in his Universe as confined to what chemists term "chemical action" among metallic substances and earthly compounds; but to acquire an incipient comprehension of the height and depth, and length and breadth of this mighty chemical operation, we must contemplate the composition of suns and planets—we must inquire into the well-nigh inscrutable causes that hold our glorious sun together in the firmament. What is it that perpetually rescues our earth from decomposing and flying instantly into a chaos of indistinguishable atoms? What saves the planets from utter destruction? The causes of all this silent and undisturbed harmony, of all this indwelling security and assurance, are not discernible by human eyes; but the spiritual powers of the soul must attempt the investigation, for even the latter can only ascertain the perfection of those chemical relations which subsist between the Great Vital Principle and its physical organism, which is the boundless Universe.

The principle of association, which is the incipient manifestation of Divine Love, flows forth from the Mighty Heart of Nature, into all the labyrinthine ramifications of organic life and animation. And chemical action is its sequence or companion. Fire, heat, light, and electricity, were the four grand, primary consequences of this principle's operation. These rudimental divisions of matter occurred just prior to the creation of the structure of the present universe. They were suitable media or vehicles for the subsequent developments of suns and planets, and for the unfolding of life and intelligence upon the surfaces of those planets which belong to the sixth circle of suns. Accompanying all these manifestations was the chemical action which indicates one mode of Divine Creation. And it informs us of the workings of immutable principles in one particular department of the stupendous Whole.

Did the reader ever ask himself the questions—What supplies the earth with elements and substances sufficient to compensate for the expenditure perpetually occurring? What preserves such justice, such a balance among all the forces and materials of Nature?—What causes such a distribution of equilibriums, and preserves such nexpressible harmony, between the supply and the demand? The perpetual refinement going on in all departments of the earth causes angular and unorganized particles to advance to the formation of mineral organizations; and, by the same law of progressive refinement and atomic ascension, the mineral advances to the vegetable; this to the animal; and the latter ascends to the formation of the great crowning kingdom, which is the human. Hence the human kingdom must perpetually draw its nourishment and subsistence from the subordinate forms and forces; and the latter must necessarily subsist and exist upon whatever is contained in the unseen labyrinths of the earth's interior. Again: meditate how the intense and incessant chemical action, which is going on every where in the earth, causes latent and dormant elements to be developed and evolved. Oxygen, hydrogen, electricity, and magnetism, are constantly being eliminated and organized, first, into water, then, into air, then, into mighty agents of universal sympathy and relationship, and finally, into the *moving—living—sentient*—and *intelligent* organism of the human soul. What a vast expenditure is here presented! Every material and spiritual element is being constantly ultimated into immortalized spiritual principles; and nearly twenty-five millions of these eternalized organizations leave the earth and go to the spirit-land every year. In truth, it may be said that, in the aggregate calculation, spreading over half a century, about *one* spirit departs from earth with every tick of the clock, or with every second of time! And the *compaction* of the particles of the elements, which flow from Nature into the soul's indestructible organism, is so indescribably minute and perfect—the atoms themselves being so exceedingly fine and attenuated—that a very large quantity of gross visible material would be, and is, absolutely demanded in order to make the organism full and entire. It requires large quantities of earthy substances (including the elements of mineral compounds, and vegetable and animal forms and forces,) to elaborate the organization of *one* human soul—even several wagon-loads or tons of these material forms and spiritual forces are indispensable to this closely inwrought and indestructible organism—and *one* of these passes from this rudimental sphere to the spirit-land every second of time! Here there is a great draught upon the resources of Nature. What saves the earth from positive diminution in its dimensions? What gives to plants, and animals, and human beings, all the water and atmosphere, all the electricity and magnetism, in the form of oxygen, heat, and light, which they perpetually require and receive unasked? I answer, it is the Chemical action of the Great Vital Principle upon the Universe. It is caused by the incessant decomposition of elements in one portion of Nature, and the impartation of those elements to such forms and combinations of matter as are suitable (according to the law of association) to receive, appropriate, and commit them to their own organism. And mineral decomposition is the primary effect of the chemical action of God upon his illimitable Univercœlum. (The reader will find a correspondence, which means analogy, between the chemical operation of God's spirit upon his universe or body, and the chemical action of man's spirit on his body; by referring o page 58 in the first volume of the Great Harmonia.) It was this investigation into and comprehensive perception of God's being and doing in his Universe, which moved me to affirm (in Nature's Divine Revelation) that Man is the perfection of all forms, and degrees of these: and that they all have ascended in a uniform and progressive manner, to the *human* form, which is the grand result of all the subordinate creations.

Again: the mineral world is like a *stomach*, whose office it is to receive, digest, and transfer particles from the still more imperfect substances of the earth. The mineral kingdom, then, as soon as established, commenced its work of unceasing activity. It is a receptacle for the influx of particles still inferior, and is an agent to modify and transfer them, by a process of refluxation, into the form of the first particles capable of associating with the vegetable world. This, in its turn, performs the same office, receiving particles into its composition, modifying them by its own qualities and properties, and transferring them to the animal world. This, in like manner, digests, re-combines, and prepares substances to enter into the *human* world. Then *this* world comprehends all the lower departments of creation, and is a receptacle for the influx of the essences and properties of all subordinate organizations. It is likewise a *microcosm* of the whole united energies and creations of Nature. Meanwhile, it stands as an indestructible representative of the original intention of the Divine Mind, by which unchangeable laws were instituted to govern materials, with a view to the production of this end. Thus Law and Matter have accomplished the first end for which they were inseparably created.

Further: the various kingdoms and forms in this rudimental sphere, are all organs for the purpose of transferring, advancing, perfecting, and sublimating all particles in the lower forms of matter, so that they may all conjoin in harmony, and produce Man. Still further: the subordinate kingdoms are forms indispensable for the purpose of communicating a proper energy and quality to each particle of matter, in order to render it suitable to associate and assimilate with the human form.

Chemists who have instituted investigations relative to matter and motion, will tell you that one substance will unite with another of like affinity; but they go no further. But if *particular* matter will only associate with that of like affinity, how is it that four or five elements are often found to exist in one composition? The truth is, there is a mutual affinity existing between all forms and substances throughout Nature, including the mineral, vegetable, and animal kingdoms. There is a constant fluctuation of all these, from, to, and through each other, acting fast or slow according to the development of the matter sustaining these mutual actions. There is a constant and unchangeable movement throughout all Nature, produced by the ultimate of matter, or what is now known to be its inherent properties of life and sensation. There is a constant, undeviating action, which produces and reproduces all forms visible and external. Composition, decomposition, recomposition, visible and invisible, are evidently performing their natural yet ceaseless work, according to established laws. Earth and atmosphere form and compose vegetable existence; and these three, in their united and energetic forces, compose their ultimates, the higher degrees of matter known as animal existence. And this last constantly gives to, and takes from, all things below *its* existence. Hence there is a ceaseless and endless chain of formation and reproduction; loss and gain; accumulation and dispersion, taking place yearly, hourly, and secondly, throughout the Universe. If there is an infected place upon the body, such as a sore or wound, you may see, in its action of healing, a representation of all Nature. You may there see the perfect operation of the two principles or forces of the anatomical and material system. What is decomposed, will be gradually repulsed from the wound; what has formed pure and healthy, by a fresh ultimation and composition of particles, is gradually and carefully deposited at the place where it is required. There is not one particle too much or too little; but the whole sustains a harmonious and united action in forming anew the parts, and repulsing the extraneous and decomposed substances, until the whole is united as before! So with all Nature: every particle of matter being governed by these laws and forces, produces harmony and union in all parts of existence. With an undeviating tendency, each particle in Nature proceeds to its destined spot, there to form what is required, or to become more refined to produce its grand effects and sublime ultimates!

Fifth, God acts upon the Universe Electrically.

In approaching a subject so vast and sublime, our minds should be almost totally divested of the impressions and influences of birth and education. We must think upon the questions as one would think who had just entered into this world of life and being, with all his intellectual and reasoning faculties in a high state of development. This state of simple-mindedness is necessary to a proper reception and understanding of the truth. In *seeking* the truth we must be like untrammeled and unsophisticated infants; but in *understanding* and *applying* the truth we must be like free-born and highly enlightened men. In this mental condition we will now proceed.

That system of mythological supernaturalism which, in truth, destroys all system and harmony in the original creation of Nature, is imperially emphatic in its opposition to a harmonial (or harmonizing) philosophy that asserts and demonstrates the gradual formation of the earth, the progressive introduction of mineral and vegetable organisms, and the steady and philosophical developments of animal and human beings upon its surface. That God made the heaven and earth and all that in them is, in six literal days—days containing twenty-four hours, according to our system of measuring time—and that he "*rested*" on the "seventh day and hallowed it" is the language of oriental supernaturalism. If the most advanced thinkers, among the supporters and disseminators of this disorderly but romantic theory of creation, will not acknowledge themselves believers in the above proposition, but say, that "days," in the original, prophetic style of writing, signify "epochs" or "ages" then it is well to inquire, why they do not consider our sabbath as *one* of those indefinite "ages" or "epochs"? why consider the six days *figurative* whilst the seventh day is accepted *literally*, and celebrated as the day on which God *rested* after a week of exceedingly hard work? This is believed to be the origin of our sabbath; but I feel *impressed* to furnish the reader with a more truthful account of its parentage and relationship to man.

The Sabbath is a day of rest, originally suggested and established by the Israelites or Jews in the patriarchal age, which age may be considered as a mediatorial or transition era, just half way between Savagism and Republicanism; the form of government to which the progressions and developments of the present age are advancing the universal family of man. Sabbath is called Sunday, because it was, subsequently to its establishment, dedicated or consecrated to the SUN, by the most ancient Druids, and also by the early religious sects in Persia. In Persia there are Magi, or priests of the Sun, who discharge what they are taught to believe to be their sacerdotal duties on that day.

Sunday was dedicated to the *Sun;* Monday to the *Moon;* Tuesday to the god Tuesco; Wednesday to the god Wednos; Thursday to the god Thor, &c.; but, for a few centuries past, the Sabbath has been set apart by man, who made it originally, for purposes of rest, meditation and worship.

As a social institution, this day is worthy of commemoration and undying respect; but as a religious institution, it may be forgotten; because it has always caused that class of persons for whom it was designed—I mean the laborer and the irreligious—to do on other days through the week, what it is *never right* to do at any time,—supposing that, by not doing the same on the Sabbath, their souls would pass to heaven free from pollution and sin. It is right to live every day as correctly as on Sunday. To live and act every day as we would on Sunday, and on Sunday as we would every day—thus living a holy and righteous life at all times—is surely more like our Heavenly Father; whose tides ebb and flow in our seas; whose birds sing; whose flowers bloom; whose Sun shines; and whose innumerable Orbs roll on through the immeasurable firmament, all just as much on the Sabbath as any other day.

Fatigued with the toils of the week, man and beast require rest and refreshment. The beast refreshes his nature, the aspirations of which are never higher than the granary; but man, whose aspirations are toward Immortality and eternal Happiness, may put aside the ideas and movements connected with material things, and repair to the sanctuary for spiritual culture and elevation. This is the rational way to celebrate the Sabbath; only let not the sanctuary, in which you worship the ONE TRUE GOD, be always composed of wood, brick and clay. No! Seek God in his universal Temple. If you are moved to read the "Word of God," go forth to the highest mountain, to the humblest valley, to the living forest, to the simplest flower; and just as much as your Love is developed and your Wisdom is unfolded, will be the magnitude and practicability of the lessons you receive from these beautiful chapters in the everlasting Volume.

This digression from a continuous consideration of the general subject before us—viz.: the electrical action of the Deity upon the Universe—is pardonable on this ground, that the supporters of philosophy and the supporters of theology (or those who *can* and *do think* for themselves, and those who *remunerate* clergymen to think for them) can not agree as to the time (or number of days or eras) the Deity required to unfold the heavens and the earth, and all that in them is. The character of geological testimonies, and the truths which perpetually emanate from this interesting department of Nature, are so utterly unimpeachable and self-demonstrative owing to their beautiful rationality, that the representatives and promulgators of oriental theology can not but admit them into the constantly lengthening category of *newly*-discovered *truths*. And it is proper the reader should remember this important fact, that—in accordance with these newly-discovered truths—all the cosmological (or world-building) and chronological (or time-stating) passages and disclosures in the primitive History are revamped and interpreted so as not to contradict, too positively and conspicuously, the wisdom and knowledge of modern days. The cosmogony of the Old Testament is not superior to that which is in the possession of the Japanese and the Norwegians. The traditional theories which these peculiar inhabitants of the earth accept from those of their most ancient progenitors, who were believed to have been divinely inspired, are far more sublime, and explanatory of many curious events in the history of mankind, than those theories which we imbibe from the correspondingly mythological cosmogony of our Primitive History. In these oriental doctrines of the earth's creation we find nothing which unfolds the mighty operations of the Deity upon his Universe; nor do we acquire from such explanations and hypotheses of creation, any new and soul-exalting, soul-expanding conceptions of the All-sustaining Mind, nor of the magnificence and dimensions of the Natural, Spiritual, and Celestial Temple which He inhabits; but on the contrary, we acquire from them the most repulsive and soul-contracting impressions of almost every thing which is really ennobling and sublime. The human soul involuntarily shrinks from the acknowledgment of a God whose character is *capricious*, *impetuous*, *combative*, and *revengeful;* because these propensities are inhuman—they belong to the animal kingdom; yet notwithstanding the repulsiveness of such a disposition, the early cosmological theories among mankind assert the existence of a malignant, implacable, capricious Deity, and they assign him a place beyond the Sun—in a court of resplendent glory.

In the absence of philosophy, how could the contemplative

chieftain of an early tribe conceive the *cause* of thunder and lightning; of earth-rocking catastrophies; of the vomiting forth of volcanic fires; of storms, floods, and destroying tempests—without referring them to the Maker of all things as the manifestations of his wrath? The oriental or mythological explanation of these physical calamities, which were of frequent occurrence in the early stages of human progression, is the best which that unenlightened age could furnish. Hence the writer or writers of the first portion of the Old Testament should not be blamed for asserting the Deity as the immediate *cause* of thunder and lightning, of the deluge, of the rainbow, &c., because it is not to be supposed that those authors, or those from whose traditions they derived many things on cosmogony, were acquainted with Nature's immutable principles, which, while engaged in accomplishing the great designs of the Divine Mind, cause the electric fluid to dart from point to point, from pole to pole, and all the multifarious operations of the (so called) imponderable elements. The doctrines of Moses on the subject of creation, of the flood, and of the confusion of languages, was entertained, in a no less romantic and unphilosophical form, by the early tribes of Central America. By impression, I know that these tribes were in existence several centuries prior to the time which is fixed upon in Genesis as the commencement of the world, (or as the earth's birth-day,) which makes the creation about six thousand years old. The patriarchal tribes of Central America entertained, in their theory of the earth's creation and destruction, many convictions in common with those who adopt the Old Testament assertions with regard to the earth's origin; and these tribes were in existence about one thousand and five hundred years in advance of the period which Moses assigns as the historical marking of the event of man's first introduction to this terrestrial sphere. In truth, the Aztecs, a tribe which once inhabited that portion of the earth, now called Mexico, entertained ideas of the Deity strongly resembling the traditions which may be found recorded in the Primitive History. The Aztecs supposed, and their Heliopolisian teachers inculcated the belief, that four successive revolutions or catastrophies had, by the direct and immediate instigation of the Deity, occurring at different periods, destroyed the whole human family. These different periods were termed sun-ages; meaning days which the God of the sun set apart for the particular display of his almighty power—or a day of universal retribution. From this myth the sacred historians received their ideas and convictions of a "Judgment Day," or of a kind of an ecclesiastical *trial* of all mankind before the Supreme "King of Kings," when "there shall be mourning at the judgment-seat of Christ," and a final settlement between every man and his Maker, in accordance with which there shall be innumerable consignments—the Evil to the lakes of inextinguishable fire, and the Righteous to the blissful realms of everlasting joy.

It will be seen that the Astecian tradition of sun-ages, or eras devoted to the manifestation and accomplishment of indignation and retribution, was adopted by the writers of early mythology. The Christians have abandoned the idea that a "judgment Day" will ever dawn upon humanity in this world, and have fixed it in the remote future—far away, in the world beyond the grave. The Aztecs denominated the first of the four successive revolutions which desolated the world, the Earth-Age. This age occurred (according to their traditions and scriptures) 5206 years subsequent to the creation of the first Sun, in which the mighty giants, who had their dominion over all the earth, were principally exterminated by a general famine, and those who escaped from this divine curse were quickly destroyed by tigers that were designed for this purpose.

The second epoch was termed the Fire-Age, and was manifested 4804 years subsequent to the preceding era. This was a judgment day in which the world was destroyed by the element of fire; and as birds could only escape the general conflagration, the good men were converted into the most beautiful birds, whilst the evil sunk into the gulf whence proceeded the devastating flames. It was believed by the Aztecs that, at this epoch, one man and a woman were preserved in a cavern composed of adamantine rocks and illuminated with shining crystals; from this pair the earth's population had a second commencement.

The third era was called the Wind-Age, and occurred 4010 years after the Age of Fire. In this Day of terrible judgment the world was destroyed by the raging hurricane and the frightful tempest; the various tribes that escaped this mighty revolution were instantly changed into the highest order of Apes or Orang-Outangs.

The fourth and last revolution, which the Aztecian traditions recognize, called the Water-Age, occurred 4008 years subsequent to the Age of Wind. In this epoch there was a universal Deluge by which every thing (including the most of mankind) was destroyed. Many human beings escaped this fate by availing themselves of their ability to be changed into various kinds of fish. But there was, however, one highly favored man and woman saved from destruction by being placed in the hollow of a tree, which was originally designed for this purpose. And it was confidently asserted that the children of this privileged pair were all born dumb, but were soon taught the art of conversation by a dove; and, for some unknown cause, the exasperation of the God of the Sun was so intense that he made every child learn from the dove to speak a different language. This caused universal dismay and alienation.

The general history of human belief with regard to the immediate interposition of God in the most terrific events and calamities which have befallen the earth, would be very instructive; because it could demonstrate the proposition that mythology, in laboring to become philosophical, has pursued a dark, circuitous path, and terminated in the theology of modern times: while philosophy, with mythology on one side and theology on the other, raises her head, like an Angel of God, and with all that majesty and humility, which a consciousness of indwelling truth and knowledge inevitably imparts to its possessor, she treads the endless paths of eternal wisdom, and conducts the honest mind into the immediate presence of pure, everlasting, and infinite things.

That the Deity bestows particular attention upon the Earth and its inhabitants, is an opinion which has been long and universally entertained by mankind. The Indian loves to believe that his tribe and lands were bequeathed by the over-ruling Sachem; that all his hunting excursions and achievements on the battle-field are rendered victorious in consequence of that Power's supreme approval. The Savage, the Barbarian and the Patriarch, are equally impressed with a corresponding conviction; but as individual and national experiences accumulate, and the principles of scientific research and civilization are unfolded, the Savage and Barbarian opinions become refined, systemized, and comparatively sublimated. In evidence of this statement, I refer the reader to the fact, that, instead of the crude and petty manifestations of Supreme attention, recognized by the Indian, we find the sublimer and more dignified exhibitions of Divine design and power, in the writings and opinions of modern Patriarchs, Priests, and Teachers. These confine their attention not so much to the mere formation of our globe, as to the marvelous and sublime manifestations of Power and Purpose, which they profess to recognize as proceeding from the Deity to his children on the Earth some hundreds of years ago. Thus, they recognize special and immediate interpositions of God in the birth and finding of Moses; in the captivity, escape, and multifarious experiences of the tribes under his control; in his enlightenment, in his miracles, in his commandments, and in his principles of government; and in all that the various Prophets were enabled to perform; and in the birth of Jesus too, in his incarnation, in his life, in his teachings, in his miracles, and in the kind of death which he ultimately experienced; and also in the endowments and incarnations of Prophet, Apostle, Pope, Priest, Bishop; and in the supreme and absolute authority invested in the Holy Bible by the institution of the sacred Canon. Thus Patriarchs and modern Teachers have advanced and enlarged upon the convictions of the Indian, who only sees the particular favor of the Deity in his successful hunting, and victorious battles.

The origin of the belief under consideration may be *primarily* traced to ignorance. It is unreasonable to expect that any individual can have a more expansive view of God than the Indian or Patriarch, if he is likewise persuaded that the Earth is the center of Creation, and that its inhabitants are the *particular* children of the Creator. Those who acknowledge a belief in supernatural manifestations, or Special Providences, have somewhere in the mind a defective understanding of the Deity and his works.

But the belief in Special Providences has also a secondary origin in Desire. Some nations and individuals have a powerful desire to be considered particularly important and righteous in the sight of the Creator. It is gratifying and supporting to some peculiarly constructed minds, to think themselves divinely favored, divinely commissioned, divinely endowed; to believe themselves to be the chosen few, particularly in the possession of a "high calling;" and thus actuated, such individuals, by first deceiving others, for the purpose of receiving the approbation and emoluments consequent upon such positions and endowments, ultimately deceive themselves. I once came in contact with an individual whose love of distinction approbation, notoriety, and personal power, were so strong, and so predominated over his imperfectly developed attributes of prudence and conscientiousness, that he was moved to set himself up as the

Jews' Messiah. At first it was but pretension; but at last he himself earnestly believed it; and did many things in demonstration of what he supposed to be his peculiar and personal mission to that unadvanced and disunited people. But the belief we are considering can also be traced to *Education;* therefore, *ignorance*, and doctrinal education, (which is mainly ignorance sublimated,) and *desire*, are, in numerous forms and states of combination, the causes of a belief in Special or Immediate Providences.

There is, however, *a belief of the understanding*, in the local and universal government of God, which is adequate to supply every demand of the pure and reasonable intellect. And this is the *belief* in the Perfection, the Unchangeableness, and in the Universality of the Principles of Divine Government and Legislation. These Principles are so admirably arranged as to comprehend, protect and govern, the Mighty Orb, the "falling Sparrow," the insect's Eye, and the human Soul. These principles are simply the rules or modes by which the Great Moving Principle governs the Universe, and bestows his universal care and blessings upon all created things. These Laws, by which He thus governs, are so unchangeable and perfect as to render supernatural manifestations both useless and positively impossible.

The miracle of changing water into wine, attributed to Jesus, is in direct opposition to the *established laws* of fluids and gases; and again, the miracle of the restoration of Lazarus to life and health, subsequently to the death and decomposition of his body, is in positive antagonism to the *determined laws* of life and organization; and so, likewise, the miraculous birth of Jesus is no less a positive violation of the *immutable laws* of reproduction and procreation.

The proof that these exhibitions of Special Providences never did occur precisely as they are related, is to be found in the *fact* that the Deity and his Laws are *perfect and unchangeable.* But, it may be said, that these miracles were performed according to preordained but previously inactive laws, which laws were called into effect, for the first time, when and where those miracles were wrought; and it may also be said, that the Deity, "knowing the End even from the Beginning," did, in order to bring about these astounding developments of *might* and *design*, institute and make an eternal provision for the *special* action of a set of principles, which, previous or subsequent to the birth of Jesus, were not intended to be brought into requisition. This hypothesis, entertained by the most intelligent theologians throughout Christendom, is refuted upon the ground that the *Deity is an unalterable Being;* that his laws are proofs of his unchangeableness, and, consequently, that he can not make a set of laws for one age of the world, which in their action will develop effects in direct opposition to his universally established modes of being and doing in every other age. For, should it be admitted that God acted at one period in positive violation or contradiction of his works in every other period, then are the unchangeableness and the integrity of his character impeached, and all true confidence in his Infinite Perfection shaken and unsettled.

But again it may be urged, that God is All-powerful, and that he, therefore, can at pleasure *suspend*, *transcend*, or *destroy*, any set of Laws which originated with him; and that the miracles attributed to Jesus and others, together with the many instances of *Divine* special attention and interposition, recorded on the pages of profane and ecclesiastical history, were developed and performed, not by violating, but by suspending or transcending the operation of those Laws which are found to be, at other times, undeviating throughout Nature. To this again the reply is, that the Perfection and Unchangeableness of the Laws of the Deity render those miracles and divine interpositions both useless and impossible. And, furthermore, it is not to be, for one moment, admitted that the Deity *did create* those Laws which operate so consistently throughout the illimitable Universe.

The Laws of Nature, like Nature itself and the human soul, were not created by the Deity, but were and are the spontaneous attributes of his divine Existence and Constitution. In other words, they are the inevitable and indispensable developments of the Divine Essence. Here I affirm that the Deity did no more create the Laws of Nature than did they create him; they are simply the outer manifestations of the internal essential principles which constitute his existence and Organization; and consequently, the Deity and his Laws are equally beyond the possibility of being *changed*, *suspended*, *transcended* or *destroyed*. All arguments concerning the possibility of *special providences*, or of supernatural manifestations and miracles of any character or extent, which are claimed and believed by many nations, sects, and individuals, can have their intrinsic value summarily determined by the syllogistic form of demonstration.*

The consoling belief which flows from the understanding into the affections, and which is capable of satisfying the reasonable demands of the soul, is a belief that God is perfect and unchangeable; that he lives through all things, and has made life, harmony, and happiness, attainable to all. When the human mind conceives and believes that God is impartial, and that he displays his natural and harmonious attributes throughout Nature, and in the deepest recesses of the Soul, *then* it will rest and be happy. An individual, thus believing, is perfectly invincible to the invasions and tirades of that fallacious education, and hereditary prejudice, which exist in the world. The convinced soul is not disturbed by every "wind of doctrine;" it is not moved by the preaching of miraculous manifestations, as demonstrating the divine commission of any man; nor

* The author has experienced and published an interesting and instructive vision on the subject of special providences. This vision comprehends the whole theme, and presents it in a new light. See "Philosophy of Special Providences."

can the doctrines of *physical resurrection*, or *final judgment*, or *eternal condemnation*, or any other absurdity and fallacy of the popular schools, affect the convinced understanding; for such know that God is an Eternal Magnet of concentrated Goodness, and that man's pathway is eternally onward and upward to the Supreme Attraction.

God is sufficiently *minute*, *local*, and *immediate*, in his providences, to impart life and beauty to every thing throughout the innumerable ramifications of infinite Creation. He possesses within himself the principles of all Motion, all Life, all Sensation, and all Intelligence. He is the Infinite Germ of the Great Universal Tree of Causation; and according to the absoluteness of self-existence, and consequent necessity, his celestial essences and essential principles unfold and flow, with the *minutest* precision, into the smallest atoms and organizations in nature.

It is not good, nor is it true or elevating, to believe that God originally designed and instituted an endless succession of consecutive causes and effects for the express purpose of giving birth to *just such an organization* as Jesus had, or such as any other individual may possess. But it is very good and righteous to believe that God unfolds and develops, from out of the inexhaustible plenitude of his Infinite Life and constitution, a vast combination of Laws and Elements which will *go on eternally*, elaborating human spirits, and will continue to improve and perfect them more and more in proportion as the circumstances of birth, of climate, of education and government, advance toward intellectual development and individual perfection. Hence it is unreasonable and unrighteous to believe that God takes special notice of those numerous transgressions, by which individuals only injure and experimentally educate themselves. Nor is it good to believe that God exerts his omnipotent power, with the express design of arresting the action of physical laws or elements, or to send rain, or to bestow *special* endowments, or signal privileges, or particular gratifications, in answer to the prayers of the (so styled) righteous. For such a belief would be admitting God to be a "respecter of persons," and also the cause of inconceivable injustices and injuries to some—yea, it would be making him a mutable Being.

Let us think of this proposition,—let us consider, that, any clergyman, (it may be the present Pope Pius,) thought by many to be a righteous man,—suppose he prays for the protection of the king, for the enrichment of the kingdom, and for the perpetuation of a monarchical or theocratical system of government. And suppose that at the same time, a representative of the people prays as fervently for the downfall of the king, and for the establishment of a republic instead of a kingdom. Of course, these opposing supplications are addressed to one and the same God. Now if the Deity who rules the universe should grant the prayer of one of these individuals, the desires of the other would necessarily be ungratified,—his particular favor bestowed upon the one party would perhaps result in immense evils to the other. Again, a righteous man, living upon the mountain side, may earnestly pray for rain, to cause his fruit-trees and agricultural productions to yield abundantly; whilst another equally righteous man, living in the valley beneath, having already had a great supply of rain upon his farm, in consequence of water accumulating in his springs from off the adjacent hills, and knowing that any more, *just then*, would injure his forthcoming crops, he therefore earnestly prays to God for fair weather. Now if the prayer of the one be granted, the other will sustain great injury in his pecuniary interests, and so, *vice versa.* Hence, to be just and impartial, God must exist and govern according to universal and unchangeable principles.

In considering special and universal providences with a belief of the understanding, the highest and greatest comfort flowing therefrom is based upon the glorious and already (to me) demonstrated *truth*, that our earth is environed by a Spiritual World. And not only is our earth thus surrounded, but so likewise are all the earths or planets belonging to our solar system. In truth, there is a *great* sphere of spiritual existences, which, touching it, girdle the material sphere, a part of which we are at present existing in; and again, encircling that sphere, is a galaxy of *greater* spheres, more refined and more magnificent; which are inhabited by spirits, drawn onward by the eternal magnet of Supreme Goodness. Thus there is a chain extending from man to Deity! And all that we can desire in the form of attention and dispensation is abundantly supplied, and handed down to us, by and through the spiritual inhabitants of higher spheres, the links in that chain of Love!

The human soul is constructed upon musical principles, which impart to it a constitutional tendency toward harmony and happiness. The various attractions to which its tones respond are Self-Love, Conjugal-Love, Parental-Love, Fraternal-Love, Filial-Love, and Universal-Love. But what I desire to impress here is, that these Loves are *innate affinities* which draw soul to soul; which cause the human mind to feel attracted to *corresponding* loves or *affinities* in other minds, without reference to time, space, age, position, education or circumstances. Therefore, should Conjugal-Love prompt an individual soul to *pray* for conjugal association, and should that soul's *true* associate reside in the Spiritual World, it is almost certain that the prayer of the yearning heart on earth will be certainly answered by the spirit, which is impelled by this irresistible attraction to seek its true companion. But here let it be remembered that all spirits and angels were once men; lived in physical organizations as we do; and died, as we die, previous to their departure for the spirit-home. And we all have relatives there—parents, sisters, and brothers, perhaps, and also relatives according to spiritual affinities. And the Spirit World is not far off; it is very near, around and above us at all times; and that which was truly joined here is not separated there; death does not divide, nor does it remove the loved ones beyond the reach of the spirit's desires or prayers. As Conjugal-Love is answered by some spirit having a corresponding attraction, so are other loves responded to by corresponding loves; and thus there proceeds to us, and that not unfrequently, a vast variety of good suggestions and righteous impulses, from some of our natural or spiritual relatives who now reside in higher spheres. And thus, too, when the soul is earnestly praying for knowledge whereby to direct social government, or for *light* upon the great problem of reorganizing and harmonizing society, it is perfectly *safe* and *reasonable* to believe that the noble spirits who have lived among us on the earth, and who are now particularly educated in these questions, draw nigh, and, perhaps, insinuate some valuable thoughts into the understanding of the praying spirit,—this would be a response to the Fraternal-Love, or the love of the neighbor. Hence we may truthfully say that Providence imparts special information—not by *direct* and *immediate* design, but by the operation of those natural and unchangeable laws whereby are governed the universal combinations of Mind and Matter. Spiritual intercourse is developed and rendered universally practicable by the Law of Association, or by the Law of Affinities. Therefore, whoever should truthfully and sincerely desire or pray for light upon governmental and social subjects, whereby to reform society and develop harmony among men, he would, probably, *if susceptible to interior impressions*, receive something, it might be, from the now educated Moses—or Lycurgus—or Solon—or Plato; for each of these individuals had their Fraternal-Love considerably developed and rudimentally educated by the friction of social and other circumstances previous to their departure for the Superior Country. So also, should any individual earnestly seek to be enlightened concerning spiritual and religious truths; should he pray to know more of God and the Universe, it is more than possible, it is *probable*, that the now advanced Paul—or David—or John—or Fenelon—or some departed relative, having the Filial-Love fully developed and in constant exercise, would impart sweet instructions, and satisfy the inquirer.

I desire the reader to seek an illustration and confirmation of this fact by disciplining and unfolding the mind to the influx of spiritual impressions.

Responses from the Spirit World will never be conflicting; and, therefore, should an individual pray and receive what he considers a reply, and should this reply contradict what others have said or revealed, then the only criterion by which to *judge* of its truth or falsehood is the unfailing standard of Nature and Reason. For instance—if a person should affirm, after earnestly praying, or while in what is modernly termed the magnetic state, that he had heard or perceived that the sun and moon were stationary during the period assigned by Joshua, then the statement must be tested by Nature, and Nature must be tested by Reason. Again, if an individual (Emanuel Swedenborg or Jacob Beman, for instance) should affirm that he perceived in the Spiritual World that the Bible is the Word of God—that it is a sacred embodiment of Truth—that it contains no errors—then the truthfulness of such an affirmation must be tested by referring it to the unchangeable and immeasurable standard of Nature and Reason.

Nature and Reason are the only mathematicians who can perfectly demonstrate and unfailingly exhibit the true or false character of every statement which the profoundly ignorant, as well as the educated mind, may be moved to make, under any conceivable circumstances.

The embracing nearness of the Spiritual World, and its accessibleness, furnish the spirit with every advantage and gratification it should desire, through the mediums of providential dispensations or Divine interposition. But if the ambitious and aspiring Christian heart is dissatisfied with the *mediate* and *indirect* manner in which its prayers to God are answered—dissatisfied because the Deity himself does not more directly hearken to its invocations, then I desire to impress that heart with this truth: that no human spirit has yet conceived a *thought*, or uttered a *word*, as it conceives of the Father, *sufficiently* magnanimous, sublime, or expressive, to be applied to even one of the exalted individuals, who, though once a resident upon some Earth, now treads the beautiful paths and flowering valleys of the Spirit Home.

Think not, because God is so inconceivable in his Greatness, so elevated above special prayer, and special action, that he is far removed from our spirits—no, he

"Lives in the soul, informs our mortal part."

And so near is he, that in him we daily and hourly "live, move, and have our being,"—we are in him and of him; and as the *body*, *branches*, *twigs*, *leaves*, *buds*, *blossoms* and *fruit* of a *tree* are unfolded and minutely developed from the essences and beginning principles which were originally deposited in its *Germ*, so does the Great Germinal Essence of the Universal Tree unfold and develop the *minutest branches*, *buds*, *blossoms* and *organizations*, which perfume and adorn the Stupendous Whole.

If a particular bud, or a chosen number of buds, should set up a claim to special blessings and attentions, and should they invoke and adjure the Germ to dispense a large share of its life and fluids to them, the other buds may remain *perfectly satisfied* that *justice* will preside over every dispensation of the moving principle which gave them birth. So, likewise, should any individual, or class of individuals, make pretensions to righteousness in consequence whereof they presume to invoke, importune, and adjure the Deity to grant them *special*, *immediate*, and *eternal* favors, other individuals may rest perfectly satisfied that the Deity and his Laws are Equally beyond the possibility of Chance, Suspension, or Separation; and hence, that *Eternal Justice* will preside over the distribution of Divine life and happiness to every flower and spirit, to every atom and seraph, that has an existence any where in the wide-spread gardens of God!

Let us now return to our investigation—viz.: The Electrical action of God upon the Universe. Electricity is a medium of universal relationship. It originally resided in the Mighty Vortex of uncreated worlds, undeveloped. In the beginning of the present structure of the Universe, all matter was in a state of diffusion and agitation in consequence of the inconceivable preparations and rarefactions that were necessary to the formation of a universe superior to the preceding structure. The four great developments of matter, Fire, Heat, Light, and Electricity; these conditions spread themselves from the Great Center through the realms of infinitude, previous to that association and organization of materials which we call planetary systems. *Fire* was the most inferior form of matter; but it contained the element of all those diversified objects and principles that beautify and vivify the earth which we inhabit, as well as all the earths or planets that begemmed the innumerable heavens of infinity. From *Fire* was developed *Heat;* from heat came *Light;* from light was developed *Electricity;* and from the aggregation and organization of these elements was unfolded the stupendous system of Nature, of which system mankind is a portion. Thus, it will be perceived, Electricity *was* the most superior and omnipresent principle in Nature; it came out of other elements, and, having gravitated to the highest point of primeval perfection, was necessarily invested with the power of perpetually pervading and inter-penetrating the vast universe of matter, which, like a shoreless ocean, rolled in boundless waves around the Supernal Mind.

So now with electricity. It is being constantly eliminated from various and innumerable founts of matter; and from them it flows into a grand sea of elements, and pervades not only all earth, but all the incalculable systems of immensity. And as it becomes refined in character and manifestation, we change its name. Thus, one modification of electricity we term Magnetism, another Galvanism, another Nervo-vital influence, &c.; yet these terms are merely expressive of the progressive refinement and superior manifestations of the One great principle. The Divine Mind employs electricity as a medium of communication to all parts and particles of the universe. Every instant of time, the Great Positive Mind causes this element to express the unchanging pulsations of his Soul through all the various ramifications of Nature. Those immutable laws, which govern the pulsations of divine vitality through the universe, are so minute and righteous that the tiny flower and revolving orb alike receive life, direction, and protection, according to their respective capacities and requirements.

It should be duly understood that electricity is *not* the cause of planetary motion, but the *agent*, or *vehicle*, of the great anatomical, physiological, mechanical, and chemical principles which emanate from the Divine Mind, and expand, equally operative, throughout the boundless universe of worlds. It has been already remarked, that, what is meant, in the Harmonial Philosophy, by attraction, gravitation, condensation, &c., is an *association of particles possessing mutual affinities.* These affinities are aided in their multifarious arrangements by the universal element Electricity. This is illustrated by the familiar phenomena of vegetation. The little germ, which is deposited in the earth, is redolent with affinities for surrounding forces and particles of matter. It draws earth, and air, and water, and heat, and light, and nourishment, from the invisible elements, into its constitution; hence a single grain of wheat will usher into existence multitudes after its own sort, several representatives of like nature—but Electricity is not the cause of this attraction among the particles, it is the agent by which these phenomena are accomplished. And so the mighty worlds, that are distributed throughout the immensity of infinitude, are incessantly reciprocating particles and substances with each other; and, in accordance with their density or rarity, with their lower or higher degrees of development, with their grosser or more refined conditions, are their (the worlds') magnitude and distances from each other determined, and their motions established. Thus, it is not owing to positive and negative electricities that the positions and motions of planets are determined; on the contrary, the law of *associative* or *elective affinities*, which law resides in and operates upon all things, is the primary cause of all planetary harmony. Hence, in accordance with the density or rarity of a planet, is its magnitude and orbit determined, and the space intervening between it and the sun around which it revolves. In this manner the Universe of worlds was originally unfolded; but (as is related in Nature's Divine Revelations) there was no *disconnected force* or *impetus* applied to the bodies thus formed, to set them in harmonious motion; no *foreign* power impulsed or guided them in order in their respective planes of revolution; but *inherent laws*—the spontaneous development and operation of God's involuntary powers; capable of controlling these great planetary manifestations, were progressively developed and brought into action, being always beautifully adapted to the *forms* to be thus acted upon.

Some philosophers have long contended for, and defended the theory which asserts the electrical origin of the universe. And it must be acknowledged that, in accordance with the rules of inductive philosophy, there are many seeming reasons upon which the vast superstructure of such a theory may be made to temporarily rest; but a deeper and more analytical investigation into Nature's immutable principles, which emanate from God's celestial constitution and control all the mighty operations of the universe, would directly convince the mind that there is no positive retrogression in any thing, in any division of the stupendous Whole. The law of universal and eternal Progression is impressed upon every thing! upon the apparently lifeless and inert stone, upon plants and trees, and animals, and man—and the free-born, untrammeled human spirit,—expanding with the indwelling sentiments of an eternal existence fraught with endless joys, made ever fresh and eternally welcome by virtue of their innumerable and progressive diversifications,—yearns to be emancipated from earth's restraints, and to yield, with all the confidence and simplicity of a child, to the sublime workings of this onward and upward principle! A mind that has experienced the inspiring emotions which a full realization of Eternal Progress inevitably awakens in the soul, can not admit the electrical origin of matter. It can not admit the proposition, that electricity, being subject to the laws of matter, was gradually condensed, becoming less and less rare, imponderable and unparticled, until finally it became dense, ponderable and particled, and formed all the animate and inanimate objects and substances of which creation is composed. No! such a mind would say: I am ready to express my convictions—a faith so strong and so well supported by all Nature, as to be identical with absolute knowledge—that all animate and inanimate objects and substances, inwrought in the mighty network of Nature, will gradually be refined, and advanced, and ultimately merged into electricity; but the reverse conclusion can not be true. The electrical origin of matter is contrary to the law of eternal and infinite Progression. The theory asserts a positive deterioration or retrogression (which means a backward or downward tendency) of the great *developments* of Nature. Electricity is made to descend from imponderability to ponderability—from a fluid to a solid, and from an element it is supposed to be condensed into a granite rock. While, in truth, the reverse is the law of Nature: ponderability progresses to imponderability—solids to fluids—and the most inanimate substance is destined to go through the great etherizing and spiritualizing processes of Nature, and finally to take a high position among the all-pervading elements of infinitude.

The innumerable effects which flow from the action of electricity upon the wide-extending fields of Creation, and the many mighty purposes which this element subserves in the countless realms beyond our limited perceptions, are too vast and overwhelming for human comprehension. But let us be duly grateful for the ability to go so far into the amazing wonders and ineffable sublimities of the Universe as to be inspired, like Dryden, with the comprehensive thought, that—

"One common Soul
Inspires, and feeds, and animates the whole."

Such a thought is antagonistic to supernaturalism, and is fatal to all the doctrines of special creation; this is, then, a very powerful reason why such a conception of God and his Universe should be cherished. And the great reason why mankind should entertain expansive conceptions of God, of Nature, and of Heaven, is this: noble and benevolent sentiments flow from noble and generous minds, and the higher our conceptions are of God and his methods of creation the more are we kind, and just, and wise, in our actions toward the different classes which compose mankind; and these classes gradually receive the good results thereof; and their hearts are made joyous and their homes happy.

The revelations of the telescope, combined with the perfect accuracy of mathematical demonstrations, have done much toward augmenting the development of human wisdom. By these means superstition has been unmasked, and its horrid deformity presented to the much deceived but presumptive devotee; and Truth has been permitted to utter her divine and eternal revelations, more in this century than in any preceding one, but her disciples are unfortunately trammeled by popular custom and the powerful restraints of social and civic life. In the secret recesses of the soul, however—

in the closet of the spirit's sanctuary—the student of Nature may not be disturbed. His thoughts, there, may dwell long and ardently upon the Goodness immense, the Goodness infinite, the boundless Love and Wisdom of God, with which the great realities of existence are beautified and adorned. And, yet, what an additional joy! what an inestimable blessing! it is to have, beating in harmony with his own, an honest, superiorly-enlightened heart, which readily listens and responds to the glorious results of his rapturous contemplations! In view of this happiness, which always should be possessed, I can not but earnestly admonish the married to seek and preserve a congeniality of faith and thought. Unless its prevention is absolutely impossible, never tread dissimilar paths in your search after salvation and truth; especially never be proud or unrighteously high-minded toward one another; because discord is generated thereby, and your "house is divided against itself;" which is a certain prognostication of the destruction of something—it may be a rupture in your affections or in your efforts to do good—and your shattered "household gods" may lie in ruins upon the family altar whence the light of *home* has departed. If you are a supernaturalist, (technically so called,) you will most likely cling (for instance) to the chronology of Moses with regard to the earth's age, and will peremptorily refuse to look at any reasons or arguments to the contrary; and if your companion be a free-thinking, honest investigator of truth, then there can not exist much pleasurable communication of thought between you—you are, in these things, unfortunately alienated. Oh, as you value the joys of life, the sacred home delights, let this not be! While you would repel all arguments against the correctness of Moses' chronology, your more generous and enlightened companion excuses, but, at the same time, deplores your ignorance and dogmatism. According to Genesis, Moses makes the age of the creation about six thousand years; yet, in addition to a vast array of geological and zoological demonstrations to the contrary, the glorious science of astronomy informs us, that even at the inconceivable velocity with which *light* travels from point to point, it would require from one hundred thousand to three hundred thousand years to pass from the (so called) fixed stars to our earth; indeed, there are planets in immensity—*planets which belong to our circle of suns*—whose light has not yet reached us, and of whose existence mankind has, as yet, acquired no knowledge, except through the agency of spiritual perception. "Well!" exclaims the supernaturalist, "what does it all amount to?" The philosopher replies: "these astronomical revelations prove incontestibly, that our earth has been in existence certainly *three hundred thousand years*, because, (granting that "the Lord made the heavens and the earth, and all that in them is," at one specific period,) it would take the light that number of years to reach our material senses; hence to compute the age of the world we must abandon the idea of counting by hundreds and thousands of years—we must add many millions of years together in order to bring the age of the world any where within the positive declarations of geological, zoological, and astronomical science.

By the unceasing operation of immutable and changeless principles the universe has been unfolded, and bedecked with motion and life, sensation and intelligence; together with all those countless varieties of forms and organizations which indicate the innumerable ramifications and omniprevalence of the Divine Essence. But human comprehension is too limited to form any thing like a just estimation of the *time* which that Divine Essence consumed even in the development of our earth; how much more oblivious, therefore, is the chronological history of the infinite Universe, whose vast dimensions no mathematician can compute, whose startling grandeur and harmonious magnificence no language can express! Yet, useless and imaginative as the inquiry may appear to some intellects, the questions—what is time? what is space? what is Eternity? what is Infinity?—will involuntarily arise in the investigating mind, and Reason will, as involuntarily, attempt their solution.

Fortunately for mankind in their present rudimental and germinal state of being, the human soul is endowed with powers and attributes of philosophical perception and understanding, which enable it to convert many past-apprehended fictions into valuable *facts*, and the most extravagant-seeming romances into the sublimest *realities* of future existence; and, on the other hand, it is equally fortunate for man, that by the exercise of the same endowments, he can convert many past-apprehended facts into *fictions*, and many supposed realities into romance.

If the mind is refined and expanded, the individual entertains correspondingly enlarged perceptions of Time, and of those things which pertain to an immortal existence. Time is only a term which is often unconsciously employed to signify the distance between one occurrence or event and another. Events, occurrences, circumstances, and objects, are separated by spaces of various lengths, and these spaces constitute what we call TIME. Therefore, Time and space are identical. Time is divided, and infinitely subdivided, in order to render it expressive of the length of the spaces which exist between objects and events. Thus Time is converted into space by dividing it into *years*, *months*, *weeks*, *days*, *hours*, *minutes*, and *seconds;* but the reason why the human mind entombs Time in that oblivious sepulchre called eternity, is, that events, objects, and circumstances, have been abandoned as applicable to the spiritual mode of existence:—consequently *nothing* and *eternity* have sustained such intimate relations in the general mind, that to pronounce them unqualifiedly synonymous is but allowing their usual definition.

As Time is divided and classified, in the same proportions, so is space. Thus: Space is measured by *miles*, *rods*, *yards*, *feet*, and *inches;* and, in order to ascertain more minutely the relation or distance which exists between objects and localities, miles and rods, feet and inches are divided and super-divided, or multiplied, and this may be done to an extent beyond the power of mind to comprehend and appreciate. Thus, also, is Time divided into years, months, days, hours, minutes, and seconds, and these are multiplied to an extent wholly inappreciable. *Time and space are consequently identical.*

It has been ascertained by optical experiments, that light travels two hundred and thirteen thousand miles in a second. This interesting discovery communicates simultaneously two distinct, yet inseparable ideas to the mind—an idea of *Time*, and an idea of *space.* Light, in its instantaneous passage from one object or locality to another, necessarily employs and develops time and distance. The element of light travels from the sun of our solar system, to the human eye, in about eight minutes; consequently we should see the sun as it was eight minutes ago, and not as it is at the moment of observation. Light travels from one of the distant suns or stars of the seventh magnitude, to the human eye, in one hundred and eighty years; consequently, should we gaze at one of them now, we see it as it was one hundred and eighty years ago; and if, through the most powerful telescope, we should gaze at one of the more distant suns (or stars) of the twelfth magnitude, we should see it *as it was* four thousand years ago, and not *as it is* at the time of observation. There are now existing Suns in the depths of immensity of such immeasurable magnitude and inconceivable grandeur, as to set at defiance every mathematical conceptive power of the human mind. And notwithstanding our earth has been in existence, and revolved upon its axis for millions of years, yet, of its inhabitants, not an eye has caught a ray of the light which emanates from one of those distant suns; but it is altogether probable that those of our brethren who shall be dwelling upon the earth ten millions of years hence, will discover another *new planet* or fixed star, which they will consider to be of the twenty-seventh magnitude; because, then, the light from one of those distant Orbs shall have, for the first time, reached our earth! Therefore the astronomer who first perceives this new planet, will see it as it was many millions of years ago; and, supposing it to be inhabited with beings possessing powers of vision equal to our own, they, if observing at the same time, would behold our earth in its primeval state—in the first stages of conglobation and consolidation.

In verification of these statements, let the reader suppose himself a resident of New York, and his brother living at Pekin, in China. If a magnetic telegraph extended between these two cities, over the earth, they might, by that means, enjoy personal communication. Now should the reader communicate to his brother intelligence of his sudden illness at the moment he was taken, that brother would learn of his condition *not* as it would be when the message reached Pekin, but *as it was* thirty seconds before, which would be the *time* occupied by the electric current to perform that particular mission.

To comprehend the philosophy of Time and Space, of Eternity and Infinity, the mind must reflect systematically. Time sustains the same relation to Eternity as space does to Infinity—the relation is distinct, identical, inseparable. Eternity is composed of *Time*—Infinity is composed of *Space*. Inasmuch, therefore, as Eternity is composed of *Time*, the conclusion can not be escaped, that events, occurrences, objects, and circumstances, will continue to exist and to be developed,—for it is only by these developments that Eternity can be in any way measured and comprehended Also, it is impossible to escape the conclusion that objects, distances, localities, miles, feet and inches, will continue to exist; because it is only by an innumerable succession and contrariety of *spaces* that any thing like a conception can be formed of Infinity. Hence, it is proper to say that Eternity is a succession of mighty and universal events. In relation to this, I refer the reader to that part of Nature's Divine

Revelations, where it will be seen that I was impressed to contemplate an *Event* or change in the universal arrangement and constitution of things which should be termed the *end of one time*, which time, according to human conception, constitutes Eternity. On the other hand, it is proper to say, that Infinity is a succession of conceivable and inconceivable *spaces* or *localities*, which, owing to their number and magnitude, extend beyond all human powers of measurement, and consequently beyond all human comprehension.

Eternity is composed of *time*, or events, as the ocean is composed of drops of water; and Infinity is composed of *spaces* or localities, as miles are composed of inches, or years of minutes. Therefore, it may not be said "Time is no more."

Comparatively speaking, there is such a thing as conceiving of Eternity and Infinity, and of the annihilation of time and space; but strictly speaking—employing language in its absolute and unqualified sense—there is no conception in the human mind which answers to an Eternity or Infinity, nor to an annihilation of time and space. Therefore, when thinking of Nature and God as existing from all eternity, the mind can not resist the impulse to inquire—when did they (God and Eternity) begin to be?

Accustomed to, and educated by, days and hours, feet and inches, the human soul can not think nor exist without them; but throughout the immeasurable *spaces*, *objects*, and *localities* of Infinity, and the *times*, *events*, and *circumstances* of Eternity, the immortal reader will perceive and understand, that—

> "With God Time is not; unto Him all is
> Present Eternity. Worlds, beings, years,
> With all their natures, powers, and events,
> The bounds whereof he fashions and ordains,
> Unfold themselves like flowers. Time must not be
> Contrasted with Eternity;—'t is not
> A second of the Everlasting Year."

Eternity is an infinite ocean, and this life is but a single drop of its everlasting waters; and if that drop be used a million of times by millions of individuals, it nevertheless remains a part of the universal ocean, indestructible. So also is Infinity an eternal expanse, and this life is but a single inch thereof; and if that inch be traversed a million of times it still remains a part of the illimitable whole, distinct, identical, inseparable. Thus Time and space, Eternity and Infinity, are identical. One is the measure and companion of the other; and, like Love and Wisdom, Truth and Virtue, Harmony and Heaven, they reside in, and proceeded from the universal constitution of the Great Positive Mind whose celestial essence moves and makes the whole alive!

The inconceivable rapidity with which terrestrial electricity travels, and the instantaneous manner in which it propagates itself, by virtue of its positive and negative prolifications with kindred elements on superior planes of action, render the problem of how the Deity "acts upon the universe electrically" one of difficult solution. Deistical and Christian philosophers have done much toward establishing a broad and almost insurmountable distinction between the operations of laws in the external universe and those manifestations of special attention and particular providences which are supposed to emanate from God alone; and the very different sciences that have been erected are mainly shaped and modeled—especially their various classifications of external effects and phenomena—to suit the elaborations of christian thinkers and speculators who are ever distrustful of that bold and comprehensive philosophy which declares and demonstrates the truth that Nature's varied and stupendous operations are but the involuntary manifestations of Deity, as, by virtue of analogical reasoning, we behold demonstrated in the phenomena of digestion, circulation, assimilation, &c., which, by the spirit's involuntary powers, are known to transpire in the economy of man's constitution. By analogical investigation and deduction the consistent reasoner can not but conclude, that, inasmuch as, through the instrumentality of different material agencies, the mind of man can actuate the blood, and the muscles, and can come in palpable contact with inanimate substances (as for instance, the handling of stone, coal, &c.,) it is, therefore, also reasonable to believe that God can and does come in constant contact with the lowest element known in physical Nature through the medium or agency of innumerable intermediates.

There is as much confusion of impressions concerning the omnipresent and voluntary omnipotence of God as he is supposed to have caused in the languages of those fabled ambitious tribes who attempted the erection of a flood-defying tower high enough to elevate them above the fluctuations and vicissitudes of present life; and the consequences of these antagonistic apprehensions of God's character, and his *method* of being and doing in his universe, are, alas! too conspicuous in the world's sectarianism—in the miserable skepticism and the profound superstition of different minds among the earth's various nations. The most erudite and enlightened intellects—those who profess great faith in Divine providence, and pray for favor and the merciful bestowment of salvation—entertain, generally speaking, no well-defined and exalted views of that Supernal organization of celestial elements and attributes, called Deity. Should the reader ask the most intelligent Christian, or even question his own mind, as to what conceptions he has formed of the Almighty, the reply would doubtless be—"He is an all-wise, all-pervading essence." Yes, but what does this mean? If the Deity is an all-pervading or omnipresent principle, then is he not "as full, as perfect in a hair as heart"?—in the granite rock as in the human soul?—can this be true? Nay, verily; because the lowest element in the soul of man contains more of the Divine life of Deity than can be found in all the granite of a hemisphere; though the latter is not altogether destitute of the all-animating Principle.

It is righteous to approach the investigation of this subject with due reverence; realizing that we are treading upon sacred ground —seeking to acquaint our affections and reasoning principle with the Holy Proprietor of Nature's magnificent Temple; but there is no reason why, because the subject is vast, and, in a great degree, incomprehensible to human minds, we should abandon the righteous effort to expand our conceptions by honest inquiry and exalted contemplations. Moreover it is not right to affirm, that the subject is too high and altogether incomprehensible for finite minds—that finite beings can not comprehend the Infinite—because the reader's mind is capable of recognizing the truthfulness of the proposition, that God's essence is not as full in the senseless stone as in man's throbbing, thinking, loving, immortal soul. Nor can it be truthfully affirmed, that God manifests the same amount of Wisdom—of anatomical and physiological skill, so to speak—in the constitution of the stone or the plant as he displays in the construction of animals and the human type. Let me be rightly apprehended. I do not assert a *lack* of Divine Wisdom in any department of God's boundless empire—for I behold marvelous intelligence in the formation of the insect's eye; in the throbbing of its tiny heart; in the construction and rainbow tints of its frail wing; and I recognize the same skill, unity, system, order, form, and harmony in all things which adorn the material universe. But I do affirm that there is a distribution of the Divine Essence, and Wisdom, and Power, in proportion always to the capacity and position of the receptacle; and hence that God is not omnipresent nor omnipotent in the sense in which those terms are ordinarily employed.

Now let us pursue this analytical investigation still further, and confess the conclusion to which it legitimately conducts us—for Truth is the Soul's highest escort and guardian. If it be conceded, that God *is not* " as full as perfect in a hair as heart," will it not also be conceded that he dwells *more in the spiritual*, than in the natural, Universe?—that he *particularly* resides in the resplendent center of the Univercœlum—which central location may be termed the Great Sensorium of the Infinite Mind—and that from thence he imparts and expands his Love-essences and Wisdom-attributes throughout the great infinitude of life and animation? In view of this truth it is no longer right to speak or think of God as being equally diffused through all things; on the contrary, when speaking or thinking of his attribute of omnipotence, we should admit, that, though the Infinite Mind has a fixed, local habitation, he, nevertheless, enlivens and actuates all existences by the unceasing emanation of his essences of Love, his principles of Will, and his attributes of Wisdom.

The Great Vortex of Positive Power, the Great Sensorium of the Divine Mind, is, therefore, the Central Spring of all action and vitality—the celestial FOUNT of unspeakable magnificence and inconceivable PERFECTION. He lives through all things, but more particularly in the great seventh spiritual sphere or SUN of the Universe. The elements and attributes, principles and essences of His inexhaustible Soul, are perpetually flowing to, and in, and out of, every thing, whether material or spiritual, that exists in the immeasurable domain of being. His Spirit fills all existence; but the most interior, and, to human minds, the most inconceivable qualities and properties of his celestial and infinite constitution have their source deep in the Center of universal being.

God is the SOUL of the Universe; hence the Universe must necessarily be the BODY of God. And unity and system are manifested every where. In the Great "stupendous whole" there can not possibly be any contradictory or antagonistic displays of Divine principles; a perfect and unbroken chain of correspondences or analogies must of necessity run through and unite all things—giving them coherency and harmonious proportions; and, therefore, since unity, order, and system, are universal, the human mind is justified in reasoning analogically, and apprehending man as a minute representation of the mighty whole—as the spirit of man lives in his body, so the Spirit of God lives in the Universe. As motion, life, and sensation are diffused through the various organs, nerves, muscles, &c., in man's constitution ; so are the essences, elements, properties, qualities, principles, and attributes which exist in the Celestial constitution of the Divine Mind diffused throughout the boundless empire of visible and invisible Nature!

Thus man is, in a finite degree, an impersonation of the Infinite—specially in the construction of his soul and body, and in the principles on which they subsist together; but inasmuch as man, in this, his first and rudimental state of being, is very undeveloped and misdirected—particularly in the affectional and moral portions of his nature—the analogy which exists between him and the Infinite extends at present only to his constitutional conformation, embracing his mind, and its involuntary operations in and upon his organism. But on a superior plane of being, man is, in his *material* or outer form, an exact *image* of the Universe; and, then, also, is his *spiritual* conformation, an exact *likeness* of the Great Moving Power, which is Deity.

Thus it is made manifest that all material things are forms, each of which is merely an external mode by which its interior essence establishes a communication between itself and the outer world, the form being only a medium of communication between the inner and the outer. Nature, then, is composed of these innumerable combinations of matter, and is a manifest type of the whole Universe. The Great Positive Mind is the Interior and Divine Essence—is the creative Cause of all external effects. The Great Divine Mind is a Soul, existing as a perfect organization of essential properties, essences, and attributes; and the *Mode* by which this Essence or Soul exists, is the Form or outward development of the whole UNIVERCŒLUM. The Divine Essence being the *Soul*, the Univercœlum is the *Body*. Moreover, the latter is a perfect representative, or, in other words, is a bold and clear expression of the interior possessions of the Divine Mind. The Universe is the Mode by which the Divine Essence exists: and the latter could not exist as an Organization without being made perfect by a corresponding exterior Form, such as is displayed in the mighty, grand, and inexpressibly harmonious Universe.

Thus it is that *form* is the express image of its interior or first principle of life and being. And the use of every thing is determined by the specificness of its own interior possessions, and especially by its relation—in form, in series, and in degrees of perfection—to all other living essences in Nature and the Universe.

It is on the same principle that the *human* form is an express likeness of the quality of its interior soul. And it has been absolutely demonstrated that man *materially* is a perfection of all matter in Nature, and that man *spiritually* is a perfection of all Motion. Therefore man as a whole, constitutes a complete system of organized *spirit* and *matter*; and thus it is that the spiritual principle of man is individualized, and is expressed by the human form, to the outer world. And thus likewise is the *body* unfolded by the specific and potential essence of its interior soul. Man is above all forms in being, and all congregations of forms; for he is the point, center, and goal, to which all other forms flow and are perfected, refined, and made useful to the whole constitution of Nature and the Universe. Meanwhile man, in reality, is *invisible* to the material senses; but all that sensuous observers know of man is derived only from his *exterior representative* and express likeness, which is the outward form that his inward being assumes.

From these considerations it is made clear that every human form possesses an organized interior principle by which the exterior is determined and developed. And as the body performs its use considered as a medium by which the inner man communicates with the *outer* world, so does the inner principle perform a use in establishing a connection with the *interior* world. So the human body individualizes the spirit in its relation to the outer world, while the spirit, now connected with the body, determines the perpetuity and identical existence of the spirit in its connection with the inner world,—the *spiritual* form being also an expression of *its* interior soul. Thus it is that the soul is a prior organization ; and when unfolding itself to the outer world, it only assumes a coating, a body, a form, suited to its existence in this rudimental sphere ot material and spiritual creation.

I have been faithful to my impressions concerning the intellectual wants of mankind, and have, therefore, premised thus somewhat elaborately the proposition of God's electrical action on the Universe in which he immutably resides. It is all-important that the mind conceive of Deity as living in the vortical *Center* of existence —which glorious center is resplendent with holy aromal emanations, and with brilliant manifestations of inconceivable perfection— and as being, as He is, the focal concentration and celestial organization of all motion, all life, all elements, and essences, all attributes and principles, which exist in the constitution of things.

It is essential to conceive of the Divine Personality ere the intellect can comprehend how God—being the superlative perfection and organization of all elements and substances—can maintain such minute and inseparable relations, to comparatively inanimate and gross forms and combinations of matter, as are indicated by the universal and changeless processes going on in all departments of Existence. Moreover, this definite conception of God is essential to a clear and logical understanding of what constitutes his voluntary and involuntary powers,—I mean the constitutional manifestations of His interior nature, which are unchangeable, and as distinguished from the exercise of those more exalted elements, which give rise to the emotions of harmony and happiness—to those deep, fathomless, boundless, inexpressible sensations of lyrical harmony—which the musical operations of the Universe, and the consonant joys of countless spirits awaken in his divine constitution.

A clear understanding of these great truths may be more easily obtained by contemplating them from a higher plane of thought. Hence, I pass to the consideration of a superior proposition.

Sixth, GOD ACTS UPON THE UNIVERSE MAGNETICALLY.

Exalted contemplation improves and happifies the soul. High thoughts invariably exalt the mind which entertains them. And the more the soul dwells and meditates upon divine themes the more will its capacity be enlarged and its affections refined and chastened. To be good, or God-like, man must make goodness his constant companion, and Deity a subject of calm, deliberate contemplation. Justified by these indisputable axioms, let us strive to contemplate the Divine Mind more definitely—to fix, if possible, in the understanding a clear and comprehensive conception of Deity; —though it is, and always will be, impossible for the human finite mind to solve the problem of the Divine Existence, or even to fully appreciate the capacity and ever-varying manifestations of a single attribute of Omnipotence. But "the pure in heart see God," and the enlightened and enlarged understanding may, in a degree, *comprehend* him. The pure, undefiled nature beholds God in every thing and every where; but the sound reason-principle must attempt to investigate his mode of Being, through scientific and philosophical instrumentalities.

As I have already said, it would be an act of supererogation to attempt to demonstrate the existence of a supreme, all-wise, good, and perfect Being; because every thing—every form, every combination and organization of matter—furnish a full and perfect evidence, which may be termed a demonstration, that there is a Divine intelligent Mind—a Ruler of the Universe. Man's faith in God is, however, subject to change and modification; it is too frequently an offspring of his religious education—too often "an image" of the structure of his own intellect; and hence, when life's pathway is thorny and tempestuous, man's confidence and faith in the goodness and wisdom, and, even in the *existence* of God, grow weak, and sometimes they desert him when his trials are great, and when a true faith is most desirable and necessary. In truth, there is no safety in a faith, or in an opinion, which has not a scientific and a philosophical foundation in the mind that entertains it. Science and philosophy form the basis of all true religion. But man can not altogether rely upon his senses for truth; for the senses may be defective, misused, and easily deceived; even the assertion of astronomical science, that the earth performs a complete revolution upon its axis once in twenty-four hours, can not be believed on the evidence of the senses; but it must be, like every other important problem or wonder in Nature, demonstrated to the understanding by a process of metaphysical reasoning and argumentation.

So likewise, in order to have a true faith and confidence in the Existence, Wisdom, Power and Love of the Supreme Being, the mind must interrogate its own depths and watch the mysterious workings of its own properties and principles. The senses, alone, can not recognize God in the forms, processes, and organizations of Nature, in the outer world of effects and phenomena; but the MIND can, through the agency of the senses, behold these multifarious indications of the Divine Principle; and in its own interior consciousness, the soul experiences a sweet and immovable faith, based upon knowledge, the nature and ingredients of which no language can properly express. Consciousness, when allowed its full and harmonious action, is a source of faith and knowledge. Philosophically speaking, faith is a CONFIDENCE in that which we strongly, and yearningly desire, or a series of desires, which may be natural and intuitive, or educational and habitual; but knowledge is that which is incontestibly and unequivocally KNOWN to the reason-principle, in which Reason sits, or should sit, on his throne, being the Lord and Governor of all the affections which live in the soul's dominion.

It is certain that "perfect Love casteth out fear," even as perfect health repelleth disease; so, in accordance with the validity of this analogy, it is as certain that perfect *knowledge* and spiritual development will displace all doubts and anxieties concerning the existence of a Supreme Personality. And how necessary it is, to mental culture, refinement, happiness and progression, that the mind be crowned with Wisdom, which is more reliable and abiding than knowledge; because the former is unfolded from the most interior elements of the mind, as flowers are developed from the earth; but the latter (knowledge) is acquired through the senses; and, though it resembles the features and manifestations of Wisdom so exactly as to be frequently confounded together, and judged indiscriminately, yet it is a comparatively ephemeral illumination of the intellect, being eminently useful and ornamental in this life, but which, when Wisdom extends his ever-abiding influence over all the territories of the soul, disappeareth like clouds before the Sun! Wisdom, therefore, is preferable to knowledge; but the two combined—I mean spiritual illumination and insight, in connection with the advantages flowing from a rich possession of what is called "worldly wisdom"—will surely shield the soul from all anxiety and skepticism concerning the existence and character of the Divine Mind and the truths of immortality. "Worldly wisdom," when exclusively possessed, may be defined as consisting of practical discernment; an unexaggerated estimate of things, events, and circumstances which enter into the sum of human experience; a clear, discriminating or scientific judgment—capable of perceiving the motives and weighing the characters of men; accurately calculating the ways and means of physical existence and subsistence; and in conforming prudentially to the popular or existing modes of life, education and habit, to the end that a superficial and temporary harmony may, at least, be preserved in the various communities. Minds of this structure seldom, or never, attempt any speculations of a poetical or metaphysical character; they never indulge themselves in the impracticable or incomprehensible; but are highly versed in the commerce and business of ordinary, every-day life—being, in every thing, sticklers for the exact sciences, for the extemporaneously useful, and for those things which yield great emolument, and make rich.

On the other hand, interior Wisdom or insight, when exclusively possessed, may be known by the eminently religious and profound contemplations in which the individual is chiefly immersed; his constant thirstings after the interior, the deep, the inaccessible, and the infinite; his meditations, cogitations, illuminations; and he is always uneasy, and nervously affected, under the multitudinous embarrassments and perplexities which flow from the selfish and corrupt social state in which mankind are existing. But it is a beauti ful combination—the union of interior Wisdom with "worldly wisdom," or acquired learning and knowledge. For the individual thus talented, is adapted to the spiritual and the natural—to an interior as well as to an exterior mode of existence; and thus he is a righteous man—a supporting and ornamental pillar in the outer world, among men—patient, temperate, industrious, hospitable, religious and superiorly enlightened. The man of "worldly wisdom" may be termed a man of *science;* because science in its broadest sense and most accurate definition, is *a system of external effects and phenomena*, with which an individual is usually well acquainted. And the man of "interior wisdom" may be termed a philosopher; because philosophy according to its true definition is *a system of Causes and Principles*, in the investigation of which the spiritually minded individual is, at all times, more or less engaged. Now, therefore, should the worldly minded or external man attempt a conception of the Divine Existence, his thoughts would surely tend to an inspection of the "events and phenomena" of external Nature. His mind would acknowledge the existence of "a power—a principle—or something" which the senses can not perceive; yet he "does not know" but this Great unseen, invisible Power may be "a law inherent in the constitution of matter"; he does not know but all nature is the effect of "a fortuitous concourse of atoms," because he "sees no special or supernatural action any where in nature or among men," which, he thinks, would probably be manifested were there in reality a self-subsisting, Supreme Being.

But the spiritually minded or internal man investigates, and acquires a conception of God, through the instrumentality of "causes and principles," which conduct him from one sphere of manifestations to another—from this series of effects to that group of causes —until he arrives at the DIVINE CAUSE of all existences, wherein his searching soul finds sweet tranquillity and abiding satisfaction. He deems all arguments, adduced to prove the existence of an all-wise, good, and powerful Principle, as useless—irrelevant—superfluous—imaginary and supererogative. He thinks it folly to discuss a subject "so self-evident." God lives in his soul—inspires him with blissful thoughts and heavenly contemplations. He "walks with God" in the fields of nature and meditation. His "pure heart" sees God in every thing;—yes—in "summer and winter, seed time and harvest," in the siderial systems, in each and every department of nature's great cathedral, the spiritually minded man sees the immutable workings of Omnipotence, and hears the lyric harmonies of the invisible spheres. To this structure of mind a belief in God and some conception of him are easily formed. The, so called, impracticable, incomprehensible, and inaccessible in existence are contemplated with a familiar, adoring vision; and the true soul—yearning, yet passive; thirsting, yet satisfied—goes within, without, and above itself, searching that Love and Wisdom which imparts life and beauty to all forms and personalities in the Universe.

32*

Accompanied by the pure in spirit—by the interior, meditative and philosophical intellect—let us proceed, with all due reverence and humility, to a just, though not complete, comprehension of the Deity as he exists in the constitution of Nature,—that we may the more easily understand how God acts upon the universal organism magnetically.

Conceive of a boundless, infinite, eternal ocean of *superlatively perfect elements;* conceive of those elements as entertaining the most perfect and *indestructible affinities* one for the other; conceive of the crystalization, interpenetration or blending of each and every atom of which those divine elements are composed; conceive of Use, Justice, and Power—of Light, and Life, and Love, and Wisdom—of all that is inexpressibly pure and celestial; conceive of all essences—qualities—properties—principles—forms—motions—forces—tendencies—beauties and harmonies; conceive of all these celestial possessions as being embosomed in those superlatively perfect elements just contemplated; conceive of these refined, perfected, etherealized, celestialized properties and principles as being harmoniously arranged and organized into one ETERNAL MIND! Conceive of this Mind as the perfect *crystalization* of all thought and feeling—of all sentiment and affection—of all love and wisdom—of all power and purpose; conceive of it as having existed and subsisted from all Eternity—as being eternal, pure, perfect, unchangeable, infinite. Conceive of this MIND as residing in the most interior and superior portions of this illimitable Universe; conceive of it as capable of seeing, not with a physical organ of vision, as man sees, but by *an immutable principle of perception;* and as hearing, not as we hear, but with a *principle of hearing* whose sweep is boundless as infinity; conceive of this Eternal Mind as being surrounded by a Great Spiritual Sun composed of innumerable elements, resplendent with auroral tints—with emanations of immortal life and beauty, pulsating with indescribable emotions, indicating the eternal life-principles which cause the Great Heart of Nature to throb perpetually, Wisdom being its coronation; conceive of this superlatively perfect Mind as giving off, "without variableness neither shadow of turning," and as breathing, through the wondrous Universe, without change, suspension, or interruption, all the essences, principles, properties, forms, motions, forces, beauties and harmonies which exist in its indestructible and inconceivably perfect constitution; conceive of the divine life and essential principles of this Mind as flowing—uncommanded, unobstructed, unlimited—through all the organism of Nature, as the blood and principles of life and sensation flow through man's body; conceive of all this, ye searchers and worshipers of the Infinite, and then it may truthfully be said that the human mind has, for the first time on this earth, formed a philosophical conception of the structure and character of that HOLY BEING, whose residence is fixed, eternal in the Heavens!

Let the mind expand its powers of imagination to their utmost capacity, and let its thoughts of Deity propagate and multiply themselves into countless numbers; let the feelings of the mind—those sentiments and emotions which stir its depths—unite and swell themselves into the sublimest conceptions of all that is celestial and heavenly; and yet the soul shall have obtained but a rude outline, a mere rudimental and imperfect *idea* of the Great Positive Mind—of the Eternal God of Nature!—of the Inventor, Sustainer, and Perfecter of all things!—of the Everlasting Soul of the Universe!—of our Father who art in Heaven! For there never was a sound formed or a word uttered that could convey the least conception of that all-pervading ESSENCE, that Great Spiritual PRINCIPLE, that Great Positive, Omnipotent MIND, which dwells in the VORTEX from which flow millions on millions of Suns, of Systems, of Universes, that extend out into indefinable space almost to the filling of space itself—and yet all constituting nothing more than an expression of *one single* THOUGHT emanating from the inexhaustible Vortex of Infinite Purity and Perfection! No word or phrase has ever been uttered—and I do not except the phrase which I have been directed to employ—that has ever conveyed to the mind of man in this, its first sphere of existence, the least possible conception of the INFINITE, DIVINE PRINCIPLE.

But the contrast—how great! how inexpressibly painful! I mean the *God of mankind* as compared with the GOD OF NATURE! Extracted from the tombs and sacred pyramids of antiquity, the mythological traditions of all sects and nations concerning a Jehovah have been molded into a single Idol, which is sought and feared by nearly every inhabitant of the civilized countries of the earth. This idol—this imaginary "King of kings and Lord of lords"—is sought chiefly through intercessors or attorneys; through creeds, and priests, and churches; through the avenue of "faith," (and sometimes works)—a faith measured out by those whose acknowledged occupation it is, to stand between the people and their Maker. If mankind were elevated and truly enlightened—if men entertained high and holy views of Nature and Heaven—they would never sacrifice their reason and understanding upon the altar of popular theology and authority—they would never seek salvation through those instrumentalities that are now deemed so essential to immortality and future happiness. Mankind, being immersed in profound ignorance and superstition, regard the existence of certain "means of salvation" as evidences of "Divine mercy"; but how insignificant or mythological this opinion, or faith, appears to the enlarged and enlightened understanding! Yea, when from the contemplations and conceptions of the God of the Universe the free-born mind is called away, then the imperfect and oriental beliefs of mankind, concerning what they term God, pass before its vision like the distorted images of unhappy dreams!

The Fetichism and Polytheism of all nations and ages, and the thoughts and the various religions and sentiments which those forms of faith excited in the human mind, are beautifully modified and organized into the Monotheism of modern days;—No! not Monotheism, (which signifies a belief in *one* God,) but rather that all the superstitions, speculations, and religious sentiments of bygone ages, are condensed, (and sanctioned by the authority of King James) into a system of Dualism, which signifies TWO—or a belief in an *absolute* GOOD, and in an *absolute* EVIL, Personality or principle. And it is to redeem the race from a sinful state (into which this supposed "absolute Evil" personage is alleged to have enticed and plunged mankind,) that the scheme of salvation was, by the exceeding mercy and forbearance of Jehovah, originally instituted. Let us, however, inquire into the details of this belief in *an evil spirit*, to the end that knowledge may be increased, and wisdom unfolded, among the inhabitants of earth.

Probably throughout the illimitable expanse of human inquiry, there are no questions considered so dreadful, so solemn, and unapproachable, as those which pertain to what is conceived to be the Supreme Good, and His eternal antagonist, the Devil. And it is both impossible and unprofitable to disguise the conspicuous fact, that, on our earth, a belief in, and fear of the Devil is almost universal; but let it here be impressed that all conceptions of the Devil, or unseen spirit of Evil, are as different among different nations as are their diverse complexions, customs, and government. But the most perfect conception of the embodiment of an Evil principle—the most splendid concentration and personification of hatred, of envy, of a voluntary love of evil, of the most unalloyed vice, of every intrinsically wicked and fiendish principle—*is the entailed property of the Christian Church.* If the reader's interior perceptions were opened, and his spirit would interrogate the labyrinths of mythology, and the mazes of heathen speculations upon Cosmogony, Theology, and Demonology, he would perceive that the most extravagant stories of Devils and Demons, indigenous to the Pagan world, do not equal the real Devil which is supposed to preside over the Theology of Christendom. Indeed, this superior Demon is not only presiding *over*, but is considered an indispensable ingredient *in*, the Theology which is promulgated by what is styled the Evangelical Order of teachers and clergymen.

The universality of a belief in a Principle of Evil is susceptible of the clearest and most rational explanation. Among the earliest inhabitants of the earth, there were minds who speculated upon the causes of evil and discord; and the love of approbation being a powerful passion in the constitution of the human mind, it became both agreeable, and convenient, to refer the causes of personal deficiences, and unrighteousness, to invisible beings or spirits. At first it was suggested that the Winds were the indications of the presence of Evil Spirits; it was not long before this suggestion, or opinion, became considered as an established *fact;* and in the course of a few generations, this *supposed fact* was not only believed and taught because of its romantic and mysterious character, but, also, for its antiquity or ancient origin. And then it was, when Paramah, Vishnue, and Siva, had their respective positions assigned them in the Eastern and most ancient cosmogony; and Siva was settled upon as the cause of human wickedness and misdirection. The general relief, afforded by this discovery of the arch-enemy of mankind, can be easily imagined and appreciated.

In consequence of this discovery, the early inhabitants experienced a kind of self-justification in whatever they attempted to perform. It was not long after Siva was made to rule over the Infernal Regions of evil atmosphere, that his name was changed, and he was promoted, from a mere principle, or breath, (spiritus,) to be a strong and influential chieftain of evil persons, hosts, and empires. This was done by Zoroaster—who, in his systematic speculations upon Cosmogony, and Demonology, styled him Ahriman.

From the Hindoo and Chaldeanic-Persian mythology, the Spirit of Evil was introduced into the Egyptian, the Hebrew or Jewish speculations, under the more mild and indefinite name of Belial and Diabolus—the former signifying simply a *libertine;* and the latter, an *accuser*, or *calumniator*. Here it is well to observe, that the Hebrew or Jewish scriptures contain but very few intimations of a belief in a personal Devil. The Jews believed in no Devil more wicked or more potent than *Belial* and his sons. And it will be conceded that an individual can not have a more troublesome, and, perhaps, direful enemy, than a *libertine* or a *calumniator;* and, from what I can learn of the Jewish and old testament writings, no other Devils, than Belial and Satan (which signify Libertine and Accuser) were ever incorporated in the Theology of the Egyptians, the Romans, and Jews. Notwithstanding the Old Testament is silent on the existence of a personal Devil, it is evident that the Jews believed in a spirit, or principle of Evil, not unlike the opinion entertained by the early inhabitants. The New Testament is more explicit upon this subject—indeed, there are several allusions in it, which give the impression that the historians and followers of Christ were thorough believers in personal Devils. They describe many experiments upon Devils; such as casting Satan (or Devils) out of persons into swine, causing the latter to run madly over precipices into the sea; and several other demoniacal demonstrations are recorded—each bearing sufficient evidence that the writers of them were believers in Satanic influences and evil personalities.

The disciples of Mahomet are believers in a personal Devil bearing the name of Eblis, who corresponds to the Christian's Lucifer. The Mahometans also name their Devil Azazel, who is made mention of in the Old Testament, in the book of Enoch,* and which signifies *refractory persons, and wicked spirits*, and also *perdition.* It is evident that *refractory* individuals, (those who are badly organ-

* One of the rejected books, at the time our present Bible was made.

ized in mind and body,) give the more advanced nations of the earth an idea of what a Devil would be in his own localities and habitations.

Thus the Devil of the whole world is a personification of the evil deeds of wickedly disposed individuals,—and the reason why he is promoted to personality and influence every where, is, that the human mind can not easily think of principles without a body, and locality; and because, also, it is found convenient to have a person with whom to contend, and gratify the superficial and unamiable propensity of combativeness and destructiveness. This is called, overcoming the Devil, and putting his temptations under your feet.

Thus, at first, the Winds were considered Devils, and were termed "Breaths"; then the multiplicity of Devils were systemized, and made to concentrate in the mythological personage who figures largely in the Hindoo, and still more ancient cosmogony, and who was named "Siva"; then came the Zoroasterian system of a Good Spirit, and an Evil Spirit who had innumerable and subordinate devils under him, and he was called "*Ahriman*." Then came the various names and modifications of Devils, flowing through the Persianic, Egyptian, Grecian, Roman, Germanic, and Anglo-Saxon channels of legendary and theological speculations; and the consequence is, that, now, the Christians have the whole contribution of evil principles and personages manufactured into a single "*Devil*," which is the very quintessence of past imaginings; and this amalgamation renders the Christian's *Satan* the most omnipotent, the most dreadful, the most insinuating, the most wicked Demon, and, at the same time, the most magnificent and powerful Prince that exists in any theology, as an antagonist to Good and the Deity. His names are various in sound and significance. He has been progressively named *Siva*, *Ahriman*, *Genius*, *Belial*, *Eblis*, *Azazel*, *Lucifer*, *Dragon*, *Serpent*, *Satan*, *Devil*, *Demon*, *Mephistophiles*, and other names of a more or less fiendish sound and signification.

Christians, having the superior advantages of wealth and education, have succeeded better in defining the appearance, habitation, and disposition of the fabulous Devil, than any other nation on the earth. And I can not but think, that, were it not for the mythological suggestions of a serpent Demon in the beginning of the Old Testament, the confirmations of, and serious allusions to him, in the New; and the independent speculations upon a Devil derived from other theological books—were it not for all this assistance to the fancy—Christian poets would have failed in their attempts to render Satan what they have, in their various classical productions.

Assisted by mythological and theological systems and suggestions, Milton imagines a splendid Pandemonium, illuminated with

> ———" a row
> Of starry lamps, and blazing cressets, fed
> With naphtha and asphaltus,"—

where resides the majestic Prince, or

> " Chief of many throned powers
> That led the embattled seraphim to war.'

This conception is nothing more than a civilization and promotion of the powerful Zoroasterian Devil, together with his subordinate angels, the genii. The most splendid and accomplished Satanic Prince, ever described to the world, is the Miltonian Devil, the materials for the manufacturing of whose physical organization, and innumerable supernumeraries, were supplied by the Persian mythology. The Persians generally believe that there lives somewhere a powerful Evil Being, whose rich possessions are too vast to be imagined, and whose servant-spirits are stationed at the various lakes, mines, mountains, caves, forests, and stars, which belong to the earth, or which can be seen by its inhabitants. In evidence of the truthfulness of this statement, I refer the reader to that world-wide celebrated collection of Persian tales, known as the " Arabian Nights' Entertainments." The genii represented in this remarkable work, are the infernal hosts which Milton describes as peopling his Pandemonium; and *Lucifer* (the splendid "Prince of darkness") is Ahriman, the Prince of the genii, who is made to govern in opposition to Ormuzd (or God) in an empire of fire, wealth and magnificence.

In order to satisfy the mind that Christian poets have infinitely sublimated and perfected all Hindoo, Arabian and Jewish conceptions of a Devil, the reader may consult Pollok's lucid description of his character—he describes Satan as having

——"his bosom filled with hate, his face
Made black with envy, and in his soul begot
Thoughts guilty of rebellion 'gainst the throne
Of the Eternal Father, and the Son."

And still further proofs that Christians have the most perfect conception of the mythological Devil, may be gathered from that profoundly imaginary and classical work, the "Pilgrim's Progress," written by the imprisoned John Bunyan. This book, probably, next to the Bible, is the most influential representative of oriental superstition, and systematic mythology, ever published in Christendom. It is influential, because it possesses many of those attractions which have insured the sale of the Arabian tales, and because it faithfully impresses upon the youthful mind the whole philosophy and mystery of the Christian theology. Here I would like the reader to understand that I do not confound religion with theology.

I think it will appear that the Devil of the Christian world is manufactured out of those kindred and homogeneous materials, which, in parts and fragments, are to be found among all nations.

The reason why a Devil, or evil Spirit, was first conceived of, is explained in the mythological tale of the "Garden of Eden." It is related that Eve was disobedient, and, having done wrong, desired to excuse herself by introducing a foreign and extenuating cause; therefore, to subserve the purposes of self-justification, she accused the serpent. Adam also sinned and *knew it*, and he sought to excuse himself by weakly attributing the cause of his evil deed to the woman; so likewise, did the early inhabitants excuse themselves by referring their personal, social, and other disturbances to unseen causes, and infernal beings. This system of referring the origin of human misdirection to foreign influences has for its foundation two causes—*Dishonesty* and *Ignorance.* Some minds are not sufficiently honest to acknowledge their own voluntary faults, and constitutional weaknesses; and other minds are not sufficiently philosophical to trace effects to their legitimate causes; and thus, between the two causes (dishonesty and ignorance) we have the profoundest disclosures and the sublimest descriptions of a magnificent Devil, and of his incalculably numerous victimized subjects. Surely, no system can equal that of Swedenborg on the philosophy of infernal influences; but even the materials of this system are to be found among the Persians, especially with the fire-worshipers, who believe that every individual is constantly attended by Evil Spirits or Genii. This habit of individuals, this fact in history, this system of nations, of referring human, social, and constitutional evils to unreal and imaginary causes, instead of *searching out* and *removing* their *real* ones, blinds the understanding, whilst it relieves personal responsibility to attribute all errors to the dangerous enemy of mankind, intent upon destruction, whose work upon the earth is admirably illustrated by Pollok. He describes the Devil as disobeying the will of God, and not consigned to utter punishment, but as being

> "Left to fill the measure of his sin,
> In tempting and seducing man—too soon,
> Too easily seduced! And from the day
> He first set foot on earth,—of rancor full,
> And pride, and hate, and malice, and revenge,—
> He set himself, with most felonious aim
> And hellish perseverance, to *root out*
> *All good,* and in its place to *plant all ill.*"

Milton and Pollok illustrate, in the most explicit and beautiful language, the fact that the human mind has put forth unsuccessful efforts to become acquainted with the source of its many and diversified afflictions. Every human description of a Devil, and his pernicious influence among men, adds only another evidence in favor of the proposition, that Ignorance and Dishonesty (or a want of candor) have implanted in the Theology of our earth, erroneous and unphilosophical explanations of evils and existing misdirections.

I feel impressed to remark that to the spiritually enlightened mind, to the clear and true-sighted intellect, this subject presents a powerful contrast between the Errors of Theology, and the Truths of Nature. On the right is seen Nature with all her beauty and loveliness; and on the left is Theology with its deified objects and principles. Theology makes all night. Nature illumines every thing with the light of day. On one side are visible the ghostly pyramids of Error; on the other the stupendous mountains of Everlasting Truths. Oh, could the reader stand upon these immeasurable mounts of intellectual elevation and divine truth, with his spiritual perceptions so opened as to scan the worlds of mind beneath, he would behold on one hand an awful night of mental misdirection;—colossal errors, residing in costly temples, bound together in sacred books, and having for their advocates and devotees the most talented minds. He would see forests of heathenism turned into the most seductive gardens of *Christian errors—revered errors of the past*,—dressed up with the garments of education and wealth, and potentialized by the spirit of antiquity. He would perceive that the hypothetical ideas and realities of the East, have been (and are) sublimated, systemized, Deified, and magnificently supported in the West; that the inhabitants of the Eastern Hemisphere supplied the germ of modern Theology in *their* mythology, and that the inhabitants of the Western Hemisphere religiously nourish the germ and perfect the flower. Upon the other hand, he would see Nature's golden Truths of Heaven gliding from mount to mount, from spirit to spirit, from flower to flower, and gilding with immortal loveliness the weakest and the strongest works of God;—he would behold that every thing declares the character and Divinity of its mission by doing its legitimate work, by obeying the principles of Nature, and consequently the Will of its Creator; and that Freedom, Truth, and Harmony, are visible in every direction.

Instead of mythological Devils, are visible the sublimest realities; and instead of false adoration and idolatry, are exhibitions of the profoundest deference and admiration. Instead of ghastly phantoms, the valley of awful shadows, and lakes of liquid fire, pregnant with frenzied children of the Most High, are visible most beauteous and unchangeable truths—the fragrant mountains of eternal progression; and the diamond ocean of Infinite Love, whose universal tide of Spiritual Life flows up, from out of everlasting founts, and which, unlike the tides of earth, EBBS NOT AGAIN!

Verily, the God of this sublime Universe has no antagonistic being, spirit, or principle, with which to contend; he is All in All—breathing his life-elements and essential principles throughout the realms and labyrinths of Infinitude—bathing the innumerable stars in the light of his nature, and sanctifying every thing by making each and all a portion of himself—an indispensable ingredient in his superlatively perfect constitution. He can not experience those fluctuations and turbulent commotions of passion which characterize man's undeveloped, undisciplined, misdirected soul. He can not be vexed and disconcerted, as man is; for he contains the principles of all harmony, all perfection and unchangeableness within himself, and is, therefore, "without variableness or shadow of turning"—is incapable of changing himself or being changed; he is the great TOTALITY of being; the Coronation of the Universe!

But the theology of Christendom is replete with opposite conceptions of God. In it, God is represented as a changeful, regretful, capricious being; as saddened when mankind are rebellious and sinful; and as gladdened when his "means of salvation" are received by the multitudes who prefer his kingdom to that of Satan—the alleged antagonist of the Deity. Surely, this theology is exceedingly mythological in its each and every assertion. It relates how, by a direct exercise of his own hands, God created the land and the sea; made animals to inhabit the land, fishes to people the sea; planted a garden with beautiful trees; formed a pair of immaculate human beings; placed them in the midst of irresistible temptations; and finally turned that pair from the garden into the wild fields; and repented—deeply, heartily repented him—that he had made man, and drove him forth to die, and cursed the ground for his sake! Thus, this theology deprives God of the attribute of omniscience, because it acknowledges that subsequently to his seeing and pronouncing every thing as "good," he fervently desired to retrace his steps and undo what he had done—especially in the creation of the human species. Surely this seems very Oriental! If this theological, or rather mythological, Deity, had possessed the attribute of omniscience, he certainly would not have made the creation of mankind a mere matter of experimental experience; in which attempt he did not, in all respects, succeed as well as he desired; his failure proving a source of deep regret and repentance to himself, and, to myriads of human souls, the cause of endless and unmitigated misery! To deny the experimental and hazardous character of man's creation by the special action of the Deity, as described in this modern mythology, would be to deny the plainest truth on the page of history. For, when it was discovered by the Maker, that, though perfect at first, man was disposed to go astray and people the earth with wicked tyrants and murderous tribes, then he "repented" himself that he had made man, and was compelled by the direful consequences thereof, to institute a new plan whereby to depopulate the earth of both man and beast, saving only germs (or two of every species) wherewith to commence the process of creation afresh, under more pure and favorable circumstances. Verily, this seems altogether unlike the "handiwork" of an Omniscient or Omnipotent Principle, or Mind; but it perfectly resembles the operations and dispensations of the Oriental Deity, who, according to the early Persianic and Egyptian conceptions (or stories) of a great, capricious, transformatory, ever-present spirit, was the special author of material things. From existing records we learn that even after man was removed from the earth by the universality of the deluge, and a new order was begun, the human species continued rebellious and abominations were innumerable. And to provide man with "means" whereby he might "wash away" his deeply-seated and "scarlet sins," and be restored to the favor and friendship of that God who authorized Joshua's soul-revolting wars and cruelties, and destroyed the multitudes of earth, by water, a still greater scheme was instituted—even the crucifixion of an innocent individual.

To the sound, enlightened, intuitive intellect, this system appears like the early dreams of imagination, combined with the fabled enchantments of the chronology and peculiar history of ancient tribes. Because the God of the Universe is unspeakably and inconceivably superior to imperfect manifestations of his formative power—in truth, He is the very essence of infinite Love, Will, Wisdom and Perfection; and from the inherent elements and principles of his perfect constitution flow forth all the form and order, activity and intelligence, which grace the fields of nature. But the God of mythological theology is the very essence of changeability and fickle-mindedness! he creates and destroys; institutes plans and repents having done so; establishes laws and repeals them; declares that "whosoever sheddeth man's blood, by man shall his blood be shed," and himself commands his favorite armies to put nations to the sword; gets joyous and angry; teaches love to enemies, and then is impatient to put all enemies under his feet; "will have mercy on whom he will have mercy, and whom he will he hardeneth"; declares himself "past finding out," but says "*all shall know him*," from the least to the greatest; proclaims "peace on earth," but bringeth "a sword"; says "thou shalt not kill," yet maketh the killing of the man of Nazareth the last, indispensable act in the moral tragedy of salvation; professes to be the friend of all men, but plunges the victims of his anger into profound, eternal misery; sends his rain and blessings "upon the just and the unjust" here, but lets fall the withering curses of his dissatisfaction upon the latter, in the life to come; causes prophets to proclaim his omnipresence, yet acknowledges a portion of infinitude to be occupied by the prince of darkness; inspires men to assert his power to be above all,—greater than all powers and principalities, all kingdoms and governments,—and yet permits quintillions upon quintillions of spirits to be irretrievably lost in a lake of fire prepared for the devil and his angels. Surely these conspicuous contradictions, in the theology of mankind, unequivocally prove its mythological origin. Strip from the present popular theology its great literary beauties and classical decorations, with the superficial or imaginary harmony of the interpretations given to its teachings—the work of Romish scholars and modern translators—and it would not recommend itself to any man's reason, which even now it does not, except through the agency of custom and education; but put away its costly drapery, and the God which it presents to the human mind is not less capricious, or more worthy of religious adoration, than the God of the Danish mythology, which ultimately became the system of sacred cosmogony, adopted by the ancient Indian tribes, and more civilized nations of Central America.

In this cosmogony, as in modern theology, the Deity is supposed to have created the sun, and moon, and stars, and the earth, and man, and every thing which is visible and invisible. But in consequence of the disobedience of one man—who builds a gorgeous palace to gratify his own ambition, instead of erecting a sacrificial monument on which should be burning a perpetual fire, as the Lord directed him to do—the Deity, glowing with terrific vengeance, sent a mighty deluge, which rose so high and was so universal that it not only swept from the earth every living thing, (including man, but extinguished both the sun and the moon! When the Deity beheld what he in his excessive rage had done—the earth and the heavens being thereby deserted—he wept bitterly for several ages; while thus he grieved, a seraph, the wife of a heavenly king of great power, came to him and promised, in exchange for some valuable gift, to repopulate the earth and restore the orbs in the heavens. The offer being acceded to, she transformed one of her own sons into a *dagger of steel* and hurled it down to earth. When it struck the ground it separated into *fifteen hundred knights* of great beauty and valor. These knights forthwith waged war with one another, and built a great fire wherein to burn whichever one of them should first fall vanquished. At length, after a long combat, the most beautiful of them, him named Zolotl, yielded; he was cast into the flames, and as his body disappeared in the consuming element, the exulting knights saw rising in the east a beautiful, effulgent sun, in which they recognized the features and translation of their supposed vanquished brother. This circumstance made them doubly adventurous, and ambitious of a still greater promotion. They, therefore, grew clamorous as to which one of their number should next pass through fire to glory! And whilst they were contending, one of th most chivalrous and beautiful among them, without waiting for the question to be decided by battle, plunged into the flames. But the heat being greatly diminished, the young knight's body burned, very slowly, away. As it consumed and vanished, however, there appeared, in an opposite part of the heavens, a pale and almost imperceptible orb—the moon. This luminary not having the luster and dazzling brilliancy which the sun possessed, deterred the remaining knights from further adventurous efforts to gratify their ambition.

The succeeding generations, (who supposed their ancestral power and dignity were traceable to the knighthood above described,) built in the East, and in Central America, two very beautiful temples, which were solemnly dedicated, one to the Moon, and the other to the Sun, in memory and honor of the deity, who, though he destroyed mankind in a moment of passion, peopled the earth again, and illumined the heavens by his merciful power!

Thus it is made distinctly obvious, that the best conceptions formed of a Supreme Being, of a Creator and Governor of worlds and mankind, are more or less mythological. Through all the religious systems existing, there runs a parallelism which the discerning intellect can not but perceive. For instance, the Danish mythology contains a conception of God, and a history of his providential manifestations among men, distinguishable from the Jewish and Christian theology only in that the latter are possessed of more historical beauties, are richer in classical embellishments, and adorned by science. Remember, I do not confound mythological deities with that Great Positive Intelligence who unfolded this stupendous system of life, activity, and order, which fills Infinitude; on the contrary, I am impressed to regard all mythology as the early manifestations of that higher and more elevating *Theology* which pervades the system of Nature. Mythology may be regarded as the first outward expression or *incarnation* of the religious sentiment; as the pyramids were, in the early and unmechanical ages, the first grand developments of the architectural principle immanent in man. Now, therefore, let it be remembered, that, while I positively repudiate the imperative, dogmatic theology taught in the schools and high places of modern times, I do not denounce the whole system as altogether false and dangerous. On the contrary, there are pure principles, and heavenly precepts, and noble examples, and historical details, and wisdom-sayings, in those ancient testamental writings, which I can not but love and inculcate; because the truths therein contained are perfectly consistent with Nature's own revealments; but it is the idea or belief that those records contain *all necessary for man to know*, and that, therefore, no man must strive to be "wise above what is written": this is what I am impressed to denounce as eminently false and pernicious. For it is undeniable that, in order to obtain any thing like a reasonable, religious, and comprehensible conception of God, the human mind must leave all forms and systems of theology, and search the magnificent framework of Universal Nature, and the mysterious possessions of its own individuality. Also, in scientific and philosophical researches, man is compelled to go frequently beyond the narrow limits of the sacred canon—far above the teachings and revelations of his most cherished institutions of religion; he must press forward to the acquisition of knowledge and wisdom far "above what is written"—or, the world would make but little progress in those things which contribute to bless man's present life and develop in his reason a profounder respect for, and, in his affections, a more intelligent love of, the Supreme Principle!

The Danish mythology, it will be perceived, teaches a doctrine of Deity, of his capricious dealings with the sinful and rebellious generations of earth, not very unlike that which, in a far more systematic and beautiful manner, adorns the pages of sacred history. To obtain, then, a full and satisfactory revelation of the *one only and true God*—the majestic Divinity who fills all the innumerable realms and firmaments of Nature with life and inexpressible happiness—the soul must be perfectly honest with itself and commune with every living thing. Some author says, "an undevout astronomer must be mad"; how much *more insane*, therefore, must be that man, who, by studying the laws and principles—the elements and attributes—which make him ONE with Nature and God, can not *see* and *feel* more true religion than is known to the idolatrous devotee of any book, priest, or temple existing on the earth! To harmonize "Nature with revelation"—to make the chronological history of our earth, as written by its geology, confirm precisely what is theologically asserted in sacred history, as written by Moses—to do this, much valuable time and talent have been unfortunately employed and expended. And yet I do not regret this expenditure; because past *errors* are powerful monitors to the sensuous observer in his search after truth; but, I feel impressed, it is now a proper age to confess that "revelations" of God in the material and spiritual universe and in the Soul—in our deep consciousness—are the *only* revealments which can be made to perfectly "harmonize" with the mighty declarations of Nature. And how cheering and encouraging it is to the seeking, yearning, investigating mind, when it discovers its sacred intuitions and honest convictions beautifully and concisely expressed, by human language, in *any* book which some illuminated mind, or minds, may have written. With the free, heaven-bound soul, the truth is precious wherever found—whether "on heathen or christian ground"—and perfect love for truth casteth out all fear of error!

www.ingramcontent.com/pod-product-compliance
Lightning Source LLC
LaVergne TN
LVHW020117110826
845151LV00001B/181

* 9 7 8 1 4 2 5 5 4 2 7 0 2 *